*Hatred and bitterness can never cure the disease of fear;
only love can do that. Hatred paralyzes life, love releases it.
Hatred confuses life. Love harmonizes it. Hatred darkens
life; love illuminates it.*
—MARTIN LUTHER KING, JR.

*Whoever destroys one life, it is as if he has destroyed an
entire world, and whoever saves one life, it is as if he has
saved an entire world.*
—MISHNA SANHEDRIN 4:5

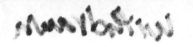

Advisor in Criminal Justice to Northeastern University Press
Gil Geis

Kathryn Watterson

NORTHEASTERN UNIVERSITY PRESS
Boston

NOT BY THE SWORD

How a Cantor and His Family Transformed a Klansman

For Zachary and for Sarah

Northeastern University Press 2001

Library of Congress Cataloging-in-Publication Data

Watterson, Kathryn, 1942–
Not by the sword : how a cantor and his
family transformed a klansman / Kathryn Watterson.
p.   cm.
Originally published: New York :
Simon & Schuster, © 1995. With new pref.
Includes bibliographical references (p.   ) and index.
ISBN 1-55553-471-6 (pbk. : alk. paper)
1. Antisemitism—Nebraska—Lincoln.   2. Ku Klux Klan
(1915–   )—Nebraska—Lincoln.
3. Weisser, Michael, Cantor.   4. Trapp, Larry.
5. Reconciliation.   6. Jewish converts from Christianity—
Biography.   7. Lincoln (Neb.)—Ethnic relations.
I. Title.
DS146.U6 W37 +
305.892'40782293—dc21   00–053406

Printed and bound by Maple Press in York, Pennsylvania.
The paper is Sebago Antique, an acid-free sheet.

MANUFACTURED IN THE UNITED STATES OF AMERICA
05 04 03 02 01   5 4 3 2 1

Contents

Preface

*I*t has been five years since *Not by the Sword* was published, and nearly a decade since the beginning of Michael and Julie Weisser's life-changing encounters with white supremacist leader Larry Trapp, a neo-Nazi and the Grand Dragon of the White Knights of the Ku Klux Klan of Nebraska.

During those years, there's been no let up in racism, xenophobia, homophobia, anti-Semitism and misogyny in our country. If anything, hatred and terrorism have become more potent forces—stimulated, on some level, by our culture's focus on violence, competition and the illusion that "everybody but me" is getting ahead. For, while our country has experienced unprecedented economic growth—today, we have twice as many millionaires as we had five years ago—the prosperity at the top has not trickled down. Over 97 percent of Americans are not millionaires; more than 80 percent have not benefited from the Wall Street boom. And while we as a society are obsessed with prosperity, one out of every five of our children lives in poverty. White men on the margins, who make up the majority of membership in hate organizations, feel more shortchanged and more threatened than ever.

I was on a book tour for *Not by the Sword* when the Alfred P. Murrah Federal Building in Oklahoma was bombed, shaking the nation. As details about the perpetrator's life emerged, so did the parallels to Larry Trapp's life. After my exposure to the hate movement, I wasn't surprised when I learned that Timothy McVeigh had found inspiration from the same Aryan Nation heroes as Larry Trapp. Both men had stockpiled weapons, studied bomb making and killing skills, and read and re-read *The Turner Diaries* to prepare for a race war that they believed would topple the federal government. ("When the day comes, we will not ask you whether you swung to the right or whether you swung to the left," it says on the back of Larry Trapp's KKK card. "We will simply swing you by the neck. This is War!")

Other terrorists with similar philosophies have struck as well. In Denver, a white man searching out "enemies" shot a Filipino-American postal worker who was delivering mail and pre-school children from a Jewish community center who were just crossing the street. In Chicago, a gunman hunting for nonwhites killed an Asian-American graduate student. Later, he gunned down a former basketball coach from Northwestern University as he was walking down the street with his family, simply because he was black. In Jasper, Texas, white racists out to beat up a black man dragged James Byrd Jr. to his death behind a truck. In Wyoming, gay university student Matthew Shepard was battered, lashed to a rural cattle fence and left to die. In California, a white supremacist beat black student Malcolm Boyd with a metal pipe outside a Fresno State fraternity party—leaving Boyd, who was about to graduate, blind and paralyzed. All these acts have been praised by hate mongers, who use the Internet to encourage one another and spread their vile blueprints of destruction.

"We're still in a country where a black man can be dragged to his death behind a car, where a gay person is tied to a fence and murdered," Cantor Weisser said during a recent conversation from Lincoln, where he continues his work as the spiritual leader of B'nai Jeshurun. "We focus on these things for a few days, and then forget about them. Most people figure if they're not hearing about hate crimes, then they're not happening, so we live in a complacent way that's not a reflection of the realities in our culture."

Today, there are some 457 active hate organizations in the United States according to the Intelligence Project, an investigative arm of the Southern Poverty Law Center. These groups include the Klan, the Aryan Nation, neo-Nazis, Skinheads and other white separatist organizations, many of which are linked to militia groups that advocate a hodgepodge of extreme antigovernment and hate doctrines. At colleges and universities around the country—places of learning assumed to stimulate open minds and hearts—there has been an apparent rise in violent hate crimes, along with an increase in frightening verbal assaults, racist and homophobic letters and e-mails, and other bias incidents. *The Review of Higher Education* recently estimated that a total of one million bias incidents occur every year on American campuses.

What are we to make of such hatred and ignorance?

Despite the inequities in our society, most people do not become so embittered that they turn to terrorism. How can we understand what drives individuals to such extremes?

Looking at Larry Trapp's life provides one way to make sense out of such a path. It's not an easy life to examine. In fact, one of the hardest things I've ever had to do as a writer was to enter the hate-filled world of Larry Trapp—to listen to the vicious messages he taped for his Klan hotline, to touch his Klan robes, to unfold his Nazi flags, to look at his swastikas and pictures of Hitler, to read his notes and his books, to literally and figuratively walk into the world he inhabited. It was so difficult for me that I wrote the first draft of this book from the perspective of the various people being attacked and harassed in Lincoln—keeping the reader ignorant until late into the story, as the community had been, of the person leading the attacks against them. In other words, I was leaving out the horrors of Larry's inner life as a white supremacist. It was only after my friend Marie read that draft and asked, "Kitsi, didn't you interview Larry?" that I realized I was treating his life prior to his transformation as a big pile of muck that I, at most, was poking with a long stick held at arm's length—unwilling to sit in it, examine its texture, know how it smelled.

And so I went back and did something I loathed: I crawled into that world, sat in the middle of a terrorist's mind and experience and wrote about it. What I found there made my skin crawl; the deeper I got into it, the more I hated it. There were days that I felt like picking up a gun myself to shoot down all the bigots of the world. But then I began to understand that my furious, knee-jerk reactions would be exactly what they wanted. Over time, I also began to see the terrible isolation and self-loathing that direct such a life. It is filled with anguish, unresolved terrors, grief, rage, depression, isolation and secrecy. Larry Trapp, who was taught the habits of hate when he was a small, abused child, felt confused, humiliated and insignificant. As he grew to be a man, guns quelled some of his fears, and hatred made him feel more powerful. To appear bigger, tougher and meaner, he spoke with his fists, acquired more weapons and built more bombs—externalizing his rage, blaming and diminishing those around him. When *The Klansman* wrote an article praising him ("We encourage and support this man who openly defies prison and even death for his convictions. He is truly a credit to the white race and an asset to the Klan"), his wildest dreams had come true; he had not only garnered the respect he'd always longed for, but he felt supported and confirmed by a big, powerful brotherhood.

Larry's life as a Klansman was pathetic; it was spiritually impoverished, a life without love. Inside that hollowness, I discovered what Michael and Julie had instinctively known: that hating the haters only confirms their view of the world. They're hitting out because they expect and want to get hit back. Their poisonous game thrives on seeing what they project coming back at them. Love, compassion and forgiveness come as a surprise, disrupt the game, change all the rules—show the way out.

Of course, while some haters may be open to change, others are not susceptible to letting down their guard. But young children in our communities can and should be reached. Today innumerable kids suffer verbal, sexual and physical abuse. When they begin to get in trouble by acting out, drinking, taking drugs or abusing others, we are more inclined to lock them up than we are to educate or help them become healthy and whole. I believe that we could dramatically stem the tide of hate in this country if we put even a tenth as many resources into understanding and supporting our children as we do into building and filling our prisons.

That's because hate mongers like Larry Trapp were almost always abused or troubled children who did not get the kindness or guidance they needed when they were young. In my mind's eye, I can still see a tiny frightened Larry sitting alone in the rain, crying and playing with worms in the dirt. How might his life have changed if he'd had an adult to nurture him? I imagine that if Larry had been attached to a positive model when he was a boy, his adult life never would have found its fuel, focus and structure in the rhetoric and recipes of the hate movement.

Cantor Weisser, who continues his human rights work and his advocacy of education and prevention instead of punishment, points out: "The time to start teaching people about the unity of the human race and the understanding of differences is in pre-school, Head Start and kindergarten. If we don't, racism and bigotry will continue forever."

And Julie Weisser, who combats discrimination wherever she encounters it—whether in the schools, at the supermarket or on the street—believes things will change only when each of us takes individual responsibility and begins to address prejudice as a moral issue. "As soon as you break down one barrier, it leads to more understanding," she says. "If you make friends with somebody Jewish or Vietnamese or black or gay, it makes you wonder about objectifying the whole group."

Despite the realities of the modern hate movement, I believe that this story of how the Weissers turned an enemy into a friend offers hope and a vision of how we can cut through hatred to build a powerful sense of community and harmony. We have reasons for optimism. In South Africa, we've seen the end of apartheid and the extraordinary work of the Truth and Reconciliation Commission, which was established to determine and acknowledge the truth concerning gross human rights violations of the past and to promote healing for an entire nation. The popularity of books, films and speakers on spirituality shows that there's an interest in this country in moving to a more fertile territory that lies beyond our focus on materialism and success. For the real poverty among us is not so much economic as it is a poverty of values, a poverty of joy, a poverty of emotional options and connections. People all around the world are cognizant of our need to come together in new ways to create peace and tolerance. I experienced a wonderful example of this universal desire one day when I was sitting in a New York studio, with headphones over my ears, taking calls on "Voice of America" from listeners in Nigeria, Burundi, Zimbabwe, Israel, Australia and New Zealand. Michael and Julie Weisser and Donna Polk were connected from Lincoln, Nebraska, and we talked directly with callers from around the world who also were looking for ways to break through the barriers that divided their people. They were fascinated by how the Weissers had turned hatred into love, and they openly discussed the need we all have to forgive, to heal, to live in the light of understanding and celebration instead of in the murky, dead-end cave of hatred.

For me, for the Weissers and for everyone whose experiences are chronicled in the pages that follow, it's gratifying to have Northeastern University Press bring out this new edition of *Not by the Sword*. I hope it provides insight into the roots of prejudice and its manifestations, blatant and subtle. I also hope that it suggests the steps we can take to make a difference, starting with ways to establish new friendships and deepen connections in our own communities. The stories in this book convey a larger vision of what is possible, of what the Rev. Dr. Martin Luther King called the power of soul force over physical force. It may be that maintaining the ability to laugh, to play, to dance the dance of life and build unity, while confronting the bigotry that invades our lives and culture on an everyday basis, can, just possibly, help to change the world.

Princeton, New Jersey
September, 2000

THE PLACE AND THE PEOPLE

Prologue

The past is prologue.

One afternoon I stopped my car outside Lincoln, Nebraska, to get a better view of the Great Plains of the United States, and my eyes swept all the way around the horizon, under a 360-degree view of nearly cloudless blue sky. A sliver of silver-white moon glinted in the distance.

Looking up into this clear vault, I realized how Willa Cather's description in *My Ántonia* captures the sensation of this place: "I had the feeling that the world was left behind, that we had got over the edge of it and were outside man's jurisdiction. I had never before looked up at the sky when there was not a familiar mountain ridge against it. But this was the complete dome of heaven, all there was of it. . . ."

This vast stretch of prairie made me imagine what it looked like millions of years ago, before this was grassland, when the place I was standing was part of a shallow inland sea filled with fish lizard dinosaurs, Ichthyosaurs and Plesiosaurs, sharks and other sea creatures. It also made me realize how what has happened in the past speaks to and exists in the present and moves invisibly yet irrevocably into a future, which will contain other people, other lives.

Long ago, the Ka-za (Swift), E-ro-ma-ha (Up Above a Stream) and other Native Americans hunted buffalo, elk, deer, antelope and prairie dogs here. This was before the land was set aside as Indian territory in 1834 and declared off-limits to white settlers, long before government men changed the rules, broke treaty after treaty. It was long before the Oglala chief and warrior Crazy Horse died here when he was betrayed and literally stabbed in the back with a U.S. Army bayonet at Fort Robinson, Nebraska, long before the government had dispossessed the tribes and claimed this land as their own.

Thousands of pioneers lured by new opportunities also passed on foot, in wagons and on horseback, through this Platte Valley on their westward trek over the Independence Trail, the Mormon Trail and the Oregon Trail when the land was still designated Indian territory, and when, as one sojourner put it in 1846, "The wolves and the deers are our travelling companions, and the wild birds and prairie winds our musicians—more highly appreciated than all the carefully prepared concerts of earth."

Today, about 94 percent of the population of Lincoln, Nebraska, comes from Dutch, Scandinavian, German, Czech, Irish, Italian, Polish or Russian ancestry. When the Kansas-Nebraska Act designated Nebraska open to settlement in 1854, land on the western side of the Missouri River was handed out to settlers and refugees who came to tame it. Among the first to arrive were Dutch who had left failing potato crops, massive unemployment and religious persecution in the Netherlands. Other European farmers soon followed.

Many of today's white population have forgotten they were once outsiders, forgotten the circumstances which drove their ancestors here. Perhaps because their heritage still makes such a big impact on their lives, the 6 percent of the population who are African-American, Mexican-American, Asian-American, Native American or other combinations* usually are more aware of their roots.

People often ask what drew African-Americans, Jews, Asians or other minorities to such a predominantly white, Protestant place in the middle of the United States. In fact, the first real settlements in Nebraska were not white and Protestant but were fur-trading posts established along the Missouri River between 1807 and 1820 by a Spanish-American Catholic named Manuel Lisa. Spanish and French

---

*According to the 1990 census, 94.5 percent of Lincoln's population is white, 2.4 percent is black, 2 percent is Hispanic, 1.7 percent is Asian or Pacific Islander and 0.6 percent is Native American.

trappers and traders who stayed long in the area often lived among and married Native Americans.

Some of the first African-Americans to cross the Mississippi and pass through Nebraska most probably were free blacks on their way west. Some African-American traders, trappers and frontiersmen may well have traveled through Nebraska as early as the 1700s. But the first black person known officially to set foot in the state was the famous Spanish scout known as "York" who helped to guide Lewis and Clark's expedition through the eastern part of the state in 1804. York served as the expedition's interpreter, guide and medicine man. He was a source of wonder to the Plains Indians, who admired his regal carriage, his ebony-colored skin, his remarkable hair, his strength and abilities as a healer. There's speculation York was released from his legal status as a slave after the Lewis and Clark expedition ended, and that he stayed among the Indians, married and became an influential chief among the Crow Indians.

The first African-Americans to settle permanently in Nebraska probably came before the Civil War, according to Bertha Calloway at the Great Plains Black Museum in Omaha. A few blacks worked in the laundry at Fort Atkinson in the 1820s. Others came with Dutch, Swedish or German settlers who moved west from New York or other slaveholding states. Like the families they worked for, the African-Americans spoke different dialects of Dutch, Swedish or German, depending on the language of the family.

In the mid-1800s, slaves escaping Missouri and other proslavery states often came through the southeastern corner of Nebraska on their way to Canada. Abolitionist John Brown made several trips in his wagon through Nebraska and Iowa carrying fugitive slaves on their way to freedom. Although Judge Roger Taney, in the Dred Scott case, had ordered "all good citizens" to return fugitive slaves, public sentiment in Nebraska was on the side of the runaways. Nebraska farmers and boardinghouse operators set up an escape route for fugitives which became part of the Underground Railroad. From Topeka, Kansas, fugitives traveled three or four days until they reached Falls City, Nebraska, where they got food, rest and protection from friends of John Brown, as well as directions to the next station, Nemaha City. After Nemaha City, they traveled to Brownville or to Nebraska City, where they crossed the Missouri, went on to Tabor, Iowa, and got outfitted for Canada. After Emancipation, some of the freed black men and women in Canada who remembered Nebraska with fondness came back to settle there.

Records at the Nebraska State Historical Society in Lincoln show that the first black settlers officially on record in Lancaster County arrived in 1868—one year after Nebraska became a state and Lincoln became the state capital. Following the Civil War, over 250,000 freed people made a mass exodus from the South on horseback, in horse- or ox-drawn wagons, in stagecoaches and on foot. Some were drawn to Nebraska by the Homestead Act of 1862, which encouraged any citizen or intended citizen over twenty-one years of age to pay a $10 fee to claim 160 acres (a quarter section) of surveyed but unclaimed public land. Some 100,000 settlers of all nationalities chose to come to Nebraska during that time. The homesteader could own his property after five years of living and cultivating crops on it.

African-Americans who came up from the South wanted to live their lives free from the intimidation, hatred and threats of violence they had lived with on a daily basis in their home states. They wanted to own their own land, earn their own living and experience the freedom of raising their children in a peaceful environment. This wasn't possible in many states where members of the Ku Klux Klan—as well as more moderate Confederates—were actively working to maintain the status quo of slavery and reverse the results of the Civil War.

Around the same time African-Americans began arriving in large numbers in Nebraska, Jewish settlers also came looking for a better life. Like African-Americans, many Jewish newcomers had left homelands where they were forbidden freedom of movement and were unable to live on land of their own choosing, buy property or vote. Like African-Americans, they wanted to find dignity and a better way of life, but first and foremost they wanted to stay alive. For just as blacks fled the murders, floggings, rapes and lynchings in the South after the Civil War, Jews likewise left their homelands to escape pogroms against them that meant destruction or near-certain death.

Many young Jews first came to Nebraska as laborers, peddlers or traders. During the mid-1860s, cargoes came by steamboat up the Missouri River to Omaha from St. Louis and St. Joseph several times a week. By that time, the Union Pacific was advertising for workers to help lay rails for the transcontinental tracks westward from Omaha, to settle the land and work for the railroad. Traders bought and sold clothing, shoes, boots, hats, blankets, revolvers and rubber goods for the tiny fledgling communities of homesteaders, stockyard workers and railroad workers. They did regular business trading with Indian tribes for beaver pelts, buffalo robes, skins, tomahawks, knives and beads.

One of the most intriguing traders was a Jewish immigrant from Prussia named Julius Meyer, who learned to speak several Indian languages. Apparently, Meyer became friends with several Native American chiefs, including Red Cloud, Sitting Bull, Spotted Tail and Swift Bear, and was known among them as Box-ka-re-sha-hash-ta-ka— "Curly-Haired White Chief with One Tongue." He was so well liked, the Pawnee elected him an honorary chief. For a while, the curly-haired white chief had a trading post called the Indian Wigwam, but later he gave it up and lived among his Indian friends. In the early 1880s, he accompanied a group of Omahas and Winnebagos to Paris, where they were guests of the French government, and where Meyer served as guide and translator.

During the 1870s and '80s, more African-Americans, Mexicans, Japanese, Eastern European Jews, Catholic Irishmen and Italians moved to Nebraska to work for the Union Pacific Railroad. The population also increased significantly because of growing agricultural demands, the stockyards and the ranches. Omaha, Lincoln and other communities were growing, which added further opportunities for incoming ethnic groups to work as laborers, surveyors, stonecutters, carpenters, preachers and teachers.

As times changed, other newcomers continued moving in. The most recent arrivals come mainly from Southeast Asia—Vietnam, Laos, Cambodia, China—and from Central and South America—Guatemala, Colombia, Nicaragua, Mexico. A few come from Russia, Armenia, Ukraine, Afghanistan and Poland. And they are all further changing the complexion of Lincoln and the rest of the Midwest. ("When we come to Lincoln from Vietnam, we see all the American people with yellow hair," says a ten-year-old, Ngon, with a joyful laugh. "But we have the black hair!")

Southeast Asians under the sponsorship of refugee resettlement agencies and various church conferences are doing what immigrants before them did: migrating to places relatives and friends have already settled. This "chain migration" provides newcomers with a strong support system—which is why Lincoln especially attracts Vietnamese newcomers to the Midwest, while Laotians go to Omaha or the small rural town of Tecumseh, in the southeast corner of Nebraska, and Cambodians often move on to Denver to join a well-established Cambodian community.

Currently in Lincoln, more than 4,000 Vietnamese have formed an active community which includes large Buddhist and Catholic congregations. Their children join some 100 other new arrivals entering the Lincoln Public Schools every year, and slowly but steadily they're moving into modest brick and wood homes beside white Nebraskans whose great-great-grandparents also arrived not speaking a word of English.

Like much of America, Nebraska is a study in contrasts. Chances for a long life are better here than anywhere else in the United States with the exception of neighboring Iowa. The slow, relaxed pace of life theoretically nurtures longevity, yet one of America's first serial murderers, Charles Starkweather, was born and bred here before he began his widely memorialized killing spree in 1958. The weather, too, goes to extremes, and is often credited or blamed for things like long life or murderous rage. The temperature is known to have fluctuated by sixty degrees in one day and tornadoes or spring floods can happen as fast as hail follows rain on a summer day.

The racial and religious aspects of the state also have their intemperate aspects. For the most part, people are friendly, prejudices seem picayune and there's not much open conflict. Everyday racism—subtle but cruel—isn't any more noticeable here than it is elsewhere, except to its targets, who often start to take it for granted. Yet like the weather, terrifying incidents of bigotry fueled by odd pockets of fanaticism can happen suddenly here and when they do, they disturb and shock the sensibility which mandates "Love Thy Neighbor as Thyself."

Memory is often short, however, when it comes to the facts and effects of the deep currents of racism and anti-Semitism that flow in our society like underground water grown dirty from waste and pollution. People surprised by the Ku Klux Klan coming to Nebraska in modern times don't seem to remember that in its many reincarnations since its birth in 1867, the Klan has been active in dozens of states in the Midwest and the North as well as in the South. Nebraskans themselves forget that in the 1920s, the KKK was vigorous throughout the state in its campaigns against blacks, Jews, foreigners, Catholics and women suffragists, as it was in dozens of other states of the Union. Family members today are often shocked and ashamed when they find records of

Klan membership or packed-away white robes of their fathers or grand-fathers in dusty attics or in basement boxes. Often, they destroy these artifacts in an effort to wipe out the traces of bigotry and the realities of racism which so clearly shaped and ruined lives.

Many people also would like to forget a story Nebraska-born Malcolm X told his biographer Alex Haley—a shaping story that became part of the way Malcolm saw his life—about a time in Omaha in 1925 when his mother was eight months pregnant with him and the Ku Klux Klan came knocking on her door. Malcolm recalled his mother telling him how she had opened the front door that night and looked up at hooded Klansmen on horseback "surrounding the house, brandishing their shotguns and rifles." The Klansmen, carrying torches, were shouting for her husband, the Reverend Little, a Baptist minister and orga-nizer for Marcus Garvey's Universal Negro Improvement Association. But Reverend Little wasn't home. Louise Little stood in the doorway and told the Klansmen she was alone with her three small children and her husband was preaching at a church in Milwaukee. The Klansmen shouted threats and warnings to get out of town, and "finally spurred their horses and galloped around the house, shattering every window pane with their gun butts" before riding off into the night "as suddenly as they came."

While some historians have challenged the details of Malcolm's story, Nebraska was definitely Klan country. That same spring of 1925, the Klan had reached its pinnacle in Nebraska, as well as in the rest of the United States. In Nebraska alone, the Klan had some 40,000 to 50,000 registered members in 1925.

The Klan had grown large following World War I, when the African-American population increased and moved north, when more and more foreigners, Catholics and Jews were coming into the country, when women were agitating for the right to vote, when jobs were scarce and when competition for those jobs was intense. African-Americans had fought unflaggingly for America during the First World War—and some reactionary whites wanted to make sure blacks didn't start thinking they were *entitled* to any new rights because of their valor and strength in combat.

All over the country, change was in the air, fear of Communists and radicals was growing, tension was palpable and the Klan milked it to their advantage. During the summer of 1919, one out of every five workers in the country was on strike—a percentage of workers striking that has never been equaled. "Race riots"—meaning armed white mobs attacking, lynching and often raping unarmed and isolated blacks, and blacks defending themselves and in some cases striking back with armed force—took place in twenty-five cities and towns during that summer. The film *Birth of a Nation,* immensely popular after it was released in 1915, contributed dramatically to the stereotyping of Klansmen as heroes and blacks as "beasts" and "savages"—labels that allowed members of Klan-led mobs to congratulate themselves for killing subhuman animals, not fellow human beings. Historians now refer to the summer of 1919 as "Red Summer" because so much blood was shed, all too often by mobs who chose to become fired up by false reports of black assaults and attacks on white women.

Nebraska wasn't immune. One of the most horrific racist incidents in this state's history happened in September 1919, when a mob of some 5,000 people in Omaha stormed the city jail to get to a young black man named William Brown, a packinghouse worker who had been accused of holding a gun on a couple, stealing seventeen dollars and raping the woman.

No charges had been filed against William Brown, and no grand jury had been convened, but the crowd in Omaha decided Brown was guilty and demanded he be turned over to them for "immediate justice." The crowd had been primed for this moment by rumors that blacks were responsible for increasing numbers of rapes in Omaha. Historian Michael Schuyler points out these rumors had nothing to do with the truth: black leaders at the time noted that thirteen out of seventeen people accused of assault in the city were white, but facts didn't stop the rumors.

The crowd, led by William Brown's accuser, a nineteen-year-old named William Hoffman, strung up the mayor of Omaha when he tried to intervene. The mayor didn't die, but he was seriously injured. Members of the mob were determined to deliver "immediate justice." They set fire to the courthouse and dragged out William Brown, who had such bad rheumatoid arthritis that a physician who knew him said later that he could not possibly have committed the rape of which he was accused.

One of the many witnesses to this incident was actor Henry Fonda, one of Nebraska's native sons, who never forgot what he saw that night. A fourteen-year-old at the time, Fonda later told his biographer he had climbed to the second floor of his father's printing plant and stood beside his father in the dark, looking down on the courthouse square, where the cursing, screaming crowd of men waved clubs and guns and burning torches. "A great huzzah went up when they saw the poor fellow," Fonda recalled. He watched while a group of strongmen put a noose around William Brown's neck and hung him from the end of a lamppost.

". . . [W]hile his feet were still dancing in the air, they riddled his body with [more than a thousand] bullets," Fonda said. "It was the most horrendous sight I'd ever seen. Then they cut down the body, tied it to an auto, and dragged it through the streets of Omaha." Another report says the crowd "hanged him from a telephone pole in front of the county court house, shot him hundreds of times, and then burned his corpse on a pyre in the middle of the street. Before the night was over, an old man and a boy also lost their lives."

After the lynching, the white mob rioted through Omaha, breaking into stores and stealing or destroying whatever was in their path—causing an estimated million dollars' worth of damage before order was restored by federal troops from Fort Crook and Fort Omaha.

Even though Brown's death preceded the official arrival of the Ku Klux Klan in Nebraska, historian Michael Schuyler points out that the William Brown lynching played a role in the Klan's establishing itself there because it proved Nebraska *had* a "race problem." Also, the breakdown of law and order following the lynching was used to insist that law enforcement officials needed the Klan's help in enforcing law and order. When the Klan came to Nebraska in the early 1920s to recruit members, Lincoln soon had the largest chapter in the state.

Some 5,000 Klansmen in their robes and hoods marched down the main street of Lincoln the summer of 1924 and held an open-air initiation. The following year on July 4, the Klan held another huge parade when 2,000 Klansmen marched in full regalia through Lincoln's business district. The procession of Klansmen riding on horseback, in officials' cars or on floats, was led by a Klansman mounted on a white horse. Some members carried banners or flags, and members of the Junior Klan Auxiliary in hoods and robes marched in step to the beat kept by a "Klavalier" drum corps.

After the parade, the Klan held an all-day picnic in Epworth Park, by the lake. Klansmen, Klanswomen, Klanschildren and the general public were invited to attend a Klan wedding, musical concerts, a baseball game, sports contests and boat rides. A newspaper account at the time reported: "Local leaders were elated at the good turnout and estimated that 25,000 people were on the grounds during the day. The ticket seller estimated that 20,000 tickets had been sold by 8 P.M." A display of fireworks was held during the evening after a Baptist evangelist from Indianapolis told the afternoon crowds, "Protestant forces which are afflicted with sleeping sickness must arouse themselves and take more of an interest in the religion in order to combat the [Catholic] program . . . working to make America Catholic." It was one of the biggest public events ever to have taken place in Lincoln.

Throughout the United States, similar gatherings were drawing hundreds of new members—each of whom paid ten dollars to join, making the publicists and leaders quite rich in the process. By 1925, the Ku Klux Klan in America had over 5 million registered members—many of them doctors, ministers, businessmen, policemen, sheriffs, teachers and prominent city and state leaders. Some Congressmen, Senators, members of the Cabinet and high military officers were said to be Klan-affiliated. Klan lecturers even claimed that President Warren Harding was sworn in as a member of the Ku Klux Klan while he was in the White House.

All of those facts from the past may seem like shameful aberrations to those few who remember them; they may seem like something that happened to other people in other places during times far removed. But in Lincoln in the 1980s, memories of the past were reawakened when the Ku Klux Klan became active once again.

SUNDAY MORNING

Chapter 1

Aizeh hu ahir . . .
Who is rich? He who is happy with what he has.
—ETHICS OF THE FATHERS

*I*t was a sunny Sunday morning in June 1991, and the mood was cheerful in the kitchen of the Weissers' new home. Julie Weisser, her husband, Cantor Michael Weisser, and their close friend Rita Babbitz sat at a long rectangular table talking and laughing over mugs of brewed black coffee. The three told stories on themselves, discussed their children and talked about the recent movie *The Doctor* with William Hurt—a doctor who had the tables turned when he became sick and had to deal with a lack of sensitivity from his medical colleagues. Julie loved the film. After she saw it, she went to the box office and bought a book of movie tickets for doctors at a local heart institute. She did it because she thought they had shown a lack of concern for Michael when he had a severe heart problem the previous month.

"Who but you would buy a book of movie coupons to give to those doctors?" Rita said with a laugh as Michael began to crack eggs into a bowl and stir them for scrambled eggs he was about to cook.

"It's quintessential Julie," Michael said as he set out rye toast, juice and muffins, and opened a can of coffee to brew another pot.

"Driven by injustice," Rita said with a smile.

"This doctor was telling me Michael didn't almost die," Julie said to Rita, her words softened by a Memphis accent she hasn't fully shed since her childhood in Tennessee. "He said, 'His heart just stopped beating,' like that was no big deal."

Half-unloaded cardboard packing boxes sat in the corners of the large eat-in kitchen. After two-and-a-half years of renting in Lincoln, Julie and Michael had finally purchased their own home—a modest but comfortable brick ranch with two bedrooms, living room, kitchen and bath, plus a tiny bedroom and recreation space in the basement. Julie and Michael had a wonderful feeling about the place when they first walked into it. And when the owner told them she would finance the mortgage herself and asked for a down payment of only $500, they knew this was their "miracle house." They had only been here a few days, but already they felt at home.

The white phone, tucked against a white wall between wooden kitchen cabinets and a yellow counter, had rung several times since Rita's arrival, which wasn't any surprise. Rita was used to it. The sound of the telephone, like the sounds of voices and laughter in the Weisser household, was part of the music, as familiar and normal as the bright blue dishes, painted yellow chairs or red wooden rooster sitting in the middle of the table. As spiritual leader for Congregation B'nai Jeshurun, one of two synagogues in Lincoln, Nebraska, Cantor Michael Weisser got calls constantly. So did Julie, who had friends scattered from Lincoln to Memphis to New York City. Add to that the calls for their three teenagers—Rebecca, Dina and Dave—and it was unusual for the phone *not* to ring.

On this particular morning, as usual, the Weisser household seemed almost like a cliché of the all-American happy family, albeit a reconstituted American family of the 1990s. Julie was missing her daughter, fifteen-year-old Rebecca Nelms, a lanky, six-foot-tall high school drama enthusiast and avid reader, who was in Memphis visiting her dad—Julie's ex-husband—and her grandparents. Fifteen-year-old Dina and seventeen-year-old Dave, the middle two of four children from Michael's previous marriage, also were absent from the kitchen. Dina, a tall, dark-haired, energetic high school freshman with a beautiful singing voice and a love of novels equal to Becca's, was in Iowa at a four-day retreat for leaders of MOVTY—Missouri Valley Federation of Temple Youth. Dave, a straight-A student and a musician with his own band, was still asleep in his room downstairs.

The natural ease and comfort here was palpable. When the telephone rang again, Ishtov, a large golden retriever, eagerly followed Michael toward the phone. Ida, a large gray cat, jumped up on the yellow counter and arched her long back under Michael's arm.

Julie and Rita were laughing loudly when Michael picked up the receiver of the phone and said "Hello."

A moment after Michael picked up the kitchen phone, Dave sleepily picked up the phone downstairs and listened to Michael's voice answering.

The man's voice on the other end of the line—startlingly harsh and hateful—seemed loud as he pronounced each word distinctly: "You *will be sorry* you ever moved into 5810 Randolph Street, Jew boy."

Then the phone went dead.

"What's the matter?! You look like someone just hit you," Julie said.

Michael sat down and finally spoke. "That guy just said, 'You *will be sorry* you ever moved into 5810 Randolph Street, Jew boy.' "

"Oh God, there's someone in the neighborhood who hates us," Julie exclaimed. "We're going to be harassed because somebody hates us."

Michael was shaking with anger.

"We should call the police," Julie said. "It has to be someone in this neighborhood. It's too much of a coincidence that we just moved into this house and then got this phone call."

"I'll bet it's the Klan," Michael said. "I'll bet it's that guy who's head of the Nebraska Ku Klux Klan."

"No, it has to be someone in the neighborhood," Julie insisted.

Dave ambled into the kitchen, his brown hair tousled, his eyes sleepy but startled. "What's going on?" he asked, putting his arm around his dad's shoulders. "What was that all about? I just picked up the phone."

"Did you hear what he said?" Michael asked.

"I heard the *o* of hello and then I heard, 'You're going to be sorry you ever moved to 5810 Randolph Street, Jew boy—click.' What are the implications of this? He knows our address and our phone number and that we're Jewish . . ."

"And so you heard him say that from the other phone?" Rita asked.

"Yeah, that was what he said," Dave said. "Wow, I wonder why anyone would do something like that?"

"It's a sickness," Michael said to him. "They don't know better or they wouldn't do it."

"It's the weirdest feeling when something like this happens," Julie said. "You just can't believe people can say those kinds of things or think those kinds of things, but they do. . . ."

"I don't think it's the Klan," Dave said. "I think it's probably just some crackpot."

"A crackpot from the Klan," Michael insisted.

A HEARTLAND *Chapter 2*

COMMUNITY

*The Torah's highest teaching is love and kindness. "What is
hateful to you, do not do to any person."*
— *THE GATES OF PRAYER*

*A*fter the telephone call, Michael, Julie and Rita sat in the
kitchen trying to figure out what to do. Michael called the police, and
an officer came by and advised them to get locks for their doors and
keys for each member of the family.

"I hate to do that," Michael said. "We've never locked our doors. Why
should we have to start now?"

Julie insisted the police officer join them for the enormous breakfast
Michael had finally started to cook. At first she refused, but Michael
and Julie's genuine welcome was convincing, and the officer sat down
at the kitchen table. Julie told her she was sure the call had been made
by some neighbor who had seen the real estate transfer in the newspaper and didn't want Jews living on their block. "A family down the
street who belong to the temple had a cross burned on their lawn ten or
fifteen years ago," she said, "and I know they prosecuted someone who
lives in this neighborhood. I think we should go to all the neighbors
and tell them what happened and see how they respond."

After the officer left, Julie dressed to go out. More often than not,
Julie's hazel-brown eyes crinkle in laughter over life's amazing com-
plexities, absurdities and adventures, but on this particular morning,
she was solemn and focused as she began to knock on doors around
the neighborhood.

A solid five-foot-five-and-a-half-inch-tall blond dynamo, Julie walked fast in her small, flat, brown shoes, like a determined woman on a mission. She was calm, friendly and direct as she collected facts, observed nuances and processed the information she got. When she knocked on the front door of the home whose occupants she had heard were anti-Semitic and explained what had happened, she watched the reaction closely. Both father and son seemed genuinely surprised; they said they were sorry to hear about the call and assured her they didn't know who did it. Julie believed them. She continued around the block knocking on doors and talking to neighbors.

Michael, whose once-black hair is thinning and beginning to turn gray, also put on a fresh shirt with his jeans and tennis shoes before he slowly meandered across the street to talk to a neighbor named Mark. Michael's strong nose, angular jawline and dark brown eyes reflect his Ukrainian and German ancestry. At five feet nine, he's overweight, but more noticeable is his easy laugh, his warm, comfortable voice and the alert, genuine curiosity and brightness lighting his face when he talks.

Mark was upset when Michael told him what had happened. "Look, if anyone bothers you or if your kids are worried, come and get me," Mark said. "I'd like nothing better than to get a hold of a couple of skinheads."

"You can pretty much tell when people are sincere," Julie said. "The woman on the other side, she's a divorced young mom with kids, and she felt really bad. I also walked around the corner and talked to Sherry Nelson, who is black and who has a young son as well as a teenager who goes to the same school as our kids, and I asked if anything similar had happened to them."

Sherry confided she'd never had a hate call, but her young child had played with white kids across the street until an old man next door to the white family said, "How can you let your kids play with that nigger?" All of a sudden, the kids couldn't play together anymore. Then the old man and his wife went on vacation and the white family let their kids play with Sherry's son again. Sherry went across the street and asked, "How can you let someone influence your mind like that?" She told Julie they were moving soon and she was glad. "My husband and I call it the Cream of Wheat city because it's so white," she said. "People are so underexposed to minorities they don't even *know* how smug and bigoted they are."

The Evanses, a couple in their eighties, came across the street to say they thought this was terrible. The Weissers' next door neighbor, Maxine, baked a sponge cake, and she and her husband, George, brought it over with fresh strawberries and a bunch of labels which said "This house is protected electronically by Security Patrol."

Michael and Julie were reassured by the response of their neighbors, but they still were troubled by the feeling something bad was about to happen. The person who had called knew their number and their address—and his words promised something ominous. They were most afraid for the kids—who were home after school by themselves until Michael got home from the synagogue or hospital visits and Julie got home from her work at a doctor's office. This also was the first time during the two-and-a-half years they had lived in Lincoln that such an open act of anti-Semitism had been directed at them. Since their arrival in October 1988, their experiences here had made them feel safe and welcome.

Like many clergymen and -women, Michael Weisser had worked in several synagogues after his graduation from New York City's Hebrew Union College–Jewish Institute of Religion, where he got his degree and certification as a cantor in Reform Judaism in June 1976. Initially, he worked as cantor and director of religious education at Memphis' largest synagogue, Temple Israel, for four years, and then he worked at synagogues in Sacramento, California; Youngstown, Ohio; and Dunedin, Florida. Michael had taken an interim job between two small congregations—one in Greenville and one in Goldsboro, North Carolina—when a rabbi friend called and said he'd noticed in a rabbinical placement list that Congregation B'nai Jeshurun in Lincoln, Nebraska, had been looking for a rabbi for four years, with no luck.

Congregation B'nai Jeshurun (Children of Israel), the oldest Jewish congregation in Lincoln, had been established in 1884. But now it seemed on the verge of dying. Michael's rabbi friend suggested Michael give the congregation a call and tell them he'd like to be their clergyman. The timing was right; Michael was ready for a new challenge. During the fifty-mile drive between synagogues in North Carolina, he'd been doing a lot of thinking about the need to break down barriers between people and how he would like to put some of his ideas about spirituality and the Jewish faith into effect in a more focused way. He called Lincoln and spoke with Marsha Plotkin, president of the congregation.

Ms. Plotkin explained that rabbinic students from Cincinnati had been flying in every other week to conduct Friday night services, but many members either had stopped coming or had transferred their loyalty to Congregation Tifereth Israel, a larger and wealthier Conservative synagogue in Lincoln. Since Lincoln doesn't have an Orthodox temple, Tifereth Israel (Glory of Israel) is attended by Lincoln's few Orthodox Jews, who require strict adherence to traditional Jewish dietary and ritual laws, as well as its Conservative Jews, who usually fall between the more strict interpreters of law in Orthodox Judaism and the more liberal practices of Reform Judaism. Services at Tifereth Israel are conducted almost entirely in Hebrew. Now some of the Reform Jews in Lincoln were also attending Tifereth Israel, but they weren't particularly happy there.

Michael Weisser told Ms. Plotkin he was intrigued by the idea of a foundering congregation—and they should think about hiring a cantor instead of a rabbi as their clergyman.

"Is it legitimate to have a cantor without a rabbi?" she had asked. Michael told her that it was rare, but according to today's laws and traditions, it was fine. Cantors who were solo spiritual leaders in the United States were few and far between—but Michael knew of one in Iowa and another in Puerto Rico.

As a solo cantor, Michael would be spiritual leader of the congregation and do the job of both rabbi and cantor. Traditionally, a cantor works along with the rabbi of a synagogue and concentrates on Jewish ceremony, Jewish liturgical music and services while the rabbi's concentration is on the Torah (the Bible and the body of Jewish literature and oral tradition that contains the laws, teachings and divine knowledge of the religion) and the Talmud (the collection of ancient rabbinic writings which delineate historical religious teachings about the Torah). The personal quality most cantors have in common is a beautiful, nearly operatic voice. In the Conservative movement of Judaism, the cantor has a public and powerful role in the synagogue as the person who sings and leads the congregation in services and in songs of prayer, and in Orthodox Judaism, the cantor plays a similarly powerful and public role.

In Reform Judaism, however, the role of the cantor is less clearly defined, since for a long time the Reform movement didn't have cantors at all. Some twenty-five or thirty years ago, most Reform congregations had choirs and very few had cantors. In moving toward a more conservative religious tradition, however, more and more Reform congregations have added cantors. Still, out of some eight hundred Reform synagogues, fewer than three hundred have fully trained cantors.*

A Reform cantor literally "cants," or sings, sacred songs of prayer and typically is in charge of the music, liturgy and education program for the synagogue, while the rabbi gives the sermons and does more of the pastoral work. Depending on the relationship between rabbi and cantor, the cantor does more or less of the rabbinical work—making hospital visits, conducting weddings and funerals and teaching Torah and Talmud. In those cases, many of the functions of the cantor and the rabbi overlap and the cantor acts as an associate and close ally of the rabbi, whereas in other cases—when the congregation is large or the rabbi is protective of his or her turf—the cantor acts more as an assistant.

Michael Weisser explained to Marsha Plotkin that cantors and rabbis have some training in common, and in the past few years, Hebrew Union College has started training rabbis and cantors together to reduce the friction and turf wars between them. He suggested Ms. Plotkin talk with her board and check out the issue of solo cantors with the Central Conference of American Rabbis, as well as with some other rabbis, to reassure herself. When she and the board made their inquiries, and when rabbinical scholars said they could find no objection to having a cantor as spiritual leader of a synagogue, Marsha Plotkin invited Michael Weisser to come for an interview.

Michael flew to Lincoln in April 1988, and he immediately liked the place. Lincoln had been "the Village of Lancaster" until its citizens successfully wrestled the status of capital away from Omaha when Nebraska became a state in 1867 and renamed their town in honor of President Lincoln. Now a city of about 213,000 people, judged by *Money* magazine as one of the top ten places to live in the United States and the third-best city to raise children, Lincoln is green, with low-slung buildings and two-story houses, small businesses, state government offices, two universities, two colleges, dozens of high schools and grade schools, two shopping malls, thirty-six hotels and motels, one county

---

*Small congregations sometimes hire only a rabbi and bring in a free-lance musician or "cantorial soloist" to sing at services.

jail and one state penitentiary. It is surrounded by the immense prairie land that was named "the Great American Desert" by a cartographer in the early 1820s. The name of the state itself comes from *nebrathka,* an Otoe and Omaha word used to describe the Platte River as "broad, flat water."

Michael felt comfortable with the pace of the city, and he especially loved the feel of the beautiful old Reform temple at 20th and South streets. Lincoln's original Jewish community, which had only twenty-eight members in the 1880s, built their first temple in 1893 on the northwest corner of 12th and D streets. But when their congregation grew with the expanding Jewish population escaping the pogroms of Eastern Europe in the 1880s and migrating to the Midwest to join friends and family at the turn of the century, they built this South Street temple—which can seat 220 people downstairs in rows of comfortable seats that curve around the deep walnut Ark, the pulpit and bimah—the raised stage—all of which was carved in Nebraska walnut during the 1920s by a Christian woodworker whose daughter later converted to Judaism and is now a member of the congregation. An upstairs balcony, with seats for 40 more people, is at eye level with beautiful stained-glass windows through which light filters into the sanctuary.

During his interview with the temple's board of directors and members, Michael was straightforward about his approach. "I believe the great failure of American Judaism has been a move away from the spiritual to the ritual," he told them. "As a community nationwide, we all too often have adopted a ritual life devoid of spiritual meaning and basic religious principles.

"Rituals can enhance basic religious principles," Michael told them, but rituals and religion are two different things. "Rituals are nice," he said. "I love Jewish ritual and ceremony, but if the ritual doesn't encapsulate spiritual ideas, then it's meaningless. Form is not what religion is about and it's not what spirituality is about.

"Essentially, I'm talking about three basic ideas at the heart of our Jewish faith—love, tolerance and nonharmful behavior. Those are the core religious principles.

" 'Love your neighbor as yourself!' We're not talking about our neighbor who is the same as we are. No, we're talking about the neighbor who is *different* from us. Tolerance requires practice. If we practice enough and become more tolerant, accepting, loving and less harmful, then we begin to attain the attributes of justice and righteousness Judaism teaches us."

During his interview, and later, during the sermon he gave at Shabbat services that Friday evening, Michael again brought up the need to try to build harmony between people. "In Jewish tradition, our role as human beings is to correct the universe," Michael said. "So how do we do that? We look at the things that we have done to place barriers between human beings and the rest of natural creation. Little by little, we need to tear down those barriers and make them disappear so we can experience the fullness of each other and the richness of the creation, which is given to us as a gift and of which we are a part."

Within this context, Michael, whose wife, Julie, had converted to Judaism, also brought up his controversial views on interfaith marriages and ecumenical work: "Remember that story in the book of Exodus when Moses is reluctant to be a prophet? He asks God what he should tell the Israelites about who is sending him into Egypt. . . . God tells Moses, 'Ehyeh-Asher-Ehyeh. Say to the Israelites, "Ehyeh sent me to you." '

"*Ehyeh-Asher-Ehyeh* means 'I shall be what I shall be,' " Michael told the congregants. "This indicates that God can be many things to many people. To one person, God may represent the growing and living things of nature. Someone else needs God to be the invisible essence of the cosmos. According to the name God gave Moses, God is everything to all people, and he will reveal himself to you in your way and me in my way, which really is all the same. If you find communion with God as a Southern Baptist, who am I to say you didn't? God is not the exclusive property of any one group. Jewish, Christian, Muslim, Baha'i, Hindu and all the many wonderful varieties of thought are potential pathways to the presence of God.

"I feel the same thing about my own children. My wife and I would love it if they have Jewish households. But the likelihood is, they will marry the person they fall in love with. And that person may or may not be Jewish. If they marry someone who is not Jewish, I have to trust it will be interesting for them and good for them.

"I have to trust that because manifestations of God are always present. They're present in the wind and in the trees and in the embrace of another human being, in the cry of a baby, in the findings of scientists."

• • •

Despite these views—or perhaps in large part because of them—the board and the membership of Congregation B'nai Jeshurun asked Michael to start work in Lincoln on the High Holy Days in September, when all the members of the congregation would come to the synagogue. Michael declined. He said he would come in October, *after* the High Holy Days because he didn't want to start his relationship with the congregation in a ritualistic way. If he came in October, he would have nearly a whole year to establish meaningful relationships before the High Holy Days came around again.

The board agreed. Michael, Julie and Rebecca moved to Lincoln in October 1988, and the cantor-as-solo-spiritual-leader experiment began. The Weissers found themselves living in a largely Christian, evangelical community. Out of Lincoln's population of 213,641, some 98,713 people told census takers in 1990 they were Christian, compared to the 795 who identified themselves as Jewish.* The Weissers would have enjoyed having a larger Jewish community and a deli that sold fresh bagels and lox, but they felt comfortable. After their first year there, Michael's then fourteen-year-old son Dave came from Memphis to live with them, and the following year, thirteen-year-old Dina also joined them. (Michael's oldest son, Daniel, was ready to begin college, and his youngest daughter, Debbie, had moved to New Jersey from Memphis with her mother.)

And as the Weisser family in Lincoln grew, so did the temple congregation. Michael later said one of the main reasons he was convinced to come to B'nai Jeshurun was the challenge. "It looked as if the congregation wasn't going to make it," he said. "The thing that impressed me in the meetings is, they told me the truth. They said, 'We don't have much money and almost nobody comes to temple.' At the service I gave, fifteen people showed up—and that was a big event because typical attendance for the past few years had been three or four people.

"It's pretty easy for a cantor to find a job and just earn a living, but here was an opportunity to try some things that I had thought about. If it didn't work out, I was young enough at the age of forty-seven to obtain another position."

*In the 1990 census, 650 people in Lincoln said they were Muslim, 600 said they were Buddhist and 440 said they were Unitarian.

At B'nai Jeshurun, beginning with his first Friday night service as solo cantor, Michael began teaching the Torah's essential messages of love and tolerance. "There's nothing anywhere in Jewish literature that says any Gentile should be excluded from what we do in our synagogues," he told the congregation that first night in October 1988. "In fact, just the opposite is true, because if you read in the prophet Isaiah, he says, 'My house shall be a house of prayer for all people.' He doesn't say my house shall be a house of prayer for all Jewish people—he says it's for *all* people."

Some of Michael Weisser's feelings against exclusivity may have come from growing up in poor, rough neighborhoods in New Haven, Connecticut, where prejudice and institutionalized bigotry flew in all directions. Michael had lived in a mixed Italian, Jewish and black neighborhood, and his friends included a number of Catholic kids. He had gone to their confirmations, and when he was thirteen years old, he was excited to invite them to his bar mitzvah. Just as a confirmation marks the Catholic child's transition into the faith, the bar mitzvah is the hallmark of the Jewish child's transition into religious responsibility. Michael was excited his friends would be at his celebration, but with the exception of a couple of them who were especially courageous, it didn't happen. That's because the Catholic priest in the parish church forbade the boys to go: it would be a sin, he said, for them to step inside a synagogue.

"He didn't do the right thing," Michael said. "Our job is to do the right thing. All Jews have a covenant with God to do what is right, what is loving. We have a covenant with God to be a light to the nations."

Congregants seemed to like what they heard and what they felt about themselves during temple services. Michael had a down-to-earth, almost street-kid quality that was appealing and accessible. More people began coming to evening services on Friday nights and to the social gatherings afterward, when they met downstairs for coffee, juice, fruit, rolls, challah (a braided bread) and conversation. They enjoyed Sabbath gatherings and religious discussions on Saturday mornings. And once they came, they usually came back. "Michael's outreach was enormous," says temple board member Alan Frank. "My wife is a dedicated Lutheran and she had never felt comfortable at synagogue before. Michael has been very affirming. He's done so much for us."

To some people, Michael's ideas were radical or misguided, but he continued to openly support interfaith couples and welcome people of all faiths to attend services. And on Friday nights, about five or six of the forty or so men, women, children and babies who turned up for Sabbath evening services were Christians who had dropped in to worship.

After his first year in Lincoln, Cantor Weisser met the Reverend Dr. Norman Leach, a Presbyterian minister who came to Lincoln from San Francisco on Yom Kippur in 1989 to head Lincoln's Interfaith Council. About six feet three, with wavy black hair, pale white skin and a large frame, Norman Leach looks as if he were once a linebacker for the University of Nebraska's Cornhuskers football team before trading his jersey for a clerical collar. In fact, as a young college student in the 1960s, Leach wasn't playing football. Instead, he was sitting in at lunch counters in Columbia, Missouri, with other members of CORE (Congress of Racial Equality), registering voters and marching in demonstrations for civil rights.

Norman Leach passionately shared Michael's ecumenical views, and the two became close friends. Dr. Leach had been executive director of the San Francisco Council of Churches, a Protestant organization which, together with the Roman Catholic Archdiocese, the Board of Rabbis of Northern California and the Jewish Religious Council, had been an active part of the San Francisco Conference on Religion, Race and Social Concerns. When Lincoln's Interfaith Council became truly interfaith rather than strictly a Christian group in March of 1989, Leach's longtime track record in civil rights and ecumenical work made him an ideal candidate to head the group.

The Interfaith Council expanded its role in the community under Leach's leadership, but dealing with anti-Semitism and bigotry in the community wasn't easy. Most of the council—called the Lincoln Fellowship of Churches when it was strictly a Christian group—had faced the reality that in addition to Lincoln's 196 Protestant churches, the city now also had 17 Catholic congregations, 1 Russian Orthodox, 1 Greek Orthodox and 2 Eastern Orthodox churches, 2 different branches of Buddhists, Muslims who worshiped in an Islamic mosque and 2 synagogues. But when the Fellowship voted to become interfaith and when B'nai Jeshurun and Tifereth Israel, the two Jewish congregations, the Unitarians, the Baha'is, the Buddhists and Lincoln Churchwomen United joined them, all but two of Lincoln's Lutheran churches left the organization. One Lutheran minister wrote to say Christians had no business being involved with Muslims, Buddhists or Jews because the focus of their lives and their work should be based on the teachings of Jesus Christ. Only one Catholic priest was active in the Interfaith Council, and he was a maverick, since the former bishop of the diocese did not allow his parish priests to become involved in ecumenical, much less interfaith, activities.

And when Norman Leach and the Interfaith Council planned Lincoln's first Martin Luther King Service, a Lutheran minister wrote to Leach protesting any event held in honor of "Martin Luther Coon." The minister enclosed some leaflets, originally from a Nazi, white supremacist newspaper, about "Martin Luther Coon" being a Communist. Leach showed the letter to Weisser, and they discussed the odd fact that Lincoln was home of the National Socialist German Workers Party (NSDAP-AO), a neo-Nazi organization founded in 1972 by Gary Rex "Gerhard" Lauck. Lauck, born and raised in Lincoln, had become the world's top supplier of Nazi propaganda to the German Nazi underground. Lauck lived outside Lincoln, but still used a Lincoln post office box for his international business of promoting Nazi organizations and disseminating his neo-Nazi newspaper, *The New Order,* and other hate publications. It seemed the protesting Lutheran minister had received some of Lauck's propaganda.

Norman Leach knew the bitter taste of deeply imbedded racism, but it still surprised him when it came directly from the head of an established religious institution. Nevertheless, Leach's English heritage gave him a certain stoicism. He, like Michael, shared a reverence and love for the beliefs and teachings of Dr. King, and they began actively to structure events and workshops to help people see that no matter who or how they worship, they could all learn to love and tolerate each other.

Through his work with the Interfaith Council, Michael Weisser also got to know Ron Drury, a Lutheran minister, Dr. Michael Combs, a Methodist minister, and other religious leaders. He also sang with the Lincoln Community Gospel Choir at a Holocaust Memorial observance. Some of the Protestant preachers Michael met started showing up every now and then for Sabbath services at the South Street temple. The Christian ministers came to the synagogue, they said, because they felt comfortable there. Also, since they were working on Sundays, Friday night services gave them a good chance to worship in a relaxed atmosphere. "When ministers are made to feel welcome and so much a part of the temple family, they become very comfortable with their relationship with Jews," Michael told some congregants who asked him about it. "When they go back to their churches and preach from their pulpits, do you think that they have anything negative to say about Jews? No. They'll say, 'When I was at B'nai Jeshurun, I felt at home.' "

Despite Congregation B'nai Jeshurun being "the little kid on the block" compared to Tifereth Israel's larger congregation of 150 families, the members of the beautiful old temple at 20th and South streets seemed to form new religious connections and feel new energy under Michael's leadership, and the life of the temple families had begun to flourish. Two-and-a-half years after Michael's arrival in Lincoln, the membership of Congregation B'nai Jeshurun had grown from 75 to 100 families—no small feat in a town with only some 300 Jewish families.

A number of the Lincoln Interfaith Council's ecumenical events were held at B'nai Jeshurun. Michael also went out to schools and churches, and to the local jail and state penitentiary to talk to prisoners interested in learning more about Judaism and the principles of love and tolerance he felt were basic to all religions.

Meanwhile, the Weisser home became known as a place to find Julie's spirited welcome, along with Creedence Clearwater on the tape deck, or Dave's guitar playing, Dina's singing and Rebecca's dramatics, not to mention Ishtov's big doggy tail wagging. At the Weissers', it was almost a guarantee you could drop in and find stimulating conversation, raucous humor, genuine, down-to-earth feeling and Michael's famous lasagna and salad, his paella, his stir-fry or his homemade bagels lathered in cream cheese. "My friends think my parents are insane," says Rebecca. "You can come over to our house any night of the week and we'll be up until eleven or twelve, messing around. Sometimes we'll dress the dog up in clothes. He's really funny. You can stick his tail through the back of boxer shorts, and he likes to wear them!"

The Weissers, like most people, didn't walk around anticipating prejudice. Of course, they knew bigotry was too much a part of the fabric of American life not to play its part in Lincoln as well as elsewhere. But it wasn't something they worried about. And since there is no way to be prepared each time bigotry slices its way into your life, the hateful phone call caught them off guard. It would have frightened them even more if they'd realized it was only a wake-up call.

THE KKK

IS WATCHING

Chapter 3

> *Because we all share this small planet earth, we have to learn to live in harmony and peace with each other and with nature. That is not just a dream, but a necessity.*
> —*THE DALAI LAMA, TENZIN GYATSO*

*O*n Tuesday, two days after the ugly phone call, Michael left the synagogue early and arrived home just before Julie pulled into the driveway. She'd put in five hours working at Dr. Timothy Fischer's office, taking patients to various rooms, weighing them, taking temperatures and blood pressure, writing symptoms down for the doctor. She also talked and listened—and for Julie that meant listening in a nonjudgmental, problem-solving way, which ranged from consoling a middle-aged man who had just put his mother into a nursing home, to encouraging a thirty-year-old that he wasn't too old for braces, to comforting an elderly woman whose husband had just died.

Julie was tired, but she left her big leather purse in the car and walked down the sloping driveway to open the large wooden mailbox. Inside, the usual cards, bills and letters were stuffed in around a thick brown manila envelope addressed with black Magic Marker in odd-looking print. The all-capital block letters to "Rabbi Michael Weisser" were irregularly spaced and looked as if they had been written at a slightly lopsided angle, with some letters overlapping or jutting up against each other.

Julie carried the mail and her purse to the kitchen table and called out to Michael she was opening a strange-looking package addressed to him. She reached into the manila envelope and pulled out an enormous stack of papers held together by rubber bands. On the top of the stack was a small card. It said, "The KKK is Watching You, Scum."

Her hands were shaking as she took the rubber bands off the stack and began to look at the flyers and brochures. "Michael, come look at this!" she yelled. "Come quick!"

Pictures of Jews with huge hooked noses and black people with gorilla heads dominated the hateful collection. One flyer showed a picture of Adolf Hitler with the warning: "DRUGS ARE TO BE USED ONLY BY JEWS, NEGROES and WHITE SCUMBAGS. PURE ARYANS DON'T USE."

Among the pages of paper were a number of threatening messages, written small and large, including: "The 'Holohoax' was nothing compared to what's going to happen to you!" and, "Heil Hitler! May his memory refresh your soul and give you inspiration!"

One said, "Your Time Is Up," and threatened "those responsible for the suffering of our White Race" (Jews, Blacks, Race-Mixers, Whites who support them) will pay the penalty for "high treason" with "Death by Hanging." A scholarly-looking brochure, *Who Brought the Slaves to America?* asserted that Jews had been the majority of slaveholders—an absurd proposition since so few Jews lived in the South during slavery. A tiny number of southern Jews owned land and slaves, but for the most part, Jews lived in cities where they worked as tailors, printers and shopkeepers—not on plantations. That distorted handout, stamped with a Ku Klux Klan insignia, came from "Christian Identity" at a post office box in Texas.

Another sheet, with a return address of the Nazi Party in Lincoln stamped on it, called the Holocaust "The Big Lie."

This and other pamphlets (*Was There Really a Holocaust?*) displayed "maps" and "historical facts" denying the Holocaust ever happened and asserting that Nazis were the only people who cared about their country. Jews—called "the Great Masters of the Lie"—were said to have fabricated facts about the Nazi extermination of the Jews. Michael and Julie had heard about neo-Nazi efforts to rewrite history, but they had never seen the actual propaganda being used to support these efforts.

The pamphlets, citing the same kind of "authorities" they quoted to "prove" the racial inferiority of blacks and other nonwhites, attempted to erase the irrefutable evidence of Hitler's plans to annihilate every

Jewish man, woman and child in Europe. The pamphlets asserted the gas chambers never existed and the deaths of more than 6 million Jews under the Nazis never occurred. Of course, they also denied that the Nazis put to death some 5 million non-Jews as well—including members of Resistance groups who actively opposed Nazism and at least a quarter of a million Gypsies, thousands of homosexuals, thousands of physically handicapped people and others classified as "mental defectives" who were condemned as "impure," "diseased" or simply "not of the Master Race."

As they looked at these materials, Michael and Julie were stunned by the gross distortions of truth. They thought of people they'd known who had survived the Holocaust, the blue numbers etched on their aging arms, and the miracle of those who had survived concentration camps and the agony of seeing loved ones sent into gas chambers. They thought of "hidden children" they'd met who were among only 11 percent of European Jews under sixteen who had survived the Second World War. Michael thought of members of his father's German family he could never know because they'd died in Nazi concentration camps.

Another flyer showed a hooded Klansman holding a Confederate flag and an American flag. It said: "Racial Purity is American's Security. While America Is Being Destroyed, Silence Is Not Golden, It's Treason."

One particularly heinous handout cited George Lincoln Rockwell, founder of the American Nazi Party, and called for the death of all blacks: "The children of today will be forced to exterminate swarms of wild niggers until all of them are finally corralled in Africa. And their children will in turn look back on you, their grandparents, and wonder how in the name of Heaven we ever let this insanity go so far without doing anything but talk."

Another flyer called for the destruction of democracy: "The 'Great Democracy' enforces your right to blow dope; turn queer; marry a nigger; kill the unborn; and do anything else to destroy America. Some people may be sick enough to accept it, but not us. We prefer to SMASH IT and replace it with a healthy White Man's Order!"

Altogether, more than two dozen photocopied letters, handouts, circulars or pamphlets were written in bizarre, authoritarian language that twisted history and religion to fit a grotesque, dehumanizing view of any human being who wasn't a white "Aryan" Christian. They contained graphic depictions of dead Jews and dead blacks and oozed with the bitter slime of hatred.

Michael and Julie were looking at a great deal of material commonly used by groups involved in a worldwide resurgence of hate-crime violence against racist and religious minorities. This propaganda is produced and circulated by a variety of white separatists in the United States to terrorize their targets, to advance anti-Semitic, racist and homophobic arguments and to stimulate division and racial conflict between blacks and Jews—their common enemy.

Lincoln had seemed like such a relatively harmless place. But as the Weissers gathered around the material at their kitchen table and contemplated what kind of mind, what kind of people could be so hate-filled as to send this ugly stuff, their feelings of comfort were shattered. When the phone rang, they both jumped, but it was just Dave calling for a ride home from work.

"We got hate mail," Julie told him.

"What do you mean?"

"We got this big packet and on top, it says, 'The KKK is Watching You, Scum.' "

What bothered Julie and Michael the most was the calling card. "All of a sudden, we had the sense that someone was watching us," Julie said.

The address on the package had spelled Randolph Street wrong—which would indicate it wasn't from any neighbor, since neighbors should know how to spell the street properly—not "Randolf." The police advised them not to open any other mail with an address like that or any unfamiliar mail.

"Why not?" Julie asked.

"Let's put it this way," one police officer said. "If the person behind this package is the local head of the KKK—which we suspect it is—he's dangerous. We know he makes explosives." The police told the Weissers the head of the KKK, a man named Larry Trapp, had called the police and said someone had sent him a letter bomb. The police went to his apartment and it *was* a bomb and they took it out and had to use specialists to detonate it. Trapp claimed someone had sent it to him, but police believed actually he'd made it himself and it hadn't been sent through the mail at all. Police thought it was a setup of some sort; perhaps Trapp had wanted them to think he had received it from some left-wing group. Or perhaps he was afraid it would go off, or wanted to see if it worked.

Michael and Julie and the kids were shaken. It wasn't as if they hadn't experienced anti-Semitism before, but each time it happened, it was startling all over again. For Michael, anti-Semitic experiences had started early. When he was a kid growing up in tough New Haven neighborhoods, he didn't usually like to fight. He liked people and had a pretty easygoing nature, but when it came to name-calling, it was a different matter. He says he never was very religious as a kid, but he was easily riled by ethnic insults. He didn't like anybody saying, "You stupid Jew," or "Hey, bagel," and so he got into a lot of fights. "They'd say something against Jews and I used to say 'Fuck you' and punch them in the face," he says. "I used to get beat up a lot, too, because I wasn't as good a fighter as I thought."

During the nine years since Julie had converted formally to Judaism, she'd been appalled at the extent of the anti-Semitism she'd seen. Julie, born Julie Ann Michael in 1952, grew up in Memphis, Tennessee, sheltered from the direct bigotry experienced by Memphis Jews and blacks—and sheltered, as well, from racial and cultural diversity. Not only did she grow up in an upper-middle-class neighborhood with a Cadillac in the garage and a swimming pool in the neatly landscaped backyard, but she also descended from Irish ancestors who had been in the United States so long no one remembered when they'd arrived. One of her great-great-grandfathers fought in the Civil War on the side of the South and died at the Battle of Brice's Cross Roads under General Nathan Bedford Forrest.

Nevertheless, Julie had become aware of bigotry at a young age. Living in the Bible Belt, she had noticed when black people had to stand on one side of the cigarette machine and white people stood at the other. She also sat in a Methodist church in Memphis at the age of twelve and found herself feeling angry about an unidentified hypocrisy she sensed around her. "I felt angry because here were a lot of people acting nice and smiling," she said, "but if they really believed everything they were saying, then where were the poor people and the people of all different colors?

"I was a real worrier like I am now—and I worried a lot about the imbalance of things. I was a kid, and I didn't know about soup kitchens or any charitable things they did, but it still struck me as this mentality about the superiority of white Christians—like oh, let's help the poor black people. And I didn't like it."

Julie also didn't particularly cherish her Confederate roots. One of her grandmothers was a member of the Daughters of the Confederacy, but Julie realizes now that in the days when her grandmother wore her DC pin, a black person could not sit beside her in a restaurant or on a bus. She wonders how her grandmother, whom she recalls as a sweet, gentle person, would have felt if that law had applied to her.

When Julie discovered Judaism, she felt she'd found her way home. She was twenty-six years old when she took a part-time secretarial job at Temple Israel in Memphis. At the time, she didn't know anyone Jewish, nor did she know anything about Judaism. But at Temple Israel, she liked what she saw and what she heard. One night she went to hear Rabbi Alexander Schindler give a lecture. Rabbi Schindler, currently president of the Union of American Hebrew Congregations, talked about distortions in the way the Bible had been translated, and Julie was fascinated.

She soon began to read and study Judaism on her own. One of the many books she read, Martin Buber's *Ten Rungs: Hasidic Sayings,* made her know her spiritual home was in the Jewish faith. She didn't feel she'd changed; she felt she had only discovered where she had always belonged. What Judaism meant to her both as a faith and as a way of life was articulated beautifully in what Albert Einstein said about Judaism: "The pursuit of knowledge for its own sake, an almost fanatical love of justice, and the desire for personal independence—these are the features of the Jewish tradition which make me thank my stars that I belong to it."

Julie loved the fact that doubts, questions and debates were integral to the faith. She loved that the study of the Torah and Talmud in the yeshiva involved arguing and heated disputes; it was a different way of looking at history and spirituality and the Bible. "Nothing was set in cement," she said. "And that's what appealed to me. It was where I fit. It was more than a religion; it was a way of life. It's like Elie Wiesel said—'There's no such thing as a marginal Jew.' I like that, because if you're a Jew, it defines you, it defines who you are."

Another thing Julie loved about the Jewish religion—particularly after she formally converted and married Michael in 1983—was that most Jewish clergy were not expected to be as pious and as perfect as Christians seemed to want their ministers to be. "People are not hesitant to tell a Jewish clergyman the latest dirty joke or have the clergyman tell them the latest dirty joke—there's not the separation between the clergy and the congregation," Julie said. "We understand in some inherent way that our rabbis and cantors are knowledgeable and capable of teaching, but they're not saints. They're human beings."

Julie's conversion to Judaism, however, continued to baffle some acquaintances in her hometown of Memphis. "How can you possibly *not* believe in Jesus Christ?" they asked. After expressing their dismay, people often told her they personally weren't prejudiced. "I have one of the nicest little Jewish customers," one older woman friend assured her. "I don't have anything at all against blacks or Jews," said another. "I think if blacks and whites want to get married, or if Jews and Christians want to get married, it's okay, as long as they don't have children."

Julie's parents simply couldn't understand why Julie would want to change her religion—even though she tried to explain that, for her, it wasn't a change. Some other people didn't understand how you could choose to "become" a Jew anyway. Didn't you have to be born a Jew? You couldn't just "become" an Indian if you wanted to, could you? In her adult life, Julie had become more and more aware of this kind of thinking and of the virulent hatred and bigotry in Memphis and elsewhere.

In Lincoln, however, the anti-Semitism had seemed subtle. It was easy to be lulled into the feeling there wasn't any real prejudice here because it was rarely overt. Rumors floated around occasionally about anti-Jewish statements at the Indian Hills Church, a fundamentalist church with the largest congregation in the community. But in the course of everyday life, bigotry seemed to stem from ignorance and lack of exposure, not malice. "I've never sat next to a Jew before," one Lincoln woman had said to Julie in all innocence. Another told her, "You're the first Jew I ever met." Julie understood this wasn't meant to be offensive; it simply was the unadorned truth.

But other things rankled. For instance, at yard sales, Michael and Julie often heard people say, "See if you can Jew 'em down"—meaning "See if you can get it cheaper." At one yard sale, they heard a lady say, "Yeah, I got that and I really Jewed him down" three or four times. Finally, Michael went up to her and said, "Excuse me, ma'am, I would like to buy that footstool and I'd like to Christian you down a little bit." Then he explained to her why he'd said that, and she was mortified;

she had no idea that what she said was offensive.

"She was a nice lady," Michael said afterward. "She didn't know."

"She wasn't a nice lady," Julie responded. "She was a bigot. She just didn't know she was a bigot."

Similar struggles were taking place in Lincoln's public high schools. At Southeast High School, for example, the administration scheduled yearbook pictures for the September day that happened to be the first day of the Jewish High Holy Days, which meant observant Jewish kids in Lincoln wouldn't have their pictures in the yearbook. When Michael called about this, the principal said if he had to honor every holiday that came along, he wouldn't be able to schedule a choir rehearsal on Wednesday evenings because the Lutheran Church has Wednesday night Bible classes. Michael told him it wasn't the same thing: Rosh Hashanah is the main event of the Jewish year—like Christmas and New Year's rolled into one. Would the principal schedule pictures for Christmas Day? The principal didn't seem to understand.

And when Jewish parents objected to junior high and high school choirs singing mostly Christian hymns and religious songs such as "Come to the river and be born again, the Lord will set you free," they were told, "There's so little music that's good for young voices." When Michael said, "Wait a minute, I'm a cantor and a musician, I'll get you fifty thousand songs good for young voices," they weren't interested.

The Weisser kids, like other Jewish students, often had been subjected to prejudice. One beautiful spring day when Dina and her friend Josie Young were walking down the hallway at East High in Lincoln, for instance, a boy walking toward them yelled "Christ killers" into their faces and ran away. More than once, Dave was asked, "How did it feel to kill Christ?" He would answer: "Read the Bible. I didn't kill anybody. Christ was Jewish; the Romans killed Christ."

These kinds of encounters started early. "In the fourth grade, my English teacher in Memphis, Miss Cutler,* said, 'Anybody who doesn't believe in the Lord Jesus Christ, our Savior, is going to hell,'" Dave remembers. "And there was me, Scott Forman and John Hedge, and we all were in the same Sunday School class at Temple Israel, so, you know, we got up and walked out, but then we got in trouble for walking out. I got paddled by the principal."

*Not her real name.

A few years later, the same teacher gave Dina's class an assignment to write "What Christmas Means to Me." Dina asked, "Can I write about what Chanukah means to me, since I'm Jewish?" Miss Cutler said, "No, the assignment is what Christmas means to you, and if you don't do it, you get an F."

When Dave dated a black girl in Memphis, he was called "race traitor" and "nigger lover," in addition to the usual anti-Semitic invectives of "kike" and "Jesus killer."

In Lincoln, Dave at first thought things weren't as bad as they'd been in Memphis. But then he decided bigotry just was manifested more indirectly. One night during a lull on his job at a local restaurant, "Nancy," as we'll call her, told Dave gay people were already in hell according to her fundamentalist Christian church's beliefs.

"What if someone who worked here was gay?" Dave asked.

"I'd quit now," she said.

Dave said, "Well, Nancy, if I were gay or bisexual, and if we were going out, how would you feel about yourself? Would that mean maybe you're going to hell, too?" Her attitude reminded Dave of the homophobia he'd seen in Memphis, when boys his age and older "would run through Overton Park, where a lot of gays sat around on blankets, and just kick the gay people in the back of the head—doing what was called 'gay bashing.' "

Another time, when Dave was stuck at work, Nancy gave him a ride home. "I get in the car and the first thing out of her mouth is, 'Do you think because you're Jewish you are going to hell?' " Dave remembers. "I said, 'Actually, Judaism doesn't teach hell. Judaism teaches God is forever, forgiveness, love and compassion. So no, I don't believe in hell, and I'm not going to hell.' She asked me, 'How can you not believe in hell?' I said, 'Like, why would I? I don't want that hanging over my head. I have bills to pay, I don't need any hell—come on. I think God understands that.' Well, anyway, we were pulling up in my driveway and I said, 'Do you really think I'm going to hell?' She said, 'Well, yeah. If you don't believe in Jesus, you're going to hell for sure.'

"I said, 'Well, thanks for the ride, lady.' I think these kids don't understand the only reason they're Christian, or the denomination of Christianity they are, the only reason I'm Jewish, or the only reason someone is Buddhist, or anything, is their parents were that faith and they were born into it. If they were out of some tribe—I mean years and years ago, or whatever—they would never know about it or think that way."

Another day when Dave was talking to his history teacher at East High, he told him about the exchange with Nancy. His teacher said, "I have to tell you, Dave, I agree with her. You will go to hell if you don't accept Jesus Christ—that's a fact."

"I can't believe you're saying this to me," Dave yelled. "You're my *teacher!* How can you say that?"

"It's what I believe," the teacher responded.

The extreme anti-Semitism expressed in the hate mail the Weissers had just received seemed more horrifying than the everyday, run-of-the-mill bigotry they had previously experienced in Lincoln. It was uglier, more deranged and represented a different quality of madness, more on the order of something that had happened to them in Greenville, North Carolina, several years earlier. At the time of that incident Michael, Julie and Rebecca were all extremely upset—but it had particularly affected Rebecca, who was only eleven years old at the time. Rebecca, who converted to Judaism when she was thirteen, remembers it all too well as her first encounter with the Ku Klux Klan. "It was around Christmastime, and I remember my mother told my friend and me to stay in the house," Rebecca recalls. "We couldn't play outside. The reason we couldn't, it turns out, was that morning, Mom went outside and she found a beheaded Santa Claus doll hanging by a noose from our doorknob on the front door. It also turns out that particular weekend the Ku Klux Klan was marching in Greenville. What a coincidence, right? That scared the daylights out of me."

But the headless Santa Claus had happened in the South, where the Klan was still active, where the Klan had shot and killed five unarmed protestors in 1979 in Greensboro, North Carolina, with the collusion of local and federal law-enforcement officials, and where the extremes of bigotry and racism seemed always ready to bubble to the surface. This was Lincoln, Nebraska, an unpretentious place in the heart of corn country and farms which seemed so calm, so welcoming, so clean and open to the beautiful vault of sky above it. Until now it had been easy to feel that prejudice wasn't as strong, wasn't as palpable, as it was in the South.

But this was palpable. Terrifying. Whoever sent this meant business. And if it was Larry Trapp—the guy the police thought it was—they were in trouble. Because certainly if he was crazy enough to have a bomb sitting in his own house, waiting for the police to come pick it up, he could do anything.

DRAGON'S LAIR

Chapter 4

From the greed of one Jew the anti-Semite concludes all Jews
are greedy and decides no single Jew can be trusted. . . . The
same is true with the stereotype of the lazy black man. . . .
In the Middle Ages, as we know, the Jew finally became one of
the incarnations of the devil, and [later] he became the radical
and antithetical enemy of the Nazis. In the same way the black
man has become one of the inferior categories of the human
species. In the extreme, racism merges into myth.
—ALBERT MEMMI

*A*s the Weissers were reacting to the documents in the package of mail he'd sent them in June 1991, a bearded man named Larry Trapp stayed busy on the southwest side of Lincoln. His job of spreading hatred was sometimes exhausting, but he maintained a fevered pace from apartment number 3 at 817 C Street. Officially the "Grand Dragon of the White Knights of the Ku Klux Klan for the Realm of Nebraska," Trapp had earned his position within the Klan through hard work— and he wasn't about to cut any slack at this point. He aimed "to build Nebraska into one of the foremost Klan enclaves in the country"—and he was doing whatever was necessary to turn that goal into reality.

Wearing frayed blue jeans, a gold swastika on a chain around his neck and a faded red T-shirt with "White Power" written in white next to a black swastika, forty-two-year-old Larry Trapp rolled his wheelchair across his apartment and gave a hoarse laugh over another "creative" letter he had just composed. "That will teach that scumbag to keep his ideas to himself," he rasped into his tape recorder.

Trapp now used a tape recorder almost constantly. He was nearly blind because of diabetes, and the tape recorder was helping him prepare for the day he would no longer have any sight to rely upon. He'd been a diabetic since childhood, but only recently had he begun to take his disease at all seriously. As a kid, he had cheated by sneaking ice cream, candy and other forbidden sweets in the middle of the night, and as an adult who worked primarily as a barber, he replaced the candy with vast amounts of beer and cigarettes until the blood vessels in his eyes began to atrophy and leave him for periods of time in a hazy pink fog. In the mid-1980s, he stopped drinking and tried to monitor what he ate, but it was too late by then to reverse or repair all the damage.

Trapp used his tape recorder to make lists of things to do, to record his thoughts, register observations and remember what he'd read, much the way many people keep inventory on lists of paper and in journals. He was a highly structured and compulsively organized person—and because his business was so fraught with paranoia, he didn't want to lose track of any piece of information, large or small, that might support his views. Trapp tape-recorded sections of books, poems and telephone conversations he wanted to keep. He tape-recorded lists of supplies he wanted to purchase, things he wanted to remember to say. Since his vision had started failing back in the late 1970s, it was harder for him to read and write, but he wasn't one to shirk learning all the things he had to learn to meet his responsibilities to his people.

He could still read under bright lights by using strong magnifying lenses, but when his left eye, which was his best one, got tired or it got too hard to see through the shadows that crept in, he'd turn on his tape recorder and listen to "Parliamentary Procedure for the Klan," review the naturalization ceremony for the Klan or listen to books such as Adolf Hitler's treatise *Mein Kampf* or other books that inspired him, such as *The Secret Diaries of Hitler's Doctor; Munich 1923; The Dispossessed Majority; The Turner Diaries,* which gave a prescription for race war; *The Fiery Cross,* a history of the Klan; or other books on tape, some of which he got from the National Library for the Blind, and some which he'd previously recorded himself.

Larry Trapp had just listened again to a passage on the Klan's belief that Jews "descended from the seed Satan planted in Eve's belly right along with the seed planted there by Adam. Nine months after eating the apple, Eve bore two sons—Adam's son was Abel; Satan's son was

Cain. Cain killed Abel. Cain's descendants killed Jesus. Now, under the banner of world Jewry, they're trying to kill all white Christians." Trapp wanted to get the information just right about Jews descending from Satan's son Cain; he considered it his responsibility as Grand Dragon to teach his members that the Klan's ideas were solidly based in Scripture and could be proved in the Bible.

As Grand Dragon, he also had to teach his members about the law. Often he used one tape recorder to play the U.S. Constitution, and a second recorder to make editorial comments about what he was hearing. When he wanted to remember what he'd said, he'd just replay that section of tape. Now being state leader, of course, he had a lot less time to do his research, listen to books on tape—and a lot more direct work to do over the phone, a lot more meetings, a lot more action.

Larry Trapp pulled up to the long table which served as his desk. A short, thick brown beard covered his chin and jawbone, and his face was marked by pores that, while scrubbed, still didn't look quite clean. The legs of his thin dirty blue jeans were tucked under his thighs, concealing the stumps of his legs—one amputated below the knee, one just above. Besides affecting his eyesight, diabetes also had caused the circulation in his feet and legs to slow to a standstill. In the mid-1980s, his toes had started turning black; one toe fell off and then two more were amputated—leaving only his big toe and his little toe on a foot which looked to him like a slingshot. In 1987, the doctors had taken off that foot and part of Larry Trapp's leg, and the next year, even though he stopped smoking completely, they took part of the other one.

Blue-gray tattoos—a skull and crossbones with "Hell's Angels" written underneath, a heart pierced by an arrow and an Iron Cross, a German military symbol used as a Nazi emblem—adorned his arms. Another Iron cross was etched in dark blue ink into the back of his right hand.

Today was a day for getting organized and getting a lot accomplished. So far, he'd written three letters, packed five envelopes with Klan materials for people who had written in with requests and made two telephone calls. Now he moved aside several stacks of pamphlets—including *Adolf Hitler on America, Proud to Be a Racist, The Rise of the White Racist Elite, Who Owned the Slaves?* and *White Workers, Who's on Your Side?*—to make space for his card file. He had a lot of work to do to catch up on his filing system on "Enemy Subversives" and "Race Traitors." Every day when he watched the television news or read the newspaper, he got another enemy name or two for the file. He'd find their addresses from telephone directories or by calling Directory Assistance. Sometimes he'd get one of the public nurses who brought him insulin and measured his blood sugar to look up a name or two for him in the directory—without telling her why he needed it, of course.

He put on thick magnifying glasses over his wide-set blue eyes and pulled a blank 5-by-7-inch card out of his file drawer. Under his bright desk light, he picked up a black Magic Marker and painstakingly printed out the name of a couple, their address and telephone number. At the bottom of the card, he wrote "Nigger Lovers" before putting it into the file. He pulled another blank card and wrote out the name Bob Wolfson and the address of the Anti-Defamation League in Omaha. At the bottom of that card, he wrote "Jew lawyer with ADL" and put it in the back of his file box. "ADL stands for Anti-Defecation League, not Anti-Defamation League," he said into his tape recorder with a chuckle.

Trapp looked at the clock and chortled at the thought the "Jew rabbi" ought to be squirming over his mail about now. Trapp got even more pleasure from the idea that one of these days the guy would open more than hate mail. One day next July, according to his timetable, that synagogue the rabbi worked in would blow sky-high—and if the rabbi was in it when it blew, Larry Trapp felt, well then, so be it. He thought one less Jew in the world could only help, not hurt. He had the explosives he needed and the detonator; the only remaining essentials were surveillance, exact timing and the right member to help him manage the job.

Larry Trapp hated Jews. The Nazi literature and books he read, such as *Hitler Youth Primer, The Aryan Warrior* and *Mein Kampf,* confirmed his views on their inherent evil. He also possessed what he called "written evidence" that Jews controlled the banks and the Federal Reserve Board and were responsible for the terrible economy. Since they were always sticking their big hairy Jew noses in other people's business, he often said, it was no wonder Jews were involved in a conspiracy to destroy the nation's economy and run the government.

Larry Trapp had gotten a great deal of information about a so-called "Jewish conspiracy" from *The Protocols of the Elders of Zion,* a forgery first circulated by Russian secret police during the late 1800s purporting to document a secret meeting of Jewish leaders conspiring to take over the world. The *Protocols,* widely disseminated by Hitler, are still popular among neo-Nazis and other anti-Semitic groups. Trapp subscribed to the newsletters of neo-Nazis and other newer paramilitary groups who also distributed the *Protocols.* He believed Klansmen couldn't afford to be exclusive anymore. Some 325 white separatist groups were operating in the United States, which included organizations such as the the White Aryan Resistance (WAR), Aryan Nations, the Church of the Creator, the Historical Review Society, the National Socialist White People's Party, the American Nazi Party, the New Order and various branches of neo-Nazi skinheads, survivalists and other Klan groups. Some 25,000 to 26,000 people were thought to belong to these and all other hate groups in America. Klan membership represented only 5,000 to 6,000 of that total. Trapp felt they should learn from each other because, after all, they were all working for the same thing.

Larry looked up at the big 36-by-48-inch red Nazi flag and double-life-sized picture of Adolf Hitler that dominated one wall of his efficiency apartment. His white cotton Klan robe, red belt and white hood, shaped like a dunce cap with a detachable front flap that could be snapped on to mask the face, hung to the left of Hitler's picture, and a large flag with a red, white and black Iron cross and a framed picture of Rudolf Hess hung next to that. Larry's great-grandparents on both sides were German, and even though his family was supposedly related to the Von Trapp family featured in *The Sound of Music* who fled from the Nazis, Larry personally felt a much closer bond with der Führer and the other Nazis who had exterminated 6 million Jews. Thinking about them, thinking about how evil they were, thrilled him. Choosing to identify with that evil, letting the feel of the hatred seep into his bones, made him feel strong and powerful. He was sorry his ancestors had left Germany and come to Omaha. Things would have been different if he'd grown up there. He was a Nazi in America, but being a Nazi in Germany would have been better, he thought. Much better.

"Fuck that neo-Nazi garbage," he said in response to a young member who proudly reported on some actions of like-minded neo-Nazis in Germany. "This word 'neo-Nazi' is a bunch of b.s. media shit—because *we're not 'neo.'* There's nothing 'neo' about us. 'Neo' is 'new.' We're the same Nazis that were around during the Second World War. We're just a more recent version of it. We have the same beliefs. Adolf Hitler is still our main man, whether he's dead or not."

If Jews had their way, Trapp told Klan members, the whole world would be Zionist-occupied. As it was, he said, everyone in the United States was living under ZOG—a Zionist Occupational Government—

and Jews were trying to dilute the white race; they were conspiring to exterminate white Christians through interracial breeding. Hitler should remind all white separatists of what remained to be accomplished, he said.

It never occurred to Trapp to notice that out of the 250 million Americans who live in the United States, only 5.5 million are Jews—less than 3 percent of the population. Larry Trapp knew practically nothing about Jews. He wouldn't have understood the humor of the joke: "What do you get when you have three Jews in the same room?" "Five opinions." Only an uninformed anti-Semite would believe Jews could organize a conspiracy to take over the U.S. government, much less a worldwide conspiracy of any sort.

But Trapp was too consumed by hatred to consider religious traditions, factual evidence or contradictions to his beliefs.

And while he despised Jews, Jews didn't rank as high on his hate list as did African-Americans. He found blacks even more loathsome than Jews. He studied "facts" about them as well—so-called "scientific reports" asserting African-Americans have smaller brains than whites—reports actually written in the 1920s and late 1930s in Nazi Germany. Trapp somehow managed to forget about black people he had known earlier in his life who had been kind to him—such as a porter named Joe at one of the barbershops where he worked in Omaha, who used to wear spotless khakis and shiny black shoes, and who was a minister in his own church. Joe had been generous to Larry Trapp, but Larry didn't remember Joe or the black counselor, Reverend Thompson, who had been so supportive when Larry was a scared young kid sent to reform school in Kearney, Nebraska, for stealing cars. He couldn't think of those individuals and still do what he did or think about people the way he did.

Trapp also hated Asians and Mexicans and Indians—whom he called Chinks, Wetbacks and Redskins. He actually didn't pay Native Americans much mind unless they got in his way. He bragged that one of his favorite pastimes before his legs had been amputated was to beat up Indians. He wouldn't kill them, he just liked to "knock 'em around."

"You know what a sap is, don't you?" he asked a young Klan member after a meeting one night. "It's a glove, the palm and the fingers are filled with shot," he explained. "I used to go to bars, wet bars, just looking for excuses. I used to love to sap Indians. They'd get in there and get drunk and they'd get all loud and say something to me, and then all the sudden, I'd whack them. They'd be on the floor wondering what hit them, you know. And I'd sit there and laugh at them. It was fun. . . ."

Larry Trapp enjoyed violence. He even enjoyed the *threat* of violence. Confrontations scared him, made his hands shake a little, but the rage that filled him when he was in the middle of any confrontation or conflict made him feel alive and electric. The rush of anger gave definition to his world, gave it form and substance and boundaries he could touch and feel. He liked the way he felt when he was blasting off—and he also liked the lull after the storm when his breath was labored and his heart still was beating fast. In most of these things, he knew, he had the upper hand. He had the power that came with a concrete conviction he was right, that he knew what he was doing, and that most of the people he dealt with were idiots. Larry Trapp needed the definition, the sharp outlines the intensity of rage provided in a day that otherwise threatened to slip into the vast realm of vague and hazy nothingness and confusion surrounding him. His rage kept introspection and depression at bay.

Larry Trapp particularly liked to scare people he thought needed to be brought down a notch or two—like Jews or blacks who "thought they were mightier than God," or women who got in his face once too often. He hated women talking back to him or giving him lip. In his personal life, women made him nervous. He couldn't figure out why exactly, because he liked them—he liked a few of them a lot, even loved them, and he liked his one-night stands. But if he was around them for too long, he got jittery and anxious. And that made him angry. He'd never known quite how to relate. He had never dated anybody until he was twenty years old, and even though he became something of a womanizer after that, on a one-to-one basis he found women hard to take.

When he was younger, it was equally difficult. Even in the Omaha neighborhood where he lived, he didn't talk to girls. In junior high, when a little redheaded girl got a crush on him—or when he decided he liked her, he couldn't remember which—he doubled up his fist and let her have it because he didn't know what else to do. When he started going out with women he met in bars, he told them his name was Jim because, as he said, "I thought it'd be embarrassing if anyone ever came into the barbershop and said, 'I'm pregnant with your kid.' "

When he first met his wife and her children, they also thought his name was Jim, and so later, when Larry married Cheryl, her children kept calling him Jim. But Cheryl got the brunt of his discomfort. When he was married for two-and-a-half years in the early seventies, he'd get sullen and hit Cheryl when he got drunk. He didn't *want* to hit her, but she'd say something that made him feel put down, and then he'd get mad and hit her before he even knew what he was doing. If he was tired, he was especially mean and belligerent. He knocked Shawn, another woman he'd lived with, through his sister's glass patio door while Shawn was holding her baby son. Both Shawn and the baby got hurt. His sister Candy was so mad at him she took Shawn to the hospital and then threw him out.

After that, Larry Trapp was scared of being with a woman full-time, scared of what he'd do to her. "I was always lonely," he would say some years later. "I wanted a wife but I didn't want a wife because I was afraid. I wanted companionship, but I was afraid of how I'd treat them and then I would lose them. I don't know, it's hard to describe really." It was easier to stick to one-night stands, which he did until after his amputations. Now he depended on a stack of porno tapes, which provided nearly all the erotic life he had left. Since he'd stopped drinking, he didn't go to bars anymore, so it was nearly impossible to pick up anyone for the night. Sometimes he propositioned his nurses, but without success.

When Larry Trapp spoke about women, they were "broads," "girls," "big bazooms," "toys," "bitches," "whores," "cunts," "lesbos" or "dykes." He thought women who spoke out in public should be locked up. A black female spokesperson was too much for him to bear. For a long time, one woman in particular had struck this particularly sensitive nerve in him. He had never met her, but she'd become the main target of his animosity—and in his opinion, she was *asking* for it. Any harassment she got, she deserved, he thought; it was her own doing. Donna Mays Polk first caught his attention back in the late 1970s when Larry moved to Lincoln. At the time, Ms. Polk was an equal employment officer for the Nebraska Department of Labor.

Larry Trapp found her nearly intolerable: not only was she a *feminist* who spoke in public with passion and confidence, but also, she was a *successful black woman.* What's more, this woman had her face on *his* television—talking about feminism, equal rights, civil rights, job rights. She was tall and graceful, with olive brown skin, short curly black hair, a low, persuasive voice and startlingly pale green eyes which calmly assessed anyone speaking to her. Interviewers showed respect for her opinions—and her status, her poise and her knowledge about a wide range of concerns felt like slaps on Trapp's own face.

Listening to Donna Polk talking on his television or radio about women's rights or civil rights sent Trapp into a rage. He had to let her know what he thought of her, try to take her down a peg. Initially, he looked up her address at the Department of Labor and made tentative contact with her by sending her anonymous postcards every now and then to tell her she was nothing but a "bitch," no matter what she tried to be.

In 1981, Donna Mays Polk wrote a book called *Black Men and Women of Nebraska*. After her book came out, she was interviewed about contributions blacks had made to the state and the country. Later, when she started an organization called the Coalition of Black Women, she was interviewed about the achievements and contributions made by black women in the state. On one show about the coalition, the host mentioned Donna had a bachelor's and a master's degree and was working on her Ph.D. in psychological and cultural studies at the University of Nebraska. That particularly burned Larry Trapp, who took her accomplishments as a personal rebuke.

He himself had a high-school-equivalency degree from reform school and a certificate as a barber. Only after becoming visually impaired and moving to Lincoln had he gone to college, and then he had taken classes in horticulture for two semesters at the University of Nebraska. He would have liked to run his own nursery or work as a horticulturist, but he had dropped out. In reacting to Donna Polk's superior education, he also was responding to the more subtle aspects of cultural racism that look upon a black person with superior scholarship, a wider command of literature, ideas, language and political sophistication, as a contradiction to the assumption of their inferiority. Donna Polk obviously confounded Trapp's view of blacks as lazy or criminal.

One day, when he saw Donna Polk's name in the paper again, he whipped off a more "personal" letter to her asking for information on the Coalition of Black Women and signed it "Katrina K. Koontz." He liked alliterations and was quite pleased with the name he made up for the KKK: "Koontz" added a double whammy—to let her know she was a "kunt" and a "koon."

Early in 1988, soon after he had begun his official association with the Ku Klux Klan, Larry Trapp grew bolder. He wrote Donna Polk an-

other note about her group on his Klan letterhead. The left side of the
stationery had a logo with a Klansman wearing the traditional white
KKK robes, white mask and white hood, sitting on a hooded horse and
raising a burning cross in his raised right arm. On the right side of the
page was an iron cross and the stamp of "Imperial Wizard J. W. Farrands." Trapp used a black Magic Marker and printed his "short,
sweet" communication in large capital letters: "I heard this organization was a front for a labor union for *nigger whores!*"

Trapp didn't sign the letter, but he included a flyer showing the pro-
file of a black man in a beret leaning back against a wall under a sign
that said "Not Responsible." Next to the picture in a box, it said, "He
may be *your* equal . . . but he sure isn't *ours.*"

By that time, the Coalition of Black Women had been disbanded. But
Trapp didn't know that, nor did he know that, in 1985, Donna Polk had
become director of counseling services at the Lincoln Indian Center. He
just knew she was *in his face*—speaking out for multiculturalism, equal
rights, tolerance—everything he hated, everything the Klan hated,
everything the Nazi Party hated, everything the White Aryan Resistance
hated.

Trapp focused his energy on writing an original, vicious poem for
Donna Polk. He had plenty of printed materials available, but he took
pride in formulating his own racist assaults. He wanted the words to
horrify and humiliate; he wanted to make her hate herself, make her feel
small and insignificant. After he finished his poem and read it aloud
several times, he sent it to her on Klan letterhead. This time he took off
the address of the national headquarters and instead stamped his new,
local address for the Klan under the logo of the hooded Klansman and
iron cross: "Nebraska State Office, Box 2297, Lincoln, NE 68502."

He laughed—a pained, tight-chested, wheezing laugh—when he
tried to imagine the look Donna Polk would have on her face when she
opened her mailbox and got his poem:

WHY OH WHY WERE SOME BORN BLACK,
WHEN ALL THEY CAN DO IS STEAL AND SELL CRACK.
WHY SAY BLACK IS BEAUTIFUL BUT TO THEM IT'S A GIVEN,
IT REALLY IS STRANGE CAUSE THEY ALWAYS WANT WHITE
    WOMEN.
SOAP WAS INVENTED SO FOLKS WOULDN'T SMELL,

BUT STAND DOWN WIND OF A NIGGER AND IT SMELLS BAD AS
  HELL
THEY DON'T LIKE IT WHEN FOLKS CALL THEM NIGGER,
THEY ALWAYS HAVE GUNS, AND ALWAYS PULL THE TRIGGER
THEY WORSHIP A NIGGER THEY CALL "MR. KING,"
HE DIDN'T LAST LONG; AINT THAT A NIG THING.
DURING BLACK HISTORY MONTH LETS ALL DO OUR SHARE,
DEPORT A NIGGER, NO TRUE WHITE FOLKS WILL CARE.
WELL THIS IS THE END OF MY POEM DON'T YOU SEE,
THEM BLACK BASTARD'S BELONG IN A TREE.

SORRY WE DIDN'T GET THIS OUT FOR "NIGGER
HISTORY MONTH." WE'LL DO BETTER *NEXT YEAR!*
NEBR. KKK

In addition to the poem, Larry Trapp sent Ms. Polk a few flyers to show her what she was in for—including a picture of three people labeled "race-traitor scum" hanging from nooses. He wanted to scare her good—get her face off his television.

When Donna Polk first started getting the anonymous postcards, she hadn't been particularly alarmed. She was used to people disagreeing with her views, and she was quite familiar as well with the small acts of disrespect that come with being a woman and being black. A practicing Buddhist, she was good at keeping her eye on the larger picture and taking things in stride. She'd grown up Donna Lee Mays with her younger brother in Southern California, where her father was a career Navy man, her mother a housewife, and where the differences separating kids in her friendly neighborhood appeared more economic than racial. Although the Mayses came from a long line of African-Americans, with some Native American heritage as well, the first time Donna had experienced active segregation was when she was twelve years old and went with her family to Maryland, where she discovered because she was black, she had to sit at the back of the bus. As an adult, she'd learned to live with racism and sexism on a daily basis, while working at the same time to educate people and expand their horizons.

But she couldn't ignore the Klan. The Klan's history of violence against blacks was legendary. In 1950, the Klan in Nebraska had mailed out invitations to "native born, white, gentile protestant citizens of the United States" with the message: "In this fight to the death for control of our country, it is necessary to oppose ruthlessness with ruthlessness." As recently as the 1980s, crosses had been burned in Lincoln.

Donna Mays Polk also knew that during her own adulthood, despite efforts of the Ku Klux Klan to put on a more polished public face, in private, various members of the different branches of the Klan had been behind the bombings of more than 130 black churches; the deaths of 4 little girls in the bombing of a black Baptist church in Birmingham, Alabama, in 1964; and the murders of more than 50 people for their involvement in the Civil Rights Movement. Since those days, the deaths of at least 300 other people had been attributed to various factions of the Ku Klux Klan.

There was no way to take any letter from the Klan lightly. Donna's only comfort had been that the letters were addressed to the Coalition of Black Women, not to her personally. But this time, the "poem" left Donna feeling slightly shaky, in large part because her own name and her home address were written out on the envelope in those strange, all-block letters she now immediately recognized. The man knew where she lived. When this happened, she, like the Weissers, felt the personal impact of the assault.

Soon after that, Donna got another hateful letter. This one ("Notice to All Niggers") talked about her family and said among other things, "Your mother was an ape and sucked on bananas."

That letter made Donna furious. "Where does he come off, talking that way about my mother?" Donna said. "I was so angry with his anonymity and with the fact that he could send mail to *my* house, and I couldn't reciprocate. If I wanted to write him a letter at *his* home, or even if I wanted to send him a subscription to *Ebony* or *Jet*—which I thought about doing at one point—where did *he* live?

"I also wondered—why is he hiding? He knows my name and he knows where I live, and yet *he* uses a post office box. So I am thinking, 'OK, I'll just go down to the post office and I will stand there, and wait until I see the person come in who has that box number.' But I didn't even know what the man looked like. I had no idea who this man was. And of course, fear created in my mind this tall, shaved-head person who could probably just kill me with a glare.

"Later on, I had a cabdriver friend who thought she knew the guy who was the head of the Nebraska KKK. She told me, 'I know where he lives.' I thought about that, but then I thought, maybe I better not deal with that. I have four sons—at that time one was living in Omaha, two were in New York and one was in Maryland—and they were afraid for me because I was way out here. So I didn't ever want to know where this KKK guy lives because I've got friends, and I've got these four sons who I know could hurt him. I didn't want them to do that.

"At that time, my oldest boy was in law enforcement in Maryland. He knew I was getting stuff like this—and when he saw some of the materials, he got concerned. He says, 'That's from the New Order—which is very dangerous, you know.' He said, 'Mom, this is serious, this isn't just the Klan, this is White Aryan Resistance and Aryan Nations as well.' "

The idea that their mother had become the target of a racist's hatred was extremely upsetting to Donna Polk's sons. At their urging, Donna turned copies of the letters she had received over to police. She also went to the FBI. "You go through this metal detector and they have a window, and I went in and I told people I had gotten these letters, and they said, 'OK, fine, thank you very much,' and I left.

"My son in law enforcement was especially concerned, really concerned," said Donna. "He starts infiltrating these groups by mail to find out what they are saying, and ordering their publications and their bibliographies and books and stuff like that." From all the literature Donna's son received, he learned a lot about the white supremacy movement—and what he learned further alarmed him. It was particularly frightening that this Ku Klux Klansman harassing his mother was connected with the Aryan Nations, the White Aryan Resistance and the New Order—racist organizations dedicated to creating a "race war" in America through violent acts.

Donna also got worried when she learned at least one Klansman was buying guns from pawnshops in Lincoln. One night when she was at a friend's house, the friend called in her roommate, Charles,* to tell Donna a story. Charles happened to have a Citizens Band radio, and one night he had heard someone with the code name "Trapper" talking about his base not functioning. Charles knew "Trapper" was handicapped, so he had volunteered to go over and fix it for him. Charles told Donna: "I go to his house—I think this was down on B or C Street—and I knock on the door and I open it and there is this man sit-

---

*Not his real name.

ting in a wheelchair with an M-16 on his lap, sitting behind this big swastika. It took my breath away. And then he found out why I was there and he said to come in, and the whole time I was working on this base unit, the guy's trying to recruit me into the Klan."

On Mother's Day, in May 1988, Donna Polk's son Mark, from Maryland, gave her a gun—her Mother's Day present. He said, "Mom, this is for you. Learn how to use it and be careful." Donna registered the gun immediately. At first she kept it at home because she thought, "I can't do this." But it wasn't long before she was frightened enough that she began to carry it with her when she drove to her office or to Omaha on business. Eventually, on her son's advice, she tried to vary her hours and drive a variety of routes to and from work to avoid predictable patterns in her movements in and around Lincoln.

"My son says, 'I don't want you to be scared,' " Donna remembers. "But I was starting to feel scared."

VIGILANTE VOICES

Chapter 5

*Everyone looks for an inferior rank compared to which he ap-
pears relatively lofty and grand. Racism offers everyone the solution that suits him best; he need only find someone smaller,
more humiliated than himself, and there he has his victim, the
target for his scorn and prejudice. Racism is a pleasure within
everyone's reach.*

—ALBERT MEMMI

*T*rapp laid his weapons out on his desk to clean them. When the
phone rang, he let it go; his answering machine clicked on after two
rings and ran his message—"Vigilante Voices of Nebraska"—which he
used as a racist hotline for the state. He listened to the sound of his
own voice:

"Welcome to the Hotline of the White Knights of the Ku Klux Klan
of Nebraska, where the truth hurts! You may contact us at Post Office
Box 2297, Lincoln, Nebraska, 68502. If you would like a large package
of racially oriented material, suitable for copying and passing around
to your friends and neighbors, please send us $4.00 in cash to the ad-
dress mentioned above and we will be glad to send this package on its
way to you. . . .

"White women, you need to stop getting abortions so that our numbers will at least compete with the numbers of offspring that those

dark-skinned races have. We have to fight for what is ours and what is our children's, so keep that in mind when you make that decision. . . ."

Trapp's Ruger .357 stainless-steel Magnum, a Beretta .380 automatic, a .38-caliber Colt and an AR-15 rifle (1300) lay on the desk. He felt an itch in his ankle. He knew it was "phantom pain," because his ankle was gone. Likewise, he often felt a deep burning or cramping sensation in his calf or his foot. It didn't make sense, but that didn't lessen the pain.

Trapp remembered the real pain in his ankle some years before, when he'd been out fishing and was breaking in a new pair of Acme boots. They fit just fine, but the seams on the insides of the boots were stiff and rubbed an ulcer on his skin. When he got back home from fishing and took off the boots, his legs ached and his feet stank from the open wound—through which he could see the bone of his ankle. It was around that same period of time that his toes turned black. Afterward, he'd told his sister Candy about how one day he pulled off his sock and noticed something in the bottom. "I reached down there and thought, 'What's a raisin doing in my sock?' " he said. "But you know what it was, it wasn't a raisin. It was my blackened toe that had fallen off and was in the bottom of my sock. My feet were in such pain that I didn't even notice it falling off. I just about got sick right there. I done a lot of trapping and skinning animals, and things don't easily make me sick, but that made me sick."

Trapp rubbed the stump of his leg to take away the stinging as he listened to more of his message on his hotline:

"You people believe everything that's said against the white race by the media. The media does come along with some truthful things occasionally, but when it comes to the white race, which is mainly their own race, they are putting it down to patronize the black and the dark-skinned races and the nonwhite races. Why? I have no idea, except it's lack of white racial pride. Blacks have black pride; Hispanics have Hispanic pride; even faggots have homosexual or gay pride. Where is the white pride of the white people?"

He pulled out his cotton rags and rods and began cleaning his Beretta, stroking the handle and fondling the chamber in the gentle way a person might pet a small and beloved dog or cat. "People are whining and crying," he heard his message saying. "They say blacks are being executed for capital offenses more often than whites. That blacks get stiffer penalties than whites. That's bullshit and you know it! Open your eyes, check it out!"

Larry nodded in agreement with himself. He liked listening to the sharp-edged tone of his voice, liked hearing his words, liked imagining who was listening on the other end of the phone. He especially liked his sign-off at the end of the message:

> "Until next time, from one of many, many white supremacists, as the media calls us, in the city of Lincoln and in the state of Nebraska, I say to you, White Power and Hail, White Victory. Because remember, the only solution is White Revolution."

Things were going well. Trapp's role as state leader of the Klan gave him confidence, made him feel authoritative. When he looked in the mirror, he saw someone tough, a man who was respected, a man who took no crap from anyone. His guns made him forget his size, his physical ailments, his relative helplessness and the shakes and anxiety he got when his insulin level wasn't right. His guns kept him safe. Often, when he got low on cash and needed some quick money, he'd have to pawn one or two of his guns for a while—and he didn't like doing that. Usually, he'd pawn his .22 rifle or something else he could do without. Over the years, he'd bought and traded most of his guns with Sheldon Kushner at the Royal Jewelry and Loan Company. He'd leave the gun with Sheldon and then get it back as soon as he could. Sometimes he'd take in his CB radio or his Coleman lantern for a trade. Sheldon was good. Because Sheldon looked out for him, Trapp had never lost anything. Sheldon knew a lot about Citizens Band radios—and they talked CB lingo together. For a long time before he was in the Klan, Larry didn't have a telephone. If Sheldon wanted to let him know he had a new gun or something for him at the pawnshop, he got a friend of his to call "Trapper" on the CB and tell him.

Now Larry avoided Sheldon as much as possible. After all, Sheldon Kushner was a Jew. Sheldon looked Jewish and sounded Jewish and he even wore one of those little hats on Fridays and spoke funny-sounding *ssshhallhushas* words to other Jews who came in and bobbed their heads and said the same things back. It was easier just to go over to the A-I Pawnshop and forget about the Royal Jewelry and Loan Company and Sheldon Kushner.

But between his Social Security check and subsidized housing and the extra money he made selling swastikas, Nazi armbands, Klan stickers and flyers, Larry got by most of the time. Glancing over at the door to make sure his MAC-10 semiautomatic assault rifle was where it was supposed to be, Trapp grinned at how upset his neighbors in the plain, one-story apartment building where he lived would be if they guessed the potentially explosive arsenal in apartment 3. His next-door neighbor—a writer-journalist who couldn't walk or talk or even use his hands, but who had graduated from the university and talked through a voice-synthesizing machine and listened to Martin Luther King's speeches all the time—he'd be especially freaked out. He'd already complained a few times that Larry's CB radio interfered with his computer, and in response, Larry had left him a few flyers in his mailbox and told him bluntly if he didn't tone it down, he'd get his fucking head blown off. The guy had called the cops on him, but when they knocked on Larry's door, Larry denied everything.

Even if the cops came again, Trapp figured he was clean. He had the right to be armed, and he had the right to his literature. He picked up his Colt .38 and started cleaning its barrel with a soft, thin rag wrapped around the end of a chopstick. As he rubbed the inside of the barrel, he wondered what would happen if the door opened right now. He always was worried about break-ins, the cops, enemies. He always kept his MAC-10 loaded in case of an emergency—which, being a Klansman, he knew could happen any day, any night, any time. He stopped what he was doing, picked up the assault rifle and set it next to his chair. He lifted it, aimed it at the door and then set it down and continued cleaning the Colt.

It was getting harder to see, but Larry Trapp wasn't worried about knowing where to shoot if he needed to. Even if he went totally blind, he thought, he could kill anybody that got into his apartment. If nothing else, he would shoot toward the sound. After all, he'd hunted and trapped in the woods at night, and he bragged he was a damn good shot. "People might say a person who's nearly blind shouldn't use a gun, but I always say it's not the gun that's dangerous," he often said. "What's dangerous is the person who handles it."

Trapp knew how to handle his firearms. Also, he could see well enough to hit his targets, especially human targets. He'd prepared himself: long before he officially joined the Klan, he'd done his homework. In 1977, when Larry Trapp was twenty-eight years old, he first noticed little floaters drifting by his line of vision. At the time, he was reading *Covert Material on How to Kill,* which described hand-to-hand fighting and various methods for killing people. He had also read books on bomb making, "man trapping" and killing techniques. One of his personal favorites was *Hit Man: A Technical Manual for Independent Contractors* by Rex Feral. He'd underlined almost the whole book because it gave such helpful and specific instructions on how to locate, observe and stalk your "mark"; how to practice silent movement and ambush; and how to chose your weapons ("The recommended handgun is the fixed barrel Ruger Mark I or Mark II"). He starred and underlined important tips: "Hollow point bullets are recommended because they deform on impact, making them non-traceable. As an added precaution, you can fill the hollows with liquid poison to insure success of your operation [by using] a hand-held one-eighth inch drill bit [to] enlarge the hollow-point openings. Fill the hollows with the liquid poison of your choice, then seal with a drop of melted wax."

The book also taught the various advantages of bare hands, knives, poisons, hypodermic needles, arson or explosives, as well as the best ways to get rid of fingerprints, evidence and the body. Most of all, it had taught him the essential skills involved in becoming a professional hit man. He looked at these materials as "job skills" necessary for his chosen work.

For two years, back in the early 1970s, Larry Trapp had been a police officer in the small town of Pierce, Nebraska. That was when he'd first started thinking about advanced methods for self-defense. By the mid-seventies, after he'd been fired from his job as a cop for sleeping on the job and was working as a barber in Omaha again, Trapp had started checking out different books on hand-to-hand combat and researching the martial arts, weapons and military operations. He soon escalated to the books on killing skills and ways to build torpedoes and bombs and other weapons from regular household supplies. In those days, he used to carry his Ruger .357 Magnum no matter where he went. After studying directions and figuring out how to do it, he made his own disposable silencer and tested it by shooting squirrels in trees outside his window at night. It worked well, and sometimes he'd go downstairs and pick up the squirrels he'd shot and cook them for dinner. In a stew, squirrel tasted something like rabbit. One night when he was feeling hungry, Larry shot a fat gray squirrel. Just as he was getting ready to go down for it, though, a big white dog came running along, sniffed the squirrel, picked it up and started to carry it off. Larry got so mad he shot the dog.

Altogether, Larry Trapp had been laying the groundwork for more years than he cared to remember, and now much of what he'd learned was being put to use in his fight for survival, his fight to the death against the enemies of the white race. He had been into survival issues for a long time. He built his own bunker back in the mid-eighties under the back porch of the house in which he was renting an apartment in Lincoln. The landlord didn't know about the bunker because Trapp built it under the back steps and worked on it at night. Following instructions from a survivalist guide, he constructed an underground room crisscrossed with wrought-iron bars. He put a hot plate down there, along with canned goods, distilled water, dried beans and a hookup for a CB radio he figured he could run off batteries if he needed to stay there to escape nuclear fallout.

In those days, in his mid-thirties, Larry Trapp spent more time outdoors. Every month or so, he would buy thirty pounds of potatoes, a couple of pounds of rice and a couple of pounds of dry beans, along with cornmeal, oatmeal and peanut butter. He killed or collected whatever else he ate. He trapped muskrat, possum, raccoon, rabbit; he pinned them down with a forked branch and shot them in the head with a pistol, "the humane way," he said, "which was only right." He fished in Salt Creek for carp and catfish, white bass or walleye. He'd also catch turtles and crab to use in soup. In the summertime, he collected wild edibles.

He wanted to be able to survive without any dependency on the government. "I don't let anything go to waste," he'd said. For instance, in cooking raccoon, "you remove as much of the yellow fat as you can. Render it down and you've got some real good cooking oil. Everything can be used."

Even though he was in a wheelchair now, Larry Trapp believed his diligence would be rewarded. When the race wars came, when whites were equipped for revolution, he'd be in the midst of the action. The main task in front of him right now was to get his message out: *White men, wake up! It's kill or be killed!*

•   •   •

In just a few short years, the Klan had not only become a vehicle for Trapp's philosophies; it had become a way of life.

Over the years, he had searched out a number of different beliefs. As a child, he had gone with his mother to Pius X Church at 63rd and Blondo in Omaha, but his father, who had been in a Catholic orphanage, told Larry how mean the nuns had been to him, and Larry couldn't forgive the Catholics that injustice. As an adult, Larry had searched for answers; he joined the Seventh-Day Adventists, he joined the Church of Christ. He became a voracious reader of the Bible, and for a while, he even talked like Jimmy Swaggart and shared passages of Scripture with his father. But his father hadn't seemed pleased or impressed, and Larry finally decided it was time to find his own way. When his research led him to discover the Ku Klux Klan was still an active organization, he thought he'd finally found his niche. "I'd always wanted to join the Klan," he said later. "But for a while I thought they might have been a thing of the past."

In Nebraska in the 1980s, Larry could have chosen from any number of fringe groups. NAPA (National Agricultural Press Association) was blaming "Jewish bankers and the Federal Reserve Board" for the farm crisis and handing out their literature at foreclosures and auctions. In October 1984, when deputy sheriffs tried to foreclose on a farmer named Arthur Kirk, NAPA made the news. Kirk was fired up by NAPA's rhetoric encouraging farmers to defend their land with their lives, and he grabbed a .41 Magnum and ordered the deputies off his property. Then he barricaded himself in his house and a short while later died in a shootout with the Nebraska state police's SWAT team.

Another organization, the Posse Comitatus, a loosely connected right-wing group of armed vigilantes in several midwestern and western states, had also made headway in Nebraska. But the Posse lost credibility when Michael Ryan, one of its advocates who had built a small paramilitary cult following on an eighty-acre farm near Rulo, Nebraska, was found to have beaten, tortured and murdered two people— a twenty-six-year-old follower and a five-year-old child. After Ryan's arrest, police found stolen farm equipment, stolen money and hundreds of bags of charcoal with which to make bombs for the "Battle of Armageddon." They also found stacks of Posse and Aryan Nations literature, along with dozens of automatic weapons and hundreds of thousands of rounds of ammunition.

After publicity about those incidents, many people involved in NAPA and Posse Comitatus went underground. Some completely dropped out. Others, more hard-core, continued, but gave their groups new names or switched over to the Identity Church movement or one of the small Nazi groups already active in the state.

Of course, Lincoln's well-publicized Nazi, Gary Lauck, who had founded the National Socialist German Workers Party in 1972, had provided another potential option. Lauck's racist and anti-Semitic newspapers were sent all over the world, and he was said to be the world's largest supplier of Nazi propaganda materials to Germany, where Nazi propaganda and activity are illegal. But the way Larry Trapp looked at it, Lauck was just a businessman who operated a one-man show, and besides that, Trapp considered him a phony: even though his real name was Gary Rex Lauck and he'd grown up in Lincoln, he called himself "Gerhard" and affected a thick German accent. In Trapp's opinion, Lauck was a bullshit artist.

Overall, Larry Trapp thought the Klan was the most solid choice. It was older, more established. Its secrecy also appealed to him. The Klan had a number of factions to choose from, but in 1988, when he was thirty-nine years old, Larry chose to be in the "Invisible Empire" of the "Knights of the Ku Klux Klan," the largest of all the Klan organizations, which operated in twenty states from the East to the West Coast—including New Jersey and California.

Trapp had a lot to offer the organization. He'd been a police officer, and, he told other members, he'd fought as a mercenary in Rhodesia, so he knew about combat; he knew how to fight. Also, since he was on disability, he could devote himself to the Klan full-time. After having his second leg amputated, he'd spent a lot of time studying television news. He watched and made notes, and, based on his analysis of Cable Network News, things were getting worse and worse. "I focused on black crimes," he said later, "and I'd think, 'Boy, I'd like to blow apart them niggers.' I had the attitude, 'I'd like to hang 'em.' " Trapp could fight boredom, depression and his lack of mobility by dedicating his energy to making the Klan and the white separatist movement his profession—his vocation and his avocation.

Larry Trapp and the Klan seemed meant for each other. Larry loved to do research, and he threw himself into reading about the Klan's history. He was inspired by the Klan's fight to protect Christian morals and uphold the rights of whites. The Klan's enthusiasm for him was reciprocal.

Soon after Trapp applied and became a member of the Klan, he talked several times personally with Imperial Wizard J. W. Farrands, national leader of the Invisible Empire. Farrands, formerly Grand Dragon for Connecticut and the first Roman Catholic ever to hold a leadership position in a major Klan group, was also the first northerner ever to be a national leader of any major Klan. Trapp felt an instant rapport with Farrands. And when he explained he didn't get around very easily, Farrands arranged for Larry to be initiated by phone, even though it wasn't ordinarily done. No other Klan leaders lived in Nebraska at the time, and so the Grand Dragon of a nearby state would "naturalize" Larry Trapp by telephone.

For the "naturalization ceremony," Trapp wore a Klan robe and hood individually sewn by a Klanswoman in North Carolina. The Klanswoman's name, an "Instruction Sheet for Robe Care" ("Store on hanger, keep out of direct sunlight") and "Washing Instructions" ("Use cold water, lay flat, press with iron") were pinned to the robe when it arrived in the mail. When Larry put in on the first time, he felt bonded with other Klansmen, past and present. Looking out from underneath the white snap-on mask, he sensed his kin, his predecessors. And even though he was alone, he knew the brotherhood was with him. The Klan leader conducted the ceremony as formally as possible, considering the circumstances.

"I am officially instructed to inform you that it is a Klansman's nature to assist those who aspire to things noble in thought and conduct and to extend a helping hand to those worthy," Larry's fellow Klansman said, his voice resounding through Larry's apartment from the speakerphone. "The Ku Klux Klan is a patriotic fraternal white movement. We do not discriminate against a man because of his religious or political creed as long as it does not conflict with Christian ideals and the welfare and furtherance of the white race."

The Klan official proceeded to tell Trapp the requirements of the Klan were simple, but they were also sacred and the Klan required as "absolute necessity" an answer to these questions:

"Are you a White Christian of no Jewish ancestry?

"Is the motive prompting your ambition to be a Klansman sincere and unselfish?

"Do you believe in the right of our people to oppose unlawful and unjust actions coming from any level of government?

"Do you believe in racial separation?

"Do you believe in religious freedom, including the right of the people to practice the Christian faith anywhere they assemble, including prayers in schools and public facilities?"

Larry Trapp answered affirmatively to each question.

Then the Klan official said to him: "The distinguishing marks of the Klansman are not found in the fineness of his clothes or in his social or financial standing, but are spiritual and racial. He is devoted to our race and our country and our families.

"With heart and soul I welcome you and open the way for you to attain the most noble achievement on the earth. We congratulate you on your courageous decision to forsake the world of selfishness and fraternal and racial alienation to join our racial community, the Invisible Empire of the Knights of the Ku Klux Klan."

The official, as part of the ceremony, gave Larry a chance to withdraw, but when Larry declined, the official said: "I will now administer the oath of the Klan. You will raise your right hand and repeat after me:

"I, Larry Trapp, do before God and man, most solemnly swear that I will and do hereby dedicate my life, my fortune and my sacred honor to the Preservation, Protection and Advancement of the White Race— and to that great order, the Invisible Empire of the Knights of the Ku Klux Klan."

Trapp couldn't find a Bible at that moment, so he put his hand on *The Fiery Cross*. He kept his left hand on the book and his right hand raised in the air as he repeated the pledge and swore to vows of Secrecy, Loyalty, Duty, Proliferation ("I swear that I will actively and diligently work to expand and increase the ranks of the Invisible Empire, therefore I will actively seek to enlist men and women of high quality and standing, high moral character, and of true and honest purpose into the Ku Klux Klan"), Fraternity, Honor and Dedication ("I believe in complete religious freedom and in the practice of the Christian faith, in public institutions but also in the separation of church and state. I will diligently fight communism and Zionism. I swear I will dedicate my life from this moment forward to fostering the welfare of the white race, and furthering the work of America's greatest movement, the Ku Klux Klan").

After he had sworn in Larry Trapp, the presiding Klan official said: "Congratulations, Brother. You are now a member of the oldest fraternal organization of white people in the world."

• • •

Soon after that ceremony, Larry received his first book on how to conduct a rally and a cross burning, what size to build the cross, how to wrap it and how to ignite it. The book also instructed him on how to build and use an altar (as in a shrine) during Klan ceremonies and initiations. He maintained contact with Farrands and others by phone and mail, and kept them informed of his Klan actions against Jews, Asians and Blacks. The Klan leadership was impressed. It wasn't long before Larry Trapp was promoted to "Imperial Representative," then to "Great Titan" (district leader) and then to "Grand Dragon, Realm of Nebraska."

It was heady stuff, and Trapp was thrilled with a sense of being immersed in history. The Klan had a language of its own—which started everything with K: Klaverns (meetings) and Kleagles (field organizers), Klonversations (conversation between Klansmen) and Kluxing (recruiting). In the 1920s, the use of Klan lingo was common. Some businesses put big *K*'s on signs in their windows—like "Klothes Kleaners"—just to get Klan customers to patronize their stores. In news stories, reporters often used the Klan method of starting words with a *K* in the text of the story—referring, for instance, to "Krusaders" who plan to attend a "Klan Klorero" and "hold kompetitive drills between Klavalier units."

Larry Trapp respected the value of rituals, and used some of the Klan language, but a lot of it seemed silly. He did use "Nighthawk" (investigator and watchdog, the person who checks out the character of prospective Klan members), "Titan" (head of a Klan province) and other indicators of a person's rank within the organization. His own title—Grand Dragon of the Realm of Nebraska—meant in Klan language he was chief executive of the statewide Klan organization (the Realm), an appointment made by the Imperial Wizard, the Klan nation's chief executive. Trapp fully intended to maintain the respect he'd gained within the organization by making an example out of Nebraska. He intended to stay effective, discreet and technically above the law.

Despite his fascination with guns, Trapp didn't have much of a police record. Having once been a police officer helped him understand how to avoid detection. For a long time, the police had only known Trapp as a troublemaker who had been arrested on a few occasions for burglary, concealed weapons, theft and once for possession of an illegal weapon.

Police also had gotten reports about threatening phone calls he had made to former landlords, and ones he reported he'd received himself.

Trapp also knew the cops must have some data about Klan activity, but Nebraska didn't keep separate records on hate crimes—and, of course, that was good for him. For a long time, the police had no way to link him to anything Klan-related. But now it was different. Now his phone was tapped, he was certain, so he was extremely careful what he said during calls. He knew the law must suspect him of sending hate mail and making threatening calls, building bombs and being the man behind some unexplained beatings and slashed tires, swastika paintings and other hate crimes in and around Lincoln and Omaha.

They might have their suspicions, but they couldn't prove anything. Trapp wasn't stupid. He knew the Constitution and the rules regarding free speech. He knew it wasn't breaking the law if you called someone and said, "I know where your children go to school" or "I'd like to see your house burn down to the ground." Those were not direct threats; those were *opinions* protected by the First Amendment to the Constitution of the United States.

Law-enforcement officials had learned about Trapp's Klan affiliation only because early in 1990 he had gone public with that news. At first he'd thought he would simply recruit new members by running a small advertisement in local papers. He thought it might give membership a boost. The cost was minimal for three days straight, so he took out an ad for the morning *Lincoln Star* and the evening *Lincoln Journal* for February 7, 8 and 9.

It was a small ad—just one column under "Personals," after advertisements for the Blue Moon Dating Service and the Magic Match Dating Service and a claim: "I can teach you to dance so that anyone will want to be your partner." Trapp's ad said simply:

> Join the Ku Klux Klan. Write to:
> P.O. Box 700, Shelton, CT 06584.

Larry Trapp never could have predicted the furor this ad would create. In 1921, the Klan had publicly announced its presence by riding into Lincoln on horseback in full regalia of white robes and hoods, carrying electric crosses. By comparison, this ad was nothing. Yet letters poured into the newspaper. Some said the Klan's presence demonstrated what an intolerant place Lincoln was, while others insisted this presence could serve as a welcome catalyst for much-needed dialogue about race. Other letters pointed to the Klan as the great-granddaddy of violent organizations in this country, the progenitor of hundreds of hate-filled offspring calling themselves by different names.

Larry Trapp welcomed the attention. If future Klansmen had missed his ad, Larry Trapp figured, they wouldn't fail to notice all this noise. Also, the negative reactions to Klan recruiting gave him new additions for his enemies' list.

Of course, some people already on his list were reacting. Donna Polk was one of them. Donna was especially upset because two months earlier, an ad she'd submitted to the *Lincoln Journal Star* (the weekend newspaper) for a letter-writing service had been turned down. When she'd asked why, a clerk in Classifieds told her, "We refuse ads *at our discretion.*" Donna learned newspaper advertising departments are never *required* to run an ad. Free speech is not at issue when it comes to paid advertising, and in fact, many newspapers have established policies *not* to run ads offensive to women or to community standards of decency. Eventually, Donna's ad ran, but it didn't run on time, and it wouldn't have run at all if she hadn't made a protest.

She wrote a letter to the newspaper: since they had a choice, why did they run this KKK ad? Also, if they wanted to run it, why did they do so during African-American History Month?

Michael Weisser was similarly incensed. Michael had tried to place an ad for a Jewish singles group and the *Journal Star* had turned it down. When he had asked why, he was told, "It's too specific." Again, the newspaper finally ran the ad, but only after a great deal of haggling. When Michael saw the KKK ad, he called up Classifieds and said, "That's a pretty specific ad, you know. Why didn't you turn *that* ad down?" The manager only said it was "policy."

The way the newspaper defended itself for running the ad also disturbed Dr. Joyce Ann Joyce, an English professor at the University of Nebraska at Lincoln. "Why is it that extreme manifestations of bigotry and racial hatred do not satisfy your criteria of 'narrow and well-grounded exceptions'?" she asked. "This hypocrisy has to stop . . . There is no doubt in my mind what you would do if I tried to run an ad in your paper for a black organization that preached racial hatred and [had] a history of murdering whites."

Within a week, another writer, Barbara Dibernard, said the newspaper had just refused an ad the previous week from PFLAG—Parents and Friends of Lesbians and Gays.

A few days after Trapp's ad, another one appeared:

Don't join the Ku Klux Klan.
Instead join churches or synagogues.
Help youth or stop crime.

Trapp assumed Donna Polk was the author of that ad, and he sent another letter to her on Klan stationery. This time, after "Knights of the Ku Klux Klan," he stamped his own name and title: "Larry Trapp, Local Representative." Blotches of ink spotted the paper, and lines of unevenly printed capital letters tilted erratically up to the right:

DEAR MRS. POLK,
 THANK YOU VERY MUCH FOR PROVING MY POINT (<u>BLACKS ARN'T VERY SMART</u>!) WHY WASTE YOUR PEOPLE'S MONEY ON AN AD TELLING PEOPLE NOT TO JOIN THE KLAN, WHEN <u>OUR</u> AD HAS ALREADY RECRUITED ALL THE NEW MEMBERS WE NEED?
 OH WELL . . . I'M HAVING TROUBLE WRITING AND LAUGHING AT THE SAME TIME, BUT I JUST WANT TO SAY <u>KEEP UP THE GOOD WORK</u>! A LITTLE COMEDY IS ALWAYS APPRECIATED.
[Signed] Larry Trapp.

In fact, the sponsor of the new ad was Jean Whitemon Newell, who had gone door-to-door with a friend and collected eighty-seven dollars to run the ad for a month. Over thirty contributors included barbers, pharmacists, single parents, secretaries and students. "Lincoln is a good town," Ms. Newell later told an interviewer from the *Lincoln Star*. "All it needs is for people to do what they know needs to be done. . . . Racism is a weed seed. If you nurture it, it's going to take over all the good things, so you pluck it."

Trapp was annoyed. Also, one of his members had brought him a copy of a petition called "Statement of Concern Regarding the Ku Klux

Klan Recruiting in Lincoln," which he'd found tacked to the bulletin board in a downtown pizza parlor. It said:

We deplore the presence of the Ku Klux Klan in the City of Lincoln and in the State of Nebraska.

We reject the violence, hatred, and racist dogma for which the Ku Klux Klan is well known. The Ku Klux Klan does not speak for the vast majority of white people in the United States of America.

We support the vision of a pluralistic, multi-cultural society in which all individuals are valued and respected. We advocate an end to racial violence and the rhetoric which supports it.

When Larry Trapp received a letter from a *Lincoln Star* reporter asking him for an interview, he felt edgy. He thought people should know more about the Klan, but the idea of going public made him nervous. He called Imperial Wizard J. W. Farrands, who gave him advice about how to handle the press and discussed the disadvantages and advantages of publicity with him.

After hanging up from the conversation with Farrands, Trapp made a few notes for himself on his tape recorder and then dialed the *Lincoln Star.* He told staff writer Linda Thomson he wanted to counter the false image the Klan was getting, so he would agree to an interview on two conditions—one, she could not describe his physical condition (for security reasons, he said, he didn't want anyone to know he was an amputee), and two, any picture taken of him could only show him from the waist up (no one should think he was an easy target in a wheelchair). With her editors' approval, Thomson agreed.

Early the morning of Tuesday, February 20, Larry Trapp bought a copy of the *Lincoln Star* and looked nervously at the front-page picture of himself in a box under "What's Inside." Under his picture was "Selling the KKK" and a summary: "His face, voice and demeanor are like those of a lot of fellows sipping coffee in local cafes. But Larry Trapp's red-white-and-blue T-shirt and cap are emblazoned with the words, 'Invisible Empire, Knights of the Ku Klux Klan.' "

Inside, under "State and Local News," he found a four-column headline: "Soft-spoken Lincoln Man Peddles Ku Klux Klan: Trapp's One-

Man Mission Is to Revive the Klan in Nebraska." Another photograph showed him in his Klan T-shirt (with the words "Invisible Empire, Knights of the Ku Klux Klan" circling the Klan emblem—a German Iron Cross centered in a red circle with a drop of "pure" Aryan blood in the center) and identified him as a "KKK recruiter." The article reported he was in his early forties, retired and "wheel-chair bound because of health problems." He planned to "distribute literature, sign up members, organize Klaverns (units of the Klan) and dispel what he termed misconceptions about the group spread by the media. . . . 'To tell you the truth,' he said, 'the main headquarters [of the Klan] had almost given up on Nebraska and Iowa until I got started.' "

In the article, Trapp insisted the Klan was not a hate organization; it had changed, and the "new Klan" couldn't be held responsible for what the old Klan had done during Reconstruction after the Civil War. " 'We don't advocate violence,' he insisted quietly. 'We advocate going through the courts, letter-writing, trying to do everything legally.' " He said if the Klan were a hate organization, he wouldn't belong to it. Ku Klux "means circle," he said, "and that's what we are, like a sewing circle and brotherhood. . . ."

Thomson wrote: "Talking with Trapp was sort of like a trip through Alice's Looking Glass. He willingly conceded minorities deserve equal opportunities . . . yet in the same breath, he lamented 'race mixing' because it led to 'mongrelization of the races.' He peddled the view he simply wanted "to rectify . . . reverse racism that impinges on the rights of Caucasians." Regarding Jews, he said, " 'We just want to keep them from taking over the country like they have been. They're big in banking.' "

Larry was happy to see one of his best quotes in large boldface: " 'I believe in racial pride. I believe black people should be proud of being black. I believe white people should be proud of being white.'—Larry Trapp"

Larry Trapp got more letters, and so did the *Star*. Readers asked why the newspaper didn't run an accompanying article to counter the assertion Klan violence took place only during Reconstruction. Thomson's skepticism was clear to an astute reader, but the headlines, boldface quotes and absence of historical context conveyed a different impression. "The article treated [Trapp] as though he were some sort of civic leader adding to the betterment of the community," Lincoln resident Mary E. Rapp wrote. "In publicizing the disgusting action and attitude of such an individual, the paper made a very clear statement as to its attitudes. . . ."

To balance Larry Trapp's assertion "today's Klan" wasn't violent, an accompanying article might easily have listed more recent crimes perpetrated by the KKK, such as a nationwide spree of cross burnings; club, baseball bat and chain attacks on interracial couples; assaults with knives and guns on civil rights advocates; and the recent convictions of two Klansmen who had kidnapped, beaten and lynched nineteen-year-old Michael Donald in Mobile, Alabama, in the 1980s. They had cut his throat and hung his body from a tree across the street from the Ku Klux Klan headquarters—because he was black.

Eventually, the *Star* ran a strong editorial countering the accuracy of Trapp's words. "Today's Klan, actually several different factions . . . is still a hate group draping itself in the American flag," it said. "[Its] very existence is a crude reflection of the deep-seated racism rooted in our culture and in our institutions. . . . We need to raise our objections to the hate groups that sprout in our midst. We also need to continue daily battle against the racism that doesn't wear a white sheet."

The *Lincoln Journal*—which Trapp called the *"Lincoln Urinal"*— also wrote an editorial against racism. But Larry Trapp had won the first round as he, like David Duke and others, maintained the Klan was only "for" whites, not "against" anyone else, and never violent. Dr. Jack Kay, chair of the Communications Department at Wayne State University, calls this "the Public Face/Private Face" of the hate movement. "In front of the cameras, it's 'We don't condone violence,' but in private, just the opposite is true," says Dr. Kay, who studies the rhetoric of hate groups. The manipulation works, he says, when the media uses sensational material without providing the background to let people know what the group has done and what it stands for. "They never show the real violence," says Dr. Kay. "They don't expose the hideous violence and the results of these crimes of assault, murder, destruction and intimidation that these groups have committed and continue to commit."

Larry Trapp had started something. A "Rally Against Racism" was held February 26, 1990, just seventeen days after his first KKK ad had run. More than one hundred people gathered on the steps of the County-City Building to hear speakers from Jewish, Moslem, Christian and Native American groups, the Coalition for Gay and Lesbian Civil Rights and other organizations. Lincoln's mayor spoke out against racism and the City Council chairman read a proclamation condemning the presence of the KKK or any hate group in Lincoln.

"It's no secret what the KKK stands for," the Reverend Michael Combs of Mt. Zion Missionary Baptist Church told protestors huddled together against the cold February wind. "It has been a foe of freedom and democracy since its founding in the 1860s."

Donna Polk, who had organized the rally, spoke of the need to work together and promised some five hundred people who signed petitions against the Klan their names would not be made public. "It's sad to acknowledge it might be dangerous to make their names known," she said.

When Cantor Michael Weisser's turn came at the microphone, he told the crowd: "The biggest crime we can commit as citizens of Lincoln is to keep our mouths shut. Let us never remain silent before the voices that say bigotry is good, because bigotry is always evil."

Seeing Donna Polk's name in the paper once again presented Larry Trapp with evidence that she was his enemy. Trapp wasn't aware of how necessary or how pleasing it was to him to maintain his grievances against his enemies. His rage was too blinding.

One night shortly after the rally, Donna Polk came home late from work. She was too tired to walk down to her letter box to pick up her mail, but the next morning, she found another letter addressed in squiggly, uneven block letters printed with a black Magic Marker:

> DEAR MRS. POLK,
> I WANT TO THANK YOU PERSONALLY
> FOR YOUR INTEREST (?) IN THE KLAN.
> I'M SORRY TO IN FORM YOU OF THIS,
> BUT YOUR EFFORTS TO STOP THE KLAN
> ARE IN VAIN. WE HAVE THE SAME
> CONSTITUTIONAL RIGHT TO OPERATE IN
> THIS TOWN AS DOES YOUR ORGANIZATION.
> JUST CHECK WITH YOUR ATTORNEY.
> IN THE MEANWHILE I WILL <u>VERY</u>

MUCH LOOK FORWARD TO (AND ENJOY)
FOLLOWING YOUR EFFORTS.
YOUR FAN,

> [Signed] Larry Trapp
> Local Representative

P.S. WE HAVE BEEN IN EXISTANCE
FOR OVER 125 YEARS AND HAVE
BEEN IN NEBRASKA SINCE THE
20's (ON AN INACTIVE BASIS), SO CHECK
YOUR NEBRASKA HISTORY BOOKS. WE
HAVE NOT BEEN ELIMINATED YET.
I RECEIVE APPLICATIONS FOR member shi [crossed out]
MEMBERSHIP EVERY DAY!
GOD BLESS THE KLAN!

From Donna Polk's perspective, the scariest thing about the letter was *it had no postmark;* not only had Larry Trapp signed his name again—but this letter had been *hand-delivered.* That night when Donna Polk went to bed, she couldn't sleep. She tried meditating, she told herself not to be afraid, but she was afraid. She moved her pillow and a blanket to the big rust-colored couch in her living room downstairs, where she felt she could better hear anyone who might have gotten into her house or who might try to get in. She had gotten sensor lights installed around her yard, but she lived in an isolated area and they provided very little comfort. She never went to sleep anymore feeling safe.

Knowing he'd sufficiently frightened Donna Polk would have made Larry Trapp happy; being cruel satisfied a twisted need inside him. He relished going over the past, savored knowing he was making progress and laying out plans to effectively meet his goals. He tapped his fingers on his desk and thought about whether he ought to try watching *Curse of the Catwoman,* one of his favorite sex videos. It had cost eighty dollars to buy it through a mail-order outlet, but it was worth it. He liked the scene where all the men took one woman down into a pit to ravish her, but the best was when the men stood around her in a circle, unzipped their jeans, pulled out their penises, and while she stripped and rubbed her own body in the center of the circle, they jerked off together.

Trapp would like seeing the tape again, but it was late and he needed to try to sleep. Carefully and methodically, he put away his cleaning tools. He placed his .357 Magnum in its holster, strapped it in, wrapped it in the soft blue towel he kept it in and placed it on his bookshelf next to some leaflets—"Chemistry of the Holocaust" and "Race Mixing Is Treason." He put his AR-15 rifle in its khaki case and hid it at the bottom of his closet. He loaded his Beretta .380, opened his file drawer and set it in the front. He hung his MAC-10 on the back of his wheelchair, hoisted himself into his bed and then moved the chair close to the bed so the semiautomatic assault rifle almost touched his right hand. If someone woke him up in the night, he'd grab it and shoot. The rest would take care of itself.

A DISEASE OF FEAR

Chapter 6

Not enough emphasis has been placed on a particular ingredient of racism, which is the uneasiness and fear aroused by differentness. The foreigner . . . is always somewhat strange and frightening. It is only a few short steps from fear to hostility, and from hostility to aggression. Loving means relaxing, yielding, forgetting oneself in the other person, identifying with him more or less. You do not forgive a foreigner until you have managed to adopt him. Otherwise he continues to be inscrutable.
—ALBERT MEMMI

*L*arry Trapp pulled off his Klan robe, folded it and laid it over a chair by his kitchen table. This had been a big day. It was November 1990, and nearly nine months had passed since he had gone public. He sat in his white T-shirt and Jockey underpants and switched on his Citizens Band radio to see what was happening. Tonight, he had "naturalized" two more members—which took a lot of preparation—and afterward he'd held a Klan meeting in his apartment. Sometimes a slow learner frustrated him, but it was reassuring that these members felt as strongly as he did against race mixing, race traitors, communism, immorality, Jew conspiracies, black crime. They knew the white race was not getting its due, and Trapp felt the burden of responsibility for directing their actions. Some of the guys were green, but he was training them and they were proving themselves.

After all the publicity in February 1990, Trapp had gotten letters from

more than forty people asking for information. He'd sent back literature on the Klan, and thirty filled-out applications had been sent back
to him. So far, however, in nine months, he'd inducted only seven new
Klansmen—counting the two from today. He had set up interviews
with others, but he screened them carefully ahead of time for weirdos,
criminals or infiltrators. He didn't want any undercover cops slipping
in. It hadn't been lost on him when Glenn Miller, leader of a militant
Klan group in North Carolina and head of the White Patriot Party, had
been convicted in 1986 by a federal jury of having used active-duty military personnel and stolen U.S. military weapons to train his recruits.
Trapp wasn't going to let anything like that happen to him. If he felt
suspicions about somebody, they were out. If they used drugs, they
were out. Druggies could too easily be bought or blackmailed. Ex-cons
were okay *only* if they were drug-free and out of crime. He didn't want
the Klan's name dirtied. In the 1970s, a state leader of the Nebraska
Klan had been charged with child molestation—which flushed Klan
membership right down the drain.

The ten members Trapp had now, he felt he could count on. He liked
a compact group. In his opinion, commitment, not big numbers, was
what got the work accomplished. His Klansmen were dedicated—and
they would inspire others to action. Sometimes it was preferable when
you motivated somebody outside the organization to act. At tonight's
meeting, a couple of the guys had asked him about doing some cross
burnings, but he told them: "It's a cross *lighting,* not a cross burning.
Unless there's a ceremony, you don't light a cross. A lot of the cross
lightings are out of order; they're not done according to Klan policy.
They gotta be done according to policy."

Personally, he said, he felt cross lightings were a matter of too much
show, not enough discipline. "As far as I'm concerned, the proof is in
the doing," he said. "Action is better than show. Racial attacks are better. Direct hits are better. They let people know where we stand." Trapp
and his right-hand man, who also was his explosives partner, had some
heavy action in mind. They planned to collect and build whatever they
needed in terms of pipe bombs, hand grenades and incendiary devices.

At the Klan meeting, Trapp explained they could go to a hardware
store and say they were farmers and needed to buy dynamite, but then
they'd have to fill out forms. He didn't want them to do that; he didn't
want to raise suspicions. It was easier to use ammonium nitrate, charcoal, fertilizer and diesel fuel to make their own improvised explosives,

or to get hidrotic acid, isopropyl ether, manganese or whatever other materials they needed from the drugstore and hardware store to make jerry-can bombs, Molotov cocktails or pipe bombs. Trapp had manuals with simple instructions—and at the end of Klan meetings, they could put the devices together. The trick was to leave out one key ingredient until the end so they didn't blow themselves up.

"Operation Gooks" had been the main topic of tonight's meeting. Next time, they'd discuss how to deal with "Martin Lucifer Coon's birthday," but tonight they instituted the first step to give Asians "fair warning." Thousands of Vietnamese had moved into Lincoln and Omaha and the rest of Nebraska—and that didn't even count Koreans, Cambodians, Chinese and other foreigners coming in. "The Gooks" had to be stopped, Larry said, before they took over everything. Even the old Presbyterian church at the corner of 26th and P streets now had a big sign on it in Vietnamese above the name Immaculate Heart of Mary Vietnamese Catholic Church. Vietnamese Catholics had purchased the building, and on Sundays after mass, they had huge, open-to-the-public Vietnamese dinners. Sometimes as many as eight hundred Vietnamese people were there at once.

A lot of Vietnamese lived in Larry Trapp's neighborhood as well, and for some reason, Trapp said with a chuckle, they kept finding their tires slit and Klan literature on their steps when they got up in the mornings. One Klansman suggested they blow up the Vietnamese church, but Larry didn't think bombing a Catholic church was such a good idea, even if it was Vietnamese. He said the better focus, or at least the first, ought to be the Vietnamese center in Omaha.

The Vietnamese Resettlement Association ran a major clearing center officially named The IndoChinese Refugee Assistance Center. Every week workers at the center helped Vietnamese newcomers join families and friends and find places to live in Nebraska. They helped them find jobs stuffing newspapers, sorting or stacking in meatpacking plants, busing at restaurants or working at Goodyear, Kawasaki or other local businesses. Often, they helped Vietnamese find minimum-wage jobs alongside recent arrivals from Mexico or Guatemala, Korea or China. Those jobs, Larry Trapp and his followers believed, took money away from white men. Thus, foreigners were to blame for the Klansmen's own lack of economic success.

Larry picked up the stack of letters his followers had written and examined them under his bright lights. Some were typewritten, some handwritten, and all were on different paper, including stationery from the New Order. But while language and syntax varied, the thrust of each message was the same. Trapp liked his own letter best:

> Dear Dog-Eating Gook, Scum,
>
> The majority of the White people of the State of Nebraska are highly agitated at your presence here.
>
> Many of us had family members that were killed in your asinine conflict almost 30 years ago.
>
> I guarantee you will not find peace in our state. You have not heard the last from the White People of Nebraska. May your filthy, rotten, savage, carcasses rot in Hell!
>
> For God, Race, and Country,
>
> A concerned <u>White</u> citizen.

Another letter advised, "[You are] unwelcome and unwanted in this state. . . . So pack your bags and get the hell outta here!!"

A letter on New Order stationery said, "To the Gook Club: First they send our boys over to the jungles of Vietnam to be killed by a bunch of goddamn rice eating orangutans, and now they're letting you slant eyed parasites into our society to mooch off of the white man's pride and joy, America. Go home Monkey-spewn [sic]."

"Nelson's" letter was simple: "Why don't you just go back to Gook land? Nebraska doesn't want you. Your entire country should have been nuked anyway!"

One long typewritten letter said the Vietnamese better not bring any more of their "own inferior race" here to "racially destroy my country" or they would be deported. "Your [sic] all nothing but a bunch of yellow-skinned, slanted-eyed, dog-eating, race-mixing bastards. You are as bad or worse than the other non-white trash that must be dealt with everyday."

Larry adjusted his magnifying lenses and addressed the big manila mailing folder, put the letters inside—with his letter on top—added a poster about "the yellow menace," sealed it and put stamps on it. The next step would be to tear the place apart.

But now it was late and time for relaxing. Larry Trapp picked up his phone and punched in the hotline number for the White Knights of the KKK in Catoosa, Oklahoma. Trapp kept up on other white supremacists' messages in much the way a doctor tries to stay abreast of his colleagues' latest research. All the white racists, however, seemed to pattern their hotlines after Tom Metzger's "Dial-A-Racist." Metzger, a television repairman in his late fifties who directs the White Aryan Resistance (WAR) from his home in Fallbrook, California, had been one of the first in the movement to use new technology. Not only did Metzger introduce telephone hotlines, but he also started a computer data bank and the "WAR Computer Bulletin Board," accessed by members and supporters. (Notices on the network include messages such as, "The fact is that the only way to be free of what threatens you is to kill it. So learn to kill. Quickly. Quietly. Without witnesses.") Metzger encouraged supporters to keep enemies' lists updated on their computers, to send messages by fax rather than by phone and to produce video shows advocating white supremacy for distribution throughout the country.

For many years, Larry Trapp had admired Metzger from a distance. "America's Most Dangerous Neo-Nazi"—as the Southern Poverty Law Center called him—had built his reputation as a young white supremacist by founding the White Brotherhood and the California Knights of the Ku Klux Klan and creating a grass-roots political base from which to run for public office.* In more recent years, the former KKK Grand Dragon had established WAR, and he and his son John had started a WAR youth group called the Aryan Youth Movement and stayed busy by organizing "border watches," picketing the arrival of Vietnamese boat people, calling for the deportation of all Jews to Israel, advocating sending dogs into the fields to attack striking lettuce workers and proposing to shoot illegal aliens entering the United States.

Now, from Oklahoma, Larry Trapp heard the familiar voice of his friend and fellow Klansman Dennis W. Mahon. Trapp switched on his speaker phone, settled back in his chair, picked up his holster and pulled out his Browning high-power 9-mm semiautomatic, which he'd just gotten back from the A-I Pawnshop.

"Do the Jews control America or do the hardworking taxpayers?" Mahon said on his prerecorded Tulsa Dial-A-Racist hotline.

"The fucking Jews," Trapp answered as he adjusted the bright light from his gooseneck lamp and then took the clip out of the Browning.

"Now, you worthless, brainwashed, two-day-old Christians out there," Mahon's recording continued, "maybe you believe that Jews are

*Metzger ran for San Diego County supervisor in 1978, in the Democratic primary for Congress in 1980 and for the Democratic nomination for the U.S. Senate in 1982—an election in which he received more than 75,000 votes.

God's chosen people. Well that's fine, you Jew-day-o-Christians can give *your* money to Israel, but don't ask us working-class white men out here trying to earn a living to give more money to that Jewish state. To hell with it! We can barely make it! The Jews are fit for destruction! Jesus Christ said that! . . . And the blacks! They're hated in every nation in the world. . . . And the Mexicans . . . they see an Anglo, they call us Anglos, they stick a knife in you and they rob you.

"Com'mon you people out there . . . American is going downhill. . . . All the jobs are going to Red China! And Haiti! And Taiwan! So there's no jobs left for your kids! You may not believe in fighting for your race, but I'll tell you what. Aren't your kids worth it? . . . You better get off your ass and start fighting, white man! White Power! Leave a message!"

"White Power!" Larry echoed from his seat by the phone. "White Power, Brother!"

Trapp put on his magnifying lenses and began polishing the gun with pipe cleaners and a rag as he listened to Mahon imitate the sound of Metzger's syrupy voice, "cute" alliterations and "special" names. Like Metzger, he called Morris Dees, cofounder and chief counsel of the Southern Poverty Law Center, who was prosecuting Metzger in court, "Morris Sleeze." Mexicans were "Mud People," police were "Jews-in-Blue" and so on. Mahon, Trapp and the others echoed Metzger's tone and sentiments, adding their own local color.

Larry was pleased about his affiliation with Tom. Metzger was a source of clarification on important political information: for instance, Metzger had told him Jews profited from abortion—that Planned Parenthood was a Jewish organization, all abortion doctors are Jews, and most abortion nurses are lesbians. This didn't surprise Larry Trapp; he was eager to believe it. He didn't need documentation.

Trapp was building a reputation, and Metzger's open recognition of him added to his stature. Metzger first mentioned him publicly when Larry reported trouble with a local nursing service and Metzger backed him up. On his national telephone hotline, Metzger had said:

DATELINE, CALIFORNIA! You have tuned to Resistance Radio, the North American voice of the W.A.R., WAR! The White Resistance. 88 on your dial; transmitting from Mud-Covered Southern California, where Spics keep pouring over the border every day. . . .

• • •

DATELINE, LINCOLN, NEBRASKA! Our friend Larry Trapp is a senior and a Klansman. And because his longtime health service found out he was a Klansman, they refused him service. Kimberly Quality Care at 7111 A Street, Suite 102, Lincoln, Nebraska, 68502. It's an anti-Aryan outfit. Drop them a line with your opinion of this act of medical care being lifted against our friend, Larry Trapp. The hotline in Nebraska to reach Larry is 402-475-9025. Give him some encouragement.

Metzger had gotten it wrong about his being a senior citizen, but after he set him straight, Trapp formed a solid bond with him. Metzger liked Trapp's dedication and Trapp liked Metzger's commitment to paramilitary training and to coordinating skinhead activity. Their hate had a harmony.

As Grand Dragon, Larry Trapp had become a force to be dealt with in the Midwest. These days, he also was turning into something of a Klan hero. In fact, the Invisible Empire's national magazine, *The Klansman,* featured Larry Trapp in an article titled "Nebraska Hero—True and Loyal Klansman" in their October 1990 issue. "Larry Trapp will serve well as a true portrait of an American hero," the article stated. "We encourage and support this man who openly defies prison and even death for his convictions. He is truly a credit to the white race and an asset to the Klan."

The Klansman praised Trapp's "brave quest" to "openly put down race-mixers" and "to expose the big lie of the Holocaust." Claiming Larry had a degree from the University of Nebraska, the article stated, "Fighting communism is not new to Larry Trapp. He fought as a mercenary soldier in what was formerly Rhodesia, in Africa. It was there that he came to despise Communism."

Another tribute, which meant as much if not more to Larry as that article, was a poem about him from a young Mississippi Klansman named Jeffrey Smith. Jeff and Larry had talked a great deal on the phone before Jeff wrote the poem "Rolling Thunder" and sent a handwritten copy of it to Larry. When he first read it, Larry said if he had been the kind of guy who cried, this would have turned him to tears. Larry now had Jeff's handwritten poem hanging in a black frame on his wall. It went:

> A brother in Nebraska, named Larry Trapp
> May ride a wheelchair
> But he doesn't take Z.O.G.'s crap.

Hindered by fate, and not by his choice,
He ignores it and fights
For our race with his voice.

From his home in Lincoln, he carries the fight
And speaks to the people
Of the Aryans plight.

He's a true White Warrior,
To this I can attest.
As a teacher and White Soldier,
He's one of our best.

Pity for himself is not in his creed,
For a man is judged worthy by his acts and his deeds,
He lives for our race,
His devotion is true,
He fights for White children, for me, and for you.

He's the perfect example of the Aryan man,
Who fights for White Victory,
In the Ku Klux Klan!

Larry Trapp had never gotten such positive attention before, never been so honored. People were paying him notice: Klansmen and racists like himself had faith in him. A couple of months earlier, in mid-September 1990, he and some of his members had gone to a public meeting of a new group called the Coalition Against Racism and Prejudice (CARP), and he had spoken out against their goal of "eliminating hate groups, racism and bigotry."

From Larry's perspective, the meeting had been a great success. Larry had been nervous, but he'd done a good job. The Klansmen with him knew it had taken courage to speak out publicly. Larry Trapp would later say his own parents had never shown faith in him "in any way, shape or form." But these people believed, followed his instructions, respected him.

•   •   •

Michael Weisser had also been at that September meeting. Earlier, Cathy Kushner, Executive Director of the YWCA, had received a phone call saying, "Imperial Wizard Ferrands" would attend the meeting along with "Imperial Representative" Larry Trapp and some eighty members of the Nebraska Klan. In fact, Ferrands did not show up, but Larry Trapp did.

Michael Weisser noticed Trapp wearing a baseball cap with a KKK logo as Trapp looked around the room. Trapp's expression radiated such a mean-spiritedness that at first glance Michael didn't notice the wheelchair. A young man whom Trapp referred to as his "Nighthawk" or "bodyguard" stood on the left side of the wheelchair throughout the meeting.

When Trapp gave his name and title and announced he had come to speak against the coalition's efforts to stop the Klan, some people objected to his presence. Trapp started shouting, and others began to shout as well. Michael Weisser intervened. "Look," he said to the group, "we're talking about being against prejudice. The guy's got a perfect right to be here just like anybody else. This is an open meeting. We don't have any bylaws that exclude him. Let him speak."

Michael believed what he said. But the black pouch hanging from the right side of Trapp's chair wasn't lost on him. Michael had noticed it at about the same time as did Bob Wolfson of the ADL and John Ways, a Lincoln police officer who also was president of the local NAACP chapter. The three of them had talked about this possibility before the meeting began, and throughout the meeting, they stood slightly behind and to each side of Larry Trapp's chair. They thought Trapp might have a gun in the pouch, and they were ready to react if necessary.

As Michael kept his eyes on Larry's hands through the first half of the meeting, an incident in North Carolina replayed itself in his mind. This incident took place during a heated school board meeting in Greenville about a proposed policy to allow the teaching of religion in school. That policy would exclude religious services and prayers, but would allow schools to teach students about various religions. Michael had gone to the podium to speak in favor of the proposal. Fundamentalist right-wing Christian groups were totally opposed. The debate was fervent on both sides.

"You know, there's a lot of hatred in this room right now, a lot of tension, a lot of bitterness," Michael had told the people in the crowded room, "and it all seems to be in the name of the Prince of Peace." He said he was in favor of this policy "because it's fair."

At that point, a man jumped up in the back of the room and screamed, "Fuck you, you Jew bastard. Hitler didn't go far enough with you sons of bitches!"

The man drew what looked like a gun from his jacket and aimed it at Michael, but a police officer and the president of Michael's congregation wrestled the man to the floor. The resolution passed unanimously in favor of the policy, which made Michael happy. But he was deeply shaken by the idea he could have been killed by someone simply for what he believed. He realized how easily he might have died, and he also realized how some people are not only capable of pulling that trigger but are eager to do so. This Klansman might be one of them.

Michael watched the pouch, and he watched the back of Larry Trapp's head move as he spoke. Trapp's voice sounded angry—jagged, constricted and pitched at a high squeak. He began with a harangue against "interracial breeding," and carried on for nearly ten minutes. "We have to protect our own," he said. "By the year 2054, the white race will be a minority because of all this interracial breeding. That's all we're trying to stop is interracial breeding, and bringing people up from Mexico. Pretty soon, the white man is going to be a museum piece."

At various points during his speech, a few voices from around the room said "Amen," which made coalition members aware that Klan supporters had come in separately from Trapp. The number wasn't certain, but no one at the meeting guessed more than five or ten at the most. When Trapp finished speaking, a few people clapped. Soon after that, the meeting broke up and coalition members filed out of the room, ignoring Trapp.

That was the last time Larry Trapp spoke publicly on behalf of the Invisible Empire. As his contacts grew nationally and internationally, Trapp decided to change his Klan affiliation. For some time, he'd thought the Invisible Empire wasn't sufficiently militant. And when he'd gotten to know the Mahon twins—Dennis and Daniel—he found a new Klan faction—the White Knights of the Ku Klux Klan—which better represented his own philosophy. Dennis Mahon, an aircraft worker for TWA at the Kansas City International Airport and the driving force behind the White Knights, had built up a potent group of some two hundred members in Kansas City, and in other parts of Kansas he'd involved some fanatical old-time Klansmen from the seventies who were committed to violence. Like Larry, Dennis Mahon was closely aligned with Tom Metzger's White Aryan Resistance. Racist activities increased all over Kansas—and were strengthened by Daniel, who was Grand Kleagle for the White Knights in the state of Oklahoma. With chapters in Kansas, Oklahoma *and* Nebraska, the White Knights of the KKK could become a real force for destruction in the midwestern United States. What's more, this force could spread. Mahon, like Trapp, praised neo-Nazi Germans for their increased firebombings and violent attacks on foreigners and political asylum seekers. Mahon had started traveling to Germany, Canada and England to organize rallies and to forge national and international links between skinheads, Klansmen and neo-Nazis. By joining the White Knights, Larry Trapp could see himself as part of a worldwide revolution.

Trapp announced his change of affiliation on his hotline. After "Welcome to the Hotline of the White Knights of the Ku Klux Klan of Nebraska, where the truth hurts!" Trapp explained the switch. "We don't believe in playin' any games like the Invisible Empire or the Knights in Arkansas does," he said. "We aren't going to be pussyfooting around like they do. We *must* fight for what is ours and what is our children's."

It wasn't unusual for Klansmen to change their alliances. At least twenty-eight different Klan groups operate throughout the United States, and most work independently from each other and involve different personalities and motivations, according to Klanwatch, the investigative arm of the Southern Poverty Law Center, which monitors hate groups throughout the country. The new groups that break off and regroup often do so because they want financial control or political power. Sometimes members change to a different Klan faction because they prefer its tactics or its open commitment to violence.

This was the case for Larry Trapp. It wasn't that the Invisible Empire was nonviolent. In point of fact, the Invisible Empire has been called by some observers the most violent of Klan groups. But the public face of the Invisible Empire was too tame for Larry Trapp. He liked the White Knights of the KKK better because they were nearby, with headquarters in Kansas City, and more importantly, they were openly militant, armed and dangerous. Mahon contended the White Knights were "the most violent Klan in America." The letterhead of the two organizations symbolized their public differences. The Invisible Empire's stationery showed a picture of the top half of a Klansman in his hood and robes, standing with his arms crossed in front of him. The White Knights' stationery showed a robed and hooded Klansman on the back of a rearing horse with a rifle in his left hand.

Larry Trapp also liked the fact that the White Knights had named themselves after an older and earlier incarnation of White Knights of the KKK in Mississippi. The Mississippi White Knights had been responsible for killing three civil rights workers—James Chaney, Andrew Goodman and Michael Schwerner—in 1964. During the 1960s, the Mississippi White Knights had caused many other deaths as well. They had bombed hundreds of black churches and several Jewish synagogues and targeted both blacks and Jews who supported civil rights. In the 1980s, White Knights Klansmen in Tennessee were implicated in the deaths of five black women in Chattanooga—one of whom was planting marigolds when she was shot.

This new Kansas City–based White Knights group, formed about 1987, had chosen their name because they admired the old Mississippi White Knights—and shared many of their views. In addition to the usual goal of ridding America of "vermin"—which included Mexicans ("Mud") coming over the border, refugees, blacks, Jews, Asians, "Jew lovers," "nigger lovers," "race mixers" and "queers," the Kansas City White Knights had an additional goal for the nineties that Larry appreciated. They aimed "to give our Aryan children a future with a land with fresh air, unpolluted water and soil." As stated in their newsletter, *White Beret,*their goal was to create "an exclusive Aryan homeland" in the U.S., where eugenics would produce an all-white society "close to a utopia."

Trapp's change to the White Knights also meant he would be openly joined to other white supremacists nationally and internationally. "One big reason I got out of the Invisible Empire is they don't believe in working with the American Nazi Party, with skinheads and other white activist groups," Larry later explained to a caller. "Now we're all working for the same goals—some are more violent than others, some are more laid back, it doesn't make any difference. We're all working for the same goal."

Trapp's new affiliation also meant he was openly aligning himself with groups that endorsed physical violence and terroristic actions on behalf of the white revolution. He wanted terrorism to lead to a race war within the United States and to white Aryan dominance throughout the world. His thinking in this regard had been shaped by literature from the New Order, the White Aryan Resistance and the Aryan Nations. All three of these groups—and another relatively new group called the Church of the Creator—were modeled after The Order, a covert military group formed during an Aryan Nations' meeting in Idaho in 1983, when founder Robert Mathews allied with a handful of young, radical racists who swore a secret vow to "One God, One Race, One Nation."

The novel *The Turner Diaries,* a futuristic fantasy about white guerrilla warfare written by William Pierce and published under the pseudonym Andrew Macdonald, was said to have inspired Mathews and others who formed The Order. In it, an underground white terrorist organization carries off "the Great Revolution" through bombings, mass murders and nuclear explosions. The Order used the book as their blueprint during the mid-1980s, when they conducted robberies and murders and planned large-scale sabotage of public utilities—all in preparation for a "race war" to establish white supremacy in the United States. ("Today has been the Day of the Rope—a grim and bloody day, but an unavoidable one. . . . If they were non-whites—and that included all the Jews and everyone who even looked like he had a bit of non-White ancestry—they were . . . started on their no-return march to the canyon in the foothills . . . The hangings and the formation of the death columns went on for about ten hours without interruption . . .") The book continued to inspire Trapp and the militant white supremacists around the country with whom he was aligned.

In 1984, The Order assassinated Denver talk-show host Alan Berg when he arrived home from work. The Order member who shot Berg at close range with an automatic pistol had sold ads for an anti-Semitic newspaper and considered Alan Berg, who was Jewish and an outspoken advocate of civil rights, the enemy. The Order also murdered a state trooper, two FBI agents and a sheriff before Robert Mathews was killed in a police shoot-out.

After Mathews' death, Metzger called for "direct action" to save "future white generations." Trapp concurred with his statement, "The easy and safe methods have all been tried. Now is the time . . . for the weapons of WAR."

Larry had come to believe he, too, would play his part in overthrowing the U.S. government. This change of affiliation meant he literally was a soldier and an officer for the white race. It meant he might have to kill enemies. He'd never had a chance to be in the U.S. Army, Navy, Marines or Air Force. He'd wanted to be a Green Beret, and he'd wanted to fight in the Vietnam War, but because he'd had diabetes since he was six years old, he was classified 4-F. And while he claimed to have been a mercenary in Rhodesia, that was not true. Now, finally, he was a soldier in the white army. If he ever was arrested in the course of carrying out his duties, his fellow supremacists would consider him a prisoner of war—and he would certainly demand that the government treat him as a POW.

When Larry Trapp was sworn in as Grand Dragon of the White Knights of the Ku Klux Klan, Realm of Nebraska, the Kansas City headquarters sent him a *Handbook for Fifth Era Knights of the Order,* containing pictures of a hangman's noose and a gun at the bottom of the page, along with regulations booklets and the materials needed for Klan ceremonies. They also sent him his White Knights of the KKK identification card with his picture, his title as Grand Dragon, his Social Security number and the Kansas City White Knights headquarters address on it. The back of the ID said the card was "Identification for Purposes of the Geneva Convention Relative to Treatment of Prisoners of War—January 12, 1949." It gave Trapp's vital statistics—date of birth, height, weight, blood type, color of hair, color of eyes—and stated:

DECLARATION OF WAR NOVEMBER 25, 1984

It is a dark and dismal time in the history of our race . . . An evil shadow has fallen across our once fair land. . . . A certain vile, alien people have taken control of our country. . . . When the day comes, we will not ask whether you swung to the right or whether you swung to the left. We will simply swing you by the neck. THIS IS WAR!

—THE ORDER

As a Klansman, Larry Trapp was finally getting his due. In addition to occasional press interviews, Larry was connected with just about every major white supremacist group in the country. He talked regularly with racist leaders in the United States and with neo-Nazis in Germany, South Africa and other places around the world. He bragged that his phone bills totaled more than $300 a month.

As a child, Larry Trapp had never been paid much respect by anyone. He had been a small, shy boy who loved to put on his swimming suit and sit in the front yard when it rained—or play with the water rushing down the gutter in the street—building dams with little sticks, looking for worms and catching them in his hand. But what little imagination he might have had somehow was squelched. His father, an amateur boxer who worked first as a welder, then as a milkman and later as a security guard and chief of security at a large furniture mart in Omaha, often belittled him, challenged him, taunted him. Larry would later say that when he was a child in Omaha, his father repeatedly beat him with his fists, called him a "little queer," and otherwise humiliated him. One time when he was about ten years old, he ran away from home. Larry later said his dad tracked him down with his car, stopped when he saw him, ran up and said, "If you're going to be a man and act like a man, I'm going to punish you like a man." Then he doubled up his fists and hit Larry in the side of the head and knocked him out.

Larry's father denied ever having abused his son. But whether that story was true or not, Larry's life as a child had felt empty, had always contained a certain hollowness he didn't understand. Larry's older sister Candy remembers how Larry started drinking excessively when he was about eight years old. "There were many times I'd go ride around the neighborhood on my bike and figure out where he might be and find him at one or another of his friends the following morning when he hadn't come home," she said. "And I'd finally find him and he and his friend would have gotten a bottle of wine and just drunk themselves into oblivion. He'd be hung over and covered with vomit, and I'd drag him home and try to clean him up.

"And then my mother would yell, of course, and he had the discipline to look forward to from my father. It wasn't as if he wasn't a lost soul anyway, but then all he had to welcome him as soon as my dad came home from work was a belting. Dad was a very strong man, and I guess it's something you grow up with and don't really think about it. Dad used a belt—and he'd make good use of it. You always trembled in fear for when Dad would come after you."

Larry's father had also taught him the habits of hate, according to the way Larry later remembered it. He modeled a diversionary form of expressing rage that, without a target, might have left him feeling depleted and helpless. Later, Larry and his sister Candy would recall how their father had always referred to black people as "niggers"—for example, "That nigger did this, that nigger did that. The only good nigger is a dead nigger." Larry and Candy also remembered Easter Sundays when they were kids and their dad would pile them in the car and say,

"Let's go down to North Omaha and see how fancy the niggers are dressing today."

Larry would also later remember his father's advice about Japanese people: "You can't ever trust a Jap. They're sneaky." And as for Jews? "The reason the kikes have so much money is that they screwed the white Christians out of it." Larry said his father taught him to make fun of differences; he taught him by example that to feel secure, you had to act bigger and tougher than other people. You needed to speak with your fists, and if that didn't work, or if, deep within, you felt afraid and humiliated, you stayed bigger by diminishing those around you.

BROKEN

BEYOND HEALING

Chapter 7

You want to kill those [bigoted] people? Do you kill a parrot for
repeating words he has been taught? Those people are reacting
as they have been taught to react. You change them by
changing what they are taught.
—MICHAEL SCHWERNER

*M*ichael and Julie Weisser hated feeling intimidated.

They had installed dead bolts, purchased extra keys, and now, every day, they locked all their doors. Like Donna Polk and others similarly advised by the police, they also had begun to lock their cars and carefully look inside the mailbox before reaching in to pull out a possible letter bomb. They felt nervous when cars drove slowly by their home. They worried about the kids being hurt. Dina, Dave and Rebecca had to let Michael and Julie know *exactly* where they were and where they were going. If they came home twenty minutes later than the agreed-upon time, they knew they'd be in trouble.

It was August 1991, two months since the hate call and mail, and by now it was clear Larry Trapp must have been the instigator behind the hate mail, phone threats and many other racist, anti-Semitic deeds happening in the Lincoln and Omaha areas. When television news stations covered the fire-bombing of an African-American home, one television station said the police were investigating any possible Klan connections. They showed a clip of Larry Trapp from an earlier interview saying, "Anyone who isn't a racist isn't proud of their own race. Blacks are racist. Jews are racist. Hispanics are racist."

When they saw Trapp on television, Michael was reminded of seeing him at the CARP meeting, and both he and Julie remembered the previous winter, when Trapp was interviewed after the KKK had plastered anti–Martin Luther King posters all over the University of Nebraska campuses in Lincoln and Omaha and a number of African-Americans had received hate mail. Trapp often wore a faded tan t-shirt out in public that had a picture of Dr. King with a bull's-eye over his forehead and the words "Our Dream Came True." But of course, Trapp didn't admit any connection to the letters or to the large handprinted KKK posters that said: "Why Not CELEBRATE the Birthday of A REAL HERO, Robert E. Lee, January 19, 1807, Instead of a Worthless Nigger 'Martin Lucifer Coon' Jan. 15, 1929."

The posters and the hate mail had stirred up a lot of angry reactions. But Lincoln Police Chief Allen Curtis had said on television: "No matter how reprehensible and personally disgusting this may be, we're in the area of First Amendment rights here. They're expressing an opinion, and nothing can be done to stop them unless the letters contain a direct threat or unless they commit a crime."

Hearing Trapp's voice again, Julie remembered the first time she and Michael had heard Larry Trapp. It was when Michael was in the hospital recovering from thoracic surgery and they heard someone yelling at a nurse. "It was this really racist, anti-Semitic, bigoted tirade about how he was going to come back and get even with this place," Julie said. "It was unbelievable. So when I found out he was with the Klan, it didn't surprise me at all because I knew he was just this totally obnoxious person."

Julie, who loves listening to stories, had also picked up a number of tidbits about Trapp from her work in local doctors' offices. "He was very vocal, and all the medical community knew him because he jumped from doctor to doctor," she said. "He was completely noncompliant, hostile and verbally abusive. He'd go to one doctor and then he'd quit and go to another one and get mad at him and go back to someone else. One nursing agency refused to send nurses to his apartment because they said he'd pulled a gun on one of their nurses and threatened her somehow."

One day after Trapp had visited the doctor's office Julie was working in at the time, she heard he had been wearing a T-shirt with a swastika on it, and she got furious. Impulsively, she said to her fellow nurses and doctors' assistants: "You know what? If Larry Trapp ever comes into the office and I'm working that day, *don't* ask me to take him back in there because I *won't* do it.

"And, hey," she also said, "if he comes in here and needs to be resuscitated, don't anybody ask me to give him CPR! If he's going to die in here, he can just die! Don't ask me to take care of him because I won't!"

Now, being so conscious of security in her own home led Julie to start thinking more about Larry Trapp. From the time she was young, Julie had worked hard to unravel the truth and understand why people chose to do what they did. At work one day, she glanced at Trapp's medical records and made a mental note of his address. Not long afterward, when she was out driving, she found herself making a detour by a plain brown, low-slung, one-story apartment house at 817 C Street. She wondered which apartment Larry Trapp lived in, and she also found herself wondering why he was doing these horrible things. What made him so hateful and so bitter? Was he lonely? Crazy? While she felt infuriated and revolted by him, she also was intrigued by how he could have become so evil.

Without understanding exactly why, Julie drove by 817 C Street again and again. "Something kept motivating me to drive by," she said later. "Whenever I went downtown, I always drove by his apartment. There was a curiosity. I was not only curious, but I had this sense there was more to Larry than what had been presented in the newspapers or on television."

One afternoon when Julie was feeling frustrated and antagonistic toward Larry Trapp, she sat down on her big blue and white living-room couch to relax and opened the Bible to Proverbs. Julie doesn't consider herself religious in a traditional sense, but she loves the Bible for its pragmatic way of discussing the challenges of being human. She believes communication with God is most possible through human actions, and she enjoys finding ideas in the Bible, in philosophical or other religious writings, which she can apply to any particular situation she faces.

As she thumbed through Proverbs, she wasn't looking for anything in particular. But then the twelfth verse of the sixth chapter seemed to jump out at her: "A worthless person, a wicked man, goes about with crooked speech, winks with his eyes, scrapes with his feet, points with his finger, with perverted heart devises evil, continuously sows discord, therefore calamity will come upon him suddenly. In a moment, he will be broken beyond healing." (Proverbs 6:12–15)

"That describes Larry Trapp!" she thought. Julie kept reading and then she enthusiastically began circling verses and writing them out on an envelope she found on the coffee table.

"Proverbs is my favorite book in the Bible because it talks about how to treat your fellow man and how to conduct your life," Julie said. "So I decided every day I was going to write a letter and send Larry Trapp a different Proverb. I went through and looked for ones about people who were angry or people who spoke lies."

That night when she saw Michael, Julie told him, "I'm going to write this Klan guy every day."

"That's okay, but I don't want you to identify yourself," Michael said. "He might have a bunch of people. If you do it, you should do it anonymously."

"No, I want to say who it's from," Julie said. "He's the one who does things anonymously; I won't do that."

Julie showed Michael some of the Proverbs she had picked out to send. The first was Proverbs 1:20–22: "Wisdom cries out in the street; in the squares she raises her voice. . . . 'How long, O simple ones, will you love being simple? How long will scoffers delight in their scoffing and fools hate knowledge?' "

Michael liked the selections Julie had chosen, but he wasn't persuaded she should write to Trapp, and he was certain that if she did, she should not sign her name.

Julie talked about her idea with a number of her friends. "Everyone said not to do it," Julie said. "They'd say, 'Are you *nuts?* You don't know the mind-set of this person. He's crazy! He's sick in the head! You don't know how he'll react. This is a *violent* person. This person is dangerous! He has weapons; he might try to *kill* you or get you killed!'

"I'd say, 'But listen to this!' And then I'd read them another Proverb.

"They'd say, 'That's great, Julie, it's a great passage, but *don't do it!'* "

In late July 1991, not many weeks after they'd gotten their own hate mail, Julie and Michael read in the *Omaha World-Herald* about a retired lieutenant colonel named Delmar Gilkensen, who had gotten some menacing mail with the return address of the White Knights of the Ku Klux Klan, Realm of Nebraska, P.O. Box 2297, Lincoln, NE 68502. Gilkensen, whose wife was Filipino, made a business out of traveling to the Philippines to find wives for single American men. The letter, which wasn't quoted in its entirety in the paper, came close to being a direct threat. It said:

Filthy Race-Mixing Scum,

It has come to the attention of this office that you are conducting a mail-order-bride business, consisting of dark-raced scum women from all over the world, and that you are helping to incorporate these low-class individuals into American life.

Shame on you!!! Don't you know that the Bible condemns inter-racial marriages and the off-spring derived from those marriages? The Bible says 'A bastard shall not enter the congregation of the Lord . . .' You, in fact, are blaspheming the name of God!!

. . . It is just a matter of time before we find out your home address. . . . Once we find out your exact address, which will not be too long from now, I am sure that my constituents in the Omaha area will take great relish in paying you and your dark-skinned whore bride a social visit. So I would advise you and your scum-whore bride to keep a constant vigilance. Until then, may your vile penis shrivel up and fall off, because of the nasty, dark, smelly places you insert it. May you both burn in Hell!

WHITE POWER!

Sergeant Bill Larsen, head of intelligence for the Lincoln Police Department, said in the article that even if this and other letters were a crime, it would still be difficult to prove who wrote it. "The post office box is registered to the Klan," Sergeant Larsen said, "but any one of its members may be using that as a return address."

Also in the news was a small article about a young black man in Omaha who had been walking home alone one night when he ran into a group of four white skinheads. The skinheads were dressed in black—three with shaved heads and tattoos and armed with what looked like bats or big sticks. They blocked the man's path. They had a large Doberman with them, and when the young man turned and ran the other direction, they started chasing him and shouting names at him. They were closing in on him when he jumped a fence and found refuge in the home of someone who had heard the commotion and opened her door to him. This incident had made the papers. But it wasn't reported as a hate crime, because Nebraska still didn't report hate crimes as part of the national hate-crime statistics network.

Michael and Julie didn't know Larry Trapp was connected directly to these events. Nor did they know that in addition to his Klan activities he also was overseeing a youth division of almost thirty neo-Nazi skinheads. Having skinheads under his command as well as Klansmen was allowing him to step up the violence and make good on his threats.

Trapp's five leading skinheads lived in Council Bluffs, Iowa—slightly more than an hour's drive from Lincoln. Originally part of WAR's Aryan Youth Movement, these skinheads had come here from Sacramento, California, by way of Fallbrook, California, where Tom Metzger lived, and Tulsa, Oklahoma, where Daniel Mahon and Dennis Mahon were living at the time. When the skinheads arrived in Nebraska, they made a beeline straight to Larry Trapp's residence in Lincoln, and after that initial visit, they'd been in constant contact. They were part of what Metzger vowed would be "a new wave of predatory leaders among Aryan youth" to carry on The Order's goal of white revolution.

Trapp felt Metzger was right about rebuilding "the hunter-killer instincts in our youth" in order to achieve victory. Since the WAR skinheads had arrived, Larry Trapp's "effectiveness" had increased, as had the violence in Omaha, Council Bluffs, and Lincoln—although no direct connections could be made to them or to Trapp. The California contingent of Trapp's youth division called themselves WAR Skins, for White Aryan Resistance, but Trapp had also worked with some Omaha Skinheads who called themselves Hammerskins because they liked to throw hammers.

Larry had wanted the WAR Skins to stay in Council Bluffs instead of Lincoln so he could spread a larger net and tighten security. From Council Bluffs, these skinheads could drive into Omaha or Lincoln, make attacks, and hightail it back over the state line to Iowa in less than an hour. Nobody would know who they were looking for or where to look. Also, they could recruit new members from local high schools in the larger Omaha–Council Bluffs area.

Their membership targets were angry young people like themselves— uneducated white kids who didn't do particularly well in school, who had been abused, "disciplined," or starved for love, and who could find a place to belong with people equally angry at the world around them. Skinhead initiation involved proving your loyalty by beating up an interracial couple, an Asian, Hispanic, Jew, homosexual, African-American or Indian.

According to Trapp, one real advantage of skinheads was their lack of concern about losing a job or a family. They had a lot more nerve than Klansmen, mainly because they were young. Older people sometimes didn't get involved because they were afraid of discrimination on the job. "They'll make racist remarks and hate other races," he said, "but they won't join an organization or play an active role because they're afraid of getting caught.

"I want people who follow orders," he said. "If you say, 'I'll prove my mettle,' but then when I ask you to do something and you say, 'Well, I don't know if I should do that.' When that happens, I says, 'Well, don't even bother renewing your dues. Don't bother about your membership because it has been canceled.' As Grand Dragon, I have the power to cancel any membership I want for any reason."

The skinheads might look like lunatics, Trapp said, but they didn't just talk about "race war"; they went out to incite it. They constantly took action. "All they want to do is kick tail," he said. "That's all they want to do." Every time the skins visited Trapp in Lincoln, for instance, they took extra time to beat up someone, break a few windows or throw a Molotov cocktail or two—actions which seemed to come naturally to them. In reality, a usual tactic of older white supremacists like Larry Trapp was to enlist and train these antagonistic younger men to carry out violent actions against "enemy forces" when they couldn't or wouldn't do it themselves. In some very real sense, the young toughs did the dirty work for the old guys, and if anyone got caught, they were it. Of course, it wasn't packaged that way—the older guys referred to these kids as "the future leaders of the white race."

Like many of the 3,000 to 3,500 neo-Nazi skinheads in America, these young white supremacists in Omaha and Council Bluffs were members of small local groups, but they made a big impact. According to Klanwatch, skinheads operating in some thirty states committed at least twenty-five murders between 1988 and 1993, in addition to beatings and other crimes against blacks, Jews, Latinos, Asians, homosexuals and members of their own groups who dared to defect.

Larry Trapp was not about to take the same kind of heat for his skinheads the Metzgers were taking, so he was careful about the ways in which he directed them. In 1990, Tom Metzger and his son John had been held liable for the murder of Mulugeta Seraw, a twenty-eight-year-old Ethiopian student, in Portland, Oregon. Skinheads trained by the Metzgers to promote racial violence had beaten Seraw to death. This court case was rare; in fact, it was one of the first times a person at the top of a racist organization had been held responsible for an act carried out on his behalf. Usually, people like Metzger—and the wealthier individuals financially backing them—are never held accountable for the acts of violence they inspire. But in this case, Morris Dees, chief trial counsel for the Southern Poverty Law Center; Klanwatch, the investigative arm of the SPLC; and the Anti-Defamation League had been able to prove connections between the Metzgers and the Aryan Youth murderers and had won their landmark civil suit and a judgment of $12 million against the Metzgers.

In Trapp's opinion, the Portland decision had been a glitch. Nevertheless, he was extra careful about exactly what he said to the skinheads, exactly how he said it. "Now listen to the way this is worded," he had told the skinheads one afternoon as he pushed a button on his recorder to play a message he had left during the height of the Gulf War for Bob Wolfson, the regional director of the Anti-Defamation League: "You know the white world is really going to laugh when Hussein kills off all you Jews over there in Israel," his voice rang out from the speakers. "Bob Wolf, why don't you go over there and get your fair share. I'd like to see you blown apart."

"You'll notice I've phrased things so he'll know what I mean," he said, "but he won't be able to prove I meant harm. You have to choose your words carefully and remember the constitutional limitations. Notice I said, 'I'd like to see you blown apart.' If I had said, 'I'll see you blown apart,' I would have been committing a crime because it would have been a direct threat. 'I'd like to see you blown apart' is just suggestive of threats. It's the expression of an opinion and is constitutionally protected. It's nothing I could be prosecuted for. In the same way, you have to think about every action you take ahead of time and then, afterwards, cover your tracks.

"Also, remember—somebody's always listening. This here phone? It's tapped. I know enough about surveillance to know that for a fact. Sometimes I hear voices in the background—when I'm having a conversation in North Carolina or in Columbia, Missouri, or something, I hear voices or whispering in the background. Other days I hear sonar sounds and pings. So, remember, they're listening, waiting for you to slip up."

The way he looked at it, it was his job to keep his skinheads directed, disciplined and away from trouble. They were tough, but they needed someone older who knew his way around the law. As Larry Trapp put it, "The reason I'm leading others, and others are not leading me, is because I do what I want to do and I do my own thing. Now granted, my own thing is usually worse than what anyone else has in mind anyway, but if you do it my way, there are fewer chances of getting caught. I don't just go out and do something, I use my mind. I use my mind, not just my hate. If you hate somebody, plus you have a halfway decent mind, you can get a lot of things accomplished."

Julie Weisser didn't know all of the abhorrent and criminal things Larry Trapp was doing. But she found more Proverbs she wanted to send to him. It was against her ethics, however, not to be open about who she was. She kept talking about her plan to write to Larry Trapp, but everyone kept telling her not to do it—or if she did it, not to sign her name. "Finally, I thought maybe everybody was right and I was wrong," she said, "and since there was no way I was going to be anonymous, I finally decided not to do it at all."

HEIL
WHITE POWER

Chapter 8

A soft answer turns away wrath,
but a harsh word stirs up anger.
The tongue of the wise dispenses knowledge,
but the mouths of fools pour out folly.
—PROVERBS 15:1-2

*I*n Larry Trapp's opinion, Operation Gooks had been one of his most thorough and satisfying missions, and he had to give his skinheads credit for contributing to its success. From start to finish, it was carried out with professionalism.

Operation Gooks had started with the Klansmen's letters to the Vietnamese center in Omaha in November 1990, as well as letters and calls to other Asians in Lincoln telling them to get out before they were burned out. Then in February 1991 the countdown started in earnest when Larry called the Vietnamese center and said, "Get out, you yellow-bellied slant-eyed Gooks, before we throw you out." His skinheads and Klansmen called with similar messages, saying, "You Gooks better move before we get angry."

By March 1991, they'd "gotten angry." Vietnamese social workers and office workers arrived one morning at the Indochinese Refugee Assistance Center of Nebraska, at 4028 South 24th Street in Omaha, to find their offices totally demolished. Skinheads had broken in and decimated the place. The destruction looked indiscriminate and complete—as though a wild, manic tantrum had been thrown on the premises. Records, papers, files, appointment and informational sheets were ripped up and burned; furniture was hacked into pieces; desks were turned over and broken; sinks and electrical wires were ripped from the walls; water pipes were broken. Telephone lines were cut. The place was totally wrecked, then torched. The wreckers had made sure neither this office nor anything in it would be ever be usable again.

Of course, the police found no evidence or proof to identify the persons who committed this damage, but there wasn't much question who was behind it. A Klan poster was tacked to a telephone pole in the alley right behind the center, and the mail, phone calls and warnings had been from the Klan and members of the White Aryan Resistance. Obviously, since the Grand Dragon of the White Knights of the KKK was in a wheelchair, he didn't do it personally; but it was a good guess he had orchestrated the event. Maybe he'd even been present, but law-enforcement officials would never know that for sure.

One of the first people called to the Center after it was trashed was Phong Huynh, a short, brown-eyed social worker from Lincoln who at the time was coordinator of the refugee resettlement program for Church World Service. Phong, whose grandparents had emigrated from China to Vietnam, where he was born, had helped translate the vicious hate mail to "yellow-skinned, slanted-eyed, dog-eating, race-mixing bastards" that had come in November 1990. Now he met with members of the Vietnamese community to discuss what to do about the attack.

Like Phong, many of these Vietnamese personally terrorized by Trapp and his associates had made harrowing escapes by boat from Vietnam in the 1970s. Now a solid five-foot-six thirty-two-year-old who jokes about his trip to "a land of giants," Phong himself was only seventeen when he arrived speaking Vietnamese, Mandarin, Cantonese, Duju and Fukienese—but not English. After working his way through high school and the University of Nebraska, he received a degree in social work. As a resident, he took on extra jobs to sponsor his father, stepmother, brother and sister's journeys to the United States. He saved lunch money, walked rather than take the bus, wore hand-me-down clothes and scrimped in innumerable other ways to buy his family a house. And now that effort, success and security was being imperiled.

Before Operation Gooks, Phong had never experienced any overt racism in Lincoln. After the center in Omaha was torched, however,

Phong like others couldn't sleep at night for fear his house would be burned. "I have to put two locks on my door," he said. "I have to watch. You never know what will they do, and this way—we day-by-day go to work, but we watch out."

Some of the Vietnamese felt the attack on the center was personal; it was war, and they wanted to fight back. Getting advice from leaders in the black community who had had similar experiences, Phong was one of several Vietnamese leaders who spoke on behalf of peaceful solutions. He said the Vietnamese Resettlement Association should contact the police instead of fighting on their own, which could cause problems to escalate. Finally, they did decide to go the legal route. They reported the attack, but within a few weeks, they had moved to new headquarters and they left no forwarding address. Never again, they vowed, would they allow something like this to happen to them.

Shortly after the center had been destroyed, Phong, who lived on C Street in Lincoln, saw a brief clip of Trapp of the KKK on a television news show, and he drew back in amazement. "I saw him before and I didn't know it!" Phong said. Phong had passed Trapp many times because he lived only two blocks away—not far from the First African Methodist Episcopal Church at C and 8th streets.

For Trapp, the whole thing had been a big success; but of course, he couldn't imagine the experience from the other side. He couldn't fathom how it would feel to be a person trying to fashion a productive new life after the atrocities of war. He didn't have a clue about the emotional distance these refugees had traveled in their lives. Nor did he understand anything about the desperation and risk, the hope and faith it had taken to make their individual journeys.

The triumph of Operation Gooks continued to draw accolades from Larry Trapp's colleagues, but Trapp's obsession in the summer of 1991 was focused on getting the best local airtime for "Race and Reason," a video produced by Tom Metzger and the White Aryan Resistance.

One afternoon in his apartment, Larry waited impatiently as he listened to a young White Aryan Resistance skinhead who was sitting across from him, drumming his long pale fingers on the pockets of his jeans as he talked. The kid, Ansel,* who was about twenty, was wear-

*Not his real name.

ing a brown shirt, a wide black belt dotted with silver spikes across his chest, black jeans tight around the ankles and black boots. Tattoos covered almost every section of skin on his arms or hands that showed. He even had tattoos on his shaved head—iron crosses and spiderwebs. He had spiderwebs on the back of his head and down his neck to the top of his shoulders.

Ansel made Larry Trapp nervous. He couldn't get used to the way these kids looked, but he was gratified by the way they put his words into action. On this particular day, he had to listen to Ansel give his report before he could get on with his agenda on "Race and Reason." The two other skinheads in Larry's apartment sat down on nearby folding chairs. "Neil," who looked even younger than Ansel, had on dark sunglasses and a blue satin jacket with pink and black stitching and one gold earring in his right ear. The girl, "Annie," wore jeans and a jeans jacket.

Even before Ansel had finished talking, Larry was breathing loudly, beginning to make comments and putting on his maroon KKK beret. He pulled his black jacket on over a white T-shirt with "White Power" written in bold red letters. He put his loaded Beretta in his pocket. He was organized, intent on business. Every minute was planned—every minute he wanted to accomplish something.

"We better get going," he said. "You got those directions? Got your pistol?" This afternoon, the skinheads were taking Larry out to the Channel 14 station to deliver the first copy of "Race and Reason." Metzger had produced more than one hundred "Race and Reason" racist videos which were being distributed to local sponsors and aired on public-access channels in some eighty-five cities around the country at the time. Trapp had applied to be the local sponsor for Lincoln, and Ansel and the skinheads had applied to sponsor it on Council Bluffs' public-access channel. The way public access worked, local residents could produce and air their own cable television shows at no charge.

Larry's application had been accepted. And on August 3, 1991, an article in the *Omaha World-Herald* announced the Grand Dragon of the Nebraska White Knights of the KKK was sponsoring a national racist "talk show" produced by Tom Metzger, founder of the White Aryan Resistance, which would be produced on public access, Channel 14. In an interview, Trapp said the show "explains the point of view of white people who are fighting for their rights. We're not going to be calling people 'niggers' and all this stuff," he told the *World-Herald*. "We're just going to say our piece. They have all the black shows on. They have a new gay show on Channel 14 now. They have a Communist show on Channel 14. We need representation, too. Equal rights, you know. Equal time."

In the same article, Dave Grooman, community access coordinator for Lincoln Cablevision, said the station couldn't refuse a show simply because of its content. As it stood, public access could only refuse a show if the program was legally obscene or was a vehicle for soliciting money or commercially promoting a product. Behind the scenes, Grooman was extremely upset about the show and tried without success to persuade the Cable Advisory Board to meet and figure out a strategy for refusing it.

Trapp had talked several times with Grooman, and today was the day to deliver the first tape and set the time for regular showings. Ansel opened the door to Larry's apartment and looked both directions. Larry could roll his own wheelchair, but he let Annie push him out the door, down the sidewalk and up into the waiting van. Ansel led the way and Neil followed. Larry had trained them to be security-conscious, and they were good at the job.

"Dave Grooman gave me instructions about where to park," Trapp said, "but we're not going to follow them." Trapp was nervous. Grooman had gotten a lot of calls objecting to the idea of "Race and Reason" being shown, and a lot of people were speaking out about it. Donna Polk said if it had to be shown, at least it should air after televisions were turned off at the local penitentiary so as not to stir up the White Aryan Brotherhood and racial problems there. WOWT-TV, the local NBC affiliate, had looked up the cable applications, which contained Trapp's number, and called him. Then on the late news, WOWT showed his channel application, with his phone number, and noted it was a matter of public record. Trapp called Grooman and said the show was a terrible security risk. After his number was broadcast, he had sat up all night facing the door with his machine gun, expecting people to try to break in.

Now he was so jittery his voice was more tight and harsh than usual. He instructed the skinheads carefully. When they got to the station, he told Neil to park in the side lot, not in the back. "The first thing you do is change the routine, never be predictable," he said. "Never rule out a setup."

Grooman, a clean-cut thirty-two-year-old blond who grew up in Nebraska City, later described the arrival of Trapp and his bodyguards at the station. "I saw the van pull up to the side entrance, and they wheeled him out," Grooman said. "He had sounded paranoid, and I think he was worried about being set up. At least one skinhead with him was from Council Bluffs and one was from Omaha. The guy from Council Bluffs had at least two spiderweb tattoos on the back of his shaved head and down his neck and he had on this spiked leather belt, and Larry had on this paramilitarylike beret.

"I opened the entry door for them, and then I opened the doors to the corridor, and Larry starts wheeling in and the skinheads are looking up and down the hallway. The skinheads wheel Larry right up to my desk, and then the one from Council Bluffs stands beside him, and the guy in the satin jacket continues to look around him, up and down the hall, like he's in the Secret Service or something. At one time, someone went to the bathroom, which was probably thirty feet from my office, and the guy snapped his head around to see what was going on. Talk about paranoid!

"I'm a bit nervous, I'd say, for a few minutes," Grooman said. "Even though my voice wasn't totally cracking, I could tell it was wavering a bit. But after the first few minutes, I thought I should handle them like any other access clients, no matter how whacked-out they were. I didn't want to show I was frightened or intimidated by them.

"They were talking about when they wanted their show on, and I said, 'Right now, 10 P.M. Tuesday evenings is open.' Larry didn't want to play it every week; he wanted to play it every other week, which was a relief. The skinheads from Council Bluffs, who were going to pick up the show after it ran here, wanted it more than once a week, and we talked about that."

Grooman explained that a tag of fifteen to twenty seconds with the name of the local sponsor had to be added at the end of the show—a requirement for "locally produced" shows. They agreed the tag for "Race and Reason" would read: "Sponsored by Larry Trapp, Grand Dragon, White Knights of the Ku Klux Klan."

Grooman says he had never thought much about hate groups before talking to Larry Trapp. "It was on the news, but it's one of those things where you kinda blank it out because you automatically think, well, that stuff doesn't happen here," says Grooman. But this experience changed all that.

"I had a feeling of what Larry Trapp and his group were capable of," Grooman said later. "After meeting them, I started finding out a lot of things. I learned that there had been cross burnings in Pioneer Park up to a couple of years ago—there were a lot of people who had been attacked. I came to realize you need to take these people seriously. It made me pretty nervous."

When the skinheads took Larry back to his apartment, he was restless and upset, even though the mission had gone well. He reminded himself he'd gotten a good time slot: 10 P.M. was perfect. He wondered whether Grooman had called the police. He worried about his legs—what would happen if he had to have another amputation? He felt jittery and his body jerked uncontrollably. He hated getting the shakes. He told himself he was just agitated because he was tired, but he must have been subliminally aware of his deteriorating condition and the specter of uncontrolled diabetes looming over him.

Larry rubbed his hands to get them warm. He could go to bed, but it was too early to go to sleep. He called Metzger in California. The line was busy. He thought about calling his sister Candy in Houston and talking to his niece and nephew, but when he dialed their number, no one was home. He cursed, dialed Metzger again and kept dialing until he got him and told him when the first show would air. Then he called Dennis Mahon in Oklahoma. Then the Imperial Representative of the Missouri office, and Thom Robb, Grand Wizard of the Knights of the KKK in Arkansas. He ended each conversation with "White Power, Brother, White Power!"

Trapp's eyes bothered him—sheets of red seemed to wave in the wind between himself and whatever he looked at. He didn't dare think about the implications of his physical condition, the implications of his vision loss. He put his "Cat Woman" video on again, shut his eyes and listened to the sounds of group sex, but he couldn't keep an erection and he couldn't ejaculate. Finally, irritated with himself for wasting time, he turned off the television.

Feeling across his desk, Trapp turned on his brightest lights, put on his magnifying glasses and punched the recording buttons to record a new Vigilante message. He tried several approaches before he decided how to announce the first airing of "Race and Reason." The way he chose allowed him to make another venomous attack on Donna Polk:

> "As for Donna Puke—or is that Donna Polk?—I guess it is Donna Polk of 349 Clifton Park Way here in Lincoln who is the head nigger in the Coalition of Black Women—for your benefit, my dear, our show, "Race and Reason," will be aired on Tuesday, August 20 at 10 P.M. on Channel 14, Public Access.
>
> "So, see, your whining and crying was to no avail. The white population of Nebraska will be victorious. After all, the only one who likes a nigger is another nigger.
>
> "Even though she says we don't have the right to do this show, she is one of those typical niggers who thinks her shit doesn't stink. Well, I believe it does. In fact, her whole body smells like shit."

Larry put Donna Polk's address on his answering machine for a reason. He hadn't actually spoken the words yet, but by giving her address, he was encouraging Klansmen or others to "pay her a visit."

This vicious personal attack was like holding a gun to her head, but the way he was doing it would leave no fingerprints. Like most white separatist leaders, he wanted to set violence in motion without getting his own hands dirty. As he would later say, "Boy, I wanted to blow apart and hang a bunch of them niggers or Jews, but since I couldn't do it so easily myself, I needed somebody else to do it for me."

HITLER'S FIRST LAWS

Chapter 9

Do not fret because of evildoers. Do not envy the wicked; for the evil have no future; the lamp of the wicked will go out.
—PROVERBS 24:19-20

*T*he Weissers avidly followed the public controversy about "Race and Reason." Before ten o'clock the night of its first showing in August 1991, several friends came over to their home to watch the program and discuss it. Michael and Julie also persuaded Rebecca, Dina and Dave to sit with them when they turned to Channel 14 and boosted the volume.

They didn't know what to expect. It was something of a surprise when the show opened with Tom Metzger describing the Aryan Fest '89 in Oklahoma and the merging of skinheads, Nazis, Klansmen, members of White Aryan Resistance and other individuals, many of whom seemed to ride Harley-Davidson motorcycles. Early in the show, the camera focused on one of the leaders—a tall, balding man wearing jeans, boots and a sleeveless leather vest that exposed a tattooed chest, tattooed arms and a rather vast beer belly. The man started his Harley and then stood beside it. Metzger gave a voice-over commentary as the camera slowly and tenderly panned the various parts of the Harley's gleaming motor.

Eventually, the camera turned to three slim young blond women in tight-fitting jeans getting out of a boat and walking away from the camera. "Stereotypes of racialist women are that they're overweight and ugly, but that's not true," Metzger says as the camera follows the rear ends of the women. "Most women in the racialist movement, like these women, are attractive, and while they may be tough, they believe in acting like women."

A French camera crew filmed themselves filming the Aryan fest, and documented the white supremacists strutting around at rallies in camouflage clothes, holding target practices with semiautomatic and fully automatic weapons and lighting crosses. It showed one rather bedraggled group in a field in Oklahoma organizing themselves into a semicircle around a large burning swastika, their arms raised in a Hitler-like salute as they shouted "White Power!"

"That was totally sickening," Dina said when the show was over. "How stupid!" Later on, Rebecca sat down and wrote a letter to the *Lincoln Star.* "I'm 15 years old and I'm Jewish," her letter began. "All around me I see people tormenting other people because of their religion, their color, or their handicaps. The organization that comes to mind when hate is involved is the Ku Klux Klan.

"One night I was watching television when my mother brought home some friends to watch a show produced by Larry Trapp. It was supposed to show how great the KKK was, but in actuality all it did was show people saluting Hitler, going fishing, getting tattoos, burning crosses and riding their motorcycles. I feel sorry for their children; they will never know the satisfaction of having a loving relationship with someone different from them. All the doors in life are closed to them.

"Our family has had its run-ins with the KKK. . . . Even in Lincoln we get harassed. I thought maybe we could forget about all the hate against Jews, but now I know that we should never forget it. If we forget, hate groups will keep doing things to offend us until we respond. We should educate the people about how wrong it is to hate. I just hope the Ku Klux Klan knows that it is a dying belief, because my generation knows it's wrong."

Michael also thought "Race and Reason" was revolting, and he was disgusted that this guy Larry Trapp was pulling everybody's chain and making them afraid. He knew that one-on-one, without a gun or a bomb, Trapp couldn't be all that dangerous because, after all, he was in a wheelchair and was going blind. But, as a police intelligence officer from the Lincoln Police Department had said, "It's hard to evaluate how dangerous he is. Obviously, his being legally blind and paraplegic would make him not seem too great a threat. However, he has a lot of weapons, and we think if he felt threatened, he wouldn't hesitate to use them." Also, the guy had followers.

Nevertheless, Michael wasn't good at sitting on his anger and not doing anything about it. While he'd never been masterful with his fists, he still had lived enough of his younger life in combative situations to have developed a readiness and willingness to challenge and confront.

"I have to call this guy," he said to Julie. "I'm gonna call him."

"Don't tell him who you are," Julie said, giving Michael the same advice he'd given her.

"Okay, I won't. But I do have to call."

Trapp's number was unlisted, but Michael finally got it from a friend who looked it up on the cable application—which was public. The day his friend called with the number, Michael was in his narrow, book-lined office at the South Street temple, where he writes his sermons, keeps up with synagogue business and writes the temple's monthly bulletin. He was working on a sermon about how prayer leads to understanding and the Jewish tradition called hesed v'rachmanut—loving kindness and womblike compassion. "When you understand deeply, you cannot help but love," he wrote. "And to develop understanding that leads to love, you must look at the situations of others with hesed v'rachmanut—loving kindness and compassion. When you fully understand, you fully love."

Michael stopped writing, picked up the phone and dialed Larry Trapp's number. What he heard was Larry's message hotline, "Vigilante Voices of Nebraska—where the truth hurts!"

Larry's vicious tirade seemed interminable. Michael couldn't believe how long the message lasted. He listened to all of it, and then he called back and timed it. It lasted eleven minutes. Larry was using his hotline that week to let people know, among other things, his opinions on hate-crime legislation. The Coalition Against Racism and Prejudice in Lincoln had initiated a resolution directing the legislature's Judiciary Committee to conduct an interim study on hate crimes, hate groups and violence, and the legislature had approved the resolution. Hate-crime legislation would require local and state law-enforcement agencies to keep separate reports on crimes motivated by religious, racial or sexual bias. ("Why isn't it a hate crime when blacks do things to whites?" Trapp said. "It's only considered a hate crime when whites do it to blacks.") He had also included a diatribe against women:

"You can tell this town is full of whores; we have our so-called college, our so-called University of Nebraska. Just recently, Playboy magazine has gone there because they know that Nebraska puts out the biggest whores in their schools. . . . Women in this town will take off their clothes for anyone—for any reason. So stop and think, people of Lincoln. If you didn't create such a bunch of whores, you wouldn't have anything to worry about with this juvenile sex offenders' facility, now would you? Hee-hee-hee. Well, until next time, all you good White People, remember this one thing: White Revolution is the only solution!"

Michael couldn't get over the venom in Trapp's voice and the awful, despicable quality of his message. At the end of eleven minutes, Michael pressed down the call button and redialed the number. Then he set down the receiver, and at the end of another eleven minutes, he hung up the phone for a second and then redialed. "At least nobody else can get through to listen to this crap," he said angrily.

That started a trend.

"I would call up and time his message," Michael said later. "I'd listen and I'd time it, and then if it was ten minutes long, every ten minutes I'd dial his number, just to keep it busy so nobody else would hear it, just to keep the line tied up.

"I did that for a week or so. And then one day a friend told me that tying up someone's line is illegal—you can be charged with harassment for that. So the next time I called, I waited for the beep because there was a place where you could leave your name and address if you were interested in information on how to become a member.

"And so this one day I waited for the beep, and I said, 'Larry, you better think about all this hatred you're spreading, because one day you're going to have to answer to God for all this hatred, and it's not going to be easy.' "

After that, whenever he thought of it, Michael picked up the phone, called Larry's number, waited for the beep and left a little message. He didn't usually plan what he was going to say; thoughts just came to him as he sat waiting for the beep. Once he said: "Why do you hate me? You don't even know me, so how can you hate me?"

Late one Tuesday night, not long after the first airing of "Race and Reason," Julie yelled for Michael to come quickly to look at the television. "This is unbelievable!" she said. "Scott Michaels is interviewing

Larry Trapp. They just flashed, a picture of him in his Klan robes! I can't believe what I'm seeing!"

The interview opened with a scene from "Race and Reason" in which a group of about fifteen men and women stood with their right arms raised in salute around a burning swastika and yelled, "Heil! White Power!" Scott Michaels, a local television reporter for Channel 11, introduced Trapp by saying the Grand Dragon of the White Knights of the Ku Klux Klan in Nebraska said he was sponsoring this racist show "to dispel myths about the white supremacy movement." In addition, Michaels reported, the show also was apparently working as "a recruiting tool." Klan headquarters in Lincoln reported they had received nineteen calls requesting membership after the first show of "Race and Reason."

The camera then focused on a person masked in a white Klan robe trimmed in red, with a tall white cotton dunce-shaped hat and white hood covering his face. Only his large, light-blue eyes were revealed through two round holes in the front of the white cloth hood. "Grand Dragon of the Nebraska KKK" flashed at the bottom of the screen. The Klansman sat in front of a huge red and black Nazi flag and a red, white and blue Confederate flag—the flag flown at official Ku Klux Klan rallies in memory of what Klansmen think of as the good old days. The cloaked and hooded man sitting against the backdrop of the anti-Semitic and racist flags made a startling picture. Draped in his white costume, he somehow looked more like a "grand dragon" than a human being.

"We sponsored this show just to let the general public know more about the white movement, to let them know that we're not the killers society seems to say we are," Trapp said from behind his white mask. "It's just to let them know we're just everyday people like the rest of them. We just have a goal in mind." As Trapp spoke, the camera shifted from his white-hooded face to his tattooed hands. It came in close on one tattoo—an iron cross—and then rested on the swastika emblazoned on his silver ring.

"The main reason we have 'Race and Reason' on is to let people know we're just like other people," Trapp said, his eyes blinking through the eye slots of his mask. The camera panned to the Nazi flag behind him, to his submachine gun casually hanging on the door, and to his framed pictures of Adolf Hitler and Rudolf Hess hanging on the wall. "We enjoy the everyday activities that other people do."

As Larry continued to speak, the camera cut away to a section of

"Race and Reason" where three bare-chested white separatists stood posed with their legs spread and automatic weapons raised toward a cutout of a human target a hundred yards in the distance. Then they crouched, began firing and advancing rapidly in jerky, wide-legged motions toward the cutout in front of them as they discharged round after round of ammunition. The rat-a-tat sound of the guns was still echoing as Larry Trapp continued. "Our life is no different from anybody else's except we're striving to keep our race from becoming a museum piece," he said.

When the interview with Trapp was over, Scott Michaels interviewed the Reverend Dr. Norman Leach on camera. Leach said he thought "Race and Reason" was pitiful. "It's pathetic in its content," he said, a gold cross gleaming over his black clerical shirt and white collar. "It's pathetic in its hateful intent, and it's a sad day that it was shown in Lincoln, Nebraska."

Scott Michaels concluded his report by reminding listeners that one hundred more episodes of "Race and Reason" had been produced and were expected to be played on Tuesday nights at 10 P.M. on Channel 14 in Lincoln. The show could air indefinitely.

After the show, Michael Weisser called Larry Trapp's number once again. "Larry, I just saw an interview with you in your Klan getup in front of the Nazi flag," Michael said. "Larry, do you know that the very first laws that Hitler's Nazis passed were against people like yourself who had no legs or who had physical deformities, physical handicaps? Do you realize you would have been among the first to die under Hitler? Why do you love the Nazis so much?"

When he listened to that message, Larry Trapp felt a momentary shock. He knew it was true, but he refused to think about it. Besides, the interview had made him jittery. Late that night, he turned on his scanner to monitor the Lincoln Police Department channel, but then he thought he heard a noise outside. He turned off the radio and sat still, listening. There was another crunch on the cement sidewalk outside. He wheeled quickly but quietly to his door, picked up his MAC-10 off the doorknob, primed it and waited. Last week somebody had thrown a brick through his window. He hoped they'd come back.

He wished like hell they'd turn that doorknob, jimmy the lock, open the door. If they did, he'd blow them into bloody bits. "Open it, you fucking faggot," he whispered. "Go ahead. I got a little surprise waitin' for ya."

Trapp's shoulders hunched in tension as he sat waiting. He didn't realize it yet, but he would later say he had been hoping for an excuse—any excuse—to kill somebody. In truth, he wanted to die himself, but he didn't believe in suicide. He sat in the middle of a terror larger than he could identify and felt almost constantly afraid—afraid for his life, afraid of his death, afraid of being alone, afraid of surviving. He had let himself become sucked into the center of a fear so large, so overwhelming and so blinding that he needed to destroy before he was destroyed, kill before he was killed.

Thinking about killing someone else was also a way for him to avoid thinking about the life-threatening disease he had, something facing him every time his blood sugar fluctuated or he had an insulin reaction. When his wife Cheryl left him after two years of marriage, Larry had lain in the street in front of the house where she was staying with her girlfriend and said he was going to lie there until a car ran over him. That was as close as he'd ever come to killing himself.

Now he sat alone in the dark, swamped by many of the same hollow feelings and unexamined yearnings he'd had in the days after Cheryl left him. Larry's mind didn't calm him—he didn't know how to look within. Instead, the echo of painful memories haunted him. Sometimes, when Larry was alone like this, his cat Max crept into his mind.

The thing with Max had happened when he'd gone back to his apartment on A Street after getting his right leg amputated at the Madonna Hospital in 1986. The doctors had cut the leg off just above the knee and he couldn't get around easily. He had a prosthesis—his dad was helping pay for that—but he couldn't use it yet, so he was stuck in a wheelchair. He was all alone and he was scared.

The problem about the cat was, Max kept defecating and urinating in the apartment, and Larry couldn't get him to stop. The smell was driving Larry crazy. Then one night Max was hungry, and he kept walking around, crying for food. Larry couldn't find any cat food. He couldn't even find a can opener.

"Shut up!" he yelled at Max. "Shut the fuck up!"

Max kept crying, and finally Larry couldn't stand it anymore. He grabbed his twenty-two-caliber pistol, screwed on the silencer, aimed at the sound and shot Maxwell in the head. Max was hit but he wouldn't die. He crawled up under a counter in the kitchen and whined and cried. Larry fired toward the sound of the plaintive mewing, but it just went on and on. Larry started calling Max to come out, but he couldn't get the cat to budge from under the counter, and he couldn't reach him. Max was giving out weak little cries and Larry couldn't even see where Max was hiding.

Finally he called Animal Control and told them a cat had wandered into his apartment and seemed to be injured—could they come and get him. The Animal Control people came and as they were carrying out Max, they asked how the cat had gotten hurt. "How would I know?" Larry said. "The cat had just wandered in crying when the door was open."

That night Larry Trapp slept in his wheelchair, his gun cradled in his arms, waiting for an intruder. But no one turned Larry's doorknob that night. The killing, if there was to be any killing, would have to wait.

YOU MAY BE NEXT

Chapter 10

*O*ne night Michael and Julie were sitting at their kitchen table eating a late-night mushroom pizza and glazed donuts as they caught up on the day's events.

It was early September 1991, and that day in his office at the South Street temple, Michael had called Larry Trapp and left another message: "How can you feel any real sense of freedom when you're doing all these hateful things? Maybe you should let all that hate go."

Now Michael took a bite of the mushroom pizza and said, "What will I do if the guy ever picks up the phone?"

Julie had told Michael the times she'd driven by Larry's apartment, she'd been struck by how lonely this person must be, how isolated in all his hatred. Even if he was surrounded by other haters who were his friends, she thought, it had to be a horrible existence. It was obvious a man so filled with malice was missing the ingredient of love in his life. Now she thought about him again, and laughed at an idea which flashed quickly into her mind.

"If he ever answers the phone, tell him you want to do something nice for him," she said. "It'll totally freak him out. And he won't know what to do. Tell him you'll take him to the grocery store or something like that. Anything to help him. It will catch him totally off guard because he's so hateful he would never expect anybody to do anything nice for him."

Michael loved Julie's idea and started looking forward to a chance to say something directly to Larry Trapp, but the opportunity didn't immediately present itself because Trapp never picked up his phone when Michael called.

Michael and Julie Weisser were not aware of just how much hate Larry Trapp was spreading, but they did watch the local news—and even though they didn't know it, they often were observing the results of Trapp's handiwork. They watched television news reports on a series of arsons in the Lincoln area during the late summer and fall of 1991. This string of nighttime arson fires endured by residents of Lincoln and the surrounding Lancaster County was part of an emerging pattern of hate-based violence in the larger community. Many, if not all, of the fires were started by Molotov cocktails—Larry Trapp's incendiary bomb of choice. Several homes damaged by these Molotov cocktails belonged to African-American families.

One of the people whose home was firebombed said he had no doubt about what prompted the arson. "I think it was motivated by hate," said Rick Carter, a large man with a kind, mellow voice. "I don't believe it was directed at me personally, but at the color of my skin. They don't know me from any other black person, but they see me as a black person, and I'd say that, based on their agenda, that's what they were after."

Police issued arrest warrants for four men suspected of seven arsons—five in Lincoln and two elsewhere in Lancaster County. They were also investigating more than thirty-five similar fires that had been started during that same period of time in and around Lincoln and trying to determine whether the same four men were involved. When officers searched the home of two of the suspects—both of whom had shaved heads and looked like skinheads—they found large amounts of Ku Klux Klan literature, grave markers, printed neo-Nazi materials, swastikas and a Nazi flag. They also found drug paraphernalia and a 9-mm Ingram MAC-11 submachine gun. The bolt for the semiautomatic weapon was missing when it was seized, possibly as part of alterations that would allow automatic fire.

While logic pointed toward Larry Trapp, his Klan organization and his skinhead Aryan Youth group, law-enforcement officials couldn't prove the suspects were members of an organized white supremacy group or followers of Larry Trapp. Nevertheless, they said they were not ruling out that connection or a connection between "Race and Reason" and the slew of fires that began about the same time as the show began to air. When the sheriff's department questioned Trapp, he denied knowing the suspects and said: "Why is it that every time a crime is committed that has more or less a racist motive, why is it always the Ku Klux Klan? Everything is blamed on the Klan! We're a constitutionally protected group. Anybody can go out and commit these acts and then say the Klan did it, and that just makes us look bad."

While no direct evidence indicated all of the arsons were motivated by racism, Lancaster County Sheriff Tom Casady said he and Lincoln Police Chief Allen Curtis were "very, very concerned about the potential connection to hate groups that are associated with activities like arson." Sheriff Casady also raised the fact he had recently seen a young man driving a car emblazoned with spray-painted swastikas. "It worries me as a parent and as a resident of this community to think that we've got these young people who don't feel the same way I do about something like a swastika—which I view as the ultimate obscene gesture," Casady said. Parents should act quickly and with outrage, he said, if their children show signs of identification with hate groups.

Police Chief Allen Curtis gave white supremacists a warning. "There's no room in our city and county for that kind of hate activity," he said. "We want the community to know and understand that, and we want the people who might engage in that type of activity to know and understand that."

At that time, of course, neither Chief Curtis nor Sheriff Casady could have known how many hours Larry Trapp had spent poring over books that gave specific recipes for effective homemade explosives nor how he had mastered the art of making Molotov cocktails and other explosives out of ordinary household supplies. One of the reasons Trapp liked Molotov cocktails best was they were so simple. All he had to do to make one was to put gasoline and soap into a bottle and follow an easy recipe. "The soap makes it adhere so it clings wherever its thrown," he told his colleagues. "The only problem is that they don't always work the way you want them to. They're not as reliable as using a detonating device to detonate explosives from a distance."

Trapp was right about that, but some people had to learn it the hard way. For instance, one of his Aryan Youth had been stupid about the way he was handling his Molotov cocktail: he lit it first, and then he stood there holding the flaming Molotov cocktail and looking for the window through which to throw it. Larry liked to do things in an orderly, efficient manner: he insisted on locating the window first, scoping out the territory. But the kid had done it wrong—and when the thing got hot and he dropped it by accident, he ended up starting a garage fire instead of a house fire.

Even if the police had known about Larry Trapp's involvement with these arsons, they wouldn't find gasoline on his hands. Legally, he played it safe. And, without a confession, it would have been nearly impossible to prove he and his followers had made the firebombs, or that his followers had thrown them and started the fires.

Nevertheless, Trapp's need for risky encounters and violent results was escalating. When he heard Jesse Jackson might come to Omaha to speak, he started planning how to assassinate him. He wanted to do it himself, and he thought being in a wheelchair might allow him access he otherwise wouldn't have. "I was planning to use my pistol," he said later. "I really wanted to kill him myself." Trapp realized he might get killed in the process, but he knew if he died killing Jesse Jackson, he would die a hero to other racists.

One day Michael called Larry Trapp's hotline and listened to one of Larry's messages, which ended with a current news item about a black woman somewhere who had used her young daughter as a front for drug sales. On his message, Larry related an exaggerated version of the woman's behavior and concluded: "Don't let them try to fool you—they put on a good front, but this is what all blacks are like."

When Michael heard Larry conclude his twisted report with, "This is what all blacks are like," the machine beeped for a message, and Michael said, "Larry, Jeffrey Dahmer is white."

Larry's voice broke in just then: "And it's too bad you're not, good buddy!" Then he slammed down the receiver. Michael hadn't even had a chance to make the obvious analogy: if that's what all blacks are like because of that one woman, does this mean all whites are like Jeffrey Dahmer—who lured young men to his apartment and then ritualistically murdered, mutilated and ate them?

"His voice was so hateful," Michael said. "I'll never forget that—it was just real hateful."

Michael and Julie followed Trapp's activities in the newspaper when they read he had been arrested and taken to court for harassing his old neighbor, freelance journalist and author William L. Rush. Trapp had begun persecuting Rush because he was physically disabled. Rush can't walk, talk or use his own voice to form words because cerebral palsy at birth damaged the part of his brain that controls muscular power and coordination. His intelligence, vision and hearing function perfectly, but not the command center regulating his tongue, arms and legs. Rush gets around town in a heavy motorized wheelchair that he controls with pressure from the back of his head.

Trapp had begun harassing the thirty-five-year-old Rush in the spring of 1990, not long after Trapp moved into apartment 3 of 817 C Street—right next door to Rush in number 1. Initially, Rush, who has a quick, ironic humor, welcomed Trapp as a new neighbor. Rush did this with the help of a stylus attached to a headband, by pressing letters and words on a computerized keyboard attached to a lap tray. By pushing certain keys linked to an electronic device inside the lap tray, Rush activates a computerized voice synthesizer, called a TouchTalker, which electronically enunciates what he wants to say. When Rush prefers, he can press different keys to make the computer print out his words instead of synthesizing and speaking them. When he greeted Trapp, however, he used his voice synthesizer.

Trapp responded to Bill Rush's initial greeting by telling Bill to let him know if anyone bothered him. He said that before his diabetes got so bad, he'd been a police officer. "I [also] used to be a mercenary in Africa," Trapp said, "so I have a lot of guns. I also have a ham radio—you know, I'm a licensed amateur radio operator—so I could call for help."

"I nodded," Bill wrote later. "Something was wrong, but I couldn't put my finger (or headstick) on it. There was something about his demeanor. I wondered why he thought that I needed his help."

The two immediately ran into difficulties.

For one thing, the wall between their apartments wasn't thick, and Rush enjoyed listening to tapes of Dr. Martin Luther King's speeches. Rush's great-grandparents on his mother's side came to the United States from Denmark and his great-great-grandparents on his father's side came from Germany, but he, like Dr. King, had daily battles against prejudice to fight. Dr. King's resonant voice urging continued courage to fight for equal rights and dream "impossible dreams" inspired him.

Bill Rush himself had turned many "impossibilities" into challenges. Despite being able to move only his neck and head at will, he had graduated from the University of Nebraska's School of Journalism and had written many articles, as well as his first book, by the time Larry Trapp moved in next door. Rush had been living independently in his C Street apartment for eight years with the help of four assistants who came in daily to aid him with various tasks. Nobody in Nebraska with his level of disability had done it before, but Rush insisted on having as normal a life as possible and had worked through all the obstacles to make it happen.

Not long after Trapp moved in next door, however, Rush started hearing voices coming out of his computer. He and an aide soon discovered the interference came from Larry Trapp's voice broadcasting over his Citizens Band radio. As a professional journalist, Bill wrote every day. He'd had articles published in local, state and national magazines, including Exceptional Parent, Popular Computing, Magazine of the Midlands, and Rehabilitation World, and he also had a job as editor of a monthly magazine, which he worked on at home. Trapp's voice on his computer made it nearly impossible to concentrate, let alone work or talk.

When Bill Rush told Trapp the ham radio was causing him serious problems, he said, "What can be done about it? I feel I'm losing my fifty-second card every time I hear your voice."

"Your fifty-second card? I don't understand," Larry said, looking bewildered.

"A full deck is fifty-two cards," Bill responded. "If you don't have fifty-two cards, you're not playing with a full deck, right?"

"Oh yeah, I get ya," Larry said. "Cute."

Trapp agreed not to do any broadcasting until after ten-thirty at night, but he didn't keep his word. The next day he broadcast on his CB in the afternoon and early evening. Bill tried to solve the problem by getting a filter for his phone, but the phone company needed Trapp's cooperation to test the filter, and Trapp wouldn't let them in. One computer-whiz friend of Bill's thought the trouble might be any one of several wires in Bill's electronic system, but again, without Trapp's participation, the problem couldn't be tracked down.

Rush was enormously frustrated not only by the interference, but also by the offensive content of the interruptions. One night, for instance, Trapp's voice broke into Rush's conversation with his girlfriend in Canada. Trapp was cursing and saying, "Tie me down and butt-fuck me," a phrase he repeated several times. Bill's girlfriend Chris couldn't believe her ears. She said: "This is too gross, Bill. I have a hard enough time understanding you without having to listen to this filth," and then she hung up.

Rush was livid. "I didn't mind his having a hobby, but I minded his vulgar interference and his using obscene language that revolted my girlfriend," he said. Without having any awareness of how many loaded weapons Trapp had on hand—or that, even if blind, Trapp might hit him with his machine gun, Bill Rush opened his door with his automatic opener and rammed his wheelchair into Larry's door. When Larry opened up, Bill yelled incoherently at him about his "damn radio."

The next day Bill felt sorry about his behavior and decided to see if he could patch things up. He opened his door and saw Larry and two other men outside trying to set up a radio antenna. Bill didn't know the men were Klansmen, nor did he calculate any personal danger when he wheeled out.

"Here he comes," said one of the men with Trapp.

"Look at him," Trapp said. "Look at how his mouth hangs open. You can't tell me that he's not retarded. Why don't he reply when you talk to him if he's not retarded? You can't tell me that there's nothing wrong with him upstairs."

"I mentally counted to ten," Bill said later. "I tried to respond, but my portable voice synthesizer had a dead battery."

"Why don't you talk to us instead of throwing a fucking fit?" Trapp said. "Look at him. He doesn't answer you. He must be a retard because he doesn't answer you."

"I started counting to a hundred," Rush later wrote. "I tried to remember, what happens around me is largely outside my control, but the way I choose to react to it is inside my control."

"Maybe he would like some information on the Klan," one of the other men said.

"That's right," said Trapp. "I'm with the Klan. I'm the head of it. I might put some literature on your door. Maybe it will get you to change your mind about your Martin Lucifer Coon."

After that, Larry Trapp called Bill Rush names every time he saw him, left hate literature in his mailbox and pointed him out to fellow Klansmen as "the fucking retard." One day when Bill's foot involuntarily kicked the wall between their apartments, Trapp's voice broke into Bill's computer and said, "Is that Bill Rush, that fucking retard, banging his head against the wall? If he sends anybody over to talk about my radio, I'll blow his fucking head off."

Another time Trapp called out: "I wonder how he graduated from college? They probably gave him his diploma because they felt sorry for him." Bill Rush went to the library and looked up newspaper articles on Trapp, and he read the racist pamphlets Trapp slid under his door. To Bill Rush, Trapp's views seemed grotesque and illogical. "He deplored 'race mixing' . . . and insisted that Jews are taking over the country," Rush observed. "It was an interesting theory, considering that Jews make up only three percent of the country's population.

"He and I had nothing in common," Bill wrote. "I admired Martin Luther King, Jr. He admired Adolf Hitler. . . . I also admired Dr. King's philosophy, which said a community should be based on agape, or Christian love . . . the only force that can bring a peaceful community into being because it fosters cooperation instead of competition."

Yet, after weeks of listening to Larry Trapp's escalating and direct diatribes against him, along with racist and sexist vulgarities over the CB, Bill Rush wanted to fight back. One afternoon he gave in to his impulse and set up his sound system with a tape of Dr. Martin Luther King's famous "I have a dream" speech from the 1963 March on Washington. Then he set the tape to play over and over again, turned the volume full blast and left his apartment to play chess for three hours. Taking that action made him feel better temporarily.

Eventually, by painstakingly unplugging one part of Bill's electronic system at a time, Bill's computer friends found his voice synthesizer was picking up the CB broadcasts. Nevertheless, even with that problem solved, living next door to the Grand Dragon of the KKK in Nebraska became intolerable. Trapp's tirades seemed unending, and the possibility of physical violence was quite real. (Trapp told Rush more than once, "I'd like to see someone blow your fucking head off.") Rush tried to get a protection order against Trapp, but since they didn't live together or have a family relationship, Nebraska law didn't provide for such an order.

Finally, after nine years in the same apartment and only three months of Trapp living next door, Bill Rush felt forced to move. He'd considered moving before, but he had always decided it would be too much of a hassle; now it was too much of a hassle not to move. In July 1990, he signed a lease and moved into a new apartment a good distance from C Street. His girlfriend, Chris, moved to Lincoln from Canada in December of 1990, and they got on with their life.

Bill didn't leave any forwarding address for the Grand Dragon of the Ku Klux Klan, but his saga with Trapp wasn't over. Trapp found him, and once again began leaving insulting and threatening messages on his telephone-answering machine.

Finally, however, Trapp threatened Bill Rush once too often.

That time came when he called in the middle of a hot summer night in 1991. Bill was out of his wheelchair and asleep in his bed without his headstick or lap tray—which meant he was unable to move or communicate. The phone woke him up and he lay in the dark listening to it ring. After his answering machine picked up and played his message, an all-too-familiar voice blasted out into the stillness of Bill's quiet apartment: "There are people beating up niggers outside your apartment building," Trapp said. "And you're next, I hope, you drooling bastard."

Maybe it was the time, the darkness or his physical helplessness. But as he lay alone in the dark, Bill felt terror he'd never before experienced.

"I didn't get any sleep for the rest of that night," Bill said later. He had to wait until morning, when a friend arrived, to tell someone what had happened. Bill's girlfriend, Chris, urged him to press charges. The message was recorded on Bill's answering machine, so he had proof of the harassment. He went to the County-City Building and spoke with the police and with the city attorney. He had material evidence, he was the complaining witness and he wanted to press charges against Trapp. As the victim, he requested that no deals be made with Trapp.

The city attorney filed the charges and Trapp was sent a notice to appear in court. On the day scheduled for Trapp's arraignment, the County-City Building received a bomb threat and had to be evacuated. No one seemed to note the coincidence, but Larry Trapp himself didn't show up. When he failed to show, a warrant was issued for his arrest.

As it turned out, this was just what the Lincoln Police Department needed. More than one person wanted to stop Trapp—or at least slow him down. A few days earlier, Trapp had put out the death threat on

Donna Polk on his White Knights hotline, suggesting that Klan members "pay her a visit and let her know what you think."

Donna Polk had learned about Trapp's threat when she got home one August night around 10:45 P.M. and heard her phone ringing as she walked in the door. She answered and it was a young man who worked for Goodyear. He said, "Donna, I need to tell you something. A white man came up to me at work today and he asked me if I know Donna Polk and I said yes, and he said, 'Call this telephone number.' So I called the number and it took me a long time to get in, but I called it and it's awful—and I'm calling to warn you."

"What are you talking about?"

"Well, it's this man and he's talking and he's calling you a bitch and giving your telephone number and address out and telling people to pay you a visit."

Donna was hysterical. "I said, 'What's the number?' And he gave it to me, and he said, 'You need to protect yourself.' He said, 'If there is anything I can do, let me know.'

"So immediately I called each of my boys and I told them," Donna recalls. "I said, 'Here's the number, would you call it?' I was too afraid to even call the number. So they said, 'Mom, just hold on, we'll call you back.' My baby boy is a lawyer in Omaha—so they were on the phone with each other from New York to Maryland to Omaha planning this strategy about what they should do. And I went out to the mailbox and there's another letter in my mailbox that very night from the Ku Klux Klan. So then my son from Maryland called me back and he said, 'Mom, I can't get in on that line so, you know, just hold tight.'

"So I called one of my colleagues who works here and I said, 'Call this number.' It took him a while, but he called me back and he said, 'God, I don't know what that number is, but I can't even get in on it.' By then it was one o'clock in the morning.

"My boy from Maryland called me back and he said, 'Mom, I want you to go to the FBI in the morning and then go to the police department.' And then one of my boys from New York called me and he said, 'Mom, I am on my way—I'll be there. I'll get a plane out today.' I said, 'Honey, wait until the Super Saver fares go into effect.'

"I told my youngest son in Omaha, I said, 'I'm going to kill him. I cannot accept this.' I wanted to kill him. My feeling was, he had crossed the line. When he made that tape and gave people my home phone number and address, he had crossed the invisible line. I just wanted to cover my tracks."

Donna got up that next morning and went to the FBI and took the latest letter. "I had been there probably two years previously, when I told them I had gotten these letters and they said, 'OK, fine, thank you' and I left. Well, this time I told them—I said, 'Well, you know I got this letter at home, and I just want you to know that I have a registered gun and somebody is going to get hurt.' And they said, 'Have a seat, we will have an agent with you in a minute.' By this time, I was so close to tears, I thought, 'I am not a bad person—why is this happening? Why is this man doing this to me?'

"So I went in and I showed them the letter and I told them about the phone number, and this FBI agent, he called it and listened to the message. And he said, 'First of all, I don't think you should call this number.' So I said OK—and he gave me some suggestions on how to protect myself, which my friend Gary Cardori, who was murdered in 1990, had already given me—hints of things how to protect myself by driving different routes and stuff like that. The FBI agent said, 'We want you to get an unpublished number and a post office box,' but I said, 'Why should I have to hide?' "

When Donna left the FBI office, she went to the telephone company to talk to the owner and president, whom she knew, and asked, "Can this guy make a message like that legally?" He said he could. After that, she went to the police department. By then, Donna was taking notes on everything that was happening. "I was just really upset and I talked to the chief and to the captain, and he said, 'Donna, I want you to know that we have a warrant out for him.' And they picked him up that day for harassing Bill Rush."

The police might have picked up Trapp for inviting white separatists to "pay [Donna] a visit," but technically his words were within the letter of the law and he hadn't done anything illegal. Also, law-enforcement officials knew the real danger to Donna Polk at this point was no longer Trapp himself, but any fanatic inspired by Trapp's message who would want to make good on the invitation. Nevertheless, Trapp's tape-recorded harassment of Rush provided a good justification for an arrest—even though it was only a misdemeanor charge for disturbing the peace.

When police officers arrested Larry Trapp at his apartment, they took him to the County-City Jail, where he spent the night. The following morning, the judge released him on a $50 personal recognizance bond, and assigned his case to attorney Susan Tast in the Public Defender's Office. Tast had some misgivings about representing Larry Trapp. "I knew who he was," she said, "and I knew Klan members don't have very much respect for women professionals, and so I thought, 'Okay, this is a client I'm going to be very, very careful with.'" Tast also had heard that Larry had a reputation for making passes at his nurses and sexually harassing them, and that a number of the nurses in the medical services refused to go to his apartment.

"When Larry first came in, I was a little apprehensive," Tast said. "He's in a wheelchair and this woman is pushing him, and he has these Klan rings and swastikas on his fingers. I had to go out of my office for a minute, and when I came back in, these rings were gone. It was strange. Anyway, I took a statement from him where he categorically denied he'd made the call. I told Larry it didn't make any difference to me what his beliefs were. My belief is everyone is entitled to a trial and entitled to the constitutional guarantee of innocent until proven guilty. After that, we had a good rapport, and Larry was always perfectly appropriate—I had no problems with him."

At his trial, which began August 28, 1991, and continued into mid-September in Lancaster County Court in the Third Judicial District of Nebraska, Trapp was prosecuted for disturbing the peace under Municipal Code 9.20.5 and for failure to appear in court for arraignment. He pled not guilty to both charges.

For William Rush, the trial was a chance to defend himself and speak his piece. "I couldn't believe I was testifying in a criminal trial," he said later. "But I didn't like the fact that he wished someone would bash in my head. I had enough brain damage in my life."

And although testifying was exhilarating, it wasn't easy. Rush found himself trying to compensate for his lack of speed by nodding yes or no to Assistant City Prosecutor Gerald Fisher instead of electronically vocalizing the words for the record. "I was nervous," he said. "Sometimes I didn't wait for the city attorney to finish asking some of his questions. It was almost like I was a contestant on a game show, trying to buzz in before my opponents."

The hardest part of the trial involved Bill Rush's need to point out Trapp's speaking patterns from the audiotape recording of the threatening message. "It was hard to reproduce his unique way of speaking on my TouchTalker with an acceptable degree of accuracy," he said. The machine couldn't, for instance, "call Afro-Americans 'niggahs.' " Also, the TouchTalker sometimes mangled longer phrases in Rush's lengthy explanations.

Defense attorney Susan Tast faulted Bill's reproduction of Larry Trapp's voice. "Bill said he recognized Larry's voice because Trapp had certain speech patterns," she said later, "like he slurred his s's, like he pronounced 'Lucifer' 'Luss-ti-fer,' and that he would say 'neggah' instead of 'nigger.' But when you hear this tape, the reasons Bill said he recognized his voice—those patterns are not on the tape." Trapp himself didn't testify at the trial, but when the recording was played, he pointed out to Susan Tast, "It doesn't even sound like my voice."

Months earlier, Trapp told his sister Candy during a Lincoln-to-Houston telephone conversation that he had a machine he put at his throat to disguise his voice so no one could identify him. He used it on her once, and she didn't recognize him—which he thought was very funny. During his trial, he called and told her he was being charged with harassment but said, "They can't prove it was me. It didn't even sound like me." Candy later wondered out loud whether he thought she was an idiot or whether he had forgotten their previous exchange on the subject.

Judge Mary L. Doyle of the Lancaster County Court didn't know about Trapp's voice-disguising machine, but she didn't buy his defense. On September 16, 1991, she found Trapp guilty and specified Trapp could not call or harass Bill Rush. Judge Doyle ordered a presentence investigation and scheduled a November sentencing date. The maximum penalty for disturbing the peace was six months in jail and a $500 fine. Public Defender Tast said she would appeal the decision because there had not been enough evidence to prove her client guilty beyond a reasonable doubt.

Nevertheless, the guilty verdict pleased Bill Rush. "I felt vindicated," he said. "Somehow testifying had given me back my self-respect. For someone who has had his personhood questioned many times, [the judge's verdict] was a victory in itself."

When Michael and Julie read "Klansman Found Guilty for Abusive Message" and "KKK Recruiter Convicted for Menacing Phone Call" in the local newspapers, they were glad. Julie still sometimes had the impulse to stop at Trapp's apartment, but when she read what Trapp had done to William Rush, she felt more like thrashing the Klansman than trying to talk sense into him. What he had done to them was nothing by comparison, so she could imagine how Rush felt. She dialed the courthouse number and asked for Judge Doyle, whom she had met socially a couple of times.

When Judge Doyle answered her phone, Julie said, "You may not be able to talk about this, but I just wanted to let you know that when you sentence Larry Trapp, I hope you send him to jail for a long, long time for what he did to Bill Rush."

Judge Doyle was polite but said she wasn't free to discuss the case or make any comment on it. Nevertheless, Julie was glad she'd called. "I *wanted* to influence her," she later admitted. "I didn't think he should have any leniency. I wanted him to get the maximum sentence because I thought what he had done to Bill Rush was really, really horrible."

At that time, in the autumn of 1991, Julie Weisser didn't have any idea what Trapp had done to Donna Polk or many others in the community. Nor did she know what Larry Trapp was planning for B'nai Jeshurun.

RICOCHETING *Chapter 11*

HATRED

*[T]heir feet run to evil and they hurry to shed blood. For in
vain is the net baited while the bird is looking on; yet they lie
in wait—to kill themselves! And set an ambush—for their own
lives! Such is the end of all who are greedy for gain; it takes
away the life of its possessors.*

—PROVERBS 1:16-19

As Larry Trapp's rage escalated, as he lobbed death threats,
bombs and assassination plans, fragments of his own hatred and fear
began to ricochet back toward him. Since he'd put out the death warrant on Donna Polk, he'd begun to be afraid he himself would be killed.
If he received the maximum sentence for his harassment of Bill Rush,
he could spend six months in jail. His lawyer told him it wouldn't happen, but still, alone in the quiet of the night, after every distraction
from group orgies on porno tapes to newly composed vendettas denouncing homosexuals, nonwhites and feminists had exhausted him,
his mind attached itself to a secret vision he had of dying in jail. In his
nightmares, black and Latino inmates came after him with razor-edged
daggers—their black eyes blazing with mirror images of his own hatred—and they slowly sliced him into pieces until he died. His own
screams and curses would wake him and he would find himself still
alive but clammy in his sweaty, grimy sheets.

Larry Trapp's daytime ordeals also unsettled him, because just as he
was escalating his terroristic stratagems in Nebraska, many of his recruits were manifesting an infuriating lack of discipline. As Grand

Dragon, he used rigorous but inconsistent standards to kick out strag-glers. "If they don't contact me when they're supposed to, how can I count on 'em?" he said. "If we're going to work together, we have to work together as a group." When two of his members were arrested on arson charges and Trapp heard on television that drug paraphernalia was found at their residences, Trapp kicked them out, even though they had done exactly what he had instructed them to do. "True Aryans don't use dope," he said. "That stuff is for niggers and Jews."

Trapp also was upset because Tom Metzger was sending the "Race and Reason" videos late from California. "They don't know what they're doing out there," he told Dave Grooman at Cablevision one day when the tape had not yet arrived for the following day's airing. "They're screwing everything up. If California can't get their act together, I'm not doing this!"

Things were also tense with the skinhead leader from Council Bluffs. One day Trapp called Dave Grooman and told him, "Ansel is on his way," Trapp said. "He's bringing you a new tape, so give him the old one." When the tattooed skinhead arrived at the station, he handed Grooman the new "Race and Reason" tape and Grooman handed him the old one.

"I don't need that," the skinhead said.

"Larry Trapp told me on the phone I'm supposed to give it back to you," Grooman said.

"He doesn't know what he's talking about," the kid said. "He's an old man."

"Both of 'em hated each other," Grooman said later. "Larry thought this kid was trying to edge in and take over here. I thought, 'Okay, great, you guys hate each other, great.' "

After that, Larry's current Exalted Cyclops, an overweight forty-year-old named John, who wore overalls, began dropping off the "Race and Reason" tapes. For Grooman, all of it was chilling. "Every time I got off work, or if I went home late, I thought, 'Those people are really out here,' " the young Nebraskan said. "I definitely didn't want Larry Trapp angry at me. I sensed what he and his group were capable of. . . ."

For Trapp, however, nothing seemed to be going according to plan. Two dogs in a yard next door to his apartment barked constantly, which gave him headaches. He got the home-care nurse who had sewn red stripes on his white Klan robes to read out loud from the book *Dirty Tricks II*, about the least-traceable method for poisoning animals, telling her he needed to get rid of some rats. But figuring out what to do about the barking dogs didn't cheer him up. His diabetes wasn't "good," his eyesight faded in and out, new ulcers had appeared on his left leg and his right stump itched. In his quiet moments alone, Larry must have known his health was deteriorating.

Life began to feel even more bleak when he got the news that his friend and fellow Klansman, Jeffrey Smith, from Tylertown, Mississippi, had been robbed and murdered on October 4, 1991. Trapp recorded a memorial to the twenty-seven-year-old who had written the poem "Rolling Thunder" for him. Larry Trapp's hotline commemoration to Smith said:

> ... This courageous young man lived and died fighting for his race, the white race. . . . [But] there's one thing about the Klan, one thing that stands out stronger than anything else. If one of our members succumbs to foul play of any sort, their passing is avenged by all members in the Klan. So the persons responsible for this man's death will receive payment in like manner for what they have done. That is a guarantee. If I didn't hate them so much, I'd almost feel sorry for what the Klan is gonna do to them.
>
> ... This young man, by the way, is Jeff Smith, one of the best friends myself and a lot of other people have ever had. So remember, Jeff Smith, you . . . will never leave our thoughts. And you will be avenged—or my name is not Larry Trapp, Grand Dragon of the White Knights of the Ku Klux Klan.

At the time he recorded this message, Trapp didn't know his friend had been killed by two fellow Klansmen intent on getting the $740 Smith had raised to buy a fax machine for the Confederate Knights of the KKK. The Klansmen had tried but failed to hire some black men to cut Smith's throat, so they killed Smith themselves by hitting him with a two-by-four. They beat him so badly his head was swollen three times its normal size. After they were arrested, each Klansman blamed the other one for doing the most damage. One even accused the other of having run Smith over with a truck, but the autopsy didn't show evidence of any tire treads.

When Trapp called Jeff's grandmother in Tylertown to express his condolences, she told him Jeff had been buried with his Ku Klux Klan robes and his silver swastika rings in the casket. "We put the Confederate flag into the casket, too," she said. "What he really wanted was a Klan Kiln [the full-blown Klan funeral, popular in the twenties], but they didn't want boycotting. So they didn't have a Klan Kiln. But all the pallbearers were Klan."

"When I go, that's what I want, too," Larry said. "I want to be dressed in my robes, and I want a regular Klan Kiln and Klan pallbearers. . . ."

Another distressing incident occurred with one of Larry Trapp's favorite nurses. None of the nursing-service nurses liked working for him; he knew that. They thought it was weird taking care of an active Klansman. But as he often said, he wasn't in this business to be loved. "I don't believe in friendship," he told his nurses. "You're acquaintances, and that's it." Two of his nurses, however, were different. One was Lynette, the director of the medical pool, and the other one was Cathy Carson. Those two knew they were in danger coming to his apartment—they could have gotten shot by someone trying to shoot him—but they came anyway. They gave him his insulin, brought him extra food from their own refrigerators, and sometimes they even came together to clean his apartment. Trapp especially liked Cathy. "She was a nice, sweet girl—married, about twenty-six years old and always very gentle with me," he later confided. "I love the sound of her voice." One time Larry asked Cathy to read some recipes into his tape recorder, and later he replayed her voice over and over.

The upsetting incident happened one morning after Larry had stayed up all night because of two strange calls he'd gotten. In one, a woman yelled, "You don't know what the fuck you're talking about when you talk all that shit!" Then she slammed down the phone. Another call came from a man who read him a poem about a fish laid against a wall with his eyes popping out. That call was so weird it scared him. When the sun came up, Larry was still sitting behind his door, holding his MAC-10, nodding off to sleep every now and then. At nine-thirty, when he heard a quiet knock at the door, his finger tightened on the trigger.

When he heard Cathy's voice, he furiously put the gun on his table, unlocked the door and backed up his wheelchair so she could get into the room. "Don't sneak up on me that way," he yelled at her. "That's dangerous! You could get hurt!"

Cathy apologized, and Larry wheeled across the room and turned on his television. He didn't look at her, but he could imagine her short brown hair and big soft eyes. He popped a cassette into the VCR because he was going to tape Montel Williams interviewing some skinheads. He could hear her opening her bag and getting out her stethoscope, getting out the insulin. He moved back by the kitchen table, and in a few minutes, she came over and said she wanted to hear his heartbeat.

"Why is the TV so quiet all of the sudden?" Larry asked.

"I turned it off because I want it quiet to listen to your heart."

"Leave your fucking hands off my fucking television!" Larry shouted. "Who the fuck do you think you are? You can't turn that off! It's on for a reason, but you're too stupid to know that!"

Larry heard Cathy suck in her breath and it looked like she was crying.

"Why don't you just get out of here," he yelled. "I don't need you here! Why don't you go home and diddle your old man or something instead of bothering me?"

"Larry Trapp, I have a job to do and then I'll gladly leave," Cathy said. She took Larry's blood pressure, listened to his heart, took a blood sample from his finger, gave him an insulin shot.

"I've never been so sad and so mad at the same time," she said. "It's like walking on eggshells to be here. One day you're so nice, and the next day you blow up. Why? Why are you so full of hate? You're too full of hate."

She got her things together and opened the door to leave. But before she left, she said, "The way you hate, Larry, it's unhealthy. It's excessive. Maybe if you didn't hate so much, your health wouldn't be so bad." And then she walked out and closed the door.

Larry opened the door and wheeled himself out after her. "Wait. Wait!" he said. "I didn't mean to blow up that way. I want you to come back."

"I don't know if I can come back," she said. "You hurt me too much."

Larry rolled back into his apartment and locked the door. He turned the television back on. He felt upset by Cathy, but he had work to do. For one thing, he had to decide what to say on his new message. He had to record it this morning.

Just as he was about to start taping some of his thoughts to hear how they sounded, his telephone rang. His machine clicked on and played through his whole message. He listened, and at the end of it, he heard a voice that was getting all too familiar. "Justice is for everybody, Larry," the voice said. "You'll have to face your justice someday, too."

Larry wheeled over to the phone, grabbed it and shouted, "Fuck you, you dirty nigger SOB," but it was too late. The caller had already hung up.

These telephone messages disturbed Larry Trapp a great deal. One day when he was feeling particularly angry at knowing he'd be getting a call any minute asking him something like, What are you going to say to God on your Judgment day? Larry left a long burst of flatulence on his answering machine.

When the phone rang, Larry sat beside the machine and waited for the caller to hear the long farting sound. Larry sat quietly waiting for what the guy would say, thinking the noise might shut him up for good. But at the end of the flatulence, a chuckle came booming over the answering machine. It was that same voice—a warm, melodic voice filled with laughter unlike anything Trapp had ever heard. When he finished laughing, the caller said, "Sounds like the voice of the Master Race to me!" Then, with another chuckle, he hung up.

Trapp grabbed furiously at the phone, but it was too late. He called the caller a string of names. Then, he didn't know why, he began to laugh. He laughed until his laughter turned into a coughing fit that made him gasp for air.

Two days later, the same guy called again, but Larry was having a meeting at the time. "Why are you continuing to do all this hateful stuff?" the caller's voice calmly said into the room. "It isn't doing anybody any good."

"That's some crackpot who keeps calling," Larry told the Klansmen.

"It sounds like you should watch out for him," one member said. "I wouldn't trust him."

Another day when the phone rang, the caller listened to Larry's hotline message and then his voice broadcast into the room again: "Larry, when you give up hating, a world of love is waiting for you."

Trapp had to put a stop to these calls. The next time he heard the same caller's voice beginning to speak, he grabbed the phone.

"Hello," he said.

"Is this Larry?" the caller asked. It was the same guy, the deep warm voice with the sound of laughter in it.

"No!"

"Yes it is, I know your voice."

"What the fuck d'ya want?" Larry asked harshly.

"I just want to talk to you."

"You know this telephone is connected to a police tap, and I'll have you arrested for harassing me," Trapp said. "Why the fuck are you harassing me?! Stop harassing me!"

"I'm not, I don't want to harass you, Larry," the caller said. "I just want to talk to you."

"I know your voice. You black by any chance?"

"No."

"Something with your voice, you sound black."

"I'm Jewish."

"You are harassing me. What do you want? Make it quick."

Michael remembered the advice Julie had given him earlier. "Well, I was thinking you might need a hand with something," he said. "And I wondered if I could help. I know you're in a wheelchair and I thought maybe I could take you to the grocery store or something."

Trapp was stunned. He couldn't think of anything to say.

Michael listened to the silence. Finally, Trapp cleared his throat, and when he spoke, his voice sounded different to Michael Weisser's ears. Michael felt certain that he heard the texture of Larry's voice soften and lose its edge of hatred.

"That's okay," Larry Trapp said. "That's nice of you, but I've got that covered. Thanks anyway. But don't call this number anymore. It's my business phone."

Before Trapp could hang up, Michael Weisser said, "I'll be in touch."

RING OF FIRE

Chapter 12

*Let us not seek to satisfy our thirst for freedom by drinking
from the cup of bitterness and hatred . . . We must not allow
our creative protest to degenerate into physical violence. Again
and again, we must rise to the majestic heights of meeting
physical force with soul force.*
—*MARTIN LUTHER KING, JR.*

*M*ichael Weisser was reading the *Lincoln Journal* when he noticed an article at the bottom of the page with the headline "Local Sponsor Pulls 'Race and Reason.' "

"Julie, come look at this," Michael hollered. "Larry Trapp is taking 'Race and Reason' off the air!"

On November 12, 1991, Larry Trapp had called Dave Grooman at Channel 14 and told him to pull the plug on "Race and Reason" because he was fed up with Tom Metzger. "Don't air Tuesday's show," Trapp said. "I'm not sponsoring it anymore—and as far as I'm concerned, no more shows will be forthcoming. Not unless they get another sponsor."

Reporter L. Kent Wolgamott of the *Lincoln Journal* called Trapp about the decision, and what Trapp told him sounded closer to David Duke's polished public party line than to Trapp's own White Knights' rhetoric: "I'm not too crazy about the black race, the brown race, whatever," he said. "But our main problem is the U.S. government. . . . I'm not backing out of the Klan or the white movement, but I think we should work for equal rights for all."

Trapp didn't mention to the *Lincoln Journal* or anyone else that Michael's telephone calls had been making him feel confused. Nor did he say he'd received a letter from a former nurse, Monica Kuhns, which had a profound effect on him. She had written, in part:

> Dear Larry,
>
> I've been wondering about something: you say you're not Christian—I'm wondering what being a Christian means to you. It's not about rules and regulations, things you can and can't do, and people who are perfect. It's about LOVE. Something I know hasn't been a very big part of your life. It's about God loving us (all races) so much that he sent his only son, Jesus, to die on the cross for our sins. The reason this world is so messed up is because of satan and sin, not blacks and Jews, etc. . . . You say you're tired of hating. Don't try to do it alone. I promise you if you give your life to Him 100% like you gave yourself to the KKK, He'll heal you of all that bitterness, hatred, and hurt, and you will be changed in ways you won't believe. I don't know why you've had so much hurt in your life but God can take that hurt and use it for good if you'll let Him. Nothing else has worked, Larry. Go to the true Healer. Give Jesus a chance. HE LOVES YOU.
>
> Your friend, Monica

The flustering effect of Mrs. Kuhns' letter had been compounded by an experience at the medical professional building, when Larry was waiting near an elevator to go up to see his eye doctor. For several days, a dense screen of red had seemed to be blotting out Larry's already narrow field of vision, and he was feeling especially disoriented. When the elevator came, he wheeled himself into the wall and cursed. Then suddenly, he felt himself being moved. A young woman had come up behind him and was pushing his wheelchair into the elevator.

"Hey, what are you doing?" Trapp said.

"I helping you on elevator," she answered in a kind voice marked by a strong accent. Inside the elevator, Larry inhaled the sweet flowery smell of her perfume and asked where she was from. "I from Vietnam," she said. Then she asked if Larry needed help into the doctor's office or anything else. "No, thanks," he said, "I'll do it myself."

When he got home and thought about her, he remembered the scent of her gardenias. He also remembered Operation Gooks and his assaults on the Vietnamese, and suddenly he found himself thinking about how he always called people like her "gooks" and "slants" and suddenly, without understanding why, he realized he was crying. Crying made him furious, and he shook himself to get rid of the sad feelings. "Look, asshole, stop it," he said out loud to himself. "Being a hard-ass is the only way you get respect. The only way."

Michael handed Julie the paper. "I've been hoping he'd do something like this," Michael said. "I know something's happening with him. I have a feeling he's waffling somehow." During their last call, Michael was certain he'd felt something shift in Larry Trapp, sure he'd heard some kind of difference during that moment Larry was so silent—right before he'd said, "That's okay . . . I've got that covered." At the least, the offer of help had shocked Larry's twisted, limited view of the world. Larry expected people to fear him and hate him back. People dedicated to hating can't forgive their enemies; the concept of forgiveness would undermine their dogma and wouldn't allow them to remain where they are.

Michael had given a lot of thought to the premise it's easy to love your friends, but hard to love your enemy. He realized his initial response to Trapp's hatred had been fueled by anger and a desire to fight back, but since their first exchange, he'd started thinking of Larry Trapp as a destructive but vulnerable, messed-up person who needed a new perspective on the world.

As unusual as it might seem, Michael knew it wasn't unlikely he and Larry had some childhood experiences in common. He didn't have to know the details of Larry Trapp's life to figure Larry probably had been an abused child who quite likely had been in trouble with the law. He didn't realize how many parallels they actually had. But Michael's father, like Larry's, had worked as a milkman for a while. Larry's father later went to work as a security guard, and Michael's father became a bus driver. Like Larry, Michael was treated unkindly as a child, and while Larry was mistreated by his father and mother, Michael was abandoned by his. When Michael was three, his parents divorced and his mother took Michael and his brother, David, and sister, Sylvia, to the Jewish Home for Children and left them there for three years. When he was six, he was reunited with his mother, who had remarried by then, but during the years he lived in "the Home," Michael was physically abused and beaten by a staff member of the orphanage. "I still don't understand why my mother put us into an orphanage, or why my father allowed it," he says now, a hurt edge in his voice. "I just don't understand it."

Like Larry Trapp, Michael Weisser also got into a lot of trouble when he was in grade school and junior high, and when he was ten years old, he was sent to reform school, the Connecticut School for Boys, for being a runaway. When he got out of reform school, he discovered a new side of life at the Roger Sherman School in New Haven. Mrs. Anna Maskel, Michael's teacher in the fifth and sixth grades, chose children from diverse backgrounds to be in her two-year-long class, and during that time, they literally celebrated their cultural differences. Mrs. Maskel herself had come from India, and one of the class projects had been to write a play to be given as a gift from the children of America to the children of India. They recorded what they'd written, and during the middle of their second year, Mrs. Maskel gave it to the United Nations ambassador from India. They later got a letter saying the Indian government was going to translate their play into different languages and broadcast it all over India.

As a child in that class, Michael had shared stories he knew about the Ukraine. His grandmother had brought in Ukrainian food, and his mother had come to class in her fancy embroidered Ukrainian blouse and brightly colored, layered dress and taught Ukrainian dances. Other mothers, fathers and grandfathers had done the same with food, clothing and stories from their own countries—which included China, Japan, Russia, Italy, Poland, Ireland. In that class, Michael had learned a deep respect for diversity; everyone was considered authentic and important—and that lesson had stayed with Michael for the rest of his life.

On the other hand, Larry, like so many people, had never understood or celebrated differences between people. Instead, he feared and distrusted anyone whose skin, features or customs were different from his own. Discriminatory cultural stereotypes seemed to explain and excuse his uncomfortable feelings about different ethnic groups. Those stereotypes not only clarified his uneasiness, but also gave him a sense of identity and power—something to make him feel like a more valid person, larger, stronger, more invincible. The trappings of the Klan and the Nazi Party also added to that illusion of bigness, control, invulnerability and purpose.

Michael thought he had a chance of getting through to Larry Trapp, and believed it was his job at least to try. He'd gotten over being so angry at him, and now the trick was to connect. Michael loved looking for this invisible energy between people; he loved forging new links.

"This energy force is part of what God is," Michael had told his congregants, "and if we continue building harmony with this force, then we eliminate the barriers between human beings . . ."

Now—on Wednesday, November 13, 1991—after reading about "Race and Reason" being pulled, Michael dialed Larry Trapp's number and got the White Knights hotline and an earful about Larry Trapp's reasons for removing the show:

". . . For any of you white activists who sent in for things advertised in various circles, there's an organization I have personally dealt with that is endorsed by Tom Metzger of W.A.R. . . .

". . . Tom Metzger is nothing but a money-grabbing fool. He cares nothing about the white movement or the white race . . .

"I recently have withdrawn his show, 'Race and Reason,' because he can't even get his tapes here to this office in time for me to show them. . . . How can I show them if they arrive after they're supposed to be shown? He doesn't care! Be warned! If you deal with this outfit, do so at your own risk. I have warned you!

". . . What have you seen Tom Metzger actually do for the white race in the recent past? Not one damn thing!

"I will use this message line not only for racial messages, but to also reveal such businesses like this in our white movement destroying our white movement from within. . . ."

Trapp also complained about Metzger asking people to send cash for posters and various items. Trapp failed to note the irony of his own hotline message, which told callers, "If you would like a large package of racially oriented material, suitable for copying and passing around to your friends and neighbors, please send us four dollars in cash."

As Michael listened, he had the feeling Larry was sitting in his apartment right beside his answering machine, listening to his own invective and waiting to hear who was calling.

He was right. When the message ended and Michael started to speak, Larry picked up the phone.

"Yeah?" he said.

"Larry Trapp, this is the rabbi," Michael said, thinking Trapp wouldn't know what a cantor was, but wanting to identify himself as a Jewish clergyman. "I hear you're pulling 'Race and Reason' off cable. Is that true?"

"Yeah, it is."

"Larry, if you want to talk about all these changes of heart that you're having, I'd love to be able to help you."

"I'm not having a change of heart," Trapp said emphatically. "I'm still a Klansman and I'm still a Nazi. But I'm just rethinking a few of the ideas."

"Okay. Still, if you want some help with it, I'll be glad to help you."

"Listen, Rabbi, I don't really care to talk to you, so it'd be better if you just left me alone."

"I also know you were found guilty and you're being sentenced this Friday by Judge Doyle on that harassment charge with Bill Rush," Michael said quickly, before Larry could hang up. "Does this have anything to do with it?"

"No, it doesn't have anything to do with it. I'm just rethinking some things."

"Okay," Michael said, "but call me. My number is . . ." Michael interrupted himself with a laugh. "I'm gonna give you my number, Larry, but I know you already have it."

Michael gave Larry his number and reminded him again, "Do let me know if I can help you because I would love to help you. I'd like to be your friend, and I'm here if you need me. I mean that."

"Thanks," Larry said. "But I'm gonna handle this on my own."

That was Wednesday. On Friday, November 15, 1991, Lincoln's Handi-Van service picked up Larry Trapp at C Street and dropped him off at the Lancaster County Courthouse on 10th Street, where he would receive his sentence. Dressed in the paramilitary garb of olive green and brown camouflage popular among white supremacists, Trapp rolled

himself into the building in his wheelchair, the bottoms of his camouflage pants tucked back below the stumps of his legs. The combination
of Trapp's paramilitary clothes, his maroon KKK beret, the ferocious
expression on his large round face with its full beard gave him the appearance of being a bigger man, someone much more substantial than
the small man whose legs had been amputated.

His face furrowed with the intensity of a concentrated internal dialogue as he rolled his wheelchair toward the inside door of the courthouse, where he met up with his helper and another Klansman from
western Nebraska. His lawyer, Susan Tast, also had been waiting for
Trapp, but she told him since she had to be in two courtrooms at once,
he should go down to the courtroom designated for his sentencing, and
she would be there soon.

As Trapp headed down the hallway toward the assigned courtroom,
he was brought to a standstill when some members of the media approached him with flashbulbs popping, bright lights trained on him
and cameras rolling. Several reporters began asking him questions
about what sentence he expected. His shoulders were hunched, and as
he looked at the reporters, his eyes and cheeks creased in fury and he
waved them away.

"I don't talk to kikes and Jews!" he shouted in the direction of Karen
Kilgarin, a reporter for Omaha's KETV-TV who is of Irish Catholic ancestry. "I don't talk to the Jews' media!"

When Gary Johnson of WOWT-TV of Omaha asked him a question,
he snarled: "You're an idiot. You and your whole damn office! You and
your half-breed bitch Pat Persaud [a WOWT-TV news anchor] from
Omaha!"

When a *Lincoln Journal* reporter said something, he shouted, "I
don't talk to the *Lincoln Urinal!*"

Throughout the courthouse, everyone, including Trapp's lawyer,
heard about his behavior. "He was surly, he was arrogant, he was an
asshole, and he was a jerk, spouting this Klan stuff which I'd never
heard him do before," said Susan Tast. "When I got with him again in
the courtroom, I said, 'Larry, where is this coming from?'

" 'I don't know,' he said. 'I don't want to talk about it.' "

In the courtroom, Trapp didn't do anything to improve his reputation. Before sentencing, Trapp told Judge Doyle if his appeal of her
guilty verdict wasn't successful, he would not abide by any monetary
terms or conditions she might impose. "I will not pay any fine," Trapp

told Judge Mary Doyle. "I'll—I'll serve jail time. I can't see payin' the State of Nebraska for something they have no proof that I ever did."

But the judge's decision had already been made. Judge Doyle said even though Trapp did not have "a serious record"—he hadn't been convicted of anything other than theft of services and carrying a concealed weapon in 1986—"the facts as the Court found them in this case" were "a serious matter."

"Mr. Rush is an individual who certainly doesn't deserve to be treated in this manner," she told Trapp. "Dealing with his life on a day-to-day basis is difficult for him and he certainly doesn't need to be harassed by you." She gave Trapp the maximum fine of $500 and the costs of prosecution. Additionally, she gave him two days in the County-City Jail.

Sentence was suspended until the outcome of the appeal. Even if Trapp lost the appeal, however, the jail sentence was minuscule. In practical terms, it meant Larry would have to serve only two more hours in jail. He would get credit for the day he spent in jail when he was picked up, and for the second day, he could go to jail at 4 P.M. and be released at 6 P.M., since, if you're in jail by four o'clock in Lancaster County, a whole day is counted as of 6 P.M. Except for the fine, he'd gotten off easily.

On his way out of the courthouse, after his sentencing, Trapp yelled and cursed again at reporters who approached him. Again, they got his performance on camera.

That Friday evening on the six o'clock local news, viewers in Lincoln and Omaha heard Karen Kilgarin and Gary Johnson, among others, report Trapp's sentence of a $500 fine and two days in jail. They also reported his response to the media and showed him shouting racial obscenities in a bitter, razor-edged voice.

On Randolph Street, Michael Weisser was reading over the text of the sermon he'd just written on "Justice" as he dressed to go to synagogue for Shabbat services that evening. "Like every other city," he read, "Lincoln has poverty, crime, violence towards children and women, racism, intolerance, homelessness. . . . Why do we say 'I am my brother's keeper' when we are not doing what we can in our actions and our deeds to build justice for all in our own community?"

Television news was on, but Michael hadn't been paying any attention to it until he looked up and saw a bearded, scowling Larry Trapp on his television screen. Trapp was sitting in a wheelchair, his shoulders hunched in his paramilitary camouflage outfit and maroon beret, and he was shouting, "I don't talk to kikes and Jews! I don't talk to the Jews' media! I don't talk to half-breeds!"

All concentration on his sermon flew from Michael's mind. Without a moment's hesitation, even before the next news item had begun, Michael picked up the phone and dialed Larry's number.

At the end of his hotline message, Larry Trapp picked up his phone and said, "White Power, Brother"—a greeting as normal to him as "Hello."

Michael was so angry he didn't bother with any semblance of polite formalities. His hope of Trapp having a change of heart obviously was an illusion—and the redeeming qualities he'd imagined about him a few days earlier had just been obliterated. "Larry Trapp, this is the rabbi," he said angrily. "I just saw you on television. It's clear you're not rethinking anything at all. Either you're the biggest liar or you're the biggest bullshit artist and hypocrite I've ever known, or you'd better have a good explanation for what you did at the courthouse today!" Later it occurred to Michael he had sounded like a teacher chastising a kid—and he couldn't explain where he had gotten such a sense of command with this man he hardly knew.

For a minute, Larry didn't say anything. Then, in a surprisingly tremulous voice, he said, "I didn't mean to do that. I'm sorry I did that. I mean, I've been talking like that all of my life, and they got in my face and they were bothering me, and I called her a kike bastard or something. I mean, I can't help it. I've been doing this forever. I'll apologize! I'll apologize to them. They had me nervous."

"Larry, do you still want to rethink things?"

"Yes, I do."

"Do you want to get out of these habits?"

"Yeah, I do."

"Well, I believe your story. Can I help you do this?" Michael asked.

"No, no, I'm gonna do it myself."

"Okay, but stay in touch," Michael said, hanging up the phone, and running late to temple.

A lively mix of people and energy filled the South Street temple that Friday night. *"Shabbat shalom"*—a peaceful Sabbath—*"Shabbat shalom,"* people intoned as they greeted each other with hugs or handshakes.

Julie sat on the right side of the sanctuary near the aisle with Rebecca, Dina, Dave and Dave's girlfriend Lisa, and leafed through *The Gates of Prayer*. Between looking at poetic passages she loves, Julie got up to greet friends as they arrived.

B'nai Jeshurun's comfortable sanctuary, with its beautiful carved-walnut bimah and stained-glass windows, had a calming effect on people who walked in through the large wooden doors and sat in comfortable upholstered seats. Standing at the dais (the reading desk) on the bimah, in his robes and tallit (prayer shawl), Michael began services with a traditional Shabbat welcome: "Our noisy day has now descended with the sun beyond sight. In the silence of our praying place we close the door upon the . . . week we have left behind. What was but moments ago the substance of our life has become memory; what we did must now be woven into what we are. On this day, we shall not do, but be. . . . On this day heat and warmth and light must come from deep within ourselves."

As he spoke, Michael was overcome once again with the sense of peace and pleasure he often feels as he leads the congregation in prayers of praise to God. His rich baritone voice moved easily and effortlessly from English into Hebrew, from spoken language into song as he intoned, *"Yihu l'ratzon imrei fi v'hegyon libi l'fanech, Adonai, tzur v'go ali*—May the words of my mouth and the meditations of my heart be acceptable before You, O Lord, my rock and my redeemer." Michael's large voice filled the sanctuary with a feeling of love as he sang another sacred prayer.

When Michael began his sermon, his down-to-earth style sounded like just a regular guy on the street talking to his friends, and yet the impact of his words, as usual, expressed a deep commitment to the basic tenets of Judaism. "If we don't communicate our love through the works of our hands, then what kind of love do we have?" Michael said. "Love means being willing to aid and serve the one who is unloved. And if we keep our tolerance to ourselves, it is not really tolerance at all, but merely silence. In order to express our tolerance, we are called to reach out to those who may seem different—reach out and make them our friends. . . .

"Justice is built through the actions of many people doing small things to refine and improve society. Justice is built through the deeds of many people influencing the attitudes of society. . . . When enough of us are showing that we care about feeding the hungry, the nation will rise to the challenge of feeding the hungry. . . . When enough of us refuse to allow people to sleep on the streets, live in cardboard boxes, be mistreated by public officials or want for proper medical care, then these injustices will begin to go away and we will be on the way to building a moral and just society, a moral and just world. . . .

"If you think about it, a big part of the mission of the Jewish people historically has been just that: the building of a better world. . . . We need to do more, so that we can make our congregation a beacon of hope here in Lincoln. Please take the time to consider the needs in our own community, and then decide, in the name of God, to do your part to help solve the problems we all face. Then shall you be among those who bring peace and justice to the world."

Before the silent prayer, Michael named members and friends of the congregation who were sick or in the hospital. Among them, he named Leslie Young, a composer and folksinger undergoing radiation treatment for cancer. He asked the congregants to include Leslie, her daughter Josie and others who were ill or bedridden in their prayers.

Then Michael turned from the dais and walked toward his seat on the bimah. Suddenly, Larry Trapp's bitter invectives against Jews, blacks and the media came to his mind, and on impulse, he turned back to the congregation. He looked out at his friends. "You need to include in your prayers tonight someone who is sick from the illness of bigotry and hatred," he said. "Please pray that he can be healed, too."

Michael and Julie Weisser and the congregation of B'nai Jeshurun didn't know it, but someone else was praying on behalf of Larry Trapp. She was Lenora Letcher—another target of Trapp's hatred—and she, too, was praying for Larry to be transformed and to find love in his heart.

Lenora Letcher, still elegant and graceful in her late seventies, has white hair and an alert, interested expression in her kind and expressive brown eyes. Mrs. Letcher radiates dignity and calm. She says when hate letters began to arrive from Larry Trapp, it was a shock.

"He terrorized me," she said. "Because I was with the NAACP, he wanted me to know I was a nigger and a smart-ass. He wanted to let me know he watched the way we worked. The letters were personally threatening to me, and they played down my heritage and they played down my race."

Mrs. Letcher, who had worked as a food manager and cook for the Beta Sigma Psi fraternity at the University of Nebraska, wasn't used to taking any personal abuse. It wasn't any lack of awareness of racism: discrimination was a fact of life that leached its way into the very water she and other African-Americans drank on a daily basis. When she had moved to Lincoln from Kansas City in 1946, for instance, African-Americans could only get housing in a segregated area referred to as "the Malone area" or "T-Town," and they couldn't get hired as teachers or receptionists, engineers, secretaries, doctors, nurses or even as sales clerks. Kresge's drugstore in downtown Lincoln hired its first black clerk in 1944—and no other black clerk was hired in Lincoln until 1951, when Lenora's friend Leola Bullock got a job at Gold's department store with the help of the NAACP and the Urban League. Blacks couldn't get work as waitresses or even as letter carriers until the late 1940s, and even then, they were harassed. Lincoln's first black mail-man, Edward Craft, had earned a degree in electrical engineering from the University of Nebraska, but that degree didn't help him get an engineer's job. When Craft began walking his mail route to deliver letters and packages, Klan members often followed and taunted him with racial slurs and threats.

Lenora Letcher also had friends in Lincoln who had had crosses burned on their lawns in the 1950s and the 1970s, and she knew that even today several black families moving into previously all-white neighborhoods had been severely harassed and tormented by racists objecting to their presence. One eighty-year-old woman she knew vividly remembered seeing lynchings when she was a child and young woman in the South. Personally, Mrs. Letcher says she had experienced very little overt racism in Lincoln, but what she had experienced had been distressing. One time during the sixties, for instance, Lenora was sitting at 9th and South in Lincoln, waiting for a bus and talking to another woman, who happened to be white. Two white men in suits came and stood beside Lenora for a while. Then one of them said, "If you were in Biloxi, Mississippi, you wouldn't be sitting talking to a white woman, and when the bus came, you'd ride in the back." The men followed her onto the bus, asked her where her husband worked, and continued to harass her until she got off the bus. More recently, she'd heard a little white girl say to her mother, "Look, Mom, there's a nigger." There had been other incidents as well, she said, but for the most part, they had been the exception, not the rule—until Larry Trapp.

"The first letter I got, I thought, 'What happened to this person?' It was a shock to me because it was so offending." The second letter was just as offending and threatening, as were the rest. "He learned about me in 1989," she said later, "and through 1990 and 1991, I received that hate mail.

"The NAACP had let us know if we got anything like this, we should be careful where we went at night, and we should stay in lighted areas. I sent the mail to the national office and let them know what I had received in Lincoln, Nebraska."

At the fraternity house where she had worked for thirty years, Mrs. Letcher had demanded respect from the white students and gotten it. "Sometimes some of the students would come up with some kind of racist remark in the kitchen, and I would just say, 'We don't like talk like that' or 'I'm not interested in that kind of remark,' " she says. "I think a lot of the students were helped because I was able to not let them offend me."

But there was no way to demand respect from Larry Trapp. "That mail had anything you could think of that was insulting towards me, towards Dr. King and his dream, towards everything. . . . They were in heavy black marker. . . . We knew he was housed here in Lincoln. I found out he lived on C Street, but I didn't have any threats for him. I heard he had an arsenal. . . ."

Mrs. Letcher refused to stay housebound or to hide. Some of her children and grandchildren wanted her not to go out, but she said she wouldn't be stopped by fear—not even after Trapp sent her an especially terrifying letter. "It showed a picture of a black woman with the words 'Five Lethal Shots in the Back of Your Head' on it," she said. "But I refused to let that frighten me." The night after she got the "five lethal shots" letter, she had choir practice at her church—Mt. Zion Baptist Church where she had been singing and directing music for years— and she wasn't going to miss it.

"I was on my way to choir rehearsal that night, and I was thinking about that letter," she said. "I had gotten to Fifty-Sixth and Vine, and just as I was crossing the street, that's when I said, 'You need to come to Jesus.' Just like that. I knew that's what he needed. I prayed in my mind he would receive Christ in his life. I prayed, 'Dear God, let him find you in his heart.' "

Maybe Larry Trapp didn't deserve the prayers Lenora Letcher was praying for him. Maybe he didn't deserve Michael and Julie Weisser's prayers or the prayers from B'nai Jeshurun's congregation. But they were praying for him anyway. And that Friday night after his sentencing, as prayers were being said for him in Lincoln, Nebraska, the swastika ring on Larry Trapp's left hand and the swastika ring on his right hand began to feel heavy and uncomfortable. For some odd reason his ring fingers began to sting and burn and itch. They'd never done that before. He took the rings off because they seemed to hurt his fingers. When his fingers felt better, he put the rings back on. All night he tossed in his bed, restless, confused and unsettled. He took his rings off again and then put them back on. An eerie feeling loomed over him, as if a large hawk were perched on a nearby chair, ready to swoop down, peck at his chest and pluck out his heart.

FACE TO FACE

> *The seed of hate is within us all.*
> *But so, too, is the light of love.*
> *The action of either brings forth a like reaction.*
> How, then, *should one address violence?*
> *Not by the sword.*
> —*RONALD L. SITTS*

*B*y a quarter to seven the next evening, Dina, Rebecca and Dave had already set off for their various Saturday night activities, and Michael and Julie were lying across their bed talking about what movie they wanted to go see.

When the phone rang, Julie picked it up. The caller asked for "the rabbi," and Julie, motioning to the phone with a question in her eyes, handed it to Michael.

"Is this the rabbi?"

Michael immediately recognized the voice. "Yeah, it is," he said. Julie whispered, "Who is it? Who is it?" and Michael mouthed back, "Larry Trapp!"

Julie said, "Oh my God!"

"I want to get out," Larry said, "but I don't know how."

"Would you like some help?"

"I don't know. I don't think so."

"Well, maybe we could talk about this tonight."

"I don't think so. Maybe later sometime." Larry's voice was tentative, unsure, as if he'd like to hang up.

"I could come over."

"No, I don't think so. That's not so good."

"Sometimes it helps to talk in person," Michael said.

"We could just talk on the phone."

"Well, that's okay, too."

"I don't know what to say," Larry said after a pause. "I'm feeling confused and kind of sick. I think this is making me sick."

"Are you certain you don't want to talk about this? I could come over."

"I don't know . . ."

"Look," Michael said. "Are you hungry?"

"I'm not really hungry, I'm worried."

"Have you eaten dinner yet?"

"No."

"Well, why don't I get some food . . ." Michael looked at Julie, who was mouthing the words "I'm coming, too."

Michael said, "We'll get some food, and my wife and I will come over and bring you some dinner."

"Well, I don't know . . ."

"We can have some food and break some bread together."

"Well, okay, I guess that would be alright. . . ."

"Okay. Look, we'll be there as soon as we can stop and pick up some chicken or something. Then we'll have some dinner and talk about what's going on. Tell me your address again? Oh, never mind, my wife is saying she knows where you live."

"I'm in apartment number three," Larry said. "It's on the right side of the building . . ."

Julie jumped off the bed. "I can't believe this! This is so incredible," she was saying. "But maybe he really has to make a change—just imagine how tiring it would be to hate that hard all the time."

"Well, he's pretty tentative," Michael said. "That was a very tentative conversation."

Still, both Michael and Julie were excited. In the spontaneity of the moment, it didn't occur to them they might be walking into some kind of ambush.

Just as they were getting ready to go out the door, Dave rushed into the house to get his wallet, which he'd forgotten to take when he went out for the evening. Michael told him where he and Julie were going. "Are you guys crazy?" Dave said. "I can't believe you're really going to

1

Larry Trapp, proud of his survivalist skills, built his own bunker in the mid-1980s in preparation for "race wars." He also fished, trapped and studied "killing skills" for the time he planned "to fight to the death enemies of the white race."

2

As Grand Dragon of the White Knights of the Ku Klux Klan in Nebraska, Larry Trapp was working to build the state into "one of the foremost Klan enclaves in the country." Trapp, also a Nazi, believed white supremacists should join forces against all non-Aryans.

3

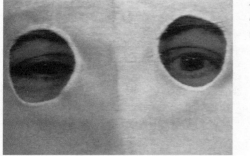

Despite Trapp's failing eyesight, due to diabetes, he stockpiled handguns, machine guns and automatic weapons.

4

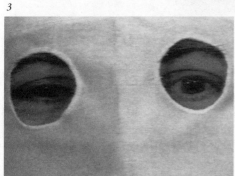

WHITE KNIGHTS of the KU KLUX KLAN
ACTIVE COMPONENT of the WHITE KNIGHTS
P.O. Box 14220 KANSAS CITY, MO 64152
WKKKK-03   DRAGON
LARRY TRAPP   507-66-6582

IDENTIFICATION FOR PURPOSES OF THE GENEVA CONVENTION RELATIVE TO TREATMENT OF PRISONERS OF WAR - AUGUST 12, 1949

DATE of BIRTH	BLOOD TYPE	COLOR of EYES	COLOR of HAIR
05-30-49	AB+	BLUE	BROWN
HEIGHT	WEIGHT	CARD NUMBER	GENEVA CONVENTION CATEGORY
5' 8"	150 lbs	Da60T096	01

DATE of ISSUE   07-31-91   SIGNATURE of ISSUING OFFICER   *Larry Trapp*

DECLARATION OF WAR NOVEMBER 25, 1984
IT IS A DARK AND DISMAL TIME IN THE HISTORY OF OUR RACE ... AN EVIL SHADOW HAS FALLEN ACROSS OUR ONCE FAIR LAND ... A CERTAIN VILE, ALIEN PEOPLE HAVE TAKEN CONTROL OF OUR COUNTRY ... WHEN THE DAY COMES, WE WILL NOT ASK WHETHER YOU SWUNG TO THE RIGHT OR WHETHER YOU SWUNG TO THE LEFT, WE WILL SIMPLY SWING YOU BY THE NECK ... THIS IS WAR!
- The ORDER

In public, Larry Trapp said, "We don't advocate violence," while in private, he and his fellow white supremacists incited and thrived on it. As his KKK identification card states, he believed "This is WAR."

5

Cantor Michael Weisser, spiritual leader of Congregation B'nai Jeshurun, and his wife, Julie Weisser, got threatening mail that told them, "Your time is up," "The 'Holohoax' was nothing compared to what's going to happen to you," and "The KKK is Watching You, Scum."

6

Built during the early 1900s, B'nai Jeshurun was another target of Trapp's. He planned to detonate a bomb in it during the summer of 1992: "Were the same Nazis that were around during the Second World War," he said. "Adolf Hitler is still our main man."

Donna Polk, director of the Nebraska Urban Indian Health Coalition, was terrorized for years by Trapp, who sent her a "Notice to All Niggers" suggesting she would die from "death by hanging" or be "exterminated" along with "swarms of wild niggers."

8

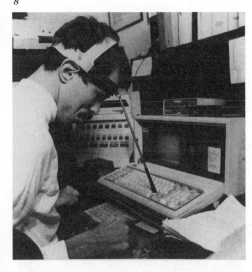

Journalist and author William Rush, whose disabilities keep him from walking, using his arms or speaking with his own voice, lived next door to Trapp until Trapp's harassment forced him to move.

9

Lenora Letcher, food manager, cook and an officer of the NAACP, received mail for "Lenore the Letch," which described ways she should die, including "five lethal shots in the back of your head." Nevertheless, she prayed for Trapp to be saved from his hatred.

Social worker Phong Huynh, who escaped by boat from Vietnam in the 1970s, was one of many Asians told by Trapp and his skinheads, "Go home you yellow-bellied slant-eyed dog-eating Gooks" prior to the time they demolished the Vietnamese center in Omaha.

11

Bob Wolfson, regional director of the Anti-Defamation League, kept tabs on the KKK and skinheads, including their distribution of this poster, in Trapp's distinctive handwriting, protesting Martin Luther King Day.

12

After Michael and Julie Weisser's visit, Larry Trapp renounced the Klan and the Nazi party and got rid of his hate propaganda. "They showed me such love that I couldn't help but love them back," he said. "It's just an experience I've never had before."

13

John Ways, Sr., president of the local chapter of the NAACP; Michael Weisser; Norman Leach, director of Lincoln's Interfaith Council; and Larry Trapp celebrated Larry's renunciation of his past at a dinner at the Weissers' home.

14

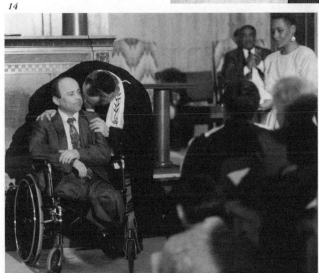

Cantor Weisser gives Larry a hug (Donna Polk is at right) after a service honoring Dr. King. Larry said, "I wasted the first forty years of my life and caused harm to other people....Now I've learned we're one race and one race only."

15

Composer and folksinger Leslie Young sang the song she wrote for Larry, "What Love Has Done," at the interfaith Martin Luther King service at B'nai Jeshurun.

Weisser teenagers Dave, seventeen, and Rebecca, sixteen, clowned with Larry and their dog, Ishtov, after Larry moved into their home on Randolph Street. "Sometimes he can be the sweetest guy," Rebecca said, "but sometimes I just want to strangle him."

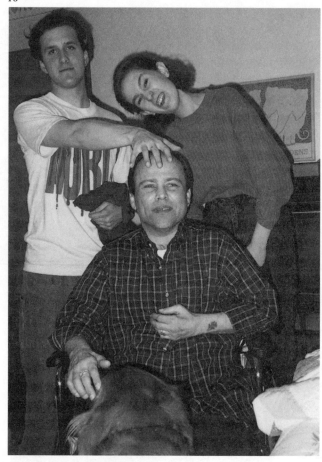

Dina Weisser, sixteen. After Larry moved in, life changed radically for the Weisser teenagers. Not only was Larry in their space, but he was dying.

As Larry's diabetes worsened, he wore his trainman's hat and spent more and more time playing with model trains. His love of trains was intertwined with previously buried memories he had of an affectionate grandfather, who had worked for the Union Pacific.

In March 1992, two university students were arrested for painting swastikas on B'nai Jeshurun. Instead of fining them $100 for a misdemeanor, the judge sentenced them to thirty hours of studying Judaism and the Holocaust with Cantor Weisser.

Larry and his father, John Trapp, of Omaha, reconciled after years of discord. "I'm ready to convert to Judaism now," Larry told Michael, "because I've forgiven my father and my father has forgiven me. I've had a Yom Kippur."

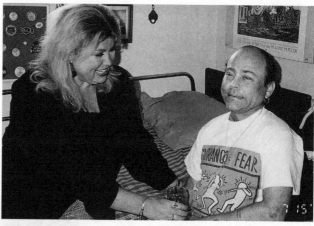

Candy Trapp Bywater, Larry's older sister, visited him from Houston in July and in August, and they laughed together over the hard times they and their younger sister, Deb, had as children. "If you don't laugh, it'll make you cry," said Candy.

On June 5, 1992, after months of intense study, Larry Trapp converted to Judaism in the synagogue he had once planned to bomb. Michael officiated and friends Charles "Griff" Griffin and David Gasser served as witnesses to Larry's conversion.

In the months before Larry Trapp's death in September 1992, he was embraced by the love of the Weisser family—Dave, Michael, Dina, Julie and Rebecca. As Michael said at Larry's funeral, "We know there is more to our lives than what first meets the eye."

do this! Don't you know when a Nazi wants to have you for dinner, he means it literally?"

"It's going to be okay, Davey," Michael said, giving his son a hug and kiss. "I know it is. Don't worry. We'll be home early."

"When's early?"

"Before midnight."

Julie also hugged Dave and reassured him.

But Dave's concern stopped Michael for a moment. "Look, I'm going to call the director of the Interfaith Council and tell him what's happening," Michael said. "If there's any problem, he'll call the police for us."

Norman Leach, at home on 17th Street having dinner with his adopted Vietnamese family, had been in some very threatening situations during his time, especially during his civil rights work with the Congress of Racial Equality, but Michael's call shocked him. In fact, he could hardly believe his ears when he heard Michael say, "Julie and I are going over to visit with Larry Trapp. If you don't hear from us by midnight, you'll need to call the police."

"Just be careful," Norman said, feeling quite worried. "For God's sake, Michael, be careful."

Michael and Julie walked out to their station wagon, got in and fastened their seat belts. But just as Michael was starting the car, Julie said, "Wait! We can't go yet. I think we really need to bring him a gift so he'll know we're sincere. He's probably as leery about us as we've been of him."

Michael agreed rather reluctantly and Julie ran back into the house. What they were doing was wild, and on some level, they knew it. But neither Michael nor Julie had a grasp of the potential death trap they could be walking into—nor were they at all aware of the extreme seriousness of Larry's Klan and Nazi activities. They'd had the one phone call and a big package of hate mail from him, but there was no way they could have known the extent of his other exploits. They had heard about the explosives from the police, but they didn't realize Larry was armed and dangerous at any time.

Neither Michael nor Julie was frightened. Larry Trapp had become a person in their minds. And besides that, Michael and Julie individually and together were risk takers. Often, it seemed, they put themselves on the line. And in this case they were doing what came naturally—which was to spontaneously extend themselves in the most hospitable way. They were like the old pioneer neighbors who would travel for two days to take water and food to a friend they heard was sick. Or perhaps like the families in Europe during World War II who worked with the Resistance, risked danger every day and never imagined another way of operating. What was different about their story was it was 1991 and not many people were in the habit of trying to rescue others.

Julie at the moment was only asking herself what to take Larry Trapp as a peace offering. "I'll take him a book!" she thought initially. "Kahlil Gibran! No, you can't take him a book—he's blind! You can't take him any clothing because you don't know what he wears or what size he is. And you don't have time to stop somewhere and get anything like candy. He's a diabetic—you can't buy a diabetic a box of candy anyway."

All these thoughts were racing through Julie's mind as she walked around their living room and then into their bedroom looking for something to take. When she started looking through a little brass jewelry box on the dresser, she suddenly saw a silver ring of intertwined strands she had bought for Michael two years earlier. Michael liked it, but didn't often wear it. "This is exactly what I want to give Larry," she said as she picked it up. She ran back out to the car and showed the ring to Michael before she put it in his hand.

"Don't you think this is perfect?" she said, fastening her seat belt. "I like it because it's all twisted up, but it's very beautiful. To me it symbolizes how somebody's life can be all twisted up and become very beautiful as well."

"Yeah, it's a good choice," Michael agreed as he gave her back the ring and backed out of the driveway. "I've always thought of it as a brotherhood ring. It's like all those strands could represent all the different kinds of people on this earth."

Julie and Michael drove to a Kentucky Fried Chicken on O Street, where they picked up three fried-chicken dinners, extra french fries and three sodas, and then headed south. They drove through the oldest part of the city, past the State Capitol Building at 16th and K streets, where in the early morning, and late afternoon, just before the sun sets, light ricochets off the Capitol's great golden dome. The dome is topped by a bronze statue of the reaper spreading seeds across the Great

Plains. They drove past the Lancaster County-City Jail, housed in the County-City Courthouse, where Larry had just made his court appearances, toward 817 C Street, between 8th and 9th Streets.

Since Julie had driven by Larry's apartment house so many times before, she knew exactly how to get there. It was an interesting drive because his neighborhood is a study in contrasts. Some of the old houses are in shambles—with boarded-over windows, old car tires, trash, broken toys and rusty bikes leaning against chipped and peeling paint. Yet these houses often share borders with the neatly trimmed and tended yards of beautifully and painstakingly restored old houses scraped and repainted in pale lavender, bright yellow or soft greens, with bright white trim. The front porches of the unkempt houses are often crowded with boxes, broken pots, shirts or old sneakers tossed here or there, while the spruced-up models boast wicker rocking chairs, hanging plants and a look of tranquility and gracious living.

In all the times Julie had had the impulse to stop and try to talk to Larry Trapp, she never had. Now as they drove toward his apartment, she said she wished at least she had sent Larry those Proverbs she had wanted to send. "I should have," she said. "I should have done it."

Often when Julie had driven by, she had noticed police cars parked outside on the street. Tonight no police cars were in sight. Michael slowed the car, and both he and Julie were silent as they passed the small white First African Methodist Episcopal Church, built in 1905, on the corner of 8th and C streets. How strange the state leader of the Ku Klux Klan and the American Nazi Party should live so near a place that had provided the African-American community so much comfort and reflection for such a long time. Yet three houses past the AME Church, Michael and Julie stopped the car outside a plain, square, one-story apartment building with the large "817" slanted at an angle above a row of battered mailboxes. A brown, flat roof jutted out over white stucco walls and brown wood paneling.

Julie looked at the building from inside the warm car and thought the front of the building could easily have been the back since it was so plain and boxlike. "It looks as if someone took a ruler, laid it on the ground, and traced a box like one you would put a small pet into," she said.

When she opened her car door and stepped out onto the icy walk, Julie noticed a small, skinny black woman sitting on the porch of 820 C Street, watching as she and Michael walked up the long concrete sidewalk toward the plain, low-slung building. Julie wondered if Larry had harassed that woman, too.

They stood at the mailboxes for a moment.

"It's number three," Michael said. They walked to the left, and eventually realized they had taken the long route around the strange, bleak building. A chain-link fence separated the apartment's uneven walk from a side yard strewn with empty beer cans, soda bottles and garbage. Two large dogs bared their teeth and barked ferociously at them from the other side of the fence. Julie noticed one of the dogs had a clean, gleaming white coat, which made him appear beautiful and oddly out of place amid the trash and dirt and ice turned into slush around the bottom of the fence. The Weissers didn't know they were looking at the dogs Larry was planning to kill with poisoned meatballs.

Finally, Michael and Julie came to a yellow door with the number 3 on it. A handwritten note in large black block letters said, "Solicitors Not Welcome."

Michael knocked on the door and a voice from inside yelled, "Who is it?"

"The rabbi," Michael answered.

Michael and Julie looked at each other while they waited. The courage of their convictions had carried them this far and now their excitement was edged by apprehension.

The door creaked open slowly and Michael and Julie saw the bearded Larry Trapp in his wheelchair. An automatic weapon—a MAC 10—was slung over the doorknob on the back of the door and a huge Nazi flag hung on the wall behind him.

Larry backed up his wheelchair to make space for Michael and Julie to step into the room. He didn't reach for his gun or even look at it. He merely looked up at them, and in that instant, Julie was struck by Trapp's appearance. She had known his legs were amputated, but his piercing blue eyes, his long dark lashes and his full, thick beard conveyed a sense of wholeness, and she felt it incongruous for a man with such a large presence to be confined to a wheelchair.

"Hi, Larry," Michael said.

"Hi there," Larry said, extending his hand.

Michael walked over and took Larry's outstretched hand in his and said, "It's good to really meet you in person."

At the touch of Michael's warm, strong hand, Larry winced as if he had been hit by a jolt of electricity. Then he broke into tears.

He didn't know what had hit him, but he looked down and began yanking at the two silver swastika rings on his fingers. He clumsily pulled one off and then pulled off the other and held them out in the palm of his hand. "Here, I can't wear these anymore," he said, beginning to cry even harder. "I want you to take these rings. They stand for all the hatred in my life. Will you take them away?"

He put the swastika rings in Michael's hand. Michael put them in his pocket, and he and Julie looked at each other in stunned silence at the coincidence—which seemed miraculous.

"Larry, we brought you a ring, too," Julie said after a moment. "I got this for Michael two years ago, and we wanted to give it to you."

Julie and Michael knelt beside Larry's chair, and Julie slid the ring on Larry's finger. "We wanted you to have this," she said.

Larry traced the strands of silver with the fingers of his other hand and began to sob more loudly. "I'm sorry," he said, trying to catch his breath between fits of weeping. "I'm so sorry for the things I've done."

Michael and Julie put their arms around Larry and hugged him and told him things were going to be okay. Larry bawled like a baby, tears pouring down his face, his nose running. Julie and Michael, overwhelmed by emotion, both started crying, too.

Larry noticed Julie crying and looked at her. "What did I do to her?" he asked Michael.

The three of them laughed, sobbed, hugged and cried, and, as Julie and Michael knelt beside Larry's wheelchair, their arms around him, this Nazi no longer seemed to be a Nazi and Klansman, but suddenly seemed to be their brother. If someone had told them four months earlier they would feel such deep compassion for this despicable racist, they might not have believed it. Yet on this night, as Larry kept crying and crying, apologizing, saying how sorry he was, how bad he felt, both Michael and Julie felt they'd known him and loved him for a long, long time.

After they all stopped crying and blowing their noses on the Kleenex Julie kept providing from her purse, Michael and Julie and Larry talked for three hours.

Julie and Michael sat on beat-up old folding chairs on each side of

Larry, listening to him talk and responding. At one point, Julie got up and found three old scarred plastic plates in Larry's dirty little kitchen area, and Michael started to serve the dinner they'd brought—chicken, mashed potatoes, gravy, cole slaw, biscuits and extra french fries.

"You people can eat chicken?" Larry asked.

"Sure!" Julie said with a laugh. "Why wouldn't we?"

"What's that meat you can't eat?"

"Pork."

"Oh, pork, yeah. I knew there was one like that."

Michael was putting chicken on the plates and he asked Larry, "What do you want—white meat or dark meat?"

"I'm not a Klansman anymore, so give me the dark meat," Larry said, trying to make a joke. "I really was going to ask you if you'd bring me a ham sandwich, but I didn't think that was appropriate."

Larry had a board across his wheelchair to use as a tray, and Julie set the plate Michael had fixed for him on it. She and Michael ate with their plates on their laps. Larry wasn't eating much—he had a big grin on his face and said he was too happy to eat.

At one point, Michael started telling jokes. Michael tells jokes as easily as most people sneeze. Larry started laughing and added a joke of his own.

Larry's joke seemed crude and adolescent to Julie, but listening to him and laughing with him surprised her. She realized she had assumed anyone so racist must be an idiot. But Larry was articulate, quick-witted with puns, even funny. It amazed her to be actually sitting there *laughing* at his jokes! But then again, it amazed her she was sitting there at all. This man was tormented by his own life, and even though jokes cleared the air, he kept going back to the subject of his changed feelings, his sense of urgency about getting out of the Klan, his anxiety about how badly he had hurt other people.

Larry showed them Monica Kuhns' letter and asked Michael to read it out loud. They all listened as Michael read: " '. . . It's not about rules and regulations, things you can and can't do, and people who are perfect. It's about LOVE. Something I know hasn't been a very big part of your life. . . .' "

"She's right, you know," Larry said. "I feel it already. She told me, 'I know you try to intellectualize everything, but some things you have to accept by faith.' It's also funny how she told me, if you give up all that bitterness, hatred and hurt, 'you will be changed in ways you won't believe.' This may sound crazy, but I already feel like I'm changed in ways I can't believe."

Larry began sobbing again as he repeated how sorry he was for everything he'd done as a Klansman and a Nazi. He told them he'd trained to be a mercenary soldier in Rhodesia before, but he knew now how everything he'd been doing all these years was wrong. He said he couldn't stand it anymore. He wanted to quit the Klan, quit the Nazi Party, quit racism—and try to make up to everyone for all the terrible things he'd done.

In Larry's cramped, dirty apartment, Julie noticed his battered dresser, his dirty kitchen, his small refrigerator and table covered with papers and junk. He had a television at the end of the bed and a box of what looked like porno tapes. Her eyes kept being drawn especially to the posters and pictures of Adolf Hitler and his pals, and to the swastikas, Nazi flags, stacks and stacks of Klan books and magazines and pamphlets, guns, dirty clothes. She was sitting next to his MAC-10 when Larry said, "I want to get rid of all of this hate stuff. I want to get all of this Klan and Nazi stuff out of my house and out of my life." He waved toward several cardboard boxes sitting nearby. Stuffed into the boxes were Klan robes, books, Nazi stickers and other racist and anti-Semitic paraphernalia. He said he'd started packing up stuff, and he wondered whether Michael and Julie would mind getting those boxes and everything else hateful out of his apartment. "I don't want any of it in here," he said. "I want it all out of my life."

Larry said he'd been thinking a lot lately about what he'd been doing most of his life—and it had seemed wrong somehow. "I've been talking to my people lately, telling them I think maybe this whole thing is goofy," he said. "It's not making any sense how we're hurting people. Our major problem is the government. The government is not giving us, us meaning all people, it's not giving us the proper tools to work with and educate all people equally."

"You've been saying this to your Klan members?" Michael asked.

"To my colleagues. They say, 'You're crazy! We gotta fight the blacks. We gotta fight the Jews.' But fighting doesn't help anybody."

Larry also talked about his life as a child. Weaving in and out of the past and present, he talked about his mother, who had died a year earlier in August. "She was really mean to me," Larry said, "but I loved her anyway." He began to cry again as he talked about both of his parents. He said his father was especially mean.

"He'd slap me across the face," Larry said, "across the head. You don't slap a child in the head or face area because of hearing damage, you know. But he'd punch me, he'd slap me around. Sometimes he'd whip me with his belt.

"But this one year, my father gave me a train set, and it was a big thing to me," Larry said, still crying. "It was the only thing my dad had ever done that made me feel real close to him. He made a board and put the train on it so it would run on the track, and it was near his work area in a storage room. It was a really big thing. I loved that train set and I loved to play with it. Anyway, my mother got angry at me about something once—I don't even remember what it was anymore—and she came down and took a can of deck paint—you know how thick deck paint is—and just poured it all over the tracks and ruined it."

Larry tried to stop crying, but just as the tears would start to dry up, he would begin to cry again, as if he had been storing tears for years and years until this moment. And as he talked and cried, Julie had the insight that even though Larry was a grown man who acted so macho and tough, he really was just a little boy who had been waiting for someone to love him and care about him and help him get out of this ugly, evil life he'd gotten himself into.

Michael was struck by what a twisted life this man had lived because his energy had been so misdirected.

Before Michael and Julie left that night, they hugged Larry and told him they loved him. They couldn't carry all the racist stuff Larry wanted out of his apartment, but they agreed to each carry off one box and promised they would come back the following day.

"I don't know what to say," Larry said between more tears. "I've been so terrible to you and to so many people. I can't believe I hated you so much. I just can't believe it. How can you ever forgive me?"

"We do forgive *you*," Julie said. "We do."

"I don't know how you can," Larry said.

"Look at it this way," Michael said. "We don't forgive what you did, but we forgive *you*. Nobody can condone cruelty, but forgiving the person who was cruel and is now remorseful is a different thing."

"I don't know what, but I . . . I just feel different," Larry said, putting the palm of his hand on his stomach. "I've never felt like this before."

"When you stop hating, you make room for love," Michael said. "Love is about the most powerful force on earth, and that's probably what you're feeling."

"I'll tell you one thing. It sure feels different," Larry said. "And it feels better. Like, I feel better. If this is love, it's a hell of a lot better than hate, excuse my language."

Michael and Julie got home before midnight—much to the relief of Dave, who had not yet told Dina and Rebecca their parents had gone to have dinner with a Nazi. Norman Leach—who had been waiting anxiously by his telephone—exhaled deeply when he heard Michael's voice.

"Norman, you're not going to believe this," Michael said. "I wouldn't believe it myself if I hadn't been there and seen it with my own eyes."

UNMASKING

THE DRAGON

Chapter 14

Our definition of healing is to touch with softness and kind-
ness, with mercy and awareness, that which has been with-
drawn in fear and judgment and distrust.
—*STEPHEN AND ONDREA LEVINE*

Sunday morning, November 17, 1991, Michael and Julie were in the kitchen with Rebecca, Dina and Dave, telling them what had happened the night before. "He was ready to be rescued," Julie said, pouring herself a tall glass of orange juice. "He basically just dumped his whole life in our lap. Everything he had wanted to say to someone, I think he said it."

"I can't believe you guys went to his house," Rebecca said, tossing her auburn hair back from her face. "If I was the adult in this situation, I would have called his little ass up and reamed him out. He would have to earn my trust first and earn it good."

Michael was holding his coffee cup in both hands. "Rebecca, Rebecca—try to use better language," he complained.

"Hey, Avi, I know, but you know what I mean," Rebecca said, calling Michael a Hebrew nickname she had given him.

"And I know what you mean, but just how fantastic is this, you guys," Julie said, sipping her juice. "I mean, here is this person who was in mercenary training in a survivalist camp in Florida and he really wanted to go to Rhodesia because he had this tremendous hatred for blacks and he wanted to go over there and fight for the whites—"

"Did he go?" Dave interrupted.

"No, he said he learned how to use machine guns and knives and make explosives, but he didn't have enough money to finish the training. He grew up hearing 'kike' and 'nigger' and all the derogatory names, and he's just spent his whole life and all his energies hating and now he's actually *quitting* the Klan and he's going to stop doing all this horrible, hateful, prejudiced stuff! I mean, isn't that an incredible miracle?"

"If it's real," Dina said, putting her arm around Dave's shoulder and leaning on him. "But remember, when we do something wrong, we have to earn back your trust—so you shouldn't be too trusting of him."

"That's right, Mom," Becca said. "Make him earn your trust. Dina should know. You grounded her for nine weeks!"

"Because of two D's!" Dina said, beginning to intertwine her long brown hair into a tiny braid down the side of her face.

"Right, but you brought home three A's and two B's the next grading period," Julie said, "so what did that prove?"

"Cruel and unusual punishment sometimes works," Dave said, moving toward the door to answer the doorbell. "It did on me when I first moved here. But just because it works doesn't make you like it."

"You have to meet him, and when you meet him, you'll understand what we mean," Michael said.

When Dave opened the front door, the first person he saw was Eva Sartori, a survivor of the Holocaust and a member of the B'nai Jeshurun congregation. Eva, along with Suzanne Kalish and Barbara Johnson Frank, had driven by to hand-deliver an invitation to Suzanne's daughter's birthday party, and they all decided to stop in for a quick visit. When they sat down at the kitchen table for coffee, Michael and Julie started telling them about Larry's phone call, Michael's return calls and the time they had spent with Larry the night before. Like Norman Leach, the three women could hardly believe their ears.

Julie carried in one of the boxes from the trunk of the car to show them some of the stuff Larry Trapp had asked them to take out of his house the previous night. "You're not going to believe this," Julie said. "There're *tons* more where this came from, too. It's just not the kind of clothing or literature most ordinary people ever see." Barbara, Julie and the kids picked up Larry's Klan robes and pieces of Nazi literature with disgust and fascination.

Eva Sartori was flabbergasted. It was difficult for her to try to equate these clothes and activities with the kind of danger she had known as a child when she and her parents hid from the Nazis and survived World War II by living with Russian partisans in the Polish forest. One-and-a-half-million Jewish children in Europe had been killed by the Nazis during the Holocaust, and Eva was one of only 10,000 to 100,000 Jewish youngsters under the age of sixteen who survived.

This stuff of Larry Trapp's was sickening, but from what she had read about Larry Trapp, she had determined he was the equivalent of an isolated, small-time thug. Examining a Klan hood with a snap-on mask which appeared to be new, however, she was shocked by a manufacturer's label sewn into the back. "I'd always thought the Klan here was more an individual thing," she said. "The fact these were mass produced alarms me. I find that very scary."

Dave was repulsed by what he saw and wasn't at all sure he wanted to go with Michael and Julie to Larry Trapp's. Rebecca said she never wanted to meet him, and Dina said even though she thought it was awesome that Michael and Julie were helping Larry, to count her out of any visits, too. Dave observed that maybe Larry *wanted* to change but wouldn't be able to. If he had to help Michael pack and help carry more stuff out of the apartment sometime in the next day or two, of course he would, he said. But he didn't much like the idea of Michael and Julie going over to the Nazi's C Street apartment for a second visit. Neither did Rebecca or Dina. The whole proposition still seemed dangerous and unreal.

Michael and Julie, however, still were thrilled from their experience of the night before. They believed they had witnessed an almost unbelievable conversion—something so extraordinary and inexplicable it seemed they literally were in God's hands. The exchange of rings in and of itself seemed like a miracle.

For the nine years Michael and Julie had been together, reaching out to people had been an ordinary, everyday thing—and so their response to Larry Trapp in and of itself didn't seem out of the ordinary. Everything about the way they lived their lives implied they would respond this way; it was part of their pattern. They always loaned their cars, loaned what little money they had, loaned their time and support and insights to their friends. If you had any kind of problem—from a sick dog you needed to drive to the vet, to counseling for a pregnant teenage daughter, to comfort for a dying friend or parent, you could call Julie or

Michael. At the same time, if you wanted to laugh hysterically or go out to a movie or dinner, you dialed the same number. Both Julie and Michael had a rare capacity to accept people with all their ugly warts, foibles and transgressions—possibly because they believed they themselves had so many flaws and imperfections. Part of the way they had coped with their own complicated and often contradictory experiences was to reach out to others, to extend themselves. Michael explained the source of his empathy: "I used to be a total jerk. Now I'm only a jerk part of the time."

Something about the previous night's experience with Larry Trapp, however, had felt transforming to themselves as well as to Larry. When they drove once again to the apartment complex at 817 C Street, they laughed with pleasure and anticipation. Maybe Larry Trapp would have changed his mind, but they didn't think so—not for a minute. To satisfy Dave's concern, they once again called Norman Leach to let him know where they were going and said they'd call on their return.

When Larry opened his door to them, the early Sunday afternoon light danced across the dust balls and grime of his floor and cast shadows that made his apartment look even more barren, dirty and dismal than it had the night before. But the man himself looked immaculate. He had gotten up early, lathered his face with soap and shaved off his thick wiry brown beard and mustache. Then he had washed his face and arms and changed into a clean shirt. Now, when he smiled, two dimples appeared in his cheeks. His small, straight nose and his wide oval-shaped face seemed to shine. Julie and Michael both noticed the difference as they hugged him hello again.

"I have to get rid of everything I've been using as a front," Larry explained, "and that included my beard. Somehow my beard seemed part of that whole life I don't want anymore."

"Larry, you have dimples!" Julie said.

"Yeah," he said sheepishly. "I never wanted anyone to see 'em 'cause they make me look too young. I never wanted to look young. I wanted to look tough."

Overnight, more than the surface had changed. The face of the dragon literally looked transformed. It had lost its hateful expression. Larry looked youthful and almost innocent—like a little boy waiting to open his Christmas or Chanukah present. Julie and Michael both were startled by the light in his bright blue eyes. And he looked at them so directly when they spoke to him, it was hard to believe he was almost blind. His eyes seemed watchful, even though their movement was never quite parallel. The light brown hair on top of his large head had grown in like down on baby geese. His skin also looked soft, almost sweet.

Larry also *felt* unlike himself. The world had a rosy glow to it that gave him an oddly alert, unusual and heightened sensation. It was as if he had awakened on some different planet. If he'd been an astronaut taking off into a different realm, he would have been more prepared than he had been for this. He remembered he'd been thinking things didn't make much sense anymore, but today he had the feeling he'd been touched by some kind of magic, something he couldn't explain. He was excited, but he also was weird and unlike himself, and he told Michael and Julie he felt as if he were on the edge of the first important day of his life. He'd wanted to make it count. After he washed and shaved off his beard, the first thing he had done was write a letter on Klan letterhead to the White Knights of the Ku Klux Klan, which he showed Michael and Julie. It said:

November 16, 1991

To whom it may concern:

Please accept this as my resignation from the White Knights of the Ku Klux Klan, effective immediately. This resignation is due to personal reasons.

L. R. Trapp,
Grand Dragon, Realm of Nebraska.

Larry had signed the letter and also made a list of all the other hate organizations with which he was affiliated, including the American Nazi Party, to whom he would write similar letters.

Then, anxiously, his hands shaking, he had dialed Donna Polk's telephone number. When he got her answering machine, he identified himself as "Larry Trapp—*formerly* Grand Dragon of the White Knights of the Ku Klux Klan," and said he wanted her to know he was sorry for everything he'd ever done to her and to the black community. He said he'd been thinking things over and he had been wrong—real wrong—to do the things he did, and he would try to make it up to her somehow. He would understand if she couldn't forgive him or believe he was sincere, he said, but he was going to work to prove to her how sorry he was and how much he wanted her forgiveness. When he hung up the phone from that call, he could hardly breathe. She must hate him. She would never forgive him, he was sure. How could she? He didn't deserve forgiveness.

Later, after he drank some water and calmed his breathing, he left a message for Robert Wolfson on the Anti-Defamation League's answering machine in Omaha:

> "This is Larry Trapp, uh, let me say *formerly* of the White Knights of the Ku Klux Klan of the Realm of Nebraska. I just want to let you know, if you want to know of my activities, you can contact Rabbi Michael Weisser of the South Side temple here in Lincoln, Nebraska. I'll be working closely with him. . . . I say *formerly* of the Klan [because] Michael Weisser is helping me. I've never thought that I could love a Jew as a brother, but him and his wife are fantastic people and I think they've helped me to start a new life. And I just want you people to know that. . . . My number is 475-9025 here in Lincoln. Please contact me at any time."

Larry hated to think about the last time he'd called Bob Wolfson and left the message: "Adolf Hitler was right and you Jews all lie! We're here to let America know that you're all a bunch of filthy liars." It was so strange: Both messages were on the same tape. This message came from the same voice, but it sounded subdued; it had lost its bitter, acid edge.

During their visit that Sunday afternoon, Larry told Michael and Julie he had a lot more calls to make. He was going to call Monica Kuhns, and he planned to call each and every person he'd ever harassed to apologize personally—he didn't care how many weeks or months it might take to get to everybody and to try to make amends. He was going to call more people in the black community and the Asian community. He said he was ashamed of how terrible he had been to them.

Then he started crying hard. Something horrible, he said, was what he'd realized during the night as he lay in bed unable to sleep. It was this: He had known all along he was being terrible. He had *wanted* to be terrible—he set out to be bad. He'd just been on a big power trip the whole time. "I *liked* being able to make people afraid," he said. "I liked being a bully. I'd roll down the street and I felt proud: 'Nobody is going to mess with me.' "

Larry rambled as he listed previous transgressions and "enemies." He said among others that he needed to call and apologize to the gay and lesbian student organization at the University of Nebraska, where he'd left ugly messages against homosexuals. Each person or organization he mentioned was a confession, a source of more tears. He had no end of calls to make, no apparent end of tears.

Once again, Michael sat on one side of Larry and Julie sat on the other. Michael's hand was on Larry's shoulder and Julie held Larry's hand and stroked it as he talked.

"Me and God haven't been on very good terms lately," Larry said, beginning to cry. "Maybe never really—even though I grew up a Catholic and all and did a lot of Bible reading, I don't think I ever was thinkin' much about God. I just wanted to impress people. I don't even know if I believed in God or not. Really, I don't think I ever believed in God."

"You know, Larry, there's so much we don't understand," Michael said. "This universe is a big place. But God exists, I know that."

"I'm beginning to think so, too," Larry said.

"Do you want to know something?" Michael asked somewhat rhetorically. "Do you want to know when I really *knew* beyond any doubt whatsoever that God exists?"

"Sure," Larry said, blowing his nose on a Kleenex Julie handed him.

"Once, when we were living in North Carolina, Julie and I had an appointment with somebody at Chapel Hill, at the University of North Carolina," Michael continued. "We got there early and we didn't want to hang around an office so we walked into the planetarium instead, and the show that day was the Milky Way Galaxy. So we're sitting there, and the planetarium goes dark and you see the sky up there and the representation of the sky. All of a sudden, the illusion that you were really under the sky was broken when a young woman, who was reading the narration, began talking and put an arrow up on the ceiling—on the dome—and she was really bored because she had done this a million times probably, and must have been a graduate student or working off a grant or something. As she spoke, and this was kind of odd in North Carolina, she didn't sound like a southerner. She said in this perfectly flat, monotone voice: 'This is the Milky Way Galaxy, a small and insignificant galaxy, one among billions of galaxies. A beam of light (and then she showed an arrow) traveling at 186,000 miles per second would take more than 120,000 years to cross the Milky Way Galaxy at its narrowest point.'

"So I heard her say that and it was like a revelation—a lightbulb went off in my head. Here is the Milky Way Galaxy, small and insignificant—right? And it would take something going 186,000 miles a second 120,000 years to cross it at its narrowest point—and, you know, she was bored with that. So when I thought of it, I thought of the immensity—I mean, I don't understand 186,000 miles a second, and I don't understand 120,000 years either. But the universe is so immense, and so unexplainable, and so incomprehensible, that for there not to be a creator of it all is ludicrous because there is no other explanation.

"I remember, also, just as a tag on to this, I went to a class one time where a professor was giving a lecture about the finite universe. He showed how there could be a model of a finite universe and the model looked like a sideways figure eight—which he drew in the middle of this big chalkboard. I don't remember all the details of it, but his idea was that the universe was finite and the reason it looked infinite to us was that it turned back upon itself—like a figure eight—so that we had the illusion that it was infinite, but it was really finite.

"So this freshman student comes up to the front of the room and says 'Hey, Professor, can I ask you a question?' The student takes a piece of chalk and draws an X above the figure eight, like about six inches above it. 'In this model of a finite universe, what's up here?' In other words, what is this universe in—this finite universe. You know, if it's finite, what's up here? And the professor had no answer. You know, this freshman student stumped him.

"It's interesting. All the people I know who are scientists, who I know personally, they all believe in God. I mean they don't believe in God according to the Roman Catholic Church, or according to Judaism, or according to some Protestant denomination, but they believe that there is no explanation for things without a God. Even Albert Einstein believed in God. He didn't follow any particular religion, you know, he was not an observant Jew or anything like that, but he understood that there had to be a God."

Larry didn't say anything when Michael had finished. He sat, his face in deep concentration as he thought about Michael's words. "Yeah," he said finally. "It makes a lot of sense. It's a long way from the kind of stuff I've been burying myself in.

"I've got a lot to learn before I can help other racists change," he said. "I've got a lot to figure out. For so long, I've just believed what Nazis say, and I haven't really investigated anything. I mean, like I was thinking about what you said last night, when you told me Jews don't run the government, and you asked me, 'Have you ever looked around at actually how many Jews are in public office? Have you ever looked at the percentages? Do you know how many Jews are presidents of banks?' Well, I don't know any of that stuff, not really. I couldn't believe there really are hardly any Jewish bank presidents. Is that really true, are you sure?"

"It's true, Larry. Jews simply don't run the banks; look at all the names of bank presidents and you'll rarely see Jews. Now psychiatrists are a different matter—and scientists. There you can find Jews, but that doesn't run the economy."

"What you said about me—that I only know one side of things, like a lot of propaganda, and I don't really see the larger picture—well, I realize it's true. It is. I still got a lot of screwy ideas I'll need to straighten out. I still got a lot of hate in me." Larry said he wanted to learn more about the way the world really worked, and he was going to try his hardest to do it.

After Michael and Julie left—with Michael promising to stop by again in the morning—Larry Trapp began making a number of other telephone calls, a process that would continue for several days. Quite a number of these calls were to his Klan members, skinheads and fellow racists, telling them he was quitting the "racialist" movement. The calls he made to apologize to people affected him, but contact with his now former colleagues affected him in a different way.

He felt a familiar nervousness as he dialed the phone numbers he knew by heart. Sometimes he would begin the call by thinking he would try to be nice and maybe make another racist begin to do some thinking, but however he began, he impulsively moved into a hostile exchange. Forty-eight hours earlier, he had been an ally, but now these racists formed something of a new enemies' list. He called his national affiliates one after the other: Dennis Mahon, Grand Dragon of the White Knights of the KKK in Oklahoma, WAR leader Tom Metzger, David Duke, founder of the National Association for the Advancement of White People in New Orleans, Thomas Robb, who was sometimes called the "Klan pastor" and was national director of the Knights of the KKK in Arkansas, and other racist leaders. Larry's habits of hate were deep, and while these weren't hate calls, the posture of combat he fell into when he connected with his old allies was the pose to which he was accustomed.

When Trapp called Tom Metzger, for instance, he called not in an effort to change Metzger, but rather to confront him and express his fury. "I want you to know I'm fed up with you and with the racialist movement," Trapp told Metzger. "The whole thing, including all this crap about race war is full of shit," he said, "and you're full of shit. I want you to know you can *count me out!*"

Metzger's response, which Trapp recorded, sounded dismissive and sarcastic: "If you want to be one of the good-for-nothing herd," he said, "then go ahead and join up with the herd."

Larry left Dennis Mahon a message that he was resigning from the Klan, and Mahon called him back. They spoke at length and Trapp tried to explain to Dennis Mahon why he was leaving the Klan and how they'd been doing the wrong thing.

"Hey, Larry, what's the deal with being friends with a Jew rabbi?" Mahon said. "What are you doing bein' friendly with Jews?"

"Listen, Dennis, what are you trying to do—pick my friends for me? I pick my own friends."

"Oh no, I'm not doing that," Mahon said. "I have a lot of Jewish friends, too, but I don't associate with 'em."

"Now that's a contradiction in terms," Larry said. "If they're friends but you don't associate with them, then they darn sure aren't friends. I've found out people aren't as bad as I thought. You've got to give people a chance."

"Sounds to me like a race traitor talking," Mahon said.

They talked some more and Larry tried to convince him that violence isn't going to solve anything, but Mahon was aggressive and the conversation deteriorated.

"Listen, Dennis, I want to hang up on you now 'cause I don't have the time or inclination to talk to racist scum," Larry said before he hung up the phone.

A split second later, the phone rang again. "Larry, don't ever hang up on me like that," Mahon said. "And don't ever call me racist scum. In fact, I think I'm going to take the next plane and fly over there to Lincoln, Nebraska, and pay you a visit so we can have a man-to-man talk."

Larry knew what "a man-to-man talk" in that tone of voice meant.

"Dennis, this is a free country and you can do whatever you want to do," Larry said in a calm, even voice. "You're more than welcome to come to Lincoln, Nebraska, or to Timbuktu or wherever you want to go. I can't stop you. But I can tell you if someone knocks on my door and you happen to be standing there, right then and there you better bend over and kiss your ass goodbye, because they are going to be sending your ass back to Oklahoma in a wooden box."

Trapp knew denouncing the white supremacist movement would make him a traitor to his former colleagues, but he couldn't worry about that, he said, because something a lot more powerful than any feeling he'd had as a Klansman had come into his life. For once, he said, he was determined to do the right thing. He'd spent his life doing the wrong things. Now he had a chance for a new beginning and he wasn't going to blow it.

When Michael Weisser stopped by Trapp's apartment again on Monday morning, Trapp told him he'd decided he wanted to share information he had about the racist movement with law-enforcement officials. He asked Michael to make a call for him to Ed Humphries, an FBI agent who had investigated him in the past. Agent Humphries had been in touch with Larry several times, and Larry thought Humphries should know what was happening. If he was going to change, Larry said, he had to prove it by following through and *really* trying to make a difference. These hate groups were only good for spreading hate, and he wasn't going to do that anymore. But he also was going to try to *stop* the hatred, stop the spread of this evil he had known and embraced so tightly.

While Larry Trapp was telling Michael about his decision, forty-five-year-old Charles Griffin was sitting in his car outside Larry's apartment waiting for Michael to reemerge. "Griff," a member of B'nai Jeshurun, a social worker, therapist and a friend of the Weissers, was worried. When he had heard about Trapp's change, his initial reaction was to say, "Michael, I don't think you want to be doing this." As a Vietnam veteran who had seen too much action, Griff was used to warfare, and he looked at any close association with Trapp as walking through something of a minefield.

"I didn't want Michael going in there without being armed," Griff said. "I thought at this point Larry really hadn't changed all that much. I also had some difficulty with it because Larry was known to have friends who could hurt you. My view was, it was dangerous for Michael to do this and I was not thrilled with it.

"I insisted on going along and waiting in the car. Our deal was, Michael would go inside and I would wait outside and pretty much if he wasn't back in X amount of time or if I heard anything, I was going to get the cops there real quick. But that was a normal precaution. I was insisting on it, I was demanding it, because it was too dangerous to do alone."

When Larry said he wanted to speak to the FBI, Michael had to suppress a smile. He knew he could trust his own instincts when it came to judging character—and he also knew change when he saw it. He appreciated Griff's concern, but he could hardly wait to tell him this news. Larry also said he wanted to contact Bill Dietrich, a police intelligence officer in Omaha who had approached Trapp and had kept a close watch on him. In addition, Larry wanted to call Robert Wolfson and schedule an afternoon session that might help Wolfson in his job of monitoring the activities of hate groups in the tristate region he covered for the Anti-Defamation League.

When Dietrich and Humphries came to Larry's apartment for debriefing sessions, Larry shared confidential information with them about his racist recruiting and about Klan and skinhead activity in Nebraska and the Midwest. "I regret everything I did," he told Humphries. "Having those thoughts, scaring so many people . . . trying to get them killed. If it hadn't been for Michael and Julie Weisser, I hate to think about what I might have done . . . I wanted to kill. I was waiting for the opportunity to kill somebody. I thank God I never got the chance."

As FBI Agent Humphries watched Larry's face and listened to his apologies and his words, he got tears in his own eyes. "This is the best thing that ever could have happened to him," Humphries said. "It's something you don't see. Larry Trapp got an opportunity of a lifetime— a second chance—and it was a beautiful thing to see."

Initially, Bob Wolfson wasn't equally moved. Even after he'd gotten Larry's message on his answering machine and talked to Michael, he was skeptical, to say the least. "When I got to Larry's apartment, I realized it was crazy for me to have gone into his room, where he had a shotgun on one side of the room and a MAC-10 on the other," Wolfson said later. "It was crazy! The only reason I did it was because I knew who Michael was. I believe in Michael. When he tells me something, I think he is a pretty good judge. Had he not been there before, I would not have done what I did. Which was nuts. I should have insisted that Larry come to me and not vice versa. I mean, look, if it happens again, and it will never happen again, but if it did, I would never do that again.

"Anyway, Larry shared information—he was very open. And he confirmed a lot of things we knew from our monitoring activities. But I didn't wake up the morning after meeting him and say, 'Now here's a man who has changed.' I never woke up and said, 'Now here's a nice guy.' I woke up and felt, 'Now here's a man who is a complicated, troubled, interesting, intelligent person who has lived a very strange life.' "

In the meantime, Michael took Dave to Larry's apartment, where they began to pack up all the racist paraphernalia Larry wanted to get out of his life. They pulled books out of the bookshelves—*Hitler and the Germans, The Goebbels Diaries, In Hitler's Germany, Hitler: Memoirs of a Confidant, Mein Kampf* and *The Dispossessed Majority,* among others. They loaded them in cardboard boxes, along with stained and ugly "White Power" T-shirts they didn't really want to touch, KKK berets, U.S. Army weapons manuals and hundreds of grotesque racist pamphlets and reprints.

"I can see why you want to purge yourself of all this garbage," Michael said. "It's pretty unbelievable."

"All this stuff deserves a fire, and a fire is all it deserves," Larry said as he watched and listened from his wheelchair to the movements and sounds of Michael and Dave packing up his stacks of papers and books.

C. J. Schepers, a young journalist who covered religion for the *Lincoln Journal,* knocked on the door of Larry's apartment as Michael and Dave were packing boxes. C. J. had called Michael earlier that morning, and he had told her Trapp had made a complete turnaround. "Cantor Weisser had been telling me off and on for several months what was going on with this guy," she said later, "and Reverend Leach and other clergy who also were concerned had given me copies of letters he'd sent some Asian people, and I had thought, 'What a creep!' Cantor Weisser had also been telling me about how he was calling this guy and trying to turn the tables on him. I had just thought, 'He shouldn't be doing that,' you know."

After Schepers had knocked on Larry's front door, she wished she had never left the newsroom. Curiosity more than anything had brought her. She didn't have a clue whether an article would come out of this visit, but she had wanted to see the Klan and Nazi stuff for herself and talk to Trapp—whom she thought must be "a real creepy, disgusting flake"—about his apparent change of feeling. Schepers admired Weisser from her coverage of religious news; she knew he was a person who reached out and made connections on a daily basis. And not only to his own congregation. Several non-Jewish people in the community had told her about the spontaneous support he had extended them. One woman, a Lutheran, told C.J. her son had been deeply involved in a cult until Michael—"that miracle man"—agreed to talk with him. Schepers also knew Weisser made weekly visits to the local jail and to the penitentiary to talk with inmates about spirituality. And every Christmas, he opened B'nai Jeshurun's doors for the distribution of some five thousand interfaith Christmas presents for needy families in Lincoln. While getting Larry Trapp out of the Klan didn't seem really possible, if anyone could help it happen, Weisser would be the one, and Schepers was intrigued by the possibility.

Actually stepping inside Trapp's apartment, however, gave her chills. "It was very strange," she said. "He had guns in a corner, and it was so peculiar. At first I just didn't know how to act around him. I felt kind of weird, I didn't want to be there . . . I guess I just basically didn't trust him. I didn't want him to pull anything over on me, so I was very leery."

Trapp seemed to intuit her discomfort. "Few people will believe I'm changed," he told her shortly after they shook hands, "and I can't blame them at all for that. But I'm going to prove it—I don't care how long it takes—I'll prove it for the rest of my life."

Trapp's eyes filled with tears as he talked about the love Michael and Julie had shown him—a love he never before had encountered.

Michael gave credit to a higher source. "I believe it's God in his life," he said. "There's no other way to understand it. I think it's a miracle."

As for Michael's assessment, Trapp said, "I'm not sure if I believe in all this reborn or born-again stuff, but I think maybe God has been there all along, and has been knocking. I think finally He just broke the door down."

Talking to Larry, Michael and Julie—who had taken a break from her job and stopped by Larry's—Schepers was moved. "After a couple of hours, I really felt there was a lot of love in the room, especially on the part of the Weissers, and I felt like Larry had given in to that," Schepers said. "Every hurt that was in him was pouring out. It was like, 'Somebody really cares about me—these people care about me.'

"Probably another thing that tied me to him was when he started talking about his home life and the abuse he had endured in reform school. I think that really struck a chord for me because I'd had an abusive home life, and I think there was a connection there. I can't explain it, but there's a connection you feel when people who have been abused have been deeply hurt and you can sense it. It's not an excuse, but it does help explain, it does help you understand their experience."

Being at Larry Trapp's apartment that day was quite emotional, but it also was disorienting, almost surreal. Listening to Larry talk about his change of heart, and having to handle and pack all the horrific literature, posters and pictures was especially unsettling for Dave. "When I went there, I didn't really believe it," Dave said. "At first I had thought, this is just like a waste of time. Julie and Dad are off on some kind of tangent. I mean, like, they're always into helping people and going out on a limb, but this was going too far. Then when I met him, I wasn't sure. I thought maybe there *is* something to this."

Julie, too, suddenly was reeling. That same day, after Dave and Michael filled the trunk of her car with boxes of Larry Trapp's Nazi and Klan stuff—which felt odd in and of itself—Julie headed back to work at Dr. Timothy Fischer's office. She drove past the Lincoln Public Library and was cruising down O Street, trying to catch the lights, when it suddenly horrified her to realize anyone looking into her back window would see a Confederate flag, a Nazi flag, swastikas and Nazi posters—overflows from the white supremacist stuff in her trunk. She and Michael had figured they would put the stuff in their garage temporarily, and after the police checked it all out, give it to a museum or something. But she couldn't believe she was driving through downtown Lincoln carrying all this filthy rubbish. What if her car broke down or she was in an accident—how could she explain it? "I thought, 'What if I have a flat tire or I have to go to a service station and I have to open up the trunk and there's all these Nazi posters, swastikas and stickers, KKK books and stationery, Ku Klux Klan hoods and boxes of hate materials in it?" Julie said. "It would be really, really embarrassing!"

When she got back to Dr. Fischer's office, Julie took one of the cardboard boxes out of the trunk and carried it up the stairs to the office, to show Dr. Fischer. "Here was all this Klan and Nazi stuff, and I was like still in amazement," Julie said, "and Dr. Fischer and everybody who worked there, they all came into the room that we sit and have coffee in and everyone was looking at it and saying, 'Oh, we don't believe this! This is not to be believed!' And I could not believe it either! I was stunned, really stunned."

On November 19, 1991, Larry sent a letter to all the news media and "other concerned individuals" apologizing for "the abusive language and racial epithets that I have used towards various races and individuals in the state of Nebraska.

"My apology may not be accepted by all members of the public, and I can understand this," he said, "but I will prove my intensions [sic] to people of all races, creeds and religions." He extended special apologies to Karen Kilgarin of KETV-TV, Channel 7, in Omaha and Pat Persaud of WOWT-TV, Channel 6, in Omaha and others he had offended by his "blasphemous remarks in the past.

"It may be hard for you to believe, but I am sure . . . you will see that you can indeed 'teach an old dog new tricks,' " he wrote. "I have a great task ahead of me. My task from this point on is working with and helping one race, and one race only . . . the *human* race." He ended his letter: "May God bless the people of all religions, colors and nations."

In his note, Trapp said he had been advised not to give any statements to the media for a period of time. But in point of fact, no one considered it a big story. A couple of local television channels announced the news of Trapp's apology, but otherwise, local journalists left it alone.

Larry's lawyer, Susan Tast, realized that for safety purposes, the less attention Trapp got, the better, and she offered to take calls on his behalf. "The change was amazing," she said. "Larry came into the office several times, and you cannot believe the difference in him. Physically! You could see it. He really was a changed person. I absolutely believe that he was genuine and that he turned his life around. I don't think this was a ploy. He had no reason as far as the court case went to turn his life around. So there was not any reason. He didn't do this to get out of trouble. That was already taken care of. He'd already been sentenced—and it was a light sentence. Larry had no reason, nothing to gain by doing this. Nothing monetary, nothing from the courts or anything else. I truly believe in my heart that Larry saw the light."

Nevertheless, Tast worried about his security.

Wolfson, too, had concern about Trapp's safety. "From the minute he decided to change, he was quite aggressive with Dennis Mahon and Tom Metzger and all those people," Wolfson said. "These are not people in my opinion who play around. I believed from the very beginning that Larry was in danger. And I was particularly worried about Julie and Michael. I felt they and their children also were exposed to danger when they were with him. I always considered violence a possibility."

It had become clear Larry should move. FBI Agent Humphries and Bill Dietrich agreed with Wolfson that Larry's defection from the Klan put him in danger, and Dennis Mahon's statement about paying Trapp a visit was no comfort. The risk might or might not be imminent, but it was no secret that defectors from the white-is-right movement often were dealt with harshly. White supremacists courted, and fed on, violence, and when one of their own became a "traitor," the traitor was punished. A few years earlier, when skinhead leader Greg Withrow defected from the Aryan Youth Movement and denounced Tom Metzger and the racist movement on national television, he barely lived to tell about it. Withrow's neo-Nazi ex-colleagues in Sacramento, California, beat and kicked him, gagged him, literally *nailed* his hands to a cross built of two-by-fours (so he wouldn't write anymore), slit his throat and chest (so he wouldn't talk anymore) and left him to die. Withrow lived only because a black couple found him, called the police and helped him get to a hospital.

Larry wanted to move because he was afraid something similar might happen to him, and if it did, he knew he wouldn't live to tell about it. He was already half-gone as it was, he joked. Night after night, he was kept awake by noises outside his apartment and by his fears of the Klan coming after him. Again he sat up holding his MAC-10 in his lap, and again he kept his shotgun loaded and ready for backup.

Two of his nurses helped him locate a new apartment at 1700 J Street, and the Red Cross scheduled a day to move him and his belongings into his new, more secure quarters. In less than a week, Larry had moved into a new apartment on the first floor of a clean white eight-story apartment building that looked like a large loaf of white bread standing end-up. This building, with two locked front doors, carpeting and an elevator bank, not only was a big step up from Trapp's C Street quarters, it also was much more secure. No one could just walk right up and bang on Trapp's door.

Larry felt safer once he had moved, but he also felt strange. As far as the public was concerned, the Grand Dragon of the Realm of Nebraska had disappeared, vanished. Likewise, Larry Trapp could no longer be found: he left no forwarding number on his old telephone, and he couldn't be located in a telephone book or through information. He got a new telephone installed in his J Street apartment, but he didn't want anyone except the Weissers, Wolfson, Humphries and Dietrich to have his number. Or his new name. With the telephone company and his new landlord, Larry had registered as "Larry Rogers." His new neighbors called him "Mr. Rogers."

Michael and Julie were awestruck at the bravery it had taken Larry to cut loose from his entire support system. "Whatever support he had had," said Michael, "whether it was a pat on the back from Tom Metzger or a poem written by his fellow Klansman about the hero in Nebraska, all the different people he could call friends were now gone.

"It was the most tremendous act of courage I've seen. He absolutely turned his life upside down in one fell swoop—with no safety net. He didn't know whether we'd be there for him. He didn't even know if we would continue to accept him."

BEFRIENDING *Chapter 15*

THE ENEMY

Love is greater than any emotion: fear dissolves in it, anger disintegrates, pain flows free.
— STEPHEN LEVINE

*L*arry Trapp bowed his head at the Weissers' dinner table, while Michael, wearing a blue yarmulke (a small head covering), said a traditional Jewish blessing. " 'Y'simcha Elohim ch'Ephraim v'ch-Manasseh,' " he said, looking at his son Dave. " 'May God inspire you to live in the tradition of Ephraim and Manasseh, who carried forward the life of our people.' "

He turned to Dina and Rebecca and said, " 'Y'simech Elohim k'Sarah, Rivkah, Rachel, v'Leah—May God inspire you to live in the tradition of Sarah, Rebekah, Rachel and Leah, who carried forward the life of our people.' " Then he raised his hands and recited, " 'May the Lord bless you and keep you; May the Lord make his face to shine upon you and give you peace.' "

A white cloth was spread across the large round oak table opened out in the Weissers' living room, and two tall silver candlesticks, which reflected the lights in the room, held glowing blue candles. That evening Larry could see shadows and light, but none of the details of the flowered place mats and napkins, the large blue dinner plates or the faces of the people in front of him. It had been exactly one week since Larry's transforming experience—a day he already was calling "my real birthday—the day I was really born and started living."

In front of Michael, a deep blue velvet cloth decorated with white embroidered Hebrew words covered two loaves of challah. Michael lifted the cloth off the challah and picked up one loaf. " '*Barukh ata . . .* ' " he began. " 'Blessed are You, O Lord our God, King of the universe, who brings forth bread from the earth.' "

Michael broke off a large chunk of the crusty white bread and passed it to John Ways, Sr., the local NAACP chapter head, who broke off a piece and handed it to Larry. Larry held it in his hand until Julie, sitting next to him, told him to break off a piece and hand it on. She took some bread and handed it to Norman Leach, who sat next to her. The challah went the rest of the way around the table.

"You know, this is wonderful," Michael said. "I'm going to interrupt myself here a minute to say breaking bread together is the only way to bring harmony to this world. That's our job."

Michael poured wine into a large silver goblet called a Kiddush cup and sang the traditional blessing. Then he lifted the cup. "*L'chayyim.*"

"*L'chayyim,*" everyone but Larry responded.

"What's 'la hem'?" Larry asked.

"*L'chayyim* is a traditional Hebrew toast," Julie answered. "*L'chayyim* means 'to life.' "

Larry tried to say it, but it still sounded like "la hem." Everyone laughed as the cup was passed around the table and Dina pronounced it again for him.

Before this dinner, Dina and Rebecca also had met Larry, and like Dave, they had begun to deal with their initial negative reactions to him. "I was really scared of him at first," Dina said. "Julie asked me to go with her to visit him, and I was freaked out. When we got there, his apartment was disgusting. It was a pigsty. There was this service that was supposed to come in and clean, but they took advantage of his blindness and everything and it was just gross. I was scared, and when I'm in there, I look at the doorknob and there's a gun on every doorknob and it scared me. Then he started telling jokes and stuff and it was funny. So I kind of calmed down a little bit.

"I just didn't know what I was going to say to him, you know? But then he made me laugh. He was just really funny. He told gross jokes. Later on, when I started looking at the Klan stuff, I thought—'cause he seemed so nice to me after I first met him, he was so funny and nice— I was looking at his stuff and I was just thinking to myself, 'How could Larry be associated with all this garbage?' They didn't go together."

Rebecca had been less persuaded. "I had a lot of apprehension," she said later. "I really didn't want anything to do with him. This was an ex-Nazi, and when I was eleven years old in North Carolina, pardon my French, I had the living shit scared out of me because of people like him. And so I really didn't want to have anything to do with him because that was my first thought. I mean, I thought, 'Yeah, he's funny all right, but he's little more than a grown child.' Eventually, though, I realized I could look beyond his bad points. He wanted to become a nice person. So I just kind of said, 'Okay, give him a chance.' "

Julie and Michael had made a special request for all three kids to be at this dinner, and they had agreed. Julie felt it was important for them to deal directly with their own issues of forgiveness. "Every religion teaches you not to rejoice when your enemy is suffering," she said. "This is true of Judaism and every religion. Larry has been suffering. And you have nothing to lose and everything to gain by trying to befriend a person who's lonely and unhappy and hateful. Whatever emotions made Larry do the things he did that were so unacceptable and repulsive and hateful to other people—we have to get past it because that was what caused his behavior.

"With Larry, I think it really was loneliness and an empty space in his life that needed to be filled. And what's the harm in trying to befriend a person like him—and what's the harm in trying to take away some of his pain and loneliness? Underneath all that stuff is a real person—a hurting person."

This moment in time was thrilling for Norman Leach. "Larry, I'll bet you never would have believed you'd be breaking bread with the president of the NAACP and the executive director of the Interfaith Council, let alone listening to Hebrew prayers in a Jewish home," he said.

"Well, no, as a matter of fact, I keep thinking I better pinch myself to make sure I'm not dreaming," Larry said, with tears in his eyes. "To tell you the truth, I never would have believed any of this, including eating dinner with a black man in a Jew's house. Now, I mean black and Jew in a good sense of the word, you know what I mean. I can't believe I feel happy about it either, but I do."

John Ways smiled. He, too, felt he was participating in a rare and extraordinary event. John had been a police officer in Lincoln for twenty-two years, and as a black man, he'd been exposed to racism in all of its various guises. In the 1980s, he had filed and won a discrimination suit against the Lincoln Police Department, and in doing so, he had weathered many personal battles. But he'd never let himself stop trying to change what he saw—including the repulsive works of Larry Trapp and his Klan. John's voice had been heard most recently protesting "Race and Reason" to Cablevision's advisory board when they finally held a public meeting in September of that year. As president of the NAACP, he also had gone to Lincoln's City Council and asked them to make a formal resolution saying the city didn't support racism or the showing of "Race and Reason," but the City Council members had talked their way around the issue and didn't act on it. Larry had sent John vicious hate mail.

But despite that, John Ways found it surprisingly easy to forgive Larry Trapp. From their predinner conversation, John felt Larry had made a genuine change. "We said a prayer, and it was very moving," he said. "I'm a Christian and forgiveness is part of my religion. Once a person says they're sorry and I feel this is from the heart, that's it. Larry expressed himself honestly and he was very remorseful for all that had transpired. I thought his plea for forgiveness was genuine and came from the heart, and that's good enough for me."

"I'm so sorry," Larry said more than once during the dinner. "I'm so sorry for scaring people and hurting people. There's so much I don't know. I still think that way sometimes, but now I know it's not right. It's not true," Larry said. "But I'm learning.

"I was always afraid of the guy who was bigger than me or a guy who had a reputation for being a bad guy. And I always thought, 'Gee, they got this power I don't have.' I was always kind of a wimp really. I was always afraid of getting into fights until I got older, and when I got older, I'd take on anybody, you know. But you know, a guy who I was afraid of naturally, he's got my respect—and it's not really respect, it's fear that he's got, it's my fear of him. Because that's how you gain respect—by having people fear you or what you could do or the organization you're with.

"I was afraid to get into fights," Larry said. "I didn't like sports. More or less, my dad tried to teach me how to box. He was faster, of course, I was a little kid, and he'd slap me around. We'd have matches with gloves on—they were eight-ounce gloves, which aren't too light. He wanted me to be tough and I wasn't. See, Dad wanted me to be a lot of things. He wouldn't accept me for what I was, and I wanted to live up to what he wanted, which is my mistake, really, you know, because not everybody can be what another person wants them to be. You have to be yourself and be happy with it, but my life has been trying to please him. When I was a policeman, he said, 'I can't imagine him running around with a gun,' and here I thought I was pleasing him, and that turned me against him. Then when I became a Klansman, that wasn't right either. I had tried for a while to be really religious, reading the Bible all the time and sharing passages with him and trying to play like a real religious person.

"But I couldn't do anything to please him. So I thought, 'Well, the hell with him. Why please him?' I thought, 'Well, I'm pleasing the KKK, I'm pleasing the Nazi Party. I'm pleasing somebody. Somebody appreciates me for being nasty, if nothing else.' I thought, 'Well, this is what I want to be.' And then when I heard Michael, I just—I just couldn't do it anymore."

Larry began crying, and everyone at the table had tears in their eyes. "I'm ashamed of the stupid things I've done in my life," he said. "I know I still have a lot of hate in me, but I'm going to work on it. I am."

At moments, it seemed unreal, yet very real. "I remember him squeezing my hand, hugging me, kissing me on the side of the face," John Ways said later. "There was a lot of warmth, a lot of hugging, and a lot of remorse. This was no show-and-tell time. He felt real bad about what he had done."

The rest of Lincoln learned about Larry's change of heart in Sunday's *Lincoln Journal Star*. After she met Larry Trapp at his apartment, C. J. Schepers had asked if she could write about his change, and he'd said no. He didn't like the media, and he was afraid for his life. On the other hand, she was a *religion* writer, and he thought his experience might help other racists change, so he finally agreed.

Convincing her editors at the *Journal* to let her write about Trapp, however, had been more difficult. "I told my managing editor about the story, and he immediately goes, 'I don't know about this,' " C. J. said. " 'Let me think about it.' After a day, he needed to think more about it, then he wanted to sleep on it. When he found out the Star wanted the story, that's when he made up his mind real quick. He said he wanted me to do the story."

Alongside C. J. Schepers' article was a photograph of Michael, Julie and Larry surrounded by all of Larry's Nazi and Klan propaganda. The story began:

> Once known as the grand dragon of the Ku Klux Klan in Nebraska, Larry Trapp of Lincoln says he has forsaken his racist beliefs forever because a Jewish man—whom he once despised as his enemy—has offered him friendship.
>
> "He showed me such love that I couldn't help but love him back," Trapp said of Cantor Michael Weisser.
>
> "That's just the way it is. It's just an experience I've never had before."
>
> Until last week, Trapp fervently fought against Jews, against blacks, against race mixing—against any minority. Today, in place of two swastika rings, he wears a silver ring given to him by Weisser and his wife, Julie.

Schepers was proud of her story, but disappointed her editors had cut Trapp's comments about David Duke, former Imperial Wizard of the KKK, who had exchanged white robes for three-piece suits. At the time, Duke was running for governor of Louisiana and saying he was no longer a racist or a Klansman. Now he spoke of "European-Americans" simply wanting *their* human rights, "just as African-Americans do."

Larry Trapp told Schepers he had talked with David Duke a number of times and Duke was still very involved, very central to the white supremacy movement. "I've talked to him personally and I can tell you, David Duke is *not* a changed man," Trapp told Schepers. "He is in the center of things pulling strings. What he's doing is the same as always; he's just using a more subdued racism for the public."

"I had that in my story," said Schepers, "but that got cut out and I thought it was very, very important. I also wanted people to know Larry wasn't doing what Duke had done. It wasn't for any gain—he wasn't going to run for politics or anything. This was a transformation. He went from hating blacks and Jewish people and Asians to 'Look what's wrong. These are the problems.' "

Schepers also was disappointed the story was placed down on the left inside corner of a page in the Regional section where few people would see it. The headline seemed small and insignificant. "I was so discouraged," she said. "I thought, 'Nobody is going to see this story!' "

• • •

The next day, however, J. L. Schmidt from the Associated Press called Schepers and said he'd seen her story and thought it was great. His editors in New York had been wanting an interesting feature from Nebraska, and this one was perfect. Schmidt rewrote the story and put it on the AP national wire.

The response shocked C.J.'s editors. Almost overnight, what had been a very private event among three people in Larry Trapp's small apartment took on symbolic significance nationally and internationally. Millions of people read or heard the story. According to an Associated Press executive, the story was picked up by some 1,500 daily newspapers and used in 3,500 radio broadcasts in the United States. In Europe, it was used by 8,500 print and broadcast outlets. The New York Times News Services picked it up, and the story also was distributed by the Jewish Telegraphic Agency. Requests started pouring in to the library of the *Lincoln Journal* for reprints of the picture of Michael, Larry and Julie. The *Lincoln Star* also ran an editorial—"Caring Friendship Transforms Hatred"—praising the Weissers for responding to hatred with kindness.

Journalists from all over the country began calling Michael and Julie, who were listed in the telephone book, asking for interviews with Larry Trapp. For several days, their telephone rang from seven o'clock in the morning until ten and eleven o'clock at night. Larry came to the Weissers' and talked on the phone to several journalists in the hopes his story would make a difference for other people. He told a number of reporters: "I was about as hardened a white racist as anybody in this country. If I can have that change of mind or change of heart, anybody can."

The Religious News Service ran one of the most striking articles on Trapp's metamorphosis by Randall Balmer, an associate professor of religion at Columbia University.

How do you explain such a dramatic turnaround? Is it the miraculous power of the divine, or should we attribute it to other factors?

Trapp claims to have been abused by his father. Alcohol has ravaged his life and destroyed his marriage. Diabetes has taken his left leg, much of his right leg and most of his vision. Trapp, therefore, seems a likely candidate for religious conversion—a fragile, broken man whose sense of bitterness and betrayal translated quite easily into bigotry. Now, feeling acceptance and friendship for perhaps the first time, even from an erstwhile adversary, he announces a turn to God.

Over the course of history many religious conversions have been similarly dramatic. A blinding light on the road to Damascus turned a persecutor of early Christians into Christianity's foremost apologist. A conversion transformed Augustine from a pagan and a profligate into the church's most influential theologian. . . .

In the meantime, Michael got a call from Jack Levine, an independent filmmaker in New York. Levine, a photographer turned filmmaker, had been a nationally recognized civil rights lawyer in Philadelphia before he started spending time behind his camera. His photographs of China and Nicaragua had been featured in New York galleries, and his habit of following his heart had led him to develop a feature film about the writer and activist Margaret Randall. When he read about this story, he was hooked. He didn't feel sure he could break even on the project financially, but he thought it was a great story and he felt compelled to explore it. He asked Michael and Julie if he could come out to Lincoln and talk to them and to Larry about optioning the rights to their story for a film, possibly a movie-of-the-week. He felt something healing, something important, was happening in Lincoln, Nebraska, and he wanted to be part of it.

Levine flew to Lincoln and spent time with Larry, Michael, Julie and the Weisser kids. Larry and the Weissers liked Jack and instinctively trusted him. From the beginning, he was a friend. None of them knew whether the film project would go anywhere, and who, if anyone, Jack might work with to produce a movie. Jack felt, however, if nothing else came of this, he had met wonderful people and gained insight into "how we all have this power to rise to the moment" the way the Weissers did.

"I just knew this was an opportunity for me to learn more about myself and what Judaism means, because I've never been really formally involved in religion in any particular way," Jack Levine said later. "I always conceived of myself as a very spiritual person, and I had deeply held moral beliefs, but I had never come to terms with my identity as a Jew. I always kind of functioned in a secular world, with a secular consciousness.

"You know, it's like sometimes the phone rings in the middle of the night and someone says, 'Do you want to do X, Y and Z?' and you know if you don't do it, you're going to miss the boat. For me, missing the boat would mean losing an opportunity to just move farther down my own road."

Daniel Levy from *Time* magazine also called and scheduled an interview and had several conversations with Michael and Larry on the telephone. He, too, felt a strong connection to the story and to the Weissers, and he set up a day to go out to Lincoln in late December for an interview.

Even after the story had gotten so much national and international attention, however, many of C. J. Schepers' fellow journalists in Lincoln still weren't persuaded. They had followed Trapp's career in the KKK and weren't impressed by any so-called change of heart. "People in the newsroom were so cynical about it," Schepers says. "First of all, when it's in your own backyard, you just don't see it, and secondly, it's the in thing to be a cynic if you're a journalist, you know. Like, if you're not, you shouldn't be in this business. You have to be hard-core; you have to look at everybody like they are the lousiest person on earth and there's no way they could change—no way good things can happen.

"I came up to a group one day and they were laughing and this reporter said, 'Oh, you know we were just laughing about Larry Trapp's so called turnaround.' She was saying she knew somebody in the doctor's office that used to treat him. And they were saying what a creep he was, how they just couldn't believe he had changed, and this all must be a big scam. And my managing editor was laughing about it with them.

"But for me, I feel different—maybe because I have the religion beat. You can't be a cynic and be in religion. I can be wary and skeptical, but I can't be a cynic, because then how could I do my job? Besides, when you get right down to it, if we don't have hope for people to change, then what do we have? We don't have anything if we don't have hope."

WHOEVER SHUNS EVIL

Chapter 16

The faith waiting in the heart of a seed
promises a miracle of life
which it cannot prove at once.
— RABINDRANATH TAGORE

*L*ocal journalists were not the only ones disinclined to believe Larry Trapp's transformation. Many people took a wait-and-see attitude. Forgiving a person who had been cruel, even if he was remorseful, seemed too much like forgiving the cruelty—perhaps even condoning it. Couldn't forgiving the actor also be interpreted as forgiving the act—or in this case the Nazis or the KKK? A number of people felt perplexed by the Weissers' ability not only to forgive Larry Trapp, but to maintain contact with him.

And when Michael and Julie enthusiastically wheeled Larry Trapp into the large, bustling downstairs reception room of the synagogue for Chanukah dinner on the evening of December 2, Cybele Londono was horrified. This young Colombian-born assistant museum curator at the University of Nebraska didn't know she would feel so upset by the sight of Larry Trapp. Julie was one of her best and closest friends, and Cybele considered Michael her "American dad." Cybele, an elegant woman with short dark hair and playful dark brown eyes, usually spent a great deal of time with the Weisser family. But when she saw how Julie had arranged the table so she and her husband David would be sitting with Larry Trapp, she couldn't bear the idea of being in such close proximity.

"I freaked out," Cybele said later. "I went over to Julie [and] I said, 'Julie, I can't do this, I can't sit with him.' I said, 'One of our guests is the child of people who were murdered in the Holocaust, and I can't do this to him.' But actually it was for me just as much . . .

"I thought, 'Ugh, I can't touch this guy.' Partly because of his problem with his legs, not having them, and partly because he had been a Nazi man. I love Julie and Michael, but I thought, 'This I can't do; I won't do this.' "

Holocaust survivor Eva Sartori and a number of other congregants felt similarly. "Maybe it was a transformation," Mrs. Sartori said, "but I never wanted to get close enough to Larry to find out. I never spent time with him, not ever. I think as far as the members of the temple were concerned, I think the majority ignored him. That's my impression. I think not everybody felt extremely compassionate about it."

These complicated feelings stirred in many people. When Donna Polk, for instance, heard Larry Trapp saying he'd changed, her immediate response was, "Yeah, and I'm the pope!" Then she listened again to his voice on her answering machine apologizing and telling her he was ashamed of his actions, he wanted forgiveness and he would try to make it up to her and to everyone by working for the rights of all people.

It sounded good, but Donna couldn't help but be incredulous. "I'll have to wait and see," Donna said. The Klan had done such terrible things to African-Americans for years, and Larry Trapp had so harassed her, that she wasn't yet ready to believe him. "I hope he has changed," she said, "but I'll have to see. It will take time for me to accept this as the truth."

But Donna Polk did forgive Larry Trapp. And she didn't wait an extended period of time to do it. On Thanksgiving Day, she called Larry Trapp at his apartment and told him she accepted his apology and would celebrate the holiday with thankfulness about his putting his energy "to work for the good of one race—the human race," as he said he planned to do. When he heard her voice, Larry was overwhelmed. He couldn't believe she could actually forgive him. If things were turned around and he were Donna Polk, he said, he would have hated Larry Trapp forever and damned him to hell for all eternity. He was so relieved by her generosity and forgiveness that he cried. And after that, whenever he spoke of her, his eyes filled with tears again.

• • •

By the time of this Chanukah dinner, the gray-bearded Vietnam vet and congregant Charles "Griff" Griffin had also dropped his guard around Larry. Griff, a solid man of medium height with light, watchful green eyes and a hearty laugh, had baked four loaves of challah for the Chanukah dinner. "I like Larry and the fact he has the chutzpah it takes, the courage, to come up and say, 'Look I screwed up, I'm wrong, I made a mistake, please, can you forgive me?' " Griff said later. "That takes a lot from a man, from any man, especially a man who's born and raised in Nebraska. Nebraska men don't like to admit they're wrong very frequently, and when they do, they'll do it in an offhanded way and in such a way that unless you're attuned to it, you don't know they're apologizing.

"I thought that was fascinating. Larry came right out and said, 'Look, I was wrong, I'm sorry. And what I guess I've learned is, at that point it's my responsibility to then try to start working very hard to forgive that individual. And that's what I did."

Songwriter and folksinger Leslie Young was another member of B'nai Jeshurun whose complicated feelings about Larry became clear at the Chanukah dinner. Leslie, born in Honduras to a Honduran mother and an American father, had been extremely upset about Larry Trapp's activities as a Klansman. During the dinner, she sang a song she had written called "For Eight Days Remember." Leslie is small, wiry, with narrow hips and shoulders and an open, feminine face—her mouth on the edge of laughter, her short brown hair framing unusually large brown eyes. She is without affectation, and her candor comes across in her music, along with a magic which allows her listeners to feel the range of emotion she feels, see what she sees, know what she understands.

After she finished singing, Leslie went down to meet Larry. "I like your voice," Larry said to her. "You have such a beautiful voice." At the time, she didn't know he couldn't see. She only realized it when he was trying to reach for his coffee cup.

Leslie told Larry she was inspired by his change. "He was there!" she said. "I mean he was at a Chanukah dinner. What's the Klan gonna be doing at a Chanukah dinner! You gotta be dumb to think the man hasn't changed. I mean, he was all hugging and kissing and crying. And a man that's not changed is not gonna do that."

●　　●　　●

Perhaps it's not surprising that the faith and belief other people had in Larry Trapp's ability to change eventually was stronger than his own. The hateful snowballing of his negative progression as Grand Dragon had stopped, but suddenly a few weeks later, Larry Trapp woke up to the fact his life was totally different. By this time, he had gone from being a hero to his fellow Klansman to being a schmuck and a traitor.

One day Larry asked Michael, "How can you believe I changed?"

"I know about change, Larry," Michael said. "I know it's possible because I've changed."

"What do you mean?"

"When we get to know each other better, I'll tell you," Michael said. "Remind me one of these days. We're not as different from each other as you might think."

After the Associated Press story had gone out nationally, Tom Metzger denounced Larry Trapp on his national telephone hotline. Larry had figured Metzger would respond, and when he did, Larry laughed with glee. Metzger's message started with his usual greetings: "You have tuned to Resistance Radio, the North American voice of the W.A.R., WAR! The White Resistance. Eighty-eight on your dial; transmitting from Mud-covered Southern California. . . .

"DATELINE: LOOO-SERRRS. Will some of the Klans and other groups quit recruiting some of those emotional loooosers that get in and then act crazy and then find looovve from a raaa-bbi and freak out? It's getting pretty disturbing.

"Recently, a Klan representative, so-called, in Lincoln, Nebraska, who obviously was not wrapped too tight, was pictured by a local— with a local rabbi—who changed his life around. Well, the rabbi gave him—oh, what else?—a carton of Kentucky fried chicken and told him how much he sympathized with him and so forth. His name was Larry Trapp.

"When you allow emotionally unstable losers into your group, they'll always change sides sooner or later. Remember Withrow, Martinez, Seymour—they all had one common problem. You could tell they were emotionally disturbed and should never be leaved—be left into any operation.

"The Jews are welcome to this freako in Nebraska. He's joining a long line of similar types who are habitual joiners and are looking for someone to hold their hand and tell them they are *wonderful* human be-ings. Give me a break. Someone has opened the gate to the funny farm.

"A suggestion: Go to a large bookstore. Buy a paperback book called the *Oosher Color Test*—the *Oosher Color Test*—and test people for their personality profiles before you bring them in. It's *much* better than a lie detector.

"DATELINE: THE U.S.-MEXICAN BORDER. . . ."

After Larry had tape-recorded Metzger's message, he kept laughing. "Now you can tell by the quiver in his voice that he's really upset about me (hee-hee) gettin' out of the Klan," he said. "He lost another man in the movement and I'll make sure he'll lose many more by the time I get through with him. Hee-hee-hee-hee-ha."

Being hated and held up to ridicule didn't bother Larry. In fact, it was useful—it gave him something to do. But his bravado, which covered up a number of feelings and fears he didn't understand, was hard to maintain without the stimulus of antagonistic events. And when the fervor of what had happened so spontaneously had subsided, media attention had died down and the threat of violence no longer seemed imminent, Larry found himself alone in a quiet and strange new apartment he didn't like. He not only had lost his old connections, but the day-to-day activity he was immersed in was *completely* different from anything he had ever known before. Doubt began to creep in on a variety of levels. His habits of a lifetime were gone, and he was scared.

Previously, Larry's extremely structured life as a Klansman had provided him with a feeling of power, focus and the stimulation of almost constant contact with like-minded hatemongers. Hatred's physical tangibility had contributed a certain electricity and a framework for his concentration, purpose and sense of direction each day. But now in his new J Street apartment, a floating sense of powerless seemed to swamp him and drag him down. His energy was diffused, and he never knew quite what to do next. He'd gone to church once with Monica Kuhns and he planned to go again. He also was going to get together with John Ways and Norman Leach, and was trying to set up meetings with some community groups. But without any action until those events took place, he felt frustrated, isolated, uneasy. And since his emotional life had such a narrow range, he reacted to these feelings in the way he knew—with anger.

His new apartment became the target for much of his rage. It was a nice place compared to his old efficiency apartment on C Street. Larry knew that. In the front of the building was a small glassed-in porch where residents perched to watch passers-by and sun themselves like birds. Visitors entered the building through the sunroom and another locked door and walked on sturdy royal blue carpet past the elevator, down a wide, well-lit corridor. Turning right, they passed two doors before getting to Larry's apartment on the left—number 103. The walls were painted white. They were clean. His nurses commented on it. But in the rush to get Larry moved to more secure quarters, no one had really noticed the new place wasn't wheelchair-accessible.

Besides that, the apartment was too big for him. It had a large living room—dining room, a kitchen area and a separate bedroom and bathroom. Larry needed four walls to define his space. In his old place, he'd been in control of his life. There, he knew where everything went, where everything belonged. Even though his vision was blurry, nearly nonexistent, he could find anything he wanted when he wanted it. In this new residence, he couldn't even find his way around.

To make matters worse, Julie started to clean—and her cleaning was no small thing. Julie gets kidded by friends for her compulsive tidiness—her daily vacuuming and washing of the kitchen floor. ("If you drop a crumb, she catches it in midair!" Leslie Young says.) In Larry's collection of dirty clothes, and even in this apartment, which hadn't built up so many layers of grime and dirt as the old one, Julie found a great challenge.

Another terrible thing for Larry was the gas stove, which was too high and had control knobs at the back. From his wheelchair, Larry couldn't turn on a flame to cook anything without burning his hand or arm. One night he told Michael and Julie: "I burned my hand on this damned stove again and the landlord better do something about it! He better fix it and he better do it right now or he's gonna be sorry." The next day Michael and Julie brought their microwave oven over for Larry to use so he wouldn't burn himself when preparing meals. Larry loved popcorn, and so they also took him microwave popcorn and a number of microwavable dinners.

But Larry wasn't happy about the microwave. He didn't want one. "I can't have a microwave in my apartment!" he shouted. "It'll give me cancer!"

Michael patiently showed Larry what to do—just in case he ever wanted to use it. He put tape over all the buttons except for the timer, the fifteen-second button and the stop button so Larry could feel exactly what he was touching and what he was doing. He could press the fifteen-second button twice if he wanted to heat up a dinner roll and press it four times if he wanted to heat up a cup of coffee.

After that, every time Julie and Michael went over to Larry's place, they found him cooking something in the microwave.

The microwave relieved a lot of Larry's fury about food preparation, but the rest of his life seemed to be spiraling out of control. As a Klansman and Nazi, Larry's relationships with other people fit into clearly defined categories. Emotional distance was built in, and life was predictable. A person's rank governed the kinds of interactions he had with them. Women weren't equals and didn't need to be considered outside the sexual realm, which had been lacking for him since his legs had been amputated anyway. Men were safe as long as they shared the same racist assumptions he did.

In his old life, Larry knew the rules and he was in charge. The patterns were simple: Fellow Klansmen didn't just drop in on him; they called ahead or stopped by according to schedule. When someone came over, the visit had a purpose. These days Michael and Julie, Dina, Griff and Leslie stopped by unexpectedly at odd times of day and for no apparent reason. Their spontaneity particularly bewildered and perturbed him. It had no pattern. And he *hated* surprises. He had no way of understanding the motivations of these impetuous people who suddenly seemed to be swarming him. How could he know what they were going to do when they never even knew themselves what they would do next? He thought they meant well, but why?

When Julie told Leslie Young about Larry's stove problem, for instance, Leslie began to drop by to bring Larry fresh foods—soup or some kind of salad—for lunch or dinner. She knew he loved potato soup, so she often made it for him. If she had time between her freelance secretarial jobs, she'd go pick Larry up and take him to her house for lunch.

One time when Leslie dropped by to make a salad for lunch, Larry was in a state of high anxiety. Julie had cleaned for him again, and he couldn't find the garbage bags he'd been looking for. He also was uptight because his heating system wasn't working and it was too hot. "I could just feel it building up," Leslie said. "And Larry's like, 'OK, I'm fine now; I want to be left alone. I don't need anybody. I can't handle this. I'm sorry. I'm not trying to be rude, but I have to be left alone.' "

• • •

Even though Larry had been determined to make amends, he started vacillating, doubting if he'd really changed—doubting if he'd meant what he said. He was creating a new life, not following established rituals, and he didn't know how to do it. He'd lost his balance and it wasn't long before he started wondering if he was losing his mind as well.

One evening, Julie stopped by Larry's to take him some Chinese food and a few groceries on her way home from work. She knocked on his door, called out to him, and when he answered, she let herself in with the key he'd given her and Michael. Larry was totally agitated and talking into his tape recorder. "This fucking apartment," he was saying. "Nothing works in here, and I want to tell you it's too cold in here. Not even the heat works right! By God, if someone doesn't do something about it, I'm gonna take everything and pile it in the middle of the living room and start a fire in the middle of this place, and believe me, I will!"

Soon after Julie arrived, he told her how mad he was because she'd moved things again the last time she'd been there.

"Don't you know you can't move a blind person's things?" he yelled. "Are you stupid or something? I don't need anybody cleaning my place. I can't even find my toothbrush and toothpaste! I always keep them together with my mouthwash and my soap and they're not anywhere! I couldn't even brush my teeth today!"

"I'm sorry, Larry. I just put them in the toothbrush holder beside the sink; I'll get them for you!" Julie said. "You can keep them exactly where you want them." Julie tried to reason with him further, but he wouldn't have any of it.

"I don't want you *touching* them!" Larry shouted. *"I'll* keep them exactly where I want them and you can *butt out!* Everybody can butt out. Michael can butt out and Leslie can butt out, too!"

At this point, Larry was screaming. "All this crap is a bunch of shit! I'm gonna forget it. Just forget it! I'm tired of you people. I'm gonna go back to doin' what I was doin' before. I'll just join the Klan again and they'll probably have me back! I don't want to do this anymore!"

Larry's face screwed up in a release of pent-up fury worse than anything Julie had ever seen. She'd been intimidated by Larry's explosive temper before, but this outburst was totally obnoxious and unnerving.

"My whole world is falling apart and I'm confused and I'm fuckin' mixed up," he shrieked. "I was much more secure the other way. You're a crazy messed-up bitch and you make me crazy and Michael makes me crazy, and I don't like all these people in my life. You've rearranged all the goddamned stuff in my goddamned apartment and I can't find any fuckin' thing. Even my goddamned toothbrush!

"I'm goin' back where I belong!"

Larry was off on a roll, and it occurred to Julie he might be having a nervous breakdown or something, but his anger was so contagious and his words so infuriating, she lost her own temper.

"Larry, what are you?" she shouted back at him, her Memphis twang taking over. "Are you like a snake that's shed its skin and you're gonna go back and look for the skin? Well, it's not gonna fit you anymore. You can go back and look for that skin, but it's not gonna fit you anymore!

"But if that's what you want, then go right ahead. You have got a chance of changing your life. But if you don't want to change your life, then I'll walk out the door right now.

"I just want you to know you're a real shithead! You're a selfish, self-centered shithead! You want to know why nobody likes you? You want to know why you don't have any friends? It's because you're mean and hateful and crappy to people. It's because you're such a jerk! You don't have a clue how to be nice to other people!"

Julie was furious. She couldn't believe it, but she was yelling and screaming at him. She was so mad and so hurt, she was crying. "And then I did something awful 'cause I have a really bad temper, and when I'm really mad, I have this instinct to strike out," she said. "Anyway, I hit him. I hit him on the back. On the back of the shoulder. I just whacked him, and I could not believe I had done that. And he was real startled by it, 'cause no one's ever told Larry he's a shit. I mean they may have said it like when he was harassing someone or something, but no one's ever said to him the reason no one likes you is because you're mean and hateful and crappy to people."

Then Julie said, "I'm leaving now."

Julie knew she'd never come back. She grabbed her purse and pulled her coat back on. She stormed to the door. But just as she was opening it to go out, Larry called out her name.

"Wait," he said in a tremulous voice. "Do you think you could come back for just one minute if you're going to leave?"

"What for?" Julie said angrily.

"Well, just come here for a minute," Larry said. "Please. Come over to the desk."

The tone in Larry's voice had changed so dramatically that even though she was still angry, Julie shut the door and walked back into the room.

At his desk, Larry had a gooseneck lamp. He wheeled over to it and turned it on.

"I just want to see your face," he said. He took the light and shined it on Julie and said, "I just want to see your face. If you're going to leave me, I want to see what you look like first. I just want to see what you look like."

Larry put his glasses on and he got out his round, black-handled magnifying glass and shined the light on Julie's face. He couldn't really see her; his vision was getting worse. If he could have, he would have seen her flushed cheeks and her large hazel-brown eyes full of tears and compassion. All he saw was a blur of blondness under a screen of red.

But Julie could see him. From the other side of the magnifying glass, she saw an enlargement of his light blue eyes, tears spilling over his long lashes and rolling down his cheeks and his nose running.

Larry was sniffling and trying to focus on Julie so he could see her face, and he said, "I don't want you to leave, I don't want anybody to leave, I'm just scared."

Watching his face, Julie felt overwhelmed at his grief and his terror. "He was real scared," she said. "This wall that he had spent so many years building up, was just gone, it crumbled. He was so lost. It was like this big turning point for him. We started having a dialogue and it was just so sweet and so sad."

After that day, Larry felt a new bond with Julie. Not only did he realize how much she cared about him, but he also knew she'd responded to him emotionally on a level no one else had ever reached. The electricity of her anger and the intensity of her concern somehow helped to create and confirm a new but tenuous sense of self-worth in him. And although he still wasn't fully trusting, more and more he shared confidences. It wasn't long before he confessed to her how much he loved plants, especially African violets. Before he officially became a Klansman and a Nazi, he told her, he had grown African violets and gone to meetings of the local African violet society. After he became a full-time racist, he was too busy for gardening or flower meetings. But sometimes even then for relaxation, after he had made a tape for "The Vigilante Voices, where the truth hurts" or listened to a tape on "The Wonders of Hitler," he would gingerly pull out a hidden tape and listen to "How to Handle Plants in a Greenhouse," "How to Take Advantage of Blooming Periods" or "Perfecting the Soil for Your African Violets."

Larry had developed an emotional attachment to plants when he was a little boy. "My [maternal] grandmother used to grow flowers outside," he said. "She had a sheltered front porch, and she used to grow the most beautiful African violets. They weren't symmetrical, the leaf shapes weren't. But she did real well with plants. I didn't know her that well, but as a little boy I'd go over there and I'd sit on her lap and she'd run her fingers through my hair and I'd get that nice kind of tingling feeling, you know." He smiled in surprise, now suddenly able after all this time to identify the feeling he had forgotten. "It's love is what it is," he said. "I loved her."

When he was about ten or eleven years old, Larry had started learning how to grow plants himself. "Mom gave me a little area in the back yard and I'd experiment," he said. "I loved irises of all kinds. I had a black iris which is the most beautiful thing you've ever seen in your life. Then I always experimented with *Gesneriaceae,* which are members of the Gesneriad family—things like African violets, *Episcia,* if you ever heard of those. They're a semitropical type of plant. So I got a lot of experience from just messing around with all that stuff, you know, both the indoor and outdoor variety. I think the first plant I ever played around with was a potato plant—when you cut a potato in half and put it in a little saucer. And I grew avocado trees—I grew them huge, and I just went on from there."

After Larry went to the Lincoln School for the Blind, he took a few courses in greenhouse management and horticulture at the University of Nebraska, thinking someday he would like to be a greenhouse owner or work on a tree farm or in a local greenhouse. "But when I applied for a job at this local nursery," Larry said, "this owner—he was Caucasian—this guy asked me, 'If you're going blind, how are you going to do things like watering the plants?'

"Well, that got me angry, but I didn't express my anger. I says, 'Well, that's ridiculous. That's a ridiculous question.' I says, 'How do I water myself? How do I get a drink of water? How do I bathe myself?' You know, I had legs and everything then. I says, 'I can do it just as well as anybody by feel. By feel I can tell whether the plant has enough water. You want the remainder of water to drip out of the bottom if you're watering from the top so you don't get fertilizer salts collected around the bottom of the pot so they burn the roots.'

"I says, 'I can raise plants just as well as anyone else. All I have to do, you know, is learn. The flowers bloom according to the amount of light they get, and all I have to do is keep in mind the photosynthetic timetables of all the flowering plants, which is not a big thing. I says, 'I can get poinsettias to bloom, I can get chrysanthemums or azaleas to grow.' But he just wouldn't give me a chance, which I thought was unfair. I should have gone to the EEOC—the Equal Opportunities or whatever they call it—but I didn't."

At one point in Lincoln, Larry had started a little plant business. He had printed up some little cards that said "Larry's Plant Clinic: Free Advice About Any Plant Ailments." People could bring in their sick plants and Larry would take care of them for a week or two and get them better and then they could take them home. He didn't take healthy plants, only sick ones.

A day or two after Larry had told her about his love of blooming plants, Julie bought a small purple African violet plant and took it to Larry as a gift. "Gee, thanks," he said, clearly delighted as he put on his magnifying lenses and began to examine it under his bright light. "It's in the *Valerina* series. It's a hardy stock—one of the easiest to grow."

The following week, Julie was at work in Dr. Fischer's office when she was called to the phone. It was Larry, and the sound of his voice alarmed her because he was crying so hard. "Julie, I accidently knocked the darn thing off in front of my scanner," he told her. "I knocked it off and then I tried to get it, but I didn't see it where it fell, and I ran over it in my chair and it's all wrecked." It took Julie a moment to figure out Larry was talking about the African violet.

"Don't worry," she said. "We can get another one.' "

"No! I don't want another one, I want this one!" he said.

Julie said, "This one is probably still okay."

"I don't think so," Larry said, still crying.

"Well, when I come over, we'll see if maybe we can fix it."

"You may think this sounds crazy, but it's a living thing, you know," said Larry. "I mean, it's like a person. I mean, it hasn't been proven, but I think plants have feelings. They can tell when you care about them and when you're neglecting them. And this one will probably think I killed it on purpose. I feel like I just committed a murder."

When Julie went over to Larry's apartment after work, she looked at the plant and thought how easy it would be to simply replace it. After all, it only cost $2.89—not a major expenditure. But Larry adamantly did not want any new plant. This one *had* to live. He convinced Julie to take him out right then to buy a new pot, pebbles for the bottom, the proper soil and food, which she did. She wanted to stop by Burger King for a chicken sandwich, but Larry wouldn't eat or drink anything until he had fixed the plant. As soon as they got back to his apartment, he carefully repotted the broken little African violet.

"You should have seen how he handled that plant," Julie remembered later. "We had the right soil and the right food and he was real gentle. When he repotted it, he told me how you shouldn't touch the leaves when you handle an African violet or they'll turn brown.

"And then he told me when I watered the African violet, I should always think about the way I like the water when I take a shower. I wouldn't want the water to be too hot or too cold, and the plant feels the same way. He also told me not to let the water get on the leaves of the African violet. He said when you water, let the water go down between the leaves into the soil until the plant feels heavy.

"He knew all that stuff because of what he'd read about flowers and listened to on tape. He knew all the different names of African violets. He knew one lady who was in the African violet society—and that year there was a story about her in the paper and she had shot her husband and then pushed him down the stairs. Larry didn't want to hear it; he got tears in his eyes, and said he couldn't listen to that kind of stuff."

Larry didn't want hate in his life anymore. But the self-indulgence inherent to the development of malicious habits is hard to give up, and often when he was frustrated, Larry would revert to angry diatribes— and become again what he referred to as "the old Larry." Julie, however, could barely tolerate his outbursts. She started teaching him how to think about his behavior in new ways. Her approach, however, also had its own combative flair.

"As soon as I figured out Larry was full of shit and how all his nastiness was a bluff, I took over," Julie says. "Like one day we went into Kinko's and he was really crappy to someone behind the counter, and I literally flew him out of this place in his wheelchair. I was pushing him about a hundred miles an hour out the door, and he got on his sliding board [that he puts between his wheelchair and the car seat] and I just

kind of like tipped it and dumped him in the front seat. I was so furious
I drove like a maniac to his apartment and I said, 'I will never go anywhere or do anything with you again if you can't treat people nicely!' I
wheeled him into his apartment and left him and slammed the door,
and I heard him say, 'But I love you,' as I was walking down the hall.

"I thought, 'I don't give a shit whether he loves me or anybody else. If
he loves us, then he'd better learn how to be nice and decent.' I went
storming back and I said, 'Hey, Larry, either you're a nice person or
you're not a nice person'—which really isn't true, but for him, because
he's so literal, it applied. I was trying to make a point with him—and he
sees things very much in black and white."

Much later Julie would say, "Larry's conversion was a liberating moment, but it didn't happen all at once. No way. I think it took him a long
time to really change. He had to let down his defenses. He has all these
layers, and so it's sort of like scraping away the muck. It happened
gradually, over time—with a lot of stopping and starting."

HELP ME UNDERSTAND

Chapter 17

For the one that hates you if they are hungry give them food to eat and if they are thirsty give them water to drink.

—PROVERBS 25:21

*L*arry's diabetes got worse one night between Chanukah and Christmas. He had eaten a boisterous, thrown-together dinner with the Weissers, and following all the noise and fun of being with Michael, Julie, the kids and a couple of their friends, Larry couldn't stand thinking about going back to his silent apartment. When Michael got up to drive him home, he said, as if doing them a favor, "Oh, that's okay, you don't need to bother. It's late and you're tired. I can just sleep here if that's okay."

Many other nights after dinner, he'd also asked, and Michael and Julie had made a pallet of blankets for him on their living-room floor. This night was no different. The first time he'd stayed over, he'd suggested he sleep on the couch, but it wasn't comfortable. "We couldn't get him off of the couch without having to pull him up by the arms," Julie says with a laugh. "Sometimes we had to pull his head! So, anyway, we'd make him a pallet on the floor, and that's where he'd sleep when he didn't want to go home."

That night Julie and Michael fixed another pallet for Larry in the living room and tried to help him get comfortable before they went to bed. Larry asked Michael to tell him something from the Torah before he went to sleep, and Michael agreed.

Michael talked to Larry about the importance of prayer, and then told him about a night years before when he'd been out walking his dog and looked up to see Orion and the two Ursas. It was one of those moments when he wanted to be reassured God was not just in his imagination. "This cloud drifted away from the moon and there was this eerie light for several moments," Michael said. "The noises of the woods and the traffic stopped so suddenly I became aware they were gone. The world was silent, and I said, 'God, please help me understand my place in the world.'

"I felt like I was transformed for a moment, and I heard, within myself, 'Teach them to pray. Teach them to pray.' Was that a message from God? Was it a message from inside myself or just the longing of my own heart? I don't know, but I do know prayer is important, Larry. I know that."

By the time Michael and Larry had finished talking, Dina and Dave had said goodnight and gone downstairs to their rooms and Rebecca had gone to sleep in her room next to Michael and Julie's, right off the living room. After they went to bed, Michael and Julie could hear Larry coughing and muttering outloud to himself. It was clear he wasn't feeling well. "He seemed just miserable," Julie remembers. "He was *so* uncomfortable. And Ishtov was lying there beside him on the floor with his nose right in Larry's face. Larry hated the smell of Ish's breath.

"In our bedroom, Michael and I started laughing because we could hear Larry saying, 'Goddamned son-of-a-bitch dog, get out of my face!' We called Ish into our room, but then later we woke up and heard Larry again and he was coughing really hard and having trouble breathing and it sounded *serious*."

Michael and Julie took Larry to the emergency room at the hospital, where doctors hooked him up to oxygen, took X-rays and told him he had bronchitis. Then a radiologist came in and looked at Larry's chest X-ray and said he thought he saw spots on it.

When the doctor talked to Larry, he said he wanted to keep Larry on the short-term floor for two or three days for more tests. The protein level in his urine was elevated. His blood sugar also was out of control, his blood pressure was way too high, and the doctor suspected that damage to his kidneys might be quite advanced.

The doctor also told Michael and Julie that Larry was typical of adults he'd encountered who'd had poorly supervised juvenile diabetes when they were young. "He said they're the most bitter, unhappy people because from a very young age they've been denied all the stuff kids get to have, like ice cream and candy and all the treats," Julie said. "He said they have the absolute worst attitude about their health and about their lives.

"Apparently, Larry's parents really didn't monitor him, and they were very inconsistent when he was growing up. He said sometimes they would go to the Dairy Queen and have ice cream and Cokes, and other times they would say, 'You can't have that.' So, he had all this conflict going on. And then you take that and put it with all the other problems Larry had. And of course when he got to be an adult, he basically didn't care. Anybody who can smoke three packs of cigarettes a day and drink like Larry used to drink, day after day, and night after night, and be in a drunken stupor all the time, knowing you're a diabetic, is just insane."

Larry's previous lack of regard toward his health had gravely exacerbated his condition. Even when he'd gotten the news he was losing his eyesight more than a decade previously, he'd used it as a way to do himself more damage. "I thought, Well, I'll go to the bar and tell all my friends, 'Oh, I'm losing my eyesight,' you know, and shed a few tears so they'd buy me free drinks," he said later. "My main motive was free drinks. And I got the drinks from their just saying, 'Well, gee, we feel so badly for you.' "

Larry had been on the wagon for several years and he'd finally stopped smoking. But now his earlier eras of neglect and abuse had caught up with him, and he was a very sick man. His face looked pale, his hands were cold, he had more phantom aches in his legs, and the ulcerated sores on the stumps of his legs seemed to look even more inflamed and pus-filled than usual. His doctors moved him from the short-term to the long-term floor and continued to run tests.

Michael called Larry's father in Omaha to tell him how sick his son was. Since Larry had left the Klan, he and his father had seen each other only once, even though the trip from Omaha to Lincoln is less than an hour's drive. "I thought you might want to come to Lincoln to see Larry," Michael said. "They don't know how serious it is."

"Well, we have a wedding we're going to," John Trapp said. "I can't get over there right now."

On January 30, Julie was working at Dr. Fischer's office, and during a lull, she asked him, "What's going to happen to Larry?" At that point,

Tim Fischer had become Larry's primary-care physician, and he'd been seeing Larry and watching the test results every day. Dr. Fischer told her Larry's kidneys were failing and he probably wouldn't live more than another six months or a year—and perhaps not that long.

Julie thought about it, and when the work day was over, she asked Dr. Fischer please *not* to tell Larry.

"I don't want him to feel like there isn't any hope," Julie said to him. "You could tell him he's real sick and his kidneys are failing. Larry already knows that anyway. But just don't put a time frame on it, because then it's like having a death sentence hanging over his head. I don't want him to have to count the time and think about whether he's going to die within so many days or so many months."

"He might want to know," Dr. Fischer said. "He might want to tie up loose ends or to take a trip or something like that."

"Where is he going to go?" Julie said. "Do you think he can go sit on the beach in Hawaii or something? He's not going to want to go anywhere—that's not the issue."

When Michael came to pick Julie up at work, he also asked Dr. Fischer not to give Larry any specific time frame for his death. He didn't think Larry could handle it emotionally. Too much had already happened to Larry too fast, he said. It had only been one and a half months since he had severed his ties with the Klan and the Nazis and started his new life. This news could be totally devastating.

Dr. Fischer said the issue of whether to tell Larry how long he had to live had ethical and moral implications he'd have to consider carefully. He said he'd think it over, discuss it with colleagues and let them know what he decided one way or another. Michael and Julie were hopeful.

The next day, Dr. Spry, a kidney specialist, came into Larry's room while Michael and Julie were there. Dr. Spry gave Larry the results of his kidney tests in layman's terms—and as soon as he related the test results, Larry understood the implications. Then Dr. Spry said, "As you may realize, you probably have no more than six months to a year to live."

Larry sat very still. He was sitting up straight and his hands were folded in his lap. It seemed he was looking right at Dr. Spry as he spoke, and he was doing everything he could not to show any emotion or shed any tears. When Dr. Spry left the room, Larry remained immobile for a few moments and then he "collapsed from the inside out," as Julie put it.

"He just couldn't believe it," Julie said. "Neither could we—because Dr. Spry wasn't his primary-care physician. He was a specialist, and we never imagined he would be the one to tell him that. Although Dr. Spry had done absolutely nothing wrong, it was still shocking. We were all in shock. I was going to follow Dr. Spry out into the hall and say 'How could you have said that?' but I was too worried about taking care of Larry."

Larry looked like a small, terrified child with his lips quivering and tears rolling down his face. Julie and Michael also began to cry, and they sat on either side of Larry, put their arms around him and huddled together, all of them crying—reminiscent of what had happened only one and a half months previously on November 16.

In a few minutes, Larry abruptly straightened up and said, "I'm okay—it's just okay." He regained his composure and wiped the tears off his face. "I don't want all this attention," he said. "Let me be by myself. Let's not talk about this anymore."

On New Year's Eve, the night after Larry got this news, Julie was sitting beside his bed talking to him. Larry had been having trouble breathing. He didn't know the prediction of six months to a year to live was a generous one. But Dr. Spry, Dr. Fischer and the other doctors discussing his case were sure Larry didn't have more than a month or two left at the most. Larry looked at Julie and began to weep—a weeping as filled with anger as it was with grief over all that he'd lost in his life and all that he'd now never be able to find.

"I don't want to die," Larry said. "I just started to live. It took me forty-two years to start to live right."

Julie looked at Larry and felt the depth of his grief. "Do you think this whole experience has made it harder for you or better for you?" she asked, thinking that somehow knowing love this late in the game magnified his losses.

"I wouldn't change it for anything," he said. "Not anything."

Julie held Larry's hand and stroked it.

"Julie?" Larry asked, "Could you hold me?"

"Of course."

Julie crawled next to Larry on the hospital bed, and held Larry in her arms to comfort him. "He was so scared," she said. "He trembled and cried. It was so terrible. It was the worst New Year's Eve of my life."

Often while he was so sick, Julie crawled up on Larry's hospital bed and held him. "I know with the nurses on the floor it must have been like the gossip of the hospital," Julie said, "because here I was the cantor's wife and I'm lying on the bed with this former Grand Dragon of the Klan and I'm holding him. But you know what, I didn't care. I really did not care. I still don't care. My feeling was that Larry needed to be held. And you can't hold a person who's sitting in a wheelchair. When people are standing up and they hug one another, they feel that fullness of a hug but when someone is sitting in a chair and you lean over and you pat them on the back and you give them a hug, it's not the same.

"So I held Larry. It was just real simple to me. It is what I would do with a child—and in many ways, Larry was a child."

A couple of days after Larry had received the news he was going to die sometime soon, Daniel Levy from *Time* magazine arrived at the hospital for a long-scheduled interview. Levy initially had seen the story on the AP wire in November and had called to set up a meeting. Traditionally, the magazine's "Interviews" were a straight one-on-one question-and-answer format, but Levy had gotten approval for doing a double Q and A with Michael *and* Larry. The only time he remembered it being done before was with the Russian writer and dissident Alexander Solzhenitsyn and his wife.

"I found this a fascinating story, but I guess like most people I really felt I had to get a feeling of who these people were," Levy said later. "I had called up, and I guess you get a bit spoiled when you work for *Time* magazine and you call people up and they're always sort of 'Wow! *Time* magazine!' And I called up Michael and he was like, 'OK, sure, come out.' I didn't realize at the time these poor people were being just so barraged by everybody. And I remember Julie—talking to Julie I kind of felt sorry for her; she sounded like she was being slightly overwhelmed. You know, I realized quite a bit later, she was sort of the unsung hero. She had all these things to do—she had kids at home and she took care of this formerly hateful man and made him into sort of one of her children—and then she had to deal with these press people as well, and I was one of them."

The night before the interview, Daniel Levy had an impromptu pasta dinner with the Weissers and went into their garage to look at the paraphernalia from Larry's previous life. "I felt this sense of horror," Levy said. "It was, for me, slightly different, but the same as going to the Holocaust museum and seeing these Nazi, anti-Semitic tracts. These were his Klan things, and boxes of hate literature containing drawings of blacks being hanged, Jews being shot, and even threats to good white Anglo-Saxon Protestants who might not toe the line."

When Levy met Larry the next day, Larry was sitting on his hospital bed with nothing on but a pair of white briefs. His upper body and the stumps of his legs looked pale and withered, and he clearly was feeling uncomfortable. Daniel noticed the stump of Larry's right leg looked liked it had been flattened, with the skin folded back into itself somehow. Long scars ran along the outside of his left leg and festering sores dotted the lower part of the stump.

After they shook hands, Larry made a joke. "I used to be five feet eight inches tall and weigh a hundred fifty pounds," he said. "Now I still weigh a hundred fifty and I'm only four feet two."

"He didn't look like some infamous leader," Levy says. "But he was this man who six months earlier, if he had use of his legs and his eyes, or if he had the chance and he felt he wouldn't get caught, he might just have killed me.

"He spoke surprisingly eloquently," says Levy. "Even with all of his stops and jerks, that sort of speech pattern, if you got beyond that and just listened to what he was saying, it was fascinating. And I had asked him why he became this way, and he told me when he was thirteen or fourteen years old in reform school at Kearney, he was gang-raped by four or five blacks."

Larry also had told Michael and Julie and several other people the same story about this alleged event in reform school, where he'd been sent for stealing cars. He said he was in the showers one day when a boy he had thought was his friend grabbed him and said, "Let's butt-fuck this little fat boy."

"I was fat at the time and I started struggling," Larry said. "We didn't have any clothes on. And about four of five of them, they just grabbed me and this one guy, John, took his turn and then the other one and so on. And this guy, Deputy Dog, they called him Deputy Dog, he didn't want to take part, but they made him because he was more or less a virgin. And I was in pain and I was crying, of course, and bleeding. And then after it happened, the counselor came in and he says, 'Well,' he says, 'apparently you got what was coming to you, didn't you?'

"From then on, I just hated blacks," Larry said. "Every time I was around them, I felt like killing them. Anybody who wasn't like me was my enemy. When I got out of there, I joined Hell's Angels. At that time, they didn't accept blacks or Hispanics and they were racists and I wanted to be like them and kick butt."

Daniel Levy knew the doctors had just told Larry how long he had to live. "I understand you've gotten some bad news recently," he said. "If you can't talk about this, don't."

"Well, they gave me this death sentence of sorts," Larry said. "But they're not going to get me that easily. The doctor told me I have six months to a year. But I think I can push it further, because I'm ornery as hell. . . . I want to try to change some minds. I know I can't change the hard-core racists, but maybe I can put something in the back of their minds that they can think about as time goes on. People who are borderline racists—maybe I can get to them *before* they cross that line. . . . I'm not going to stop just because I'm sick."

During their interview, Rebecca called Larry from Memphis, where she'd gone to visit her father. "When she called, Larry sort of brightened up in the room over this young girl," Daniel Levy said. "It was funny how he was always saying how beautiful things were. Obviously, he was blind. He would see strange shifts of light and darkness, yet he would always refer to people and things as 'very beautiful.' "

At another point, Larry began to cry. He cried several times during their two-hour interview, and Daniel Levy stared at him in amazement. "I remember looking at this man and repeating to myself, 'This is the Grand Dragon of the Ku Klux Klan. This is the supreme white race,' " Levy said. "Here is this fellow sitting on this bed with these juvenile sorts of tattoos on his body, and he's being comforted by a cantor. Michael sat along side of him during the whole interview and when things were tough, Michael would put his arm around Larry and comfort him.

"I think it was then I began to realize what sort of a man Michael was," Levy said. "Here was somebody who was the focus of Larry's hatred and he had transcended it. He wouldn't let it get in the way of possibly being able to reach Larry on some sort of level. If somebody called up leaving messages on my phone saying 'You're going to die, Jew,' I would not bring food over to his house unless it was laced with arsenic,

PCBs and other things. But Michael was able to move beyond that anger and hatred. He's a man who really tried to love his enemy."

Daniel Levy was so taken with Lincoln and the Weissers he stayed an extra two days—and in the process, he learned more about Michael. "I decided to do this in a relaxed manner," he said. "One day I went with Michael to Wesleyan University, where he met with a small class and talked about religion. And it was so wonderful to see how he made it very accessible in talking about the close similarities between Judaism and Christianity. He showed many little connections—like how the Last Supper was a Passover. And this whole idea of baptism goes back to the whole idea of *mikvah* and purification. He showed those connections and sort of the wholeness or oneness of everybody, how there's really very little difference between us. I had known a lot about religion—I went to yeshiva school when I was a kid—and to see somebody go beyond that intellectual debate about it and try to bring some sort of substance and understanding to it was quite remarkable."

Another day, Michael asked Daniel Levy if he wanted to go to his weekly meeting at the County-City Jail. "I said I was game," Levy later recalled. "But here I found myself in this town where there are no Jews in prison, or maybe one or two, and here the minister for this super-maximum-security jail is this cantor.

"I remember going into this concrete bunker where all the doors were worked by electrical bolts. We walked from chamber to chamber, and we finally came into one of their pods, which is the central area with the cells around it. And instead of having bars around it, there were steel doors. As we got in that room, this gate bolted shut behind us, and I thought to myself 'We are going to die.'

"I was envisioning the *New York Times* reporting a prison break, fifteenth day, cantor and *Time* magazine reporter still in there. As it turned out, we went into this small room, and there were like eight of us at the table, and Michael read a part from the Bible. And it was quite appropriate. He told the story and I remember him saying, 'Do you have any questions?' Of course, there's silence. So he says, 'Well, let's all hold hands and say a prayer.' So I was just sitting there holding hands with guys with 'Love' and 'Hate' tattooed on their knuckles, and we said a small prayer.

"We also went out to a state penitentiary called the Lincoln Correctional Center, outside of Lincoln, where he met with an inmates' club. It wasn't just getting out of a cell; they wanted to use their minds and there was a good bit of give and take. It was a group of about twenty or so. There was genuine interest, and I know Michael was quite pleased with that. Many of them had heard the story of Michael and Larry Trapp, and they knew people like Larry and said they could never forgive them or even want to try to understand them. Michael said, 'I felt the same way. This is really what's happened, and in a sense it has changed my life.' He didn't have to do any of this. He didn't have to go there. But it actually seemed very gratifying for him."

What Daniel Levy didn't know at the time, but what Michael eventually told him, his friends and his congregation, explained in many ways why Michael Weisser worked so hard to make other people's lives better, why he seemed to want so much to give people an opportunity to change and to overcome the divisions separating them. It explained why his thinking had taken such a spiritual direction—and why he didn't look at his work as a job, but rather as his life.

FLICK

OF A TAIL

Chapter 18

And I tell you the good in us will win,
Over all our wickedness, over all the wrongs we have done.
We will look back at the pages of written history, and be amazed,
and then we will laugh and sing,
And the good that is in us, children in their cradles, will have won.
— GATES OF PRAYER

*S*omeone who did understand a great deal about Michael
Weisser's motivating history was Marshall M. Glatzer. Cantor Glatzer
had been one of Michael Weisser's professors during Michael's five and
a half years at Hebrew Union College—Jewish Institute of Religion's
School of Sacred Music in New York City in the mid-1970s. He had retired in 1987 after heart surgery and was enjoying his retirement in
Yardley, Pennsylvania, when he picked up a newspaper one day and
read an article about his former student reaching out to the Grand
Dragon of the Ku Klux Klan. Cantor Glatzer was particularly thrilled
because he knew Michael had overcome tremendous impediments in
his own life before he had become a cantorial student.

Cantor Glatzer sat right down and wrote a letter: "Dear Michael: You
can imagine my surprise upon opening my [newspaper recently] to
find you smiling back at me from the page. Let me add my congratulations and a sincere 'Shalom' to you for being so successful in turning
an enemy into a friend—one of the most noble of our traditions. Knowing your background, and recalling your own story, this was especially

moving to me. I can readily understand your easy empathy for your new friend. I trust this note finds you and your family well and wish you continued success in all that you do. . . ."

Cantor Glatzer remembered Michael with fondness. "I was his teacher—and when Michael and I got close, he confided in me about his past," Glatzer recalled. "I was pleased to find that somebody could rise above his background and overcome it."

Michael rarely explained the painful personal experiences which made him understand how Larry Trapp or anyone else could change. Yet Michael fathomed these seeming impossibilities because he himself had changed from a benumbed, selfish and harmful young thief into the person he now was. There's a Buddhist saying, "Our fortunes change at the flick of a horse's tail," and this is what had happened to Michael. But the truth was too complicated, too shameful and had happened too long ago to explain very often. He was afraid people might not understand. And if they didn't, it might be more difficult for him to continue making his own amends and doing his own good work.

When Larry told the story of his father punching him in the jaw and knocking him out when he ran away, Michael remembered how he felt when his parents divorced and his father, Louis, the milkman turned bus driver, virtually disappeared from his life. He remembered the way his chest hurt as his mother walked him, his brother David and sister Sylvia to the orphanage where he stayed from the time he was three years old until he was six.

Michael remembered how he hated the big dormitory room he shared with other children, how he hated the food and the narrow bed he made every morning, how he ran away from the orphanage and found his way to his Grandma Sophie's house in New Haven. He would never forget how he was picked up there by a smiling Mr. Major,* "the bad man" at the Jewish orphanage. Mr. Major laughed with Grandma Sophie, but refused her offered cup of coffee. As soon as he got Michael back to the home, Mr. Major beat him mercilessly with a rubber-soled shoe. Michael was four years old at the time.

Michael talked freely about how once his mother had remarried and he was home again, they moved from house to house in New Haven.

*Not his real name.

Michael rarely lingered on how, when his good-natured stepfather, Morris Rubinsky, was working at the shoe store, his mother, who worked long hours as a waitress at Chuck's Luncheonette, sometimes flew off the handle and beat him with a belt or a shoe. "That's what people did in those days—especially from the lower economic strata—and they still do it," Michael said. "They don't see it as abuse. When a child is out of line, they just say, 'I'm going to beat the hell out of you.' We didn't really know there was anything wrong with that because everybody we knew was in the same boat."

Michael had said several times that some abused children somehow miraculously come through the experience without inflicting pain on others. But more often than not, he said, abused children turn that pain back on themselves or on others. What Michael did not say was how dramatically he had turned his own pain back on himself and on others. He didn't say he had done a lot of wrong—and caused a lot of harm—before he started doing the right thing. Nor did he say he'd paid the price for his wrongs many times over.

Michael first got into trouble when he was ten years old and ran away from home—partly because he was rebellious and partly because he just wanted to be somewhere else. He remembers one time when he ran away and got himself to the Merritt Parkway. "I was wearing a big, huge, bulky white sweater and a pair of jeans and it was raining," he says. "I was hitchhiking, which was common then. So this young couple picks me up and I get in the back of the car drenched like a rat, and the guy turns around and says, 'Where are you going?' I said, 'I'm goin' to New York.' And he looks at me and kind of smiles and said, 'Why are you going to New York?' I was trying to be a tough guy, right, so I said, 'The cops are after me.' So he said, 'OK, I'll take you and the cops will never get you.' I felt this guy was cool, you know, he was going to take me to New York, but he got off at the next exit and brought me to the state troopers' barracks.

"So they had me. And then I was in a cell at the police barracks—they had to keep me somewhere. The state troopers were nice to me. They gave me something to eat, and the next thing I know, somebody came and got me. But I had to go to the Juvenile Court for being a runaway." Michael was sent to a "reformatory"—the Connecticut School for Boys—for a year.

There, he attended classes *and* learned how to polish floors. "The drill was, on the weekend, all of these boys in a row with blankets under their knees and blankets on their hands, went back and forth, up and down this room until Mr. Roberts, who had a hair-trigger temper, thought it was perfect. Sometimes it was an hour, sometimes it was three hours, sometimes it was a whole Saturday. The most humiliating part wasn't the floors. Every second week they would march us downtown to Meriden to go to the movie. I hated it. You had to march to the theater, double file, and all the people in the community would be staring at you because you were all wearing the same baggy state-made jeans and white shirts and black shoes, and everybody knew where you came from. It was humiliating, it was terrible, and people would be saying things, 'state kids,' you know."

Like any kid sent to "reform" school, Michael also learned about crime. "Until I got there—I had no idea you could break into a store or steal a car," he said. "It never crossed my mind—because basically I was scared of doing stuff like that. But there were kids there who were experienced child criminals and I got to be friends with some of them."

The first crime Michael ever committed was when he and a couple of his friends escaped. The three boys waited until the night-duty guard fell asleep, and then they walked down the stairs, crawled out a window and took off into the woods. "On the way, we broke into a service station," Michael remembers. "It was really relatively easy to do. We got in there and one of the guys popped open a cigarette machine, so we stuffed our pockets with cigarettes, and whatever money was in there, and we took some candy bars, and then we split up. I think I was gone for a day and a half and the other kids were gone a comparable time before they were caught and brought back.

"The police picked me up just as a person who didn't belong somewhere. We didn't get caught for the breaking and entering in the service station. When I got back, I was put in the hole, and the director came and said to me, 'You would have been going home in thirty days, but now we are going to have the pleasure of your company for another six months.' So that was probably a big mistake."

Larry Trapp spent a lot longer time in reform school than Michael did—and he spent most of his adolescence there. But the biggest difference between his experiences and Larry Trapp's, Michael has said, was Larry had diabetes and he didn't, and Larry's parents were racists and his weren't. Also, Michael always had all different kinds of friends.

"Even in New Haven it wasn't really cool to hang out with black kids or Puerto Rican kids," Michael says, "but I always did—partly because we lived in a crummy neighborhood and our neighbors were black, so I knew we were all the same. When I was in junior high at Augusta Lewis Troup Junior High School—it was a tough school, but all schools in New Haven were tough—I had a singing group we called Two Days and a Night because it was two white guys and a black guy. I know we weren't any good, but we did it anyway, and we even once performed at the Whalley Avenue Theater during a talent show between all the Saturday movies. That was pretty good. I did that for a while and I kind of liked that. People used to make comments about it like, 'Why do you sing with that nigger?' But I really didn't see things that way."

By the time he was a teenager, Michael was trying to cover his feelings of powerlessness by being tough. He showed up at school in a leather jacket with chains hanging off of it. He wore his hair in a ducktail, dressed in heavy engineer's boots, blue jeans and white T-shirts with his packs of Lucky Strikes rolled into the sleeve. He got something of a reputation when one time outside a drugstore near Hillhouse High School, he hit a bully named "Speed" in the jaw and the other side of Speed's head hit the corner of the building, which caused both jaws to break. Speed was in the hospital and everybody thought Michael had some kind of secret weapon. The truth was he had always been afraid of Speed, and for three years the kid had pushed him around and hit him. That day he'd just gotten fed up. Nobody realized the building had done the bulk of the damage. When Speed's father came to their house, Michael's mother and stepfather thought they were going to be sued. But Speed's father said, "Michael broke Speed's jaw in two places and, you know, it's about time that happened to him because he's been screwing around with people forever and getting away with it."

Michael hated being in school, but he had paper routes and a job in a gas station pumping gas and selling belts or hoses and made fairly good money, which he turned over to his mother. He and two of his friends—Richie and "Fly Face"—sang together in their free time, and every now and then they sang at dances. Occasionally, they'd take a neighbor's unlocked '49 Chevrolet (which didn't need a key to start) for a midnight joy ride and then return it to the same parking space so the guy would never know it had been gone.

When Michael was seventeen, he quit high school, and he and his friend George, who was black, enlisted together in the Army. Michael became an artillery man in the Third Army Missile Command at Fort Bragg. A "flick of the horse's tail" came for Michael with the notification of the death of his beloved stepfather, Morris Rubinsky. Michael was nineteen years old when the Red Cross sent a telegram: FATHER DIED IN CONNECTICUT—ARRANGE TRANSPORTATION. At first Michael didn't know which father they were talking about—was it Morris Rubinsky or his biological father, Louis Weisser? Michael couldn't believe it was Morris. Morris had been his rock—the person who got him out of "the Home," who laughed with him, wrestled with David and him and told them stories at night. One of the highlights of Michael's childhood had been when his mother Ann first brought Morris to meet him at the orphanage and he'd looked up into those calm, kind eyes and seen the man who was going to be his new father. Michael had liked him from the beginning, and Morris had been a soothing, steady presence in his life.

The worst part of Morris' death was that he'd committed suicide by jumping off a bridge. Michael was devastated; what stands out in his memory about going home for Morris' funeral was the weather. "It was so cold," he says. "It was so bitter cold." Michael himself was chilled to the bone. Afterward, nothing was the same. Nothing mattered. Whatever sense of hope he'd had was gone. "I just didn't care about anything," Michael says. "I didn't care what happened to me." At the time, Michael couldn't comprehend the emotional damage he'd experienced from having been abandoned three times in his life—first by his father, then by his mother, and now by Morris—all with no explanations. When he got out of the Army, he went to Florida, then Baltimore—anywhere but Connecticut—and worked at low-paying jobs that ranged from making desserts in a restaurant to selling magazine subscriptions.

In the early 1960s, he wound up in New York City. Within a couple of days of being in Manhattan, Michael met a guy named Al from Boston who was a professional thief. Al was a couple of years older than Michael, and he and Michael started hanging around together at a rock-and-roll bar on 45th Street called the Wagon Wheel. "We were really sleazy people," Michael says. "I mean, Al looked nice and I looked nice, and these other people looked nice, but now looking back, the people we knew and hung around with were really the dregs of humanity.

"Anyway, this one night, Al said to me, 'Come on, let's go over to Jersey and make some money.' So I went, and we went into this warehouse building in the middle of the night and he opened the safe in about thirty minutes and took the back pages out of the checkbook and wrote up a whole bunch of payroll checks on their machine. He wrote the amounts for $89.76, $112.14, numbers like that, and then the next day we went to a lot of grocery stores and bought $3.00 worth of groceries and cashed bunches of the checks and split the money.

"Another thing he taught me how to do in those days was to buy an airline ticket with a phony check. You would go to the bank, open an account with $25.00 and they'd give you a book of checks. Then you would go to an airline office and buy a ticket, and then you'd go to another office and cash it. There were no computers then, and they would just give you your money for these airline tickets. So we were thieves, and that's how we were making our living. We did that for quite a while."

One June night a kid named Arnie led Al and Michael to an apartment in Manhattan for a burglary. Arnie had said, "Look, I know this place where a guy keeps a lot of diamonds and jewelry and money—and I know when he's not home." Al rented a car and the three drove to Greenwich Village, where they broke into the third-floor apartment of a restaurant owner who allegedly was at work. The kid had been half-right: the man's apartment was filled with beautiful antiques, expensive jewelry and cash. But Michael, Al and the kid were busy bagging things up and stashing them by the door for a quick exit when the man came home. He unlocked his own front door and walked into Al, who started hitting him on the head with a gun. Michael was stunned. "I didn't know Al had a gun," Michael said, "but Al pistol-whipped him and tied him up." Then they left.

The next day the banged-up restaurant owner, with stitches in his head, identified Arnie because he'd seen him in Kelly's bar on 45th Street. When the police picked up Arnie, he gave them the names and descriptions of his accomplices. Michael was arrested at his hotel room and booked into the old city jail, the Tombs, where he was held in lieu of bail. When the police picked up Al, they learned he was wanted on a warrant for armed robbery and forgery in Massachusetts. Al made a deal: in exchange for having the New York charges dropped against him, he would turn state's witness against Michael and give testimony about the burglaries in New Jersey as well as this incident in New York.

That way, the charges from New Jersey and New York would come in on Michael, but not on him, and he would be extradited to Massachusetts to face prosecution there.

Even though Michael hadn't been armed and didn't hit the man, he was equally guilty under the law for armed robbery and assault and battery. He didn't blame Al, and he didn't try to cut a deal. This was the price he had to pay for what he'd done. He pled guilty to one count of felony robbery, assault and burglary in New York and to seven counts of breaking and entering, larceny and attempted breaking and entering in New Jersey. He was convicted and sentenced to two consecutive prison sentences: two to five years in New York and two to five in New Jersey.

The prisons he served time in were no playgrounds. As a first-time offender, he was sent to Elmira State Reformatory, but when a hunger strike broke out there, he was transferred with a number of other prisoners to Auburn State Prison—where he served the remainder of his New York time. After two years in New York, he was paroled directly to Trenton State Prison, where he stayed another two and a half years. In each of these prisons, Michael lived confined behind thick walls and in barren steel cages, getting up, standing in line, walking in the prison yard and working with thousands of other men wearing identical prison clothes who lived in an environment oddly akin to infancy, where every decision is made *for* you—where every movement is watched, where you can't buy a shirt, make a phone call or order a pair of glasses for yourself.

At Auburn, he worked as a typesetter in the print shop and learned the ropes of prison life. He became a weight lifter for self-protection, and in the process became friends with a guy named Bruno, who weighed about 350 pounds and was a little bit crazy. If you were a friend of Bruno's, nobody would bother you and you never had a problem. "Bruno didn't care if his friends were white or black," Michael said. "The weight-lifting box was integrated and nobody dared say anything to him because he would just break you in half, you know. So I was a friend of Bruno's—and Bruno was a good guy, but he was nuts. I knew he was nuts. But it meant I managed to live a pretty calm life."

During that time, in the silence of his nights on his hard cot in his cell, Michael began to examine his life and how he had gotten where he was. Often, before the morning light broke, he was up writing down his thoughts. In the process, he faced his own dishonesty. "My hands perpetrated their own indignities," he wrote. "While I was speaking of man perpetrating indignities on man, I knew the meaning of hypocrisy." In poems, stories, letters and journal entries, he struggled with the shame of his actions and the waste and disgrace of his imprisonment—which he believed he never could overcome. He wrote: "The stigma of an ousted man / remains until his death, / hunted, harried, chased, and more / until he takes his final breath. Even then he isn't free / his memory's despoiled / his children's reputation spoiled."

Days, weeks and months passed slowly. But after four years of inhaling Camels, blowing out the smoke and watching the steam rise from his coffee cup in the mornings as he sat writing on a board propped between his lap and a small table beside his cot, Michael began to envision the end of his sentence. He began to dream about the possibility of a real life.

In one of many letters to his mother in New Haven, he wrote: "It will be some feeling to be able to be a human being again. Do you have any idea what it is like to get up to a bell? To eat to a bell? To sleep to a bell? To do everything in life to a bell? That isn't life. It's security, yes, but . . . it's something less than life. The only thing left to men in prisons that they can call their own is self-respect. And though it is so precious, so irreplaceable once lost, there are many who throw it away with no thought of what they will be without it."

In the solitude he'd found in prison, Michael had begun to discover who he was. "I think I've found, finally, that I am relevant, if not to anyone else or anything else, then to myself," he wrote. "I have come to see a lot of things in a different light in the past few years. I think I'm becoming aware that material things are not so important after all. They are nice, yes, but not nice enough to be worth tossing away years of my life. Now I am able to see the follies of my own life. . . . My own idiocies seem much greater than before because I understand the motivations and the results—and for perhaps the first time, I know them for what they really amount to—which is *nothing*."

While he was in prison, the Vietnam War was escalating along with antiwar protests, the Beatles were touring America and the Kerner Commission Report observed, "Our nation is moving toward two societies, one black, one white, separate and unequal." From inside prison, as if from another country, Michael watched and read and felt connected to all these events. He heard the words of astronaut Neil Armstrong's planned speech—"One small step for man, one giant leap for mankind"—as American astronauts walked on the moon for the first time. When Martin Luther King, Jr., was assassinated, Michael cried for the first time since he had been a young kid. When Bobby Kennedy was murdered in Los Angeles, he cried again.

He got weary listening to prison narratives about excess wealth and superhuman feats—tall tales men told to cover their feelings of insignificance. "Why can't everyone be contented with what they are, who they are?" he wrote his mother, Ann. "I can think of several people who are really big, huge-hearted folks who have somehow lived their lives with thoughts of others in their minds. All of them are good people, people who seem to care when they hear of someone's troubles. I think they all bleed a little bit every time they see the horrible numbers in newspapers denoting boys dead in Vietnam. . . . I think they feel for the struggle of black people in America and for the plight of the Jews in Israel and for convicts in prisons. I think what it all boils down to is that these people, these little insignificant small people who possess no axe to grind are really the important people of the world."

Michael spent the last year of his sentence at Jones Farm, a minimum-security facility, where he lived in barracks with 140 other men and was allowed to leave the prison to work an eight-hour job every day and then come back to the prison. The job he got at a small factory involved cutting out patterns for swimming-pool liners and pool covers. "I feel pretty satisfied with myself for the first time in quite a few years," he wrote his mother. "Also, I'm going to send you enough money to pay your rent every month, so don't say no because the check will be in the mail every month anyway. The rest of what I'm earning, I'll save and use for expenses." Michael loved working eight hours a day and being back in the normal world. ("My experiences in the world of real people and things have so far left a very sweet taste in my mouth. People are genuinely good and moral.") At night back at Jones Farm, he read an enormous number of books, participated in discussion groups with a graduate student from Princeton University and started feeling like "a somewhat normal human being."

Before he was paroled, Michael had figured out the way he wanted to live his life: "I know I don't need a big car and a big pile of money," he wrote to his mother. "A little share of happiness and a chunk of peace of mind will take pretty good care of me. . . . I've learned to view all men as my brothers. I love—a lot. Does this sound like me? . . . Mother, the love I'm talking about goes beyond the abstract kind of love reserved for only causes and generalities. It goes to the family, to you, to friends whose names can be counted on the fingers of one hand. When I say I love, I'm not being fancy or glib or flip. I used to think I was a little odd because I can't remember ever having hated anyone. Ever. Not in my entire twenty-eight years. Hate sometimes seems like a necessity in this world of ours, but I've discovered love is just as strong and even stronger. So I guess I'm not such an oddball after all. . . . It's taken this much of my life to figure this out, but I suppose that it's been worth the effort and the hassles and the hang-ups and the problems and troubles, because the compensations inside of my head are so tremendous as to be indescribable. I think I'm at total peace with myself and with the rest of the world."

Michael's process of change was well underway by the time he got out on parole, found an apartment in Jamesburg, New Jersey, and began to fall in love with a small, dark-haired young woman named Louise who worked at a local dentist's office. Besides Louise, another person he met was about to make his life change dramatically. That person was a rabbi Michael ran into one day when he stopped after work to buy tickets for a rock-and-roll concert. The concert was a benefit and tickets were being sold at a Conservative synagogue named Congregation Beth Or. While Michael was buying the tickets for himself and Louise, a tall, thin man named Rabbi Isaac Moseson came out and said, "Are you Jewish?"

"Yeah."

"So how come I never see you in the synagogue?"

"It doesn't interest me much."

In prison, Michael had started going to Jewish services again—at first just to have someplace to go. But he'd found a solace there that surprised him. He'd also begun to read the Bible. Still, he did not consider himself religious. After that first meeting, however, Michael seemed to see Rabbi Moseson everywhere—sitting in a restaurant eating dinner, in a café at lunch, in the supermarket, at odd places. Every time Rabbi Moseson saw Michael, he spoke to him. Eventually, Michael ended up going to a Friday night service with Louise, who had begun converting to Judiasm before she met Michael. At the service, Rabbi Moseson mentioned a new friend of his was visiting the synagogue that night.

Rabbi Moseson lured Michael in slowly but surely. Soon, Michael was attending services fairly regularly. One day Rabbi Moseson asked Michael to help him out. "I'm in a real jam," he said. "I've got these two couples coming in who are studying for conversion. I have to be somewhere else for a meeting. Could you teach them about Passover?"

"No," Michael said. "I don't know anything about Passover."

"Come on, please. They're coming in next Thursday and I can't be here. I'll give you a couple of books and you can look it over. It doesn't matter—and they don't know a whole lot about it anyway." Michael, who was working at an aluminum company at the time, finally agreed; he read ahead, met with the two couples and had a successful session.

Little by little, Rabbi Moseson got Michael even more involved. Rabbi Isaac Moseson's father had always told him, "If a person has a potential, push him to his potential"—and he'd spent his life as a rabbi trying to do just that. In Michael, who was unsure of himself when they met, Isaac saw a spark of genius—and beautiful promise. One day he asked Michael to help him conduct part of the service. Michael said, "I don't know how to do that. I don't remember any of the songs." But the rabbi said, "Ah, it's not for two weeks. I need you to do it. You can look it up." So Michael did it.

Then one day the rabbi asked Michael if he could help him with the bar mitzvah kids. "Look," the rabbi said, "you've got this great job that ends at three o'clock in the afternoon and the kids don't come until three-thirty. You can do it—you know, three-thirty to five, twice a week."

"I don't know any of this stuff," Michael said.

"That's okay. You'll be a page or two ahead of the kids. You'll be fine."

Michael only knew Hebrew from his own bar mitzvah, so he read slowly, but he practiced. He also had an instant rapport with the bar mitzvah kids, who started excelling and wanted to please Michael. It became apparent he was doing a good thing.

Before long, a woman came in and said to Michael, "The rabbi told me I should talk to you about private bar mitzvah lessons for my son." The woman told Michael her son was going to be thirteen in a couple of months, and hadn't been in Hebrew school because he was mentally retarded. "The rabbi said whatever way you wanted to handle it would be fine."

When the woman left, Michael went upstairs and asked the rabbi, "What are you doing? I don't know anything about mentally retarded kids!"

"Look, Michael," Rabbi Moseson said. "If anybody can teach this child, you can. It doesn't matter what he accomplishes. Whatever little bit he can accomplish will be wonderful."

Michael set up a series of appointments with the boy, and they met twice a week for almost two years. At the end of that time, the boy was able to chant the blessings for the Torah and for a Haftorah reading at the Sabbath service. People had packed the synagogue for his bar mitzvah because the boy's mother was well liked and everyone thought she was courageous for doing this. The boy recited the Torah blessings before and after Rabbi Moseson read the special Torah reading for him. The boy then recited the first blessing and read the Haftorah. Michael recited the concluding blessing afterward. It was an extraordinary experience, and everyone in the sanctuary was in tears.

A few months after that, Rabbi Moseson asked Michael if he could drive him to New York for a meeting. He said he had a heart condition and he was supposed to take it easy, so he needed a driver. When they got almost all the way to the Upper West Side of Manhattan, Rabbi Moseson explained to Michael he'd set up an interview for him at Hebrew Union College—Jewish Institute of Religion, where Michael could study to become a cantor. He hadn't told him about it ahead of time, he said, because for once he didn't want to have to hear Michael say no. Rabbi Moseson had heard Michael sing when he had filled in at services occasionally. He thought Michael had a beautiful voice and would make a wonderful cantor.

"Look, I'll go through with this, but it's a farce," Michael responded. "It's ridiculous. I mean, I feel like going up there and telling these people that you're full of shit."

"Don't do that," Rabbi Moseson said with a laugh. "Look, I'm a rabbi, and the word will get around that I'm full of shit. Don't do that."

During the interview, the admissions panel asked Michael what he knew about seminary and he said he didn't know very much, "but Rabbi Moseson thinks I do. Rabbi Moseson thinks that what the world needs is one more cantor."

When Michael was accepted into the institute, Rabbi Moseson

arranged for him to get a fellowship for the first year as well as another part-time job. By then Michael and Louise had gotten married and she was pregnant with the first of their four children. And so when Michael Weisser was twenty-nine years old, he began a regular commute to New York City to study Jewish history, Hebraic and liturgical studies and sacred music. After Michael began his studies, the institute called Rabbi Moseson and said, "Don't worry about another fellowship. We're giving him a four-year-scholarship. He knows more as an entering student than a lot of our graduating students." Rabbi Moseson's confidence was more than fulfilled. Michael won top awards as a cantorial student and was graduated with highest honors from Hebrew Union College–Jewish Institute of Religion on June 5, 1976, and got his Board of Cantor Certification that same date.

"It was a blessing," Rabbi Moseson says. "Never in his life did Michael dream he would be a cantor. He felt he didn't deserve it because of his past, but I accepted him for his present and for his future and told him to let go of what was behind him. I told him, 'God takes care of all fools, me included. If you live long enough, there's always a tomorrow.' "

Cantor Glatzer, who hadn't seen Michael since his graduation, remembers Michael as "more serious than most cantorial students—or at least more serious than many of the others." Only the admissions committee and a few people at the seminary knew about Michael's background, and they advised Michael it wasn't something people needed to know. But when Michael talked to Cantor Glatzer about what he had done and how he had been in prison for five years and on parole for two years, Cantor Glatzer wasn't shocked. "He had some rough edges, as I recall, so I wasn't too surprised," he said. In fact, on some levels, Cantor Glatzer was quite delighted by the news.

"In the Jewish tradition, we're quite open to change," he said. "The Jewish tradition praises the man who comes back from doing wrong and does the right thing. Now all of that was a long long time ago, and Michael's more than proved himself since then."

WORKING MIRACLES

Chapter 19

The repentant sinner should strive to do good with the same
faculties with which he sinned. . . . If his feet had run to sin, let
them now run to the performance of the good. If his mouth
had spoken falsehood, let it now be opened in wisdom. Violent
hands should now open in charity. . . . The trouble-maker
should now become a peacemaker.
—*RABBI JONAH GERONDI (13TH C.)*

*M*ichael pushed Larry's wheelchair into the living room just after Julie had carried in another two bags of Larry's clothes. An early
January snow drifting down outside made the carpeted living room
with its big blue and white couch and comfortable chairs especially
warm and inviting. Remembering Larry's initial call, Michael said,
"Larry, you're going to be *really* sorry—no, I mean *really* happy—you
ever moved into 5810 Randolph Street!"

Since Larry had gotten out of the hospital, he had never slept another night at his own apartment. Later, nobody would remember exactly when and how it was decided he should move into the Weissers'
home, but they would recall it seemed the right thing to do. It also
seemed practical: Julie and Michael wouldn't have to run back and
forth from Larry's apartment several times every day because of one
crisis or another, and Larry could have good care and a loving home
until he died.

The nurses from Medical Personnel Pool who stopped by twice a day to measure Larry's blood sugar, take his blood pressure and give him insulin shots were able to stop calling ahead to see whether he was at home or at the Weissers'.

Otherwise it was anything but practical. Between them, Michael and Julie had five children—with three at home. They had a limited income and a small house. An extra person naturally meant extra expense. Larry got a Social Security check, but he didn't manage his money well. Already, Michael had paid a $187 grocery bill Larry owed so Larry wouldn't be prosecuted. Also, a sixth person would make their already cramped house more crowded—especially since that person was disabled and terminally ill. Larry would need Rebecca's bedroom because it was on the main level and involved no stairs. Rebecca would have to move downstairs to live with Dina and Dave in a dormitory-style basement arrangement.

Michael and Julie had talked to Dina, Rebecca and Dave about moving Larry into their home—and the kids agreed, although later they would remember it all slightly differently, would remember it all happened quickly, much too quickly, and they sometimes wondered whether it should have happened at all.

"It was all such a whirlwind," sixteen-year-old Rebecca remembers. "It was like I had come home one night—and they had mentioned it to me in passing. Like, 'How would you feel about giving up your room if Larry wanted to come live with us?'

" 'Excuse me?'

"I don't even remember ever really saying 'Yes, okay.' But apparently I did, I'm assuming I did, because I come home one night and all of my stuff is in the living room. They had moved my bed downstairs. I said 'What the hell is going on?'

"They said, 'Don't say anything or he'll feel bad.'

" '*He'll* feel bad! What about me? I've just been thrown out of my room!' I hated the hell out of him.

"Everybody in the house said all this sappy stuff about how I would learn to be a better person," Rebecca said. "I don't know, I mean, I feel a certain caring about Larry, and sometimes he can be the sweetest guy, but sometimes I just want to strangle him. On the other hand, it has forced me to take on more responsibility than I normally would have at this age, and it gives me an experience other teenagers haven't had."

Dina, who helped move Larry's things from his old apartment, also had mixed feelings about Larry's living with the family. During the move, Michael had taken Larry and a load of his stuff over to their house, and Dina was in Larry's apartment with Julie when the phone rang. "I answered it all cheerful," Dina said, "and this voice says, 'Is Larry Trapp there?' "

"I said, 'No, he's not, may I take a message?'

" 'Yeah. This is the Grand Wizard of the KKK. Tell him I called.'

"It scared the shit out of me," Dina said, "and I am crying, I am freaking out. I didn't know what to say to this guy. And then this voice goes, 'I love you, Dina.' It scared me to death, and he was laughing. I called back and I said, 'That is *not* funny, Larry! That is the most shitty thing to do to a kid!' So I just hung up on him. I was fourteen years old and I didn't talk to him for a day. That's the longest time I ever held a grudge, but I was so mad.

"Sometimes it's fun having Larry live with us, and sometimes it's just like a half-and-half thing," Dina said. "If I'm on the phone, and Julie has to go get something and I'm staying with Larry while he's asleep, I'll be talking and they'll say 'What are you doing?' I'll say, 'Oh, listening for Larry.' 'Who's Larry?' Then I have to go, 'He was a Klansman, but now he's not a Klansman, he's becoming Jewish and he's sleeping. So that's the whole story.' "

For Larry, moving into the Weissers seemed like a dream. "I never thought I was good enough to have anyone love me like this," he said. "It's still unbelievable. I thought my days were over with, but they've just begun. They began on November sixteenth. I had no will to live before—I didn't care one way or another. Now I've got everything in the world I want. I've got more than I ever wanted . . ."

A number of people weren't nearly so thrilled about Larry's move into Randolph Street. Julie's father, for one, was quite upset. In his and her mother's opinion, Julie always took on too much responsibility—but this was ridiculous. Julie's brother Dan had described the madhouse when he returned to Memphis from a visit to Lincoln, and Julie's father called, meaning to calmly discuss this with his daughter and talk some sense into her head. He ended up yelling, "Who do you think you are, Mother Teresa? You can't have that man live in your home!"

Some friends and members of the congregation were equally upset. "I had just gotten pregnant and so everything seemed weird, but my reaction was 'They've gone crazy,' " Cybele Londono said. "I thought,

'They've gone out of their minds. This is too much pressure; it will destroy their marriage.' We had all been very scared of the Klan—we had never expected that to happen in Lincoln—and when the Nazi man moved into their house, I thought 'What is happening here?' I thought, 'They're not rolling in money! How can they accept the financial burden of this?' I thought, 'Knowing him is one thing, moving him into their house is another.' Michael had picked up the ball, but Julie was running with it. I know of *nobody* who could have gotten into a situation like that."

"I was furious at Michael," said David Gasser, Cybele's husband, who works for a pharmaceutical company. "I thought he wasn't as available and it would take away from the time he spent at the temple. Also, the community was offended and upset with Julie because she wasn't showing up for Hadassah meetings and she stopped coming around as often. People expect more from the cantor's wife."

But for Michael and Julie, this was a personal decision, a family decision. They had a commitment to do what felt right to them—and this felt right, even if it was slightly crazy. Larry Trapp was dying—and they had the opportunity to give him support and a loving family until he died—and that's what they intended to do.

"Just because Michael is a person who's in a goldfish bowl because of the nature of what he does, I don't really think the personal decisions we make are really anyone else's business," Julie said. "This is just something we did on a very personal level, and we had no way of knowing it would have such a big ripple effect. Truthfully, I feel resentful sometimes that people feel they can pass judgment on a personal decision we made in our family. It's really not something that concerns them. And if they have negative thoughts about it, then maybe they should call us—knowing that we are pretty open-minded people—and talk about it. And if they have any doubts about Larry, all they have to do is meet him."

It was a tight squeeze on many levels, including the alien nature of this person coming to live and to die in the midst of the spontaneous daily dramas and chaos inspired by two rather zany adults, three teenagers, innumerable friends, a cat, a dog, a ringing doorbell and a ringing phone.

At first it looked odd just to see Larry and his hospital bed in Rebecca's room. ("Here's the former head of the Klan sleeping in Becca's Laura Ashley room—with Laura Ashley wallpaper and curtains," Julie said to her friend Rita, laughing at the sight.) Michael and Julie had a separate telephone line installed for Larry so he would be able to maintain independent contact with the outside world. They put up shelves for his books and put in a desk and a table for his tape recorder and boxes for his many tape recordings and books on tape. If Larry wanted to go somewhere on his own without Julie or Michael, he called a taxicab to take him.

For Larry, the physical changes also were dramatic. Suddenly, he was not only smiling a lot, but he was eating balanced meals, taking showers every day, wearing nice clean clothes and sleeping on soft pillows in clean sheets with a soft, pretty patchwork quilt covering him. "I have these horrible visions of Larry in his old efficiency apartment lying on dirty sheets with no cover," Julie said. "He didn't know he was cold because his circulation is so bad he has no feeling in his lower body. His sheets were dirty, his towels were sour and felt like sandpaper, and the kitchen was caked with food on the stove and the cabinets were filthy. Now he's clean, he smells good and he's probably receiving the best medical care he has had in years."

The exterior of the Weisser home also changed. It wasn't wheelchair-accessible until Michael and Julie got the League of Human Dignity, a state organization, to build a wide wooden ramp from their small front yard up to the front door. This also allowed Larry greater freedom—and less strain to the backs of whomever had to assist him. Within no time at all, it seemed, the wooden ramp which began just off the driveway and wound gracefully around wooden birdhouses and hanging plants looked as if it had always been there.

The external transformations seemed only a dim reflection of what was happening internally. Larry had changed his mind about the way the world worked, and was busy trying to catch up on new information. But by locking horns with Julie and Michael, who were challenging his assumptions and pointing out fallacies in his thinking, Larry was beginning to change his behavior as well. From the beginning, Julie had recognized how the Klan had empowered Larry and given him a sense of being somebody, and she appreciated how defenseless he felt without that support. Now she was particularly intent on helping Larry learn about life and grow as a person in what time he had left.

As part of her "growth plan," which evolved on a day-to-day basis,

Julie began to take Larry places he'd never been to before—places that made Lincoln seem like a new and glorious city to him. Larry had never really had the fun of seeing normal life in Lincoln—Americans of all sizes, shapes and colors dressed up in slacks, high heels or shiny shoes going to work or relaxing in T-shirts and Levi's, Nike, Adidas and Reebok sneakers. And although his limited vision didn't allow him literally to *see* much more than shadows, shapes and sometimes color, he could envision all of this from Julie's vivid descriptions. Everything seemed novel; until now, he hadn't sat around in booths of Chinese restaurants listening to animated conversations around him or waited in lines at McDonald's, Wendy's or at Zach's Yogurt, where he could hear a variety of different languages and smell a startling assortment of food and body odors. He hadn't ever just driven around in a car listening to music and having fun. For the first time, Larry went to the university museum, where Julie read to him about the American Indian exhibits; the university bookstore, where he bought a set of the Zohar, five volumes of Jewish mysticism, for Michael and a silver necklace with a globe on it for Julie. ("I'd buy you the world if I could," he said when he gave it to her.) Julie also took Larry to The Way Home bookstore, where he smelled the deep musky aroma of incense, heard about UFO's landing in the Midwest and listened to New Age music; to antique stores, where Julie would hand him brass signs and dolls and birdcages to look at and feel; and to the Train Cellar, where Larry began to examine and admire model trains, which he decided he wanted to collect.

Larry looked forward to Michael's coming home at night so he could tell him about all the things that happened during the day. Michael was a calming influence on him—and between Michael and Julie, Larry's ways of thinking about life were taking on new dimensions.

"It's fun smiling at people and tryin' to make 'em feel good," Larry later said. "I've gotten to the point where I can love everybody. It's a lot easier now for me to love than to hate. I can't force myself to hate now. It's difficult. I used to go for the hard thing, not knowing it would be hard. I didn't realize it was hard, but Michael has shown me how hard it was. I thought, well, this makes me a tough guy. If I can show them I hate them, then I can make them afraid of me, and by having them afraid of me, I'm showing them my power.

"I used to think fighting was the way for anything. My wife and I would battle until I got what I wanted. Julie has taught me to talk things out. At first I didn't agree with anything she said. Like being a liberal. I was never a liberal in all my life. I was always a conservative-type person. But she made me think in a liberal-type manner, and now I'm satisfied that I'm thinking that way."

Besides taking Larry around Lincoln and to his doctor's appointments, Julie also drove him on his missions to apologize, make amends and try to erase the ugly trail he'd left in his wake. Some days Larry was too sick to get up, but more often than not, his willpower propelled him to try to make up for lost time. "I want to do anything I can do to correct the damage I have done," he said. "I don't care if I have to stay up twenty-four hours a day to do it, I am going to do it. People have to stop thinking 'This is a situation I can do nothing about' or 'Somebody else will take care of it.' If everyone has that attitude, nobody will be there to take care of it. Everybody should get involved one way or another."

Larry called one of his former young bodyguards—a boy who was a university student—and talked to him at length about the way he felt. At one time, the young man had talked a lot about how much he hated students of other nationalities or ethnic groups being on campus. After several conversations, the young man said, "You know, I'm getting kind of sick of this, too, all this hating all the time," and he, too, dropped out of the Klan.

He also called the leader of the Klan in Missouri to try to get him to change. The man remained cordial, talked to Larry, and even sent him notes, but he didn't leave the Klan.

Larry called Donna Polk for suggestions about where he could make a contribution toward change in Lincoln, and she suggested the county's juvenile jail, among other places. Soon after that, Julie began driving Larry twice a week to meet with juveniles at the county's youth detention center, euphemistically called "The Youth Attention Center," where he talked with the kids—many of whom were living adolescent lives similar to his own. Some of them were awaiting sentencing; some would be headed for Kearney, where, he told them, he himself had spent more than five years off and on in reform school. It was at Kearney, he told them, he got his high-school-equivalency degree and his barber's license. He talked about his bad attitude, how he'd stolen cars when he was a kid, how he hadn't cared about anybody and how as a Klansman he had wasted his life.

"Love can work miracles," Larry told the collection of boys and girls gathered in a small room to talk to him. "My life today is an example of that."

Talking about kids he'd met at the youth detention center, Larry said, "I've given these kids T-shirts now, black kids and white kids and Hispanic kids, and I've told them I care about them. There's this black kid, Joe, who doesn't like whites. I bought him this T-shirt with the continent of Africa on it with all the states colored in. He's proud of it, and I'm showing him I do indeed love him. I think it will help him straighten out his thoughts like I've straightened out mine.

"When I saw him the last time I was there, I said, 'No matter if you're home or you're out of the center, if you need something, here's my number. Just call me and I'll be there for you.' I meant what I said. This isn't just talk. Saying you're going to do something and then not doing it isn't going to help anyone. But if you follow it through, then you can help someone. You show 'I love you.'

"The thing is, with these centers, they do something wrong to get in there in the first place, but when they get in there, the local government doesn't do anything for them except make it worse. They think these kids are troublemakers so they don't deserve anything."

With some real trepidation, Larry called Bill Rush, the journalist in a wheelchair who had taken him to court and won. When he called, he identified himself and said he wanted to apologize. Larry didn't realize he was being offensive, but after all he had done to disrupt Bill Rush's life and terrorize him, Larry addressed Bill as "good buddy" on the telephone. For an apology, he said, "I'm sorry for the inconvenience I caused you."

Julie, who was sitting in the room with Larry while he called, realized Larry couldn't bring himself simply to say "I'm sorry," so the result was very businesslike and far less than heartfelt—a fact Julie was sure would not be missed by Bill Rush.

Julie couldn't stand the macho game. "Larry, tell him you're sorry!" she whispered.

"Bill, I'm sorry," Larry said, starting to cry as soon as the words came out of his mouth.

Bill agreed to meet in person, and Larry, thrilled and anxious, bought two large posters of Martin Luther King—one to give to Bill and one to put up in his own room. Julie drove Larry downtown to Bill's new apartment, where Bill and his minister were waiting for them in the lobby.

As soon as Julie rolled Larry's lightweight manual wheelchair up to Bill's three-hundred-pound motorized wheelchair—"a Sherman tank compared to Larry's Volkswagen," as Bill put it—Larry started crying and asking Bill's pardon. Bill smiled and then laughed when Larry said, "You're never going to believe it, but I'm going to go to an NAACP meeting."

Before they left, Bill's minister gave Julie a letter for Larry to read later. In it, Bill let Larry know he didn't have the right to be condescending, to call him "good buddy," or refer to "inconveniencing him," after having called him a "fucking retard" and literally run him out of his home. Bill Rush had had to fight all his life simply for the right to become educated and to prove he was intelligent, and he wasn't about to be compromised now. He was glad Larry had found love in his life and changed his viewpoint. He also was glad for Larry that he no longer was as isolated as most disabled people are. Beyond that, he wasn't eager to be one of Larry's "good buddies." Soon after their meeting, however, Bill Rush wrote Larry another letter, a generous one, congratulating him on his change and thanking him for the poster, which he liked very much.

The Rev. Dr. Martin Luther King, Jr., had replaced Hitler as one of Larry's heroes, and he was looking forward with excitement to the second annual Martin Luther King Day celebration being planned by the Lincoln Interfaith Council and the Coalition Against Racism and Prejudice. The interfaith service was going to be held at B'nai Jeshurun, and Norman Leach had asked Larry to address the gathering. Of course, the irony of asking the same man to speak who had been responsible for the "Don't Celebrate Martin Luther Coon" posters the year before wasn't lost on him.

Norman Leach believed Larry's participation at the interfaith service would vividly illustrate the spirit of reconciliation advocated by Dr. King. "You were somebody desperately needing love in your life—and when you found it, it changed you," Leach said to Larry. "Your experience is an example of what Dr. King called physical force being overcome by soul force."

Larry prepared himself by listening to speeches by Martin Luther King on tape. It horrified him that he used to hate Dr. King's voice coming out of Bill Rush's room and that he traditionally had written "Fuck the Nigger" across the space over Martin Luther King Day on his calendar. Now he loved Dr. King's words. Every time Larry listened to another speech, he learned something new, felt something surprising—as if a shaft of light actually was illuminating ideas he only now was beginning to absorb. At night, from their room, Michael and Julie could hear Dr. King's voice ringing from Larry's room:

". . . I have a dream my four little children will one day live in a nation where they will not be judged by the color of their skin but by the content of their character. I have a dream today!"

Other nights, Larry listened to books about Gandhi and Malcolm X. And he started going through a list of books on Judaism he'd asked Michael to recommend. More than once, Michael and Julie heard Larry's voice as he talked into his tape recorder:

"Test one, two, three, test one, two, three. . . . These are some various notes from the book *One Thousand and One Questions and Answers About Judaism.*

" 'The strong belief in God's oneness is apparent in the following six-word prayer that's a basic prayer in Judaism:

" '*Sh'ma Yisrael Adonai Elohenu, Adonai Ehad.*' This means, 'Hear O Israel, the Lord is our God, the Lord is one.' "

AMAZING

Chapter 20

GRACE

*If I can die having brought any light, having exposed any
meaningful truth that will help to destroy the racist cancer
that is malignant in the body of America—then, all of the
credit is due to Allah.*

—MALCOLM X

Larry Trapp sat in his wheelchair on the end of the second aisle
in B'nai Jeshurun's sanctuary. He pulled at the blue and red tie he was
wearing and nervously smoothed down his white shirt and the jacket
of a navy blue suit of Michael's that Julie had gotten altered to fit him.
He was terrified of speaking in public. He'd tried to back out, but
Michael had told him, "People are counting on you. You're in the program."

"What if I forget what I want to say?" he whispered. "What if I mess
up? What if I can't say anything?"

"You're going to do a wonderful job," Julie said, beginning to rub the
circulation back into Larry's hands to warm them. "You will, I promise."

"Do I look alright?" he whispered.

"You look great," Julie said as people wandered into the synagogue
and took their seats. "You look handsome in that suit. Your haircut
looks good, too. Do you want a drink of water? I have some in my bag."

"Julie's jolly medicine bag," Larry whispered with a laugh. "Have any
extra legs in there? I could use a couple."

"What's funny?" Rebecca asked, leaning forward over her mother's shoulder. She, Dina, Dave and several of their friends were sitting in the row behind Larry and Julie.

"Larry asked me if I have any extra legs in my purse."

"It's big enough," Rebecca said.

Behind and to the side and front of them, people of every color, size, shape and ethnic background in Lincoln filed into the seats—an impressive demonstration of Lincoln's truly multicultural community. When all the seats in the sanctuary and the balcony were filled, kids sat down on the floor in front of the first row and dozens of people stood lined up in the back of the room and leaned against the walls up and down the aisles. Among the people sitting in the sanctuary that evening were many families and individuals Larry had once terrorized.

C. J. Schepers was there for the *Lincoln Star.* Having the ex–Grand Dragon of the KKK speaking at a ceremony for Dr. King sounded like a great story to Scheppers, but once again she'd had to fight for permission to cover it.

"Where's Michael?" Larry whispered, looking around through the haze of people and motion around him.

"He's on the bimah," Julie whispered, looking up to where Michael stood in his long black robe and tallit exchanging last-minute plans with Norman Leach, who was in a white robe with white tassels and a large white cross around his neck. Sitting onstage with them were Phong Huynh, Norman's adopted son Tha Chanh Lam and Donna Polk. The Lincoln Community Gospel Choir stood at floor level in the front of the dais in black robes embroidered with "L.C.G.C."

The service began when Norman Leach introduced his friend Phong Huynh, coordinator for the Church World Service's refugee resettlement program, to give the opening prayer. Looking at Phong Huynh standing at the microphone in a dark suit and tie, it was hard to imagine how he must have looked years ago after his escape from Vietnam. Yet as Phong enunciated his English words clearly, graceful traces of his Vietnamese accent were a reminder of his roots. "I want to work on behalf of strangers in a strange land," Phong said. "Today is the day to celebrate the life of Dr. Martin Luther King, Jr. Today is to celebrate freedom and justice. It is a day when we come together as one—to celebrate all races, religions and classes and to put aside differences and join in a spirit of togetherness—if for only one day—to bring to life the vision of freedom which is Martin Luther King, Jr.'s dream. Amen."

Norman Leach stepped back to the dais and said: "A little word of pride, being a new father at the age of fifty-one—I want to mention now that my son Tha Chanh Lam will come up later on to share his words," Norman said. "My son Tha arrived in Lincoln from Cambodia last May not speaking one word of English, so it is with special pride to me, and I hope it will be to you, when Tha later shares his words with us."

After the Lincoln Community Gospel Choir sang, Michael Weisser stepped up to the dais. "I'd like to call upon Donna Polk to read the Scripture, Psalm Number 8," he said.

Larry could feel sweat on his forehead. He elbowed Julie and said, "Is Donna Polk up there?"

"Yes, she's going to read the Scripture," Julie whispered.

Donna Polk stood at the podium and looked out at the audience. She composed herself and leaned slightly forward to the microphone. "Before I read the Scripture, I'd just like to say publicly, this is a very important night for me," she said in her deep, rich voice. "I'm here because of Dr. King, and I'm here because of Mr. Trapp. And I hope all of you understand the significance of the actions that caused Mr. Trapp to bring us together here tonight. He wants to make amends and I want to say publicly, *I accept your friendship.*

"Now I'll read Psalm 8: *'O Lord, our lord, how majestic is your name. . . .'* " When finished, Donna Polk walked back to her seat by Michael Weisser and sat down as the gospel choir began to sing "Precious Lord." Larry tried to maintain his composure.

When the choir finished the last refrain of the song, Norman Leach again came to the podium. "Dr. King had a dream that envisioned the day when persons who were black and white, Jew and Gentile, could be in brotherhood and sisterhood with one another. Tonight's celebration honors that dream in a most poignant way by the inclusion in our service of the former Grand Dragon of the Ku Klux Klan, Mr. Larry Trapp . . .

"We are not here, however, to focus undue attention on Mr. Trapp himself, but rather on the fact that through God's wonderful love we have witnessed the reality that someone whose life was heretofore dedicated to hatred and prejudice can repent and begin a new life. What has happened to him is possible for others.

"Preachers often talk about the transforming power of unconditional love, and we say those words, and I think we mean those words, but it isn't often we see that lived out in reality. . . ."

It was Larry's turn.

Julie pushed Larry's wheelchair around to the front of the sanctuary as Michael came down the steps from the dais to meet them. Kids sitting in front of the first row stood up to make room as Michael pushed Larry the rest of the way, where he turned Larry's wheelchair to face the people in the sanctuary.

From Larry's visual perspective, he was facing a shadowy, barely visible sea of humanity, but this evening he felt the presence of the people more than he saw them. Many of the people in the sanctuary were seeing him for the first time in person—and they saw a short, dignified-looking man with a receding hairline and a round face in a good-looking gray suit sitting in a wooden wheelchair. Most of them couldn't see the pant legs of his suit tucked back up under his thighs or even quite remember the times they had seen him on television when as Grand Dragon of the KKK he wore a beard and a permanently angry, menacing expression. Those who were close enough to the front tonight could see the smooth, soft skin on his face and a sweet, calm expression that gave him a radiant look as he cleared his throat and began to speak.

"First of all, I'd like to say thanks to Mrs. Donna Polk," Larry said in a raspy but clear voice loud enough to be heard throughout the sanctuary. "I really owe her a lot for her acceptance of my apology. Her acceptance of my apology gave me strength at the beginning of this to go on with other things. I thank you, Mrs. Polk.

"Right now before I go on, I'd like to ask you all to shake hands with the person next to you, your brother or your sister, because we're all brothers and sisters."

Everyone in the sanctuary turned and shook hands with the people sitting beside them and in front or behind them, and noise rippled through the room. After some of the activity died down, Larry started talking again.

"I had wasted the first forty years of my life and caused harm to other people until I believe God stepped in to give me Cantor Weisser as a messenger to show me that I could receive love and to show me the love that I could give to others," he said. "I've learned we're all the same, we're all in the world, we all have to face the same situations and people, and we have the same purpose—no matter whether we're white people or Oriental people or black people. Once we get that under our belt and we realize we are one race and one race only, then and only then will we progress as a society.

"My term as Grand Dragon of the Ku Klux Klan is not anything that I look back on with any pride. My robes, I don't want to be near them anymore. I don't want to think about them, I don't want to think about the Nazis.

"People like them, they've been hated. You can think, 'I hate the Nazis, I hate the Klan,' but we have to reach out and show them we love them as our brothers—and possibly they'll go through the same change I've gone through because Cantor and Mrs. Weisser reached out to me and showed me unconditional love.

"I think that's what Dr. Martin Luther King's message is all about— love, reaching out, getting along and making a difference. . . . If we do his works and God's works, society will be a lot different.

"That's about all I have to say," Larry said, clearing his throat again. "I'm a little shell-shocked. Basically, I want to tell you all *I love you*. Anything I can do to help correct the situation I helped cause, I'll be very willing."

Michael and Donna Polk came down from the dais together and kissed and hugged Larry as everybody in the sanctuary clapped and gave a standing ovation. When the applause had died down, Michael said, "We have something that wasn't on the program—a young woman who has a song to sing which she wrote for Larry. She's Leslie Young and the song is called, 'What Love Has Done.' "

Leslie, looking small and young in an orange sweater and corduroy pants, came up to the front and hugged Larry. She had written this song for Larry only and it had never occurred to her as she was writing she would sing it for anyone else. Now, standing near him in the sanctuary, she pushed her glasses up on her nose and said, "This song is about the love that transformed Larry into the person he was all along. He was just covered up like many of us are because of something that happened in our lives or bad choices we made. It just took love to get him out—and it gives us hope that maybe if we follow the example of what we saw through the Weissers maybe other people can be transformed into what God meant them to be all along—and who they are deep down inside but just don't know it at that time. This is for you, Larry."

Leslie sat down on the edge of the bimah and, looking at Larry, strummed her guitar. Her clear, beautiful voice filled the sanctuary as she sang:

Look what love has done . . .
Turned a stone heart into gold
Made a new life out of old
Anyone can plainly see
That it was love that set you free.

Now we're brothers you and I
And I'll love you 'till I die
We are brothers all because
What love has done.

It used to be, you hated me,
You didn't understand
That every race and every man
Were fashioned by His hand.
That we're all the same within
'Neath the color of our skin
Yes you and I, we're all the same to Him.

Look at what love has done . . .
When I look into your eyes
And you smile, I realize
What a miracle there'd be
If this whole world would come to see
That the greatest gift of all
Is to answer to love's call.

Yes, we are brothers all because
What love has done. . .

When Leslie finished singing the chorus again—"Yes, you and I, we're all the same to Him"—sniffling and crying could be heard throughout the synagogue. In his dignified suit, white shirt and tie, Larry was crying, and tears were in Michael Weisser's eyes as he pushed Larry back to his seat beside Julie. When Michael came back up on the dais, he said, "Please pass the Kleenex," and everyone laughed. Then he said, "The Lincoln Gospel Choir is going to sing a song that seems appropriate right now."

The song, "Amazing Grace," was written in the late 1700s by an Englishman named John Newton, a crew member and later a ship captain in the slave trade who had begun to wake up to the heinousness of his work after hearing himself say "God have mercy" during a terrible storm. Eventually, Newton became a minister and one of the most effective abolitionist voices in England. Even without knowing the history of the song, however, few people singing along with the gospel choir that evening could have failed to appreciate the words: "Amazing Grace, how sweet the sound, that saved a wretch like me. I once was lost, but now am found, was blind, but now I see."

At the end of "Amazing Grace," tall, slender Tha Chanh Lam walked to the podium and stood looking at the audience. Norman Leach's adopted son had arrived in Lincoln from Cambodia the previous spring weighing barely more than a hundred pounds. He was nineteen years old now and a student at Lincoln High School, but this was the first time he had spoken in public in his entire life. He looked at the audience and said, "Let there be peace on earth, and let it begin with me."

And then the gospel choir and everyone else began to sing, "Let there be peace and let it begin with me."

At the end of the service, everyone stood, singing "We Shall Overcome" along with the gospel choir. They clasped hands of every shade and texture and raised them in the air as they sang loudly and swayed from side to side. The spirit of Dr. Martin Luther King seemed to hover over them.

Not long after the Martin Luther King Service, John Ways, Sr., invited Larry to a meeting of the NAACP at the Malone Community Center. Larry had asked to go so he could share information and answer questions about racist organizations *and* apologize for what he had done to the black community. Some of the members were hesitant about it, but they'd agreed to meet with him.

This was the first time Lenora Letcher had seen Larry up close. Shortly after John Ways introduced Larry, she reminded him of the hate mail he had addressed to her as "Leonore the Letch," and told him her response had been, "Here's a person who needs to come to Jesus."

"To look at you, you have a very pleasant face," Mrs. Letcher said. "And I don't see a person of hatred. I want to say I am glad you had this decision to change. Whether my thinking had anything to do with your changing or not, my prayers were answered."

"What you said is exactly what happened," Larry answered. "People's prayers turned me around. . . . I had a lot of wrong thoughts, but I don't have that kind of violence in me anymore."

Leola Bullock listened carefully, and with some skepticism, to Larry's words. Mrs. Bullock had moved to Lincoln from Mississippi with her husband in 1950, had picketed Kresge's and Woolworth's in 1956 in support of the civil rights demonstrations, and had always been actively committed to change. She'd been the first black sales clerk at Gold's department store in downtown Lincoln, and she was used to seeing racism in its many guises—including liberal white racism, which reached out to "inferiors" to help "pull them up." She wondered where Larry fell into the spectrum at this point—and as always, she was curious about the roots of white racism.

"It seems that racism is a part of white Christianity," she said. "They talk about a white Christ and all that. My question is, how can Klansmen consider themselves Christians and *hate?* Where I come from, Christianity is about love."

"The ones who say they're Christians—like the Christian White Knights or Christian Identity—they brainwash themselves," Larry answered. "They make the Bible say what they want it to say. They're confused people, the Klan and the Nazi Party; they're—I think they really hate themselves is what their problem is. They don't want to punish themselves, so they want to try to punish someone else. Basically, I think that's what the problem is."

"I saw a lady on TV talking about her Klan activity," Mrs. Bullock said, "and she said God had spoken to her and told her to join the Klan. God had talked to her. I just don't understand."

"I understand what you mean," Larry said. "I got a book a while back that you can only order through white supremacist channels, and it was called *I Found Jesus Christ Through the Ku Klux Klan.* That's not a joke. It has nothing to do with the teachings of Jesus Christ. The Klan is very anti-Christian. The whole thing is confusing, but let's face it—a white supremacist is a confused person.

"God touched my life. I thought I was a Christian and this, that and the other, but God really came into my life through a messenger—Michael Weisser. Through the love he extended to me, just our phone conversations, I could feel the love in his voice. I didn't know how to act. He was a shock to me."

"It seems to me, even if the Klan thinks it's based on Christianity, why isn't Christianity trying to help these folks?" Mrs. Bullock said. "It's interesting it was the Jewish people who were able to help you overcome your prejudice and hatred."

Donna Polk, who was also at the NAACP meeting, asked Larry what he thought his reaction would have been had a nonwhite person approached him and extended a hand of friendship like the Weisser family had done.

"It would have hit me the same way," Larry said. "I wouldn't have known what to do."

"Would you have been as open to the people?"

"More than likely," he said. "I would say definitely. Because I have been shown love—and if a person, I don't care what race or color, religion or anything they are—if people show love, you can feel it. I don't know if it's because I'm blind or what, but I've got a way of sensing if people are sincere. I would have had second thoughts right then."

Donna also asked Larry about the scope and the threat of white supremacist groups. "My friend Gary Cardori was murdered a couple of years ago—he was a private investigator who had been hired by the Nebraska legislature to investigate the Franklin Credit Union scandals, and he had gone to the Nazi camp in Idaho," Donna said. "When he came back, he told me about some things he'd heard up there and asked me to read *The Turner Diaries.* And I came back and tried to get black people interested and concerned about what I'd learned about white supremacists in terms of their planning race riots and a general takeover of the government, and their paramilitary activities, some of which are in Nebraska. Can you speak about some of that? Am I crazy or was Gary telling the truth when he was talking about that?"

"Oh, you bet he's telling the truth," Larry said. "The name of the camp he was talking about—now listen to the name of this place. It's Aryan Nations, but you know what it's called? Church of Jesus Christ Christian is what they call it. You're not off the wall at all. This is really occurring. And the general public is not aware things are this bad. They say the Ku Klux Klan is something that's fading away; the Nazi Party is nothing. But the Nazi Party is almost the same strength now with Germany united as it was during World War II. And racists are more sophisticated.

"At one time, David Duke was a blatant racist and he'd say anything he felt like. Now he's subdued and even more dangerous because of it. He and others like him call themselves 'white separatists'—not white supremacists—to sugar-coat their true message. His real end goal and the goal of the white separatist movement in this country is the complete annihilation of all nonwhites. There is talk of setting up purely white colonies here in the United States. That way they'll have their economy established when the rest of the U.S. is taken over by the whites. What they are talking about is basically tyranny.

"*The Turner Diaries* more or less represents the philosophy of the white separatist movement. They talk about pregnant white women hanging from trees and lampposts with signs on them saying 'I was a race traitor,' with their belly cut open, their baby cut out. This is what they plan on. They also plan to get into smaller terrorist groups and do a lot of terrorist acts. This is what I fear more than anything.

"It's a dangerous situation, not just for the black race or the yellow race, but for the United States. What we need is love to lift the United States and the whole world back up again."

Not long after that meeting, Larry gave a talk about his experiences with the Klan to Donna Polk's students in a multicultural education class she taught at the College of St. Mary. Larry surprised Donna when he told the class he targeted her because she was black, because she was a leader and because she was a woman. "It surprised me because I knew he was a racist," Donna said, "but it never occurred to me he was a sexist, too." Larry told Donna's students he had deeply resented the fact that people listened to Donna and that she had power and influence in the community.

"What did you want to happen to me?" Donna asked Larry in front of her class.

"I wanted someone to kill you," Larry said, tears welling up in his eyes. "That's the truth. I'm ashamed now, but at that time, I wanted to kill you."

A FAMILY'S VISION

Chapter 21

In the faces of men and women, I see God.

— WALT WHITMAN

*L*arry Trapp rolled his wheelchair up to his spot at the kitchen table, and Dina kissed the top of his head. It was late Saturday morning and Rebecca strolled in, gave Larry a hug and peered into the refrigerator. "Mom, don't we have any food in this house?" she yelled to Julie, who was in the bathroom. "We never have any food in this house!"

"I think there's some cheese," Larry said.

"I was thinking about maybe getting a little diamond stud in my nose," Rebecca said, shaking an almost-empty milk carton.

"Don't ever pierce your nose—that's nasty," Dina said.

"I don't think it's a good idea either," Larry said. "That would make a hole in your nose. Hey, hole sounds like mohel.* Want to hear my latest mohel joke?"

"Not really," Rebecca said with a laugh.

"Ditto," Dina said. "No really, Larry, it's okay. Tell us."

"I'm just too funny for you," Larry said. Since Larry had learned a Jewish "mohel" performs the circumcision at birthing ceremonies, he had started making up puns about mohels. They ranged from "What's the name of a fancy night club in Paris? The Mohel-on-Rouge" to "What disease do you get from mosquitos who've bitten too many mohels? Mohel-aria."

*Mohel is a Yiddish word which sounds like "moil" or "moyle" but is pronounced by Larry and many Americans as "mole."

Now he asked, "What do you call a nervous mohel?"

"We don't know."

"Give up? A mohel-shake."

Since Larry Trapp had moved in, life had changed radically at 5810 Randolph Street. As the snow blew and the season began to change from winter to spring 1992, the focus had shifted more and more from the kids to Larry. Often now, the doorbell also rang for Larry. Charles Griffin frequently came by to help him study the Talmud in preparation for his desired conversion to Judaism. Since February, Larry had been studying in earnest with Michael, but Griff was adding to his knowledge and discussing religious issues with him. Griff and Larry also spent a lot of time talking about war and what motivates men to fight. Additionally, they shared a common interest in model trains.

Besides Griff and Leslie Young, other frequent callers included Ron Drury, who shared Larry's love of fishing, and Bill Brda, a tall, pale, blond Christian of Czech decent with a long narrow face, who said that when he walked into the South Street temple three years previously, he had felt a tremendous peacefulness, a feeling he continued to have when he was there. When John Ways came over to visit, he and Larry sometimes compared stories about being police officers. Norm Leach talked to Larry about his life with the Vietnamese community and Anne Kennedy, who taught English to new arrivals from Vietnam, Afghanistan, Africa and other countries at Elliott Elementary School, told Larry stories about her students. Whenever Bob Wolfson drove down from Omaha, he, too, stopped by.

A surprising regular was Cybele Londono. For a long time, Cybele and her husband David had stayed away from the Weissers and from the synagogue. Cybele had even stopped going to choir practice so she wouldn't have to see Michael. "I think there was some jealousy they were spending so much time with him and not so much with us," Cybele said. "I got to the point where I was missing Julie and Michael, and I said to myself, 'Why am I behaving this way? If I am a friend, I have to behave like a friend, and therefore I am going to try to force myself to understand . . .' Because we were being so judgmental. So I went back to choir and I sort of started opening up to the whole situation. I stopped by the house when I left work at the museum. At first I was afraid to even talk to Larry, I didn't feel comfortable talking to him.

"I guess it was Larry who changed my mind. I wasn't afraid to touch him anymore, I wasn't afraid to talk to him. Now I kiss him and hug him. I like him. I couldn't believe how funny and sweet he could be. David was still so furious at Michael, but then I started telling David, 'You have to see what is going on with your own eyes. You can't continue to judge Michael and Julie, you really have to make an effort to see this.' "

Just as Cybele and other friends of the Weissers had felt some jealousy, so had Dina, Rebecca and Dave. But their resentment felt selfish and confusing to them. They felt they should be more accepting. This man was dying, and besides that, he was blind and disabled. How much could they resent him? In reality, a lot. Larry literally was in their space. Not only were they cramped together downstairs, but they no longer could express themselves freely.

Dave couldn't wake up and play his guitar and sing like he used to because it might wake up Larry—who slept late every morning. Dina couldn't walk around singing or practicing a speech whenever she felt like it. Rebecca couldn't turn up the music to dance or talk as loudly as she used to on the phone or practice her dramatics in the living room. They couldn't even cut up in the basement. Julie taped a sign to the downstairs bathroom door: "Please open and close this door *very* quietly. All the noise from the downstairs comes up through the vents into Larry's room. Thank you, Julie xxxooo."

Privacy, it seemed, had also become a thing of the past. Everyone had to tiptoe around when Larry was sleeping. Although they understood Larry often was awake during the night and needed to sleep during the day, it wasn't fun to curtail their spontaneity or to have to go outside the house to practice music or laugh out loud. They particularly hated the times Larry got stressed out and reverted to being angry.

"I was cutting oranges for him the other day, and he was yelling at me," Dina said. "He told me, 'Cut them in fourths and then in halves!' That's exactly what I was doing. I thought it would be nice if I peeled them for him, but he said, 'What's taking so long?! Don't peel them!' So I put them in a bowl and he says, 'Just hand me a plate.' So I hand him a plate and he dumps the oranges and misses the plate. So he says, 'Give me a napkin.' So I give him a napkin, and he goes, 'Paper towels, not napkins!' After he calmed down and got the oranges exactly how he wanted them, he goes, 'Oh, thanks.' "

"I wanted to say, 'Look, you have no right to yell at Dina,' " Rebecca said. " 'We do everything for you. Quit acting like an asshole.' But my mother thinks it's not our place to put our foot down."

On the other hand, as much as they resented it at times, each of the teenagers at the Weisser residence knew Larry was getting the benefit of Julie's intense and protective attention. They knew how committed she could be. Each of them had gotten their turn with Julie's nurturing. Julie herself had sloughed off high school—and she wasn't about to let that happen to her kids. "I took diet pills from the tenth grade to the twelfth grade," she says, "so I weighed a hundred and ten pounds. My pediatrician had prescribed them for me because it wasn't horrible back then. Doctors would say, 'Oh, your kid's got a weight problem— here, let me give her this amphetamine.' I had hepatitis in the eleventh grade because I was so thin and I was so sick. I didn't want the kids to repeat my high school days of sleeping until I heard a bell ring and people shuffling past me out the door with the sound of slamming lockers for an alarm clock. I was a mess."

Julie doesn't remember college as much better. She went to Lambuth College in Jackson, Tennessee, in 1970, the same year she graduated from high school, and attended classes for about two weeks. After that, she slept until noon every day when her friends would wake her up for lunch or a ride to the park. Some days her roommate, her roommate's boyfriend, who happens to be black, and her best friend, Michelle Mc-Carley, took her along with them to do campaign work for Albert Gore, Sr. At that time, Julie didn't care anything about politics, but she was drawn to the interests and activities of her friends, and she liked campaigning for Senator Gore.

One day when they were at a campaign rally, a news photographer took their picture, and relatives of Julie's parents sent them a copy of their daughter's photograph on the front page of the *Jackson Sun*. That ended Julie's college career. Julie's roommate's interracial love interest, Julie's work for the Democrats and the company she was keeping, not to mention the neglect of her studies, did not go over well at her Republican home. Not long after that, her father drove up to Jackson and ordered Julie to pack up and get into the car. She was going home.

Back in Memphis, Julie lived with friends in a duplex near Memphis State University, where she spent her time smoking dope and lying on the floor listening to Joe Cocker, the Moody Blues and the Jefferson Airplane. She had no real direction, and although she was working as a secretary at the time, she continued using drugs—experimenting with LSD, uppers, downers, Quaaludes and mushrooms. She floated without apparent direction until 1974, when she met Gordon Nelms. He was seven years older than she was, had a stable job and nothing to do with the drug scene. Julie was ready for a change, and after a short period of dating, she married Gordon. Rebecca was born two years later, but Julie's life as a young wife and mother didn't solve her problems, and she continued to struggle with substance abuse off and on for several years.

Julie didn't really begin to find her own footing until after her marriage was coming unraveled and she had taken her part-time secretarial job at Temple Israel in Memphis in 1978. It was there, after a very difficult period, that she first began to feel her own strength as a woman and began to develop a focus that would stay with her. The study of Judaism—with its ethical guidelines, its range and flexibility—had set a standard for Julie to build upon both intellectually and spiritually. When she and Michael married in 1983, she also had become immersed in the Jewish community and found new meaning in being alive.

Now she wasn't about to let her kids take as long as she had to figure out what life or the world was about. "I have gone the opposite way with my kids," she says. "I want them to know they have to work their tails off in school. I want them to understand they can't walk around with their heads in the clouds. They've got this whole life ahead of them and they're bright and they can do important things—things that matter to them."

As an only child, Rebecca had her mother's undivided attention for thirteen years until Dave moved in. Before that, she had met her stepbrothers and stepsisters—Dave and Dina, Danny and Debbie—on vacations, but otherwise she didn't know them well, and she'd had her mother to herself for talking, going places, making up and performing silly plays. She could sit with Julie and paint or draw for hours, write poems or go out shopping. Since she was ten, she'd also been able to talk to Michael anytime she wanted to without competition. But then Dave had moved in, and then Dina. "That was okay," Rebecca said. "They didn't take that much of my mother's attention, and my mom and I used to run errands together and we'd communicate when we were doing that."

Fifteen-year-old Dave had showed up in Lincoln two-and-a-half years earlier chain-smoking Marlboros, doing drugs, drinking and hanging out with older kids. He also had a negative outlook, a history of poor grades and a record of truancy in Memphis—167 absences in one school year. "Michael always just kind of lives life like 'Well, every-thing will work out,'" Julie says. "So when Davey moved here, it was like Michael thought some magic dust was going to fall over him and he was going to become this great kid. But it didn't work like that. It took me months and months of saying, 'This is what you have to do.' The minute Davey did something wrong, I was at the principal's office. He would skip school and he'd be at the principal's office and I'd walk in and he'd go, 'Hey, what are you doing here?' I'd say, 'I'm here be-cause you skipped school.' He'd be so surprised. He tested us for about six months before he started getting it together."

After a year under Julie's strict supervision—he was once grounded for a month for lying—Dave was totally off drugs, he'd stopped smok-ing cigarettes, stopped drinking, was playing music in a band and had made great friends. When the school called to say they were going to test Davey for the gifted program, Michael started crying—an unchar-acteristic thing for him at the time. "I want to thank you 'cause if it weren't for you, Davey wouldn't be doing what he's doing," Michael told Julie. Davey not only got into the gifted program, but he had be-come a straight-A student enrolled in advanced-placement classes. He was realizing he could go to college and keep his life in order.

"Davey feels really good about himself now, and he should," says Julie. "He's smart and he's turned his life around."

Dina had had different struggles, but she also had arrived in Lincoln unhappy and failing school. Besides that, she was severely overweight. She also experienced Julie's tight-reined nurturing when she got grounded for not doing her chores, grounded for not making good grades, grounded for a bad attitude. "And in this house, grounded means grounded," says Dina. "Everything. Grounded from the phone, the TV, friends, social life. Ask Dave. It's grounded." But the discipline had worked for her, too. By the end of the year, she had lost her excess weight, had brought up her grades, was singing in the sophomore cho-rus, performing and singing in school plays. She came in third in her division for a dramatic interpretation of "The Little Moon of Albany," and Larry saw her sing a solo, "The Greatest Love of All," in a spring show at East High.

Now it was Larry's turn. Julie, who always had been there for them, was totally absorbed by someone else. ("All of a sudden, Larry's got to be with us always, always, always," Rebecca said. "We never go any-where without him.") When Larry got sick, Julie attended him with the fervor of a mother caring for a newborn. She had been the kind of mother who crawled out of her baby daughter's room on her stomach so as not to awaken her. She now sometimes behaved in an analogous fashion toward Larry.

On a day-to-day basis, she was distracted, often tense. She ate choco-late for energy, stopped checking Dave's breath for cigarettes and started smoking herself. ("She doesn't even notice if I smoke anymore," Dave said wistfully. "I never thought I'd miss that kind of attention from her.")

As the weeks passed, Julie become Larry's ethics teacher, his best friend, his sister, his mother, the love of his life and his confidante. At first Julie spent almost all of her time with Larry except for the two-and-a-half days a week she worked at Dr. Fischer's. But when she was at work, Larry was a problem. He said he could do fine on his own. But he didn't. Julie would get home and find he hadn't taken his medicine and hadn't eaten food she had set out for him.

While Larry had managed being home by himself for hours and years at a time before this, once he had Julie's attention, he couldn't bear for her to leave him. "He didn't need daily reassurances that we loved him, he needed hourly reassurances," Julie said. "He was like a starving person who had finally gotten food. It had been such a long time since he'd gotten any real love or affection or attention or kind-ness that, once he got a taste of it, he couldn't get enough and he just wasn't about to give up a drop of it."

As Larry's diabetes progressed and he got sicker, he got even more anxious. If he couldn't see or hear Julie, he was afraid she'd disappear. "He was a scared and lonely and worried person," Julie said. "He was really complicated, but it was a little like having a new child here. He was forever testing us to make sure we still loved him. I told him, 'The only reason you trust me is because I've proven to you I'm going to stick by you through thick and thin. I've proven you can trust me. Even if I'm not here for a few minutes, I'm not going to disappear and I'm not going to desert you.' "

Julie empathized with Larry's separation anxiety. "I always thought my parents were going to disappear if they weren't in view. I remember going to first grade, and every time the teacher turned her back, I would run home." But sometimes Larry drove her crazy. One night when she was vacuuming, for instance, she realized Larry was calling her name because he needed a towel. She got him a towel, but just then the phone rang and someone else knocked at the door. Julie escaped to the laundry room, but within minutes, the downstairs phone rang. It was Larry, calling from his room.

Julie started yelling. "I can't have five minutes to myself!" she shouted. "No one will leave me alone!"

"I thought you liked me to call you on the phone," Larry said.

"I do like you to call me," Julie said. "But not every five minutes."

Nevertheless, it wasn't long before Julie told Dr. Fischer she needed a leave of absence to take care of Larry full-time until he died. Since Larry had developed congestive heart failure and his kidneys were failing, his body was processing everything more slowly. Instead of needing an insulin shot every twelve hours, Larry needed one every eight hours. His nurses didn't want to come after 5 P.M., so Julie had started filling in. Also, Larry didn't want anyone else giving him shots, taking his blood pressure, checking his blood levels, measuring his urine or holding his head when he vomited. When he fired his nursing service entirely, Julie's years of nursing work came in handy.

Dr. Fischer understood Julie's protective feelings, and told her she could have a leave for as long as she needed it. In the meantime, he continued to oversee Larry's care.

Just as having Julie so totally focused on Larry was hard on the kids, sometimes it was hard on Michael as well. It was quite clear to Michael, however, that Julie was as much a mother figure to Larry as Michael was a father figure, and that within these relationships, important things were taking place emotionally. "He speaks to me as if I'm his compassionate dad taking the place of his not-compassionate dad," Michael said. "He treads lightly around me, but he trusts me."

In fact, one time when Julie was mad at him, Larry said, "You can't kick me out. Michael won't let you."

It also became quite clear as Larry got more ill how closely his love for Julie was intertwined with feelings about his mother. A few times Larry actually slipped and called Julie "Mom" instead of "Julie." One night as he was settling down and getting ready to sleep, Rebecca came in, and Julie read her some of the letters some students had written to Larry after he gave a talk at one of the schools. Afterward, Larry said goodnight to Rebecca and Julie. Julie was leaving the room when she noticed Larry crying.

"Larry, what's wrong?" Julie asked.

"I don't like to talk about my mother," he said, "because no matter how mean she was to me, I did love her."

Sometimes Larry told Julie, "You smell like my mother."

"At night after I've washed my face and put on my Keri lotion particularly," Julie says, "he comments that I smell like his mother. He has a really good sense of smell and he relies on that a lot. He identifies who comes into the room by the way they smell. I don't like the sweetness of women's perfume, so I've always worn men's cologne. And not long after we met Larry, he said, 'What you're wearing smells like men's cologne.' I said, 'That's 'cause it is.' Larry said, 'I don't like it.'

"After that, the first thing he did, even though he had no money, he went to a department store and spent sixty dollars on a bottle of perfume for me. And he said, 'This smells really good, wear this.' And so I started wearing all these perfumes, and that's not really me, but I wear it 'cause he likes it. There is this real strong connection there. A couple times he's even said, 'You and Michael are doing for me what my parents should have done. You're taking care of me.' "

As time passed, life seemed to become a bit more "normal," if not predictable, with Larry as part of the scene. Rebecca, Dina and Dave began to feel closer to Larry and they each appreciated the effort and energy Larry put into trying to make up for the wrong he'd done. He went everywhere he was invited to speak. One of those places was their school, East High, where he talked about his life in the Klan to their fellow students. He also met with students from a Jewish youth group in Omaha who had gone to visit concentration camps in Germany the previous summer. Initially, this was one group Larry turned down. Griff had called and asked him to meet with the kids, and Larry's response had been no—he would rather be talking to black kids because that was mainly where he had done so much harm.

"That's also bigoted, Larry," Julie said. "These kids may be white, but they're called 'kikes' and 'Jew boys' and they need to hear you, too. You threatened them as well! Everybody can learn from this.' "

Larry recognized Julie's point and told Griff he'd like to meet the group of teenagers, so they came over and met with him in the living room for more than two hours. They were curious and interested in Larry's story and asked a number of questions. When Larry talked about hurting people and what he had done as a Klansman, he couldn't stop himself from crying.

One boy was very quiet as he listened to Larry talk. At the end, he said, "I just got back from Germany and I went to Auschwitz and Dachau, and I saw all the concentration camps. The whole time I was there, I couldn't cry. But today you made me cry."

ATONEMENT   *Chapter 22*

In the sayings of the Fathers, we read: 'Who is wise? He who
learns from all men. . . .' We can learn not only from those
whose occupation is to teach, but from every man, even from
a person who is ignorant or from one who is wicked, you can
gain understanding as to how to conduct your life.
— MARTIN BUBER

*E*arly one Monday morning in late March 1992, the phone
started ringing before Julie and Michael were awake. "Michael, you
better get down to the temple *quick*," one of his congregants said.

Michael pulled on his jeans, shirt and jeans jacket with a feeling of
dread. It was about eight o'clock when he parked in back of the synagogue and walked around to the front, where he looked up at large
white Nazi swastikas spray-painted across each of the three sets of
huge wooden doors.

An angry weariness seemed to wrap itself around him as Michael
climbed the stairs to his office and called the police. He knew this was
not representative of the community, but it was depressing, and he was
only slightly cheered by the number of messages on his answering machine expressing outrage and concern. Many schoolchildren on their
way to Prescott Elementary School had seen the offensive swastikas
and reported them to their teachers. One woman identifying herself as
a Baptist said the Nazi signs gave her "a sick feeling" and she'd like to
come over to help repaint the doors if she could.

A police officer who came to take a report told Michael it was almost impossible to catch people who did something like this unless they caught them in the act. "I know," Michael said. "I just needed to report it."

This time, however, the police did catch the culprits. A Lincoln police officer, flipping through the previous evening's reports, found an account from an officer who had approached two young men sitting in a car not far from 20th and South. It was after nine o'clock, and the officer had written down their driver's license numbers and told them to move on.

When they were called into the police station, both confessed almost immediately to having spray-painted the swastikas. Both were charged with vandalism, an offense which carries a maximum penalty of six months in jail and a $500 fine, and released on their own recognizance.

When they left the police station, they called Michael. It was about 6:30 P.M. and he was still at the synagogue. They wanted to apologize, but Michael said, "No, that's too easy. You can't call me on the phone and apologize for what you did. If you want to apologize, you need to come here to this building and apologize to me in person."

The two men were later identified as twenty-three-year-old students at the University of Nebraska. But their names hadn't hit the newspapers when they went to the synagogue and sat down to face Michael. "The thing that struck me the most was that one of these guys is a twenty-three-year-old sociology major at the university and the other one is a twenty-three-old philosophy major," Michael said with great emotion, "and they had *no* idea of the import of what they had done."

Michael appeared at the arraignment of each man and suggested there should be some sort of accountability. The judge and prosecutor agreed, and both men were "sentenced" to thirty hours of the study of Judaism and the Holocaust with Michael. "It's pretty certain the worst that would have happened otherwise would have been a hundred-dollar fine," Michael said. "And what would they learn from that?"

The week before the swastikas were painted on the synagogue, two other upsetting incidents had occurred. The first happened when State Senator Elroy Hefner made a biased remark at a session of the state legislature during a debate about rural people wanting farm animals and farm equipment to be exempted from personal property tax and urban people wanting business inventories to be exempted. One state senator stated there was absolutely no difference in principle between a cow and a cash register: a cow is an asset, he said, and a cash register is an asset. If one is taxed, the other should be taxed as well. In response, Senator Hefner said he didn't compare cows to cash registers at all. "When I think of a cash register," he said, "it reminds me of a Jewish piano."

When Michael heard this, he called Senator Hefner's office. Senator Hefner's secretary told Michael, "I don't know why everybody's making such a fuss; it just means the Jews are good with money." That afternoon, Senator Hefner and Michael met for two hours, and afterward the senator issued a public apology and said he intended to work toward a more tolerant society.

"He truly did not know how offensive that remark was," Michael said later. "That's the kind of institutionalized racism that makes people think they haven't done anything wrong when they say racist things. Senator Hefner is a good, decent person who grew up in a little town in northeastern Nebraska. He had heard this kind of thing all his life."

The other disconcerting event of the previous week involved Larry's seventy-five-year-old father, John Trapp, who gave an interview to the Sunday *Omaha World-Herald* denouncing his son's conversion and denying Larry's allegations he was an abusive and racist father. John Trapp said the idea he beat his son was "a total, out-and-out lie." Also, he said, he never used racist terms. If he had, how could he have worked for twenty years at a furniture store owned by a Jewish family?

The senior Mr. Trapp said Larry's charges had upset his life and hurt his reputation. "Pearl Harbor was nothing compared to this. This hurts more," John Trapp told reporter Paul Hammel. "What does he gain by dragging his mother and father down? I just want to be left out of the whole thing.

"It hurts me to lose him. I'm getting older, too. But I've got other things to worry about and straighten out." John Trapp said this was all especially painful because Larry was his only son and he had been the one who got up at 4 A.M. to give Larry his insulin shots when he was a child. He said while he may not have supervised Larry as well as he might have, "I have two daughters who turned out okay." As for what he had thought of Larry's Klan activities, he said he and Larry's mother had considered it just another of Larry's "fantasies" that would "eventually peter out."

Larry told Paul Hammel he regretted the remarks he made about his upbringing and he didn't blame his father anymore, but what he'd said was true: "If people want to be warned on how not to become a racist," he said, "then I have to tell the truth."

The connection between Larry and his father always had been tenuous, but when Larry didn't attend his mother's funeral in the summer of 1990 and then refused to go to his father's new marriage ceremony a few months later, John Trapp sent him a paid-up life insurance policy with a note saying he was severing all ties with him and no longer claimed Larry as a *son*. "I just got tired of a lifetime of abuse and disrespect," John Trapp said, "so do not attempt to communicate with me from now on! Any attempt of your doing so will be dealt with *legally!* I do not threaten—*I ACT.*"

Now John Trapp was not only belittling his son's transformation, but he also was accusing the Weissers of exploiting Larry and standing in the way of his seeing his son. In truth, it was at Julie and Michael's urging that Larry had called his father shortly after moving into his J Street apartment. His father had come to Lincoln, appeared on a TV news story with Larry and had lunch with him. That had mended some of the bad feeling between them, but then John Trapp read a story reprinted from the *Des Moines Register* in which Larry talked about his "shameful" life as a white supremacist and said that "his father's racial hatred influenced his views as a child."

Also, Daniel Levy's two-page interview, "The Cantor and the Klansman," had appeared in the February 17, 1992, *Time* magazine, and an enormous wave of media interest had followed. Now there was even talk of a movie contract, and John Trapp felt it was time to speak out in his own defense.

While the media attention was threatening to John Trapp, it was an imposition at Randolph Street, where the telephone often started ringing before seven o'clock in the morning with calls from journalists. Larry, Michael and Julie found they were spending hours on the phone.

It was eye-opening to Julie that, as a woman without a title, she was "invisible" to some of the people who called. Her role in Larry's transformation often was ignored totally. Julie might answer the phone just after Larry had told her another gruesome and revealing story about his childhood, but the reporter on the other end of the line would almost invariably ask to speak to Michael or Larry. Julie began to get annoyed as the months progressed, her caretaking of Larry intensified and the majority of the articles, headlined like *Time*'s "The Cantor and The Klansman" still focused mainly, if not exclusively, on the relationship between the two men.

As much as she resented the sexism, however, Julie cared about people understanding what had happened to Larry. Talking about it also gave her an outlet for the intensity of the experience. "Inside Edition" came to Randolph Street to film the family with Larry. ("Why did you reach out with love?" the on-camera reporter asked. "Larry gave us an opportunity to practice our religion," Michael answered. "It was a gift for us to get to practice the commandment that teaches us to love our neighbor, to be tolerant, to want justice.")

People magazine ran a three-page article ("Living With the Enemy: Facing a Klan Bigot's Hatred, a Jewish Family Gives Him Love—and a Home") with pictures from the Weissers' Passover Seder and Larry shopping for cards with Julie. ("As always over the ceremonial supper, the youngest child—this time a family friend—asked, 'Why is this night different from all other nights?' As always, Weisser gave the ritual response, commemorating the Jewish exodus from biblical Egypt. He made no mention, however, of the most startling difference. Sitting at the table with him was Larry Trapp . . . 'I didn't understand some of the words,' says Trapp, 'but I listened. It helped me understand what the Jewish people have gone through.' ")

It was odd to all of the Weissers to be the subject of this much attention. ("It said in this article I 'bound and giggle,' " Rebecca observed. "I never giggled in my life.") But while it took a toll on their time, the Weissers thoroughly enjoyed many of the journalists and camera people who came to Lincoln. They had fun bantering and making the discoveries that come with exploring ideas out loud.

And while Larry had never liked or trusted journalists, he now was spending a great deal of time with them trying to analyze the process that had gotten him to where he was. Among other things, he explained how he used to distort information: "The white separatist movement takes one small fact and builds it into a myth to 'explain' the biological inferiority of other races, for instance," he said. "And once you have that racist attitude, you build on it by looking for what you want to see on the news. You find 'evidence' everywhere you look to confirm your views."

"I think sometimes God chooses very unlikely spokespeople," Julie said one day after Larry had done an interview with National Public Radio's Maria Hinojosa. "I'm serious. If you look through the Bible, you'll see—everyone who was anybody in the Bible was always a really flawed character. Moses was a very unlikely choice. He murdered an Egyptian who was beating a Hebrew slave, and then he hid the body and fled the country so he wouldn't have to face the consequences of what he had done. So many people who made a difference in the Bible were these really misguided people, but something happened in their lives to change them."

That Larry's father was so distrusting and angry about the attention his son was getting was upsetting to Michael and Julie. "The thing I'd like most is for Larry to reconcile with his dad," Julie said. "He won't really be at peace with himself until he does that." Both Julie and Michael called John Trapp to try to talk to him about his son's health and the possibility of a visit, but he wouldn't talk to them. One day when Larry was quite sick, Michael called to tell John Trapp about it. John Trapp didn't give him a chance to talk. "Keep your big Jew noses out of my business!" he said before he slammed down the phone. Another day he did return a call, but he got Rebecca on the phone and told her, "Tell your mother to stop playing games." When the Weissers called again, he disconnected his telephone and got an unlisted number.

"HEAR, O ISRAEL . . ."

Chapter 23

It's a basic Jewish law. If someone hurts you and sincerely asks forgiveness, you must grant it. If you're still upset, the law recognizes that you might refuse once, even twice. But after the third request, you must forgive them.

—RABBI JOSEPH TELUSHKIN

O*ne* day in late May, not too many days before his forty-third birthday, a red-faced and teary-eyed Larry rolled his wheelchair into the living room and asked Michael to "please step into my office" because he wanted to talk to him privately.

Michael went into Larry's room and sat down on the bed. Larry sat beside him in his wheelchair and said, "I'm ready to convert to Judaism now."

"Why today, Larry?"

"Because I've forgiven my father and my father has forgiven me. I've had a Yom Kippur."

Larry explained he'd just finished a telephone conversation with his father in which each of them had acknowledged the wrongs they'd done to one another. Larry knew that forgiving his father for the pain he'd experienced as a child prepared him on a deep level for the conversion to Judaism he had been anticipating and working toward during the last six months.

Forgiving his father was a letting go of his deep resentments and his desire for revenge and punishment. It also gave him an inner sensation he'd never had before—a feeling of softness around his heart. "It's a great thing just to ask for forgiveness and to receive forgiveness," Larry said later. "I'm still a little wary of my father, but I love him because he's my father—and he knows it. He apologized for the way he'd been and I have truly forgiven him. It makes him feel better, too. It's like a ripple effect. You forgive a person and then they can go out and forgive someone they've had a problem with, too, and the whole process of forgiveness can spread and spread and spread."

The process of Larry forgiving his father had begun in early April when Julie had taken Larry into a Hallmark card shop to buy a birthday card for Dina. That day, like most days, they'd stopped at Herman's Hutch, Larry's favorite store, right across from Union College. Larry had bought a number of special model trains from Herman, the owner of the store, and spent hours talking to him about railroad life. In the card shop, he was still talking about trains before he suddenly said, "My dad's birthday is April fourteenth. I should really buy him a card. I should do it out of respect." Julie helped him pick out a nice card and she also bought one for John Trapp from herself, Michael and the kids. On the bottom of her card, she wrote, "It would be very nice if Larry could hear from you. Every child needs approval and love."

A few days later, Julie answered the phone and it was John Trapp. "I just want to thank you for the birthday card," he said. "Could I speak to Larry?"

Julie was excited as she ran to tell Larry his father was on the phone.

"Did he apologize to you?" Larry asked.

"No, but that doesn't matter."

"I'm not talking to him—no way!" Larry said. "Not until he apologizes to you first. He owes you an apology."

Julie ran back to her room and closed the door. "Mr. Trapp," she said. "Could I have your number? Larry would love to talk to you, but he'll have to call you back in a few minutes."

When she hung up the phone, Julie stormed back into Larry's room. "Larry, if you don't call him back, it's really wrong! You can't open a door and then close it on him!"

"I'll only make up with him if he apologizes to you!"

"Larry, it's between you and your father. He doesn't have to apologize to me, but you owe him a call back right now."

"I'll do it," Larry said, "but it's only for you."

"No, it's for *you*," Julie said. "You've been reading all those books on

Judaism. And you want to be a Jew? If you've learned anything at all, you know Judaism is just like every other religion! It teaches you *not* to rejoice when your enemy is suffering—and that enemy certainly includes your father! It teaches you to be just, and never to be cruel!"

Larry spoke to his father, and not long after that, Michael and John Trapp sat down for a long talk. During their discussion, Mr. Trapp alluded to the fact he hadn't been the best father, nor had he been the best husband.

"Look, you've spent your whole life not accepting your son," Michael said. "You still have time to show him love before he dies."

John Trapp and his wife Margaret began to visit Larry regularly— usually on Friday mornings. Margaret, a thin, attractive woman with a gentle smile, had been widowed before she married John Trapp, and she seemed to bring a great deal of warmth and dignity to the visits. John Trapp initially seemed more uncomfortable, but he was strong, nice-looking and robust. At about five feet nine, he looked like a pleasant midwestern businessman. He clearly made an effort to be congenial and positive with both Larry and the Weissers.

Most of the visits weren't easy. Starting on Thursday evenings, Larry would start chewing Maalox because his stomach was upset. He always felt nervous about seeing his father. He liked Margaret, however, and she softened the sharp edges of the encounters. And when his father gave him a brass belt buckle with a train on it, Larry was thrilled. He wore it with his jeans—and sometimes even with his striped engineer's overalls.

Julie thought the visits were important for Larry, but sometimes they were grueling. Once, in the kitchen, Larry put the stump of his leg up on the table as he was sitting and talking with his father and Margaret. Larry had a lot of phantom pain in his leg, and that day, like other times, he jerked and grabbed at his leg. It burned and itched, but he couldn't do anything about it. He rocked back and forth and then waited for the feeling to pass. When he stopped rocking, he left the stump on the table. Julie was horrified, but she couldn't say anything about it in front of the Trapps. She wondered what they thought as they looked at that stump covered with sores—and she wondered how it made them feel, but neither Margaret or John Trapp acted repulsed. Larry didn't explain what was happening, and Julie figured she, too, just had to let the moment pass.

The day after Larry made his announcement that he'd forgiven his father, he called a cab and went out alone on a mysterious mission. When he returned, he brought Julie a dozen yellow roses. On a small card to her, he had someone at the flower shop write this message: "To the most beautiful woman who helped me with my transformation from a dragon to a butterfly."

Shortly after that, Julie got out of her car and saw a huge, dead monarch butterfly laying on the pavement. It had delicate black and gold wings and seemed to be a perfect specimen. Julie picked it up and put it on top of a shelf in the living room, beside Larry's card.

In addition to his reconciliation with his father, Larry had done a lot of other preparation for his conversion to Judaism. Soon after he moved into Randolph Street, he had gotten a list from Michael and started ordering and listening to books on tape about Jewish history and religion. He had study sessions with Michael at least two or three times a week, and his Vietnam-vet and therapist friend, Griff, also spent a lot of hours talking to him about religious issues, Israel, the Middle East situation and Larry's misconceptions about Judaism. Michael, Ron Drury, Bill Brda and Griff took turns reading him passages from the Torah and from books he couldn't get on tape.

Larry studied the meaning of the holidays, customs and traditions even though he hadn't been able to experience all of them. In the process of his studies, he'd realized that in Judaism, cruelty is a great sin; kindness and compassion are stressed over and over, and *behavior* is considered even more important than *belief.* As a Catholic child, he'd thought the greatest sin was nonbelief in Christ. He also was surprised to learn that when the Romans of the first century controlled Palestine, they executed enormous numbers of people for various "crimes." Jesus was the most famous Jew crucified by the Romans, but the Romans also executed 50,000 to 100,000 other Jews as well. Each new thing he learned interested and amazed him.

Larry prayed every day. And night after night, he practiced Hebrew with Michael. Michael loved the Hebrew language and he explained the way it worked. "There are only twenty-two consonants and the letters are always pronounced the same way," he said, "so once you learn how to speak it, you can always predict how to say things. Also, Hebrew is spoken in families of words. For instance, in English, you can say someone is an *author,* she writes a *book,* and her book is kept in a *library.* In English, those words have no relationship. But in Hebrew, the writer is a *sofer,* she writes a *safer,* and the *safer* is kept in a *safria.* There's a relationship between the ideas and the words. It's a very logical, coherent language."

Often when he was trying to pronounce a word, Larry would say, "I can't say that." Then he'd speak the word, and Michael would say, "See, you said it!" Michael was impressed with how hard Larry worked and how he mastered one of the hardest sounds in Hebrew—the *h* sound made in words such as *Ehad.*

"I'll never get that sound right," Larry said.

"Think of it as the German *ach* and then say it backwards so the *h* part comes out first," Michael said. "It's like an *h* that touches the back of the roof of your mouth."

"Like ok'he'y dok'he'y?" he said, making "okey-dokey" sound like Hebrew words.

"Yes, ok'he'y," Michael laughed.

Larry pronounced *Ehad* correctly and then repeated the entire prayer, *Sh'ma Yisrael Adonai Elohenu, Adonai Ehad.*

"Just about all my life, I've been searching for a religion I could understand," Larry said, "and Judaism is that religion. The people who brought this miracle into my life and the people I love most are Jews. So there again is another reason for converting to Judaism. That doesn't mean I love anyone else less—it just means Jews have done so much for me."

In extraordinary understatement, Larry said, "Being a Jew is something I never wanted to do. In fact, a couple of years ago, I would have said a Jew is the last thing I would ever become. Of course, if someone had ever told me I'd give a person a fair chance, I would have said, 'No, you're out of your mind, man. You're wrong.' I never believed in giving a person a fair chance. I believed the strong shall survive.

"Now I believe the ones who will survive are the ones who are just in their ways—they're righteous individuals. God will help them survive. Of course, four years ago, I didn't believe in God. I didn't believe in God until less than a year ago. Now I live my life for God."

Michael also felt Larry was ready to become a Jew.

And as spiritual leader for B'nai Jeshurun, it was his judgment that counted. Of course, his decision to convert Larry had larger implications for a number of people. Some members of the Jewish community in Lincoln felt Michael was too quick to convert people to start with, and the idea of converting a person who had been a Nazi and a Klansman was less than appealing.

In all of the United States, there are only around 185,000 converts to Judaism. Converts, for the most part, have reached out to Judaism rather than vice versa, since Judaism traditionally doesn't recruit new members. Non-Jews who want to join the religion have to work hard. They not only study the Torah, but they also attend weekly study sessions for a year or more, depending on their branch of Judaism. In some Orthodox communities, converts must spend five years preparing for conversion and then must pass testing by a panel of three rabbis. In Reform Judaism, the length of study sometimes is as short as three months, but usually it lasts at least a full year so the novice can study and experience each of the Jewish holidays. Larry Trapp had been studying Judaism for only four months.

In Michael's opinion, that was adequate. Larry did not have a year left for further study, nor would he be able to go through all the holidays. He might not even have another month. Initially, Michael had tried hard to get Larry to be a Methodist or a Lutheran, but Larry's determination to become a Jew had impressed Michael. Through talking books, Larry had read about seventy-five books on Judaism, and he continued to ask Michael to discuss religious ideas and study with him. After witnessing Larry's efforts, Michael became convinced Judaism was right for Larry. When Larry said he was ready after he had his "Yom Kippur" with his father, Michael was moved by Larry's earnestness and by his understanding of the meaning of Yom Kippur. He felt Larry was "spiritually ready."

Certain aspects of the conversion ceremony would have to be adapted to Larry's failing physical condition. A *mikvah,* the ritual immersion, wouldn't be possible, nor would a circumcision ceremony. Larry himself had wanted to have his Iron Cross tattoos removed before conversion, but the risk of infection was too great.

Larry's conversion ceremony was scheduled for June 5—and the only sadness for Larry was that Rebecca had to visit her father and grandparents in Memphis and wouldn't be there. She called when she arrived, however, and later wrote a letter, which said: "Hey Larry, I'm very proud of you. I wish I could be there to see you convert, but I'll just have to rent the video when it comes out. I can see it now: 'The Conversion' starring Larry Trapp as Clint Eastwood. 'Go ahead, punk, light my sabbath candles.' Anyway, I'm having lots of fun here in Memphis, but I can't wait to see you. Love, Rebekah.*

On June 5, a small informal gathering of the Weissers and several friends, including Bob Wolfson and Ron Drury, congregated at B'nai Jeshurun for Larry Trapp's conversion ceremony. Alan Frank, a professor of law at the University of Nebraska College of Law, also made a point of being there "to represent the temple family" and the board of trustees. Larry sat in his wheelchair between Michael and Julie. He was wearing shorts, a T-shirt that said "Ignorance = Fear, Silence = Death," and a small white yarmulke.

Michael, in his black clerical robes, white prayer shawl and white yarmulke, sat on Larry's right and led him step-by-step through the conversion ceremony, while Julie sat on his left.

"Do you of your own free will seek admittance into the Jewish faith?" Michael asked Larry.

"I do."

"Have you given up former religious affiliations?"

"I have."

"Do you pledge your loyalty to Judaism and the Jewish people amidst all circumstances and conditions?"

"I do."

"Do you promise to establish a Jewish home and participate actively in the life of the synagogue and the Jewish community?"

"I do."

Before the close of the service, Larry said the Sh'ma in Hebrew and Michael placed the Torah in Larry's arms. At the feel of the heavy ancient scrolls wrapped in beautiful blue velvet cloth, tears streamed down Larry's face. "Your Hebrew name is Keter Hillel—meaning 'crown of an honorable man,' " Michael said, placing a white prayer shawl around Larry's shoulders. "*Birkat Kohanim* . . . May the Lord bless you and keep you and make His face to shine upon you and give you peace."

Afterward, everyone hugged and kissed Larry, and then Griff and David Gasser, Larry's official witnesses, signed papers. "I've got citizenship in Israel now, too, since I'm a Jew," Larry said, beaming with

---

*Rebecca sometimes uses "Rebekah," a transliteration of the Hebrew spelling.

pride. "I can go over there anytime I want to without citizenship papers. I can live two places at once if I want. But I guess I have enough trouble as it is living in one place."

Bob Wolfson had been teary throughout Larry's conversion ceremony. "The yarmulke feels at home on my head," Larry said to him. "I'm honored to be a Jew. I think it's probably the happiest and best thing I've done in my life."

Charles Griffin, too, was tearful. "There's something here that's greater than our understanding," Griff said. "I'm a religious person, and I can't help but believe that God has a plan here, that there's a major purpose here . . ."

After the ceremony, everyone at the service was so happy for Larry that they weren't focused on the irony of this event: Larry had become a Jew at the synagogue he had planned to blow up this very same summer. In all likelihood, had he stayed in the Klan, a bomb would have exploded there in less than a month.

Forgiving your enemy is one thing, but letting him become a member of your family is another. Alan Frank didn't know Larry well, but he'd overcome his ambivalence and discomfort about talking to him, and since their first encounter at the temple, he'd felt comfortable about the sincerity of Larry's turnaround.

Alan also had no problems with Larry's conversion. "I know Michael had tried to get him interested in Christianity because of his roots, but when he decided he wanted to turn to Judaism, I thought that was fine," Alan said. "I guess to some people it might have seemed rather quick, but I had talked to Michael enough to know A, there wasn't a lot of time and B, Larry really had done an awful lot of studying. I wanted to be there anyway personally, but it was good for somebody to be there from the board of trustees to give our support to it. I was glad I went. It was a moving experience to be there; it was really affirming."

It concerned Alan to realize Larry might want to become a member of the temple family. Nevertheless, in his role as vice president of B'nai Jeshurun, Alan sent Larry a letter congratulating him on his conversion, saying he was pleased to be there, and enclosing the basic information he normally sent people who expressed interest in joining. Larry filled out the application, and pledged to contribute ten to twenty dollars a month for his "fair share dues." For his "time and talent pledge," he cast aside reality and enthusiastically volunteered to (1) work on temple grounds, (2) lead adult education sessions on fighting racism and anti-Semitism, and on brotherhood and unity, (3) be a youth group leader, (4) be a Cub Scout den leader, and (5) join the Social Action Committee.

Normally, the board of trustees of B'nai Jeshurun agreed to new applications for membership with little or no comment. This application was different because a number of board members were uncomfortable about how other congregants might react. In their representative capacity, they knew some people were quite upset about the prospect of this ex-Nazi being part of their temple. It was one thing his becoming a Jew, but having him belong to the congregation was another matter.

"A lot of people think because Larry wanted to become Jewish, Michael tapped him on his head with his magic wand and made him a Jew—and there are a lot of people who do not agree with that and never will," said David Gasser. "I understand Michael enough to know that for him if Larry's spirit is committed to being a Jew, that essential thing is good enough for Michael. But it is not good enough for many others. When Michael converted Larry, he lost a great deal of support from the mainstream and conservative Jewish community here in Lincoln."

David Gasser had been a witness to Larry's conversion because Larry asked him to be and because personal contact had tempered his aversion. Even though he would have liked for Larry to study for a longer period of time, he wanted to support him. In fact, on May 29, when David and Cybele's son Alex was born, Cybele had called Larry from the hospital and asked him to come see their baby. Larry had held Alex and fallen in love with what a little miracle he was. David understood how much Larry wanted to erase his past, but he also sympathized with people who had the feeling Michael sometimes was "too Christ-like" in "turning the other cheek." He especially understood the horrified reaction some Jews had when they saw a picture of Larry holding the Torah.

Several of the board members wanted to put off the decision about Larry's membership until they had more of a consensus. Others, like Alan Frank, felt they should just go ahead and accept him right then and there. "Larry is Jewish, he applied for membership and we should accept him," Alan said. "I'm not about to put some kind of a past-behavior clause on whether somebody should be able to join or not. I don't think that necessarily would be wrong if some rapist or murderer wanted to join, but I'm not prepared in this case to draw lines between people who are Jewish and want to join the temple. I think we basically should accept them all."

A number of ideas were floated, including having an open meeting for people to come and express their opinions. Others insisted it wasn't fair to put Larry Trapp through special proceedings. After a heated discussion, the board had a secret ballot to vote on his membership.

"I voted for Larry becoming a member of the temple," said Holocaust survivor Eva Sartori, another member of the board of trustees. "I had some positive and negative reasons for voting for Larry Trapp. It seemed to me if he had become properly converted by Michael, then if we had any confidence in Michael, we had to accept his judgment that Larry had become a Jew. Otherwise there was no point in having Michael around.

"It seems to me it's possible that anyone can be rehabilitated. And then I thought, too, it was giving Larry too much importance to deny him membership. Because I thought he was a punk. Not outstanding in any way. Someone who didn't have too much going for him, who was a small-time hood. To demonize him as a Nazi, someone who was super-human evil, was giving him too much stature."

A board member who had threatened to quit over the issue stayed, but another member of the synagogue resigned because he was uncomfortable being a member of the same temple as Larry.

"By and large, the whole thing turned out not to be very significant in the life of the temple," Eva Sartori said. "I think the board was nearly unanimous in voting to give him membership. I think there may have been a couple of abstentions, and maybe a negative vote, but by and large the board supported the decision to let him be a member."

Julie understood how some people would never be able to forgive Larry; he had done horrible things simply unforgivable to many people. "I told Larry we had one member of the temple who quit because of him. Michael didn't want me to. He said, 'Oh no, don't, it would hurt him.' I said, 'Yeah, but it's true.' Michael would never have told him, but I thought that it was important for Larry to know that because of all the shit he did there was actually a person who would no longer come to the temple if he were a member. I thought it was part of the reality. He mainly had a lot of support, but there were other people who would never ever forgive or accept him because of what he did."

• • •

Besides wanting to join the temple, Larry also had applied for membership in the NAACP. Not surprisingly, a number of NAACP members had equally strong reservations about Larry Trapp actually joining and becoming part of their organization. Many people in the black community still felt the reverberations of Larry Trapp's previous actions. Although they didn't know Larry Trapp had been behind the Molotov cocktail attacks that had burned several homes the previous summer, his apologies for what they knew he had done still couldn't take away what "still sticks right in my heart and puts a knot in my stomach," as one woman put it.

"I understand the whole perspective where you've been and where you are," one NAACP member said to Larry. "I guess right now the letters and materials I received from you—I still have them on the inside of me. It's not that I don't believe you. But right now I have to sort through my own feelings. I'm going to be watching you; I'm going to be listening to the things you say for I don't know how long. I'm happy you have taken that step and renounced the things you were involved in, but I have to work through my own thoughts. I'm not ready right now to say, 'Larry Trapp, I believe everything you're saying to me.' I'm saying, 'You have to show me first.' "

Larry had begun attending regular NAACP meetings while Lenora Letcher was president of the Lincoln chapter. Larry's wish to become a member was "most challenging" for her. "It was up to me because I was president," Lenora said. "John [Ways] had resigned. It was very hard. I had accepted Larry's apology, and now I had to decide if he could become a member. A number of people made comments about it and were a little apprehensive.

"I talked to the Nebraska-Iowa Conference [of the NAACP], and I mentioned Larry Trapp wanted to become a member. Some of them objected. I prayed about it, and in the long run, I decided I was using my own conscience, and I decided yes. I had prayed he would change, and with my faith in God, I had to believe my prayers were answered. So I had to accept his membership.

"The way I look at it," Mrs. Letcher said, "is if you have any kind of faith at all and you pray about it and see the answer, you can't doubt your prayers or you doubt to whom you are praying. After seeing this man change, I can't say my prayer didn't have something to do with it. So my faith was challenged right there. I had to acknowledge my faith, my prayer. That was one of the things that convinced me. You pray about a lot of things, and sometimes the answer is no. The answer here seems to have been yes."

As for the people unable to forgive and embrace Larry Trapp, Lenora said, "I want them to look forward, not backwards. At times, I've become discouraged. But I think, if my grandmother and grandfather and my mother were able to go through slavery and bigotry and not become discouraged at the anger and the hatred, then we can do this and not become discouraged. You have to not let anger and hatred become a part of you. Because if you do, you get so bitter you can't really see that a change can be made and then help make that change.

"I remember my fourth-grade teacher telling me, 'Anger can destroy you if you let it. But you can overcome anger if you try,' " Lenora Letcher said. "You know, there's a will to have a mind to do the right thing, and there can be a will to just be mean and hateful. I think everybody needs to *try* to do the right thing and to overcome hatred and bitterness.

"We're all human beings. We're all in America. We're all Americans, regardless of race. We have to *live* as Americans, not as separate people, not to lose your culture, but to live as one people."

THE TRAIN— *Chapter 24*

MAN'S TRACKS

In every man there is something precious, which is in no one else. And so we should honor each for what is hidden within him, for what only he has, and none of his comrades.

—MARTIN BUBER

*A*s time passed, anything violent or any reminder of violence seemed to upset Larry terribly. One day when he'd seen Jesse Jackson on television, he'd begun weeping. "I wanted to assassinate him!" he cried, "and now I'd vote for him for president!"

This evening, he was calm. He'd eaten, taken his medicine and become quite involved in examining a New York Central Line engine he planned to give Griff as a present. More and more, as the intense heat of summer warmed the sidewalks, rose from the earth and hung in the air, Larry sat playing with his trains and listening to recordings of engines traveling over train tracks and blowing their whistles.

Larry had begged Julie to be with him when he died, and so every time she left the house without him, which was rare these days, she fretted. Tonight she and Michael drove to the shopping center together for a few quick errands. The kids were home in case Larry needed anything. Besides, Julie and Michael expected it would only take fifteen or twenty minutes to return a movie video, cash a check and pick up a treat for Larry—some corn on the cob from Long John Silver's restaurant.

"You know, Michael," Julie said on the way, "I feel like a worker bee who has to keep working for the queen bee. Larry is the most demanding, manipulative person sometimes."

"You let yourself be manipulated."

"I know it, but he's *dying*. I know it's crazy, but I just don't want him to die unhappy after a bad day. I want him to die after a *good* day. It may sound altruistic, but it's not. You know it works two ways. As difficult as he can be, he's given me so much in return."

"Isn't it ironic that you're working so hard to keep alive this dying man you used to despise?" Michael said. "Remember when you said you'd never do CPR on him if he needed it?"

At Long John Silver's restaurant, Michael went inside to get the corn and cash a check, while Julie stayed in the car to have some time alone. As she sat there, she got an uneasy feeling. She got more worried as time started crawling by. As soon as Michael got back into the car with a bag of hot corn, she said, 'Michael, something is happening at home.' "

"Okay, we'll take the movie back and then go home."

"No, I want to go *now*. Something is happening."

Everyone around Julie felt she'd gone overboard in taking care of Larry; they felt she was too extreme about her commitment and didn't set enough limits. Michael was no exception.

"You're so far into this, you can't see the forest for the trees," Michael said with a sigh as he turned the car back toward home. Julie was extreme, but Michael respected her passion and her instincts, and appreciated that when she put her mind to something, she wouldn't let it go.

In fact, when he turned the corner onto Randolph Street, Michael was shocked, but he wasn't all that surprised to see Julie had been right. An ambulance was in their driveway and a fire truck was parked in the front. They jumped out of the car and ran inside, where Dave, Rebecca and Dina were standing huddled together. Larry, whose skin looked the color of slate, was on a gurney with an oxygen mask covering his mouth and nose. Several paramedics were standing around him. One was monitoring Larry's pulse.

Apparently, after Michael and Julie had left, Larry had called Dave on the telephone downstairs. "Don't be afraid," he said, "but I think I'm having a heart attack."

"Who is this?" Dave asked.

"It's Larry."

Dave, Rebecca and Dina ran upstairs. Rebecca called 911, and the fire truck arrived within minutes.

One of the paramedics told them it looked as if Larry had had a heart attack. As the attendants wheeled him out, Larry lifted up his oxygen mask, grinned and said, "Hold the corn."

Even though he retained a sense of humor, Larry was getting sicker by the day. It was July. He had lived through the heart episode and rallied for a few days, but his kidneys were worse and medical crises were becoming more frequent. More and more often, Larry literally couldn't get a deep breath of air into his lungs, and trips to the emergency room were becoming commonplace.

Eventually, they got a tank of oxygen for him to have at home whenever he needed it. ("I'm not wearing that oxygen mask out in public," Larry said in all seriousness. "I don't want to look conspicuous.") Julie put "No Smoking" signs up on the front door with warnings about flammable oxygen in the house. Almost every morning, Julie emptied pans of Larry's vomit and put cold cloths on his forehead. She held a pan under his chin and watched him wrench with the pain causing his nausea.

Some days Larry was so weak she and Michael had to help him from his chair to the bed or the car and from his chair to the toilet and back. On those days, Julie helped him brush his teeth—and often had the feeling she had picked up where she'd left off seventeen years previously. But taking care of Rebecca as a baby had been easy by comparison. This was equivalent to having an extremely sick infant.

Julie had never had anyone close to her die before, and she dreaded Larry's death. When Michael had had a malfunction in his heart the previous April and passed out on the bathroom floor, all her nurse's training had become useless. She'd run around the house screaming and never thought of dialing 911 or attempting CPR.

It was clear, however, that the end of Larry's life was approaching, and everyone needed to prepare. Friends urged Julie and Michael to call a hospice. At first Larry resisted, but Julie explained to him that hospice gave tremendous support to terminally ill people and their families and it would be a better for all of them. The hospice also could help with the ever-increasing expenses and the growing necessity for intensive care for Larry. Larry wanted to die at home, and they wanted that for him, but it was traumatic; the kids were frightened, she was frightened and they all needed help.

"You're just doing this because you guys don't want me to die in your house! You want me out of here!"

"Larry, if you really think that's true," Michael said. "Then why don't you just get out! I'm tired of hearing you say that kind of stuff. People are just trying to help you! Why are you saying that?"

"Look, I'm really scared. When I talk to Julie about dying, it doesn't seem real."

Later that night he said, "I feel so cheated. Just when I've started living my life, I'm going to die."

The following week, Jan Branting, a registered nurse for the Hospice of Tabitha, came to the house. Jan had grown up in a small Nebraska town of about 1,500 mostly blond-haired, blue-eyed people with Swedish Lutheran roots. Jan's Swedish-born grandmother, who had lived in a sod house, had traveled to Nebraska in a Conestoga wagon. As a nurse in Lincoln, Jan was fascinated by diversity and sought out patients with totally different backgrounds from her own. When she heard Larry Trapp was going to be a hospice patient, she volunteered for the job.

Larry didn't want to meet her. So Jan went to Randolph Street assuming she'd only meet Michael and Julie. When she arrived, Michael answered the door. "With Michael, when you look into his eyes, you can just see all the way down to his soul," Jan said. They sat in the kitchen to talk, and Jan told him his being a clergyman would be a benefit to the team effort of the hospice, where doctors, nurses, social workers and the family work together.

They had talked for quite a while when Julie pushed Larry into the room. "At first he was rather stiff and just really had a wall up," Jan recalled. "But Julie was like Michael—no pretenses. You just cut right through to the bottom, and I love that."

Jan was there for three hours that first day, and eventually Larry relaxed and began talking and laughing. Toward the end of her visit, Jan risked mentioning the hospice, and got out papers for Larry to sign. She didn't pull out the "Do Not Resuscitate" forms because she didn't want to press too much, but nevertheless, when she said goodbye to Larry and told him she'd see him soon, he panicked. "No!" he said. "You can come to see Julie, but you can't come and see me."

"For a while, Julie would call and say this and this is happening, and

I would tell her what to do," Jan said. "But I needed to come at least once every two weeks so Medicare would cover it. Well, it didn't take long. I was there within the next week and then it was continual. Larry did not ever refuse to see me. Sometimes he was asleep and I didn't awaken him. I would observe his breathing and take a pulse on him." Larry had congestive heart failure as well as kidney failure, and since diabetes works on all the vessels, and because Larry's circulation was so poor to start with, Jan sometimes found it almost impossible to find his pulse because it was so weak.

"It was kind of a balancing act to get all of the symptoms in control, because about this time—even though he wasn't admitting to it—Larry was getting physically sicker real quick," Jan said. "He was sleeping more, and he had more and more anxiety. And sometimes that manifests itself with pain. The first few weeks I was there, I was increasing the pain medication just bing, bing. Pretty soon it got up to quite a high level, and I'm thinking, 'Wait a minute here, what kind of pain are we talking about?' Then I realized it was anxiety. At that point we increased his Xanax to calm him down more, and then his pain was more under control. All the symptoms kept happening and he was very frightened because he was not ready yet. He hadn't totally reconciled with his past; even though he was scared, he needed to do that."

As Larry became sicker, he also became more childlike. He regressed more and more into a little boy who spent time playing with his trains. "I think the true Larry is what we started seeing in the end," Jan Branting observed. "He had put up a front so much of his life, been this big racist tough guy, this real nasty person, to cover up that scared little boy."

During exchanges with friends and visitors, Larry spoke of himself as an "antique train collector." "Just one of these trains alone is worth between $290 and $450," Larry would say. "See, this one—this Union Pacific 4013 is imported from Italy. Julie and Michael and the kids gave it to me for my birthday. Anyway, this train is valuable now, but it'll be even more valuable later—feel how heavy it is! And this Southern Pacific beauty has the engine behind the car instead of in front of it."

But while he could hold forth on the history of the Union Pacific, the Burlington Railroad and the Southern Pacific, Larry's passion had more of the quality of a little boy's excited energy about his latest toys.

Larry's love for trains, train things and the sounds of trains was intertwined with certain happy memories of childhood and his maternal grandfather, Roger Barton, who had worked in the shop for the Union Pacific Railroad.

Sometimes when he was young, Larry would walk with his dad to the Union Pacific depot to visit his grandfather. Larry also remembered going to Playland Amusement Park with his grandpa, going out for ice cream and then going back to his grandparents' house for watermelon. At Grandpa and Grandma Barton's, Larry would get to examine animal lighters and other cigarette lighters his grandpa collected. He would pick up and stare in wonder at their bronze Statue of Liberty with a red thermometer in it. At Grandpa Barton's, Larry slept upstairs under an afghan and quilts Grandma Barton had made herself, and both Grandma and Grandpa talked to him about the animals he loved and tried to care for—everything from snakes to bullfrogs to rabbits.

For years, all of these memories had been buried. He had forgotten how, after his grandmother died, Grandpa Barton couldn't come to the house anymore because his cigarettes fell out of his fingers and burned things. But now as Larry became more ill, Grandpa Barton seemed to be sitting watch. Nearly every day, Larry wore his trainman's cap, his big stopwatch and the belt with the train buckle his father had given him. Often, Larry asked Julie to read to him from train collectors' magazines, and she would circle the items he wanted to have.

Setting up a model-train track became a matter of urgency with him. He was eager to set up a train track and landscape with stop signs, crossing signals, lanterns, stations and all the paraphernalia. He could hardly wait for more accessories: he wanted houses, barns, railroad stations. He was always trying to decide what he needed to get next. Whenever he felt strong enough, he asked Julie to take him to Herman's Hutch, where Herman would say, "Shut up, Larry, and let me tell you about this train!"

Julie and Michael both indulged him. Julie took him to the Union Pacific Historical Museum in Omaha, where he had the time of his life talking to Murphy Poe, another train buff and a black man who in his own lifetime had stood up to the Klan. Murphy and Larry established a friendship and often talked on the phone about life and about trains.

At home, both Michael and Julie got involved in following Larry's directions on how to build his model-train display.

"It's ironic," Julie said. "Larry controlled our lives when he was a

Klansman and all this first started, and we had to get keys for our doors and we were worried all the time. But now he has even more control over us. Michael is in the kitchen, building a service station for the train set, and he has me building a cattle bridge out of balsa wood."

After Julie finished building the cattle bridge, Larry felt what she had put together and said, "The cow's head can get through the slats there! The slats are too wide. The cow could fall off that bridge!"

Julie started to argue and then began to laugh at the absurdity of the conversation. "Larry, the cow is not going to fall over the bridge!" she said. "He's plastic! That cow is not real and so he won't fall off the bridge!"

For all his love of trains, Larry had never ridden in a real railroad car pulled by a real engine on a real track. So when Julie suggested she take him for an actual train ride on the Fremont and Elkhorn Valley Railroad, which runs a dinner train with two dining-club cars from Fremont, Nebraska, to the Elkhorn Valley at Hooper, and then back to Fremont, he was thrilled. It was thirty miles round-trip and took about three hours.

For days, Larry looked forward to the train trip. But when the Friday morning of the event arrived, he was sick. "I'm sick of being sick and tired," he cried. Nevertheless, as the day progressed, he rallied. Nothing was going to stop him from taking this ride. In the early evening, Michael helped Larry dress in a white shirt, tie and the same suit of Michael's altered for the Martin Luther King ceremony. Larry also wore his brand-new blue and white yarmulke embroidered with his Hebrew name, Keter Hillel.

Julie drove them to the train station in Fremont, about an hour from Lincoln, with Larry's oxygen in the back seat. Getting on board the train was the evening's only glitch: Larry's wheelchair wouldn't fit between the doors. The conductor and engineer solved the problem by helping Larry transfer to a dining-room chair outside the train. Then they carried him aboard as if he were royalty, and seated him at a table in the Elkhorn River Car, a restored dining-room car the Pullman Standard Company originally built in 1947 for the Illinois Central Railroad. When the train pulled out of the station, Larry felt he had been lifted onto Cloud Nine.

"I didn't have a drink," Larry reported afterward. "During dinner, I just had coffee. I wanted to have all my faculties to enjoy the evening. I had never had so much fun in my whole life being sober! It was the best time of my life."

As much as he had changed, Larry still had occasional regressions to his old, nasty behavior. His friend Griff, who also is a therapist, said backsliding was inevitable. "That's normal for a person whose hatred has been a defense for the deep pain he has," Griff said. "It would take years for him to move fully beyond it, and unfortunately he doesn't have that time."

One day in August, when Julie took Larry to the lumberyard to get some wood for the base of the train platform, Julie was feeling very uptight about spending money, and she said, "Larry, you have no money, we have no money, and we shouldn't get this."

Like a petulant child, Larry said, "But I have to!"

Julie reluctantly picked up the wood. As they were leaving, right when Julie was paying the lumberyard man, Larry said, "I've never met a woman with any brains."

Julie looked at the lumberyard man, raised her eyebrows and said "Help!" in a joking way at what Larry said.

When they drove off, Larry was furious. He said, "Don't you know crying 'Help!' is like crying 'Fire!' That guy could have thought I was trying to hurt you. He could have pulled out a gun and shot me!" Larry pouted—and when they got home, he ate sixteen pieces of hard candy.

Julie said, "Now I don't know what to do about your insulin!"

"You don't have a license behind your name!" He said, "Get out of my fucking room! I hate living here! I hate this family!"

"Your insecurity is controlling your life!" Julie responded. "This is bullshit! The only time you act nice is when you think you're dying."

Larry called the hospice and told Jan Branting he needed help because Michael and Julie were putting him out of the house, but by then Jan knew Larry, and she told him to calm down, everything would be alright soon.

A bit later Julie went back into Larry's room to change his pain-medication patches, but he told her not to touch him and to go away. Pain medication needs to be maintained at a certain level in one's system to be effective, so without it, Larry soon began having terrible withdrawal symptoms, and he called out for help. His arms and legs were cramping and jerking, and his pain was so intense that his body was twisting. Michael rubbed Larry's legs and Julie rubbed his back. "Give me anything!" Larry begged. Julie called the nurse to see what they could do, and in the midst of this, Larry started bawling like a baby. "I'm sorry, I didn't mean any of those things I said! I'm so sorry! Now you hate me!"

"We don't ever hate you, Larry, but this has got to stop," Julie said. "We love you, but you have to stop screaming at everyone when you're frustrated and angry."

That night Larry started discussing death. He asked Julie to read him the literature the hospice had left for him. Julie was reluctant because it upset her so much, but Larry insisted. He particularly wanted to know about the signs of imminent death. The hospice literature said one sign is you sleep more. Another is you sometimes lose control of your bladder.

"Dying is very degrading," Larry said. "I'm going to hate that. It's going to be so embarrassing."

"Larry, listen," Julie said, trying to comfort him. "It won't bother me. Everyone's the same. I've taken care of you; I've helped you shower." The truth was, Julie herself didn't really know what to expect and was on the verge of tears simply discussing this.

"I appreciate you taking care of me," Larry said. "You like to see me laugh, too, don't you? Yeah, I can tell that. I know how much you love me."

"I do love you."

"I know. Michael worries about me. I wish everyone didn't worry so much about me."

"Everybody worries about you because you have a lot of friends who love you, you know."

"This may sound odd, but there's something fascinating about how when you die, your body shuts down," Larry said. "Your body tells you when it's time to go. The whole process of dying is pretty interesting and intriguing. But sometimes I get scared of things. Really scared."

That night Larry asked Michael if he would put a mezuzah on his door. "I want it on my door because I'm proud of being Jewish," he said. A mezuzah (Hebrew for "doorpost") is a small boxlike container which holds a tiny scroll with the Sh'ma and a quotation from Deut. 6:4–9 and 11:13–21 and initials that express the belief that there is one God and one God only. For thousands of years, Jews have attached mezuzahs to their doorposts to remind them as they come and go of the high level of behavior they should maintain both inside and outside the home.

Michael got a mezuzah and told Larry he would attach it to Larry's door at his eye level, so he could touch it from his wheelchair when he went into his room.

"Michael, I've been listening to my *Thousand Questions about Judaism,* and it says that the rabbi or the cantor has to nail the mezuzah in with his forehead."

"I was hoping you hadn't gotten up to that point," Michael said with a chuckle.

Michael nailed in the mezuzah, touched it with his fingertip, kissed his finger and said the special blessing for it: " 'Blessed are you, Lord our God, King of the Universe, who has sanctified us with His commandments, and who has instructed us to put up a mezuzah.' "

After that, Larry began to tie up a number of loose ends. His father brought Larry's younger sister, Debbie, down from Omaha, and he got to tell her he loved her and say goodbye to her. Debbie, short and dark-haired, was eight years younger than he and had been the favored child. Larry said they'd never been very close—in part because during most of Debbie's childhood, Larry had been in reform school. Larry also had been jealous of her, and now he apologized for whatever mean things he'd done to her.

He talked often by phone with his older sister Candace, who lived in Houston with her two children and her husband Lloyd. Candy was eighteen months older than Larry, and the two of them had been extremely close as children. In July and again in August, Candy came to visit.

Larry was dwarfed by his big sister, who is six feet tall, with auburn, shoulder-length hair, a lively face and long, manicured fingernails painted to match her lipstick. Candy had led the way for the Trapp children, and she spoke with the boldness, humor and pathos of a person who's made her way to safe ground through a hard life. "Dad never beat us when he was drunk," she says. "No, he beat us when he was sober. When he was drunk, he beat Mom."

Larry also made amends and covered a lot of ground with Candy. During one conversation, Candy told him about the last holiday they'd all spent together in 1985. Candy remembered packing up part of their traditional Christmas Eve dinner in a care package for him before she and Debbie drove him back home to Lincoln from Omaha. "That was the first time I'd ever seen that particular apartment where you lived," she said. "It was the little duplex where you go in from the back entrance—it was a fairly nice little place, kind of an efficiency, right?

"Anyway, after we helped you up the dark sidewalk, you opened the door, and you know, the first thing I saw when you flipped on the light was the KKK flag. Then there was the robe and the hood hanging on a coatrack right by the front door. It was suspended in air like it was some kind of a ghoulish greeting on Halloween there in front of you in midair, like no gravity, just hanging there. If I remember correctly, you had one of those crazy automatic rifles and a couple of those guns propped there right by the front door, so it was as if we were entering this fortress in this really weird museum of some type."

"That was my MAC-10 and my sawed-off shotgun," Larry said.

"Well, Deb and I didn't dare say a thing because we didn't want to precipitate your half-hour dissertation on the Klan and on the Holocaust and we didn't want to go through that again.

"We looked at each other and her eyes were rolling and my eyes were rolling and we were trying not to comment, and you said, 'Did you see the robe up there?' 'Did ya see the wall?' 'Here's all my pamphlets here on the TV table and here's all my stuff about the KKK.'

"And we said, 'Oh, yeah, we saw that.' You were so eager to share your enthusiasms, but we kind of passed it off and said, 'Larry, we've got a long trip back, and the road's starting to get bad, so we probably better get going.' We knew not to encourage you on things like that because you'd preach forever.

"So we kissed you goodnight and wished you happy holidays and we got back in the car, and we were both just tombstone quiet; we were both just absorbed in our thoughts. We pulled out of the alley and drove down the street—and I think it was before we got to the highway before we said anything. Usually I'm kind of quick to share my opinions, and Deb is pretty good that way, too, but neither one of us said a thing.

"We were driving down the highway toward Omaha, and then I said, 'I have only two things to say about that whole experience.' And Deb just looked at me so sober—and her eyes—she always kind of looked at me like she half respected me and half worried about what I was going to say. She looked at me real funny and I glanced over at her and I said: 'Number one, I don't know why they cut the holes in the hood, because he can't see anyway. Number two, it's too damn long even for short legs, and without legs, he only needs it about waist-high.'

"She just burst out laughing. We just were in tears still by the time we pulled into Omaha. It was one of those tension breakers—and we decided, Hey, it's just like everything else, you've got to laugh it off; if you take it seriously, it's just gonna kill you."

Larry laughed with Candy, but then he said in all seriousness: "Well, Candy, they did make it shorter for me. I gave them the measurements. They allowed for the fact that I didn't have my legs."

One day Jan Branting from the hospice was staying with Larry when his father came to visit. Larry's father arrived looking like a trim golfer in slacks, a knit shirt with a collar and a white windbreaker. He went into Larry's room, where he and Larry sat talking. During their visit, Jan heard Larry and his father say they loved each other and were sorry for all the things that had happened between them.

"I'm out in the living room crying because I could hear them in there," Jan said. "It was really special. After that, Larry was making more steps, making more peace toward dying."

A few days later, Larry said he needed to talk to Jan, and she went to see him. "I didn't do anything medical that day," Jan said. "I just sat and talked to him for a long, long time. He just shared different things with me. I thought, I can't even imagine this sweet little round-faced, dimpled person was ever that other person who lived that awful life.

"I told him, 'I'm there for you.' He had a terrible headache, and I just massaged his head. Sometimes you can't take every symptom away, and I told him that. I said, 'We'll do the best we can and it's just not much fun.' But he really fought it. It's not as difficult when people are older and they've lived a real good life. Anytime someone has a lot of turmoil in their life, I know the last part is going to be more of a fight and more difficult, too, because there's so much more to resolve."

HEALING TRUTHS

Chapter 25

For everything there is a season, and a time for every matter under heaven;

a time to be born, and a time to die;

a time to plant, and a time to pluck up what is planted;

a time to kill, and a time to heal . . .

—*ECCLESIASTES 3:1-4*

Larry woke up in a sweat, screaming for Michael.

He'd dreamt he was stuck in a circular saw and was being cut up into pieces. "I'm so scared I'm going to die in the middle of a nightmare and be stuck there forever," he said. "Please, please pray for me. Pray for me."

When Larry went back to sleep, he thought he was wide awake and he had a sensation of either being born or dying. It was so vivid, he was sure it was happening to him. He wasn't scared. He wasn't upset, but he really couldn't decide which it was—whether he was being put together or taken apart.

But Larry Trapp still wasn't ready to die.

All his work wasn't done. He was appalled by his own cruelty and tortured by what a heinous person he had been. Over and over again, he dreamt his mouth was full of mud. He had to spit the mud out of his mouth; he would open his mouth and mud would pour out. He dreamt he beat up a retarded boy who had some fishing lure he wanted; he took the lure—and woke up crying at what he'd done. He wanted to erase his past, but his life as a Klansman and Nazi continued to haunt him. He still talked about getting the Iron crosses and "Hell's Angels" tattoos removed, as if this would wipe away the traces that plagued him. His remorse was tremendous, and his burden was magnified by unfinished business.

One Sunday in mid-August, Julie and Michael noticed Larry had been seeming more depressed. He was sleeping more, and he didn't want to bathe. Julie's fortieth birthday was coming up on Tuesday, and she'd told him she was going to go out to lunch to celebrate it. Larry was very tearful, but Julie herself had been going off the deep end. She was deeply fatigued and depressed from the strain. Not only was she exhausted from staying up most nights, but she also was sad from listening to Larry. Every night, it seemed, after she had soaked and bandaged the stump of his left leg, Larry purged himself of more of his past.

"It's been a catharsis for him and a lot of sleepless nights for me," she said. Many nights after staying up with Larry, Julie would lay awake thinking about all the lonely people in the world who do hateful, repulsive things to others. It made her sad to think about all the passion Larry had poured into being a Nazi and a Klansman—and all the people he'd hurt simply because he felt like such a nobody. Jan Branting and Tim Fischer both told her she had to have sleep and she had to get out of the house—just what Michael, the kids and her friends had been telling her all along. Now, however, she knew she had to listen or she wouldn't be any good to anyone.

"I've been real respectful of what you need, and now it's time for you to be respectful of what I need," Julie said to Larry. "Tonight a hospice nurse is going to come and stay in your room overnight and give you your medications and calm you down if you need it so I can sleep. On Tuesday, I've been invited out for lunch and I'm going to go—Jan will stay with you while I'm gone."

On Tuesday when Julie came back from lunch, Larry was asleep, but he woke up hysterically sobbing. On Wednesday, Larry cried all day. "I don't know what's wrong with me," he said. "If I hear you go into the other room, I miss you."

Julie didn't know what was going on, but she told Jan and Dr. Fischer she had a sense something was about to change. Larry was getting more and more anxious, and he had tremendous panic that caused him to tremble almost uncontrollably. He ached in all his joints and his abdomen. Phantom pains raged through his legs, and his shoulders, back and head throbbed with pain. He was used to feeling miserable, but now he was sure he was going to die any minute.

Julie called Jan at the hospice, and Jan said she thought a lot of Larry's pain might be more emotional than physical. She said if necessary, they could increase his dose of Thorazine. Then she talked to Larry and reassured him, "It's going to be okay. I'm coming over in the morning and we'll talk about all this."

Larry was so uptight, the muscles in his chest and back began to cramp and pull with agonizing severity. Julie began to rub his back. She massaged his arms and said, "Larry, you can let everything out. Whatever you're holding in, it's okay, just let it out." Larry began to sob.

"Why are you crying?" Julie asked. "Please tell me."

"I wish I hadn't put you through this."

"What are you talking about? Larry, I wouldn't have it any other way. You haven't put me through anything except something wonderful."

"I wish I hadn't."

"Why are you upset? I need to know."

"You're going to hate me if I tell you," he said. "It will hurt you. I just don't want to hurt you."

"You don't ever hurt me. What are you worried about?"

"If I tell you, you'll never love me."

"I will, I promise."

"I've told you a lot of lies," he said. "Lots of lies. I lied to you."

"You have? If you have, that's okay."

"I never was in Hell's Angels."

"That doesn't surprise me," Julie said. "In fact, I figured that all along. Those didn't look like official tattoos."

"And I never was a mercenary," he said. "I wanted to go to Rhodesia to fight, but I never made it that far. I didn't even go to mercenary training like I said I did. I wanted to go, but I didn't ever have the money.

"Also, I didn't quit my job as a policeman," he said. "I was fired because I didn't check a building I was supposed to check. I didn't check it because I was drunk. And I was a terrible father to my two girls— Cheryl's daughters. I was real mean to them. I treated them the way my father treated me. I was so mean—and they needed a father. I was mean to Cheryl and she was a nice woman."

Larry began to sob again. "The biggest thing—the worst thing, you will hate me for this," Larry said. "Michael will hate me, everybody will hate me."

"It's okay, nothing will make us hate you—never."

"The thing in Kearney," Larry started to say. He choked on his words, sobbed and started again. "The thing in Kearney that I told everybody? The rape? *It never happened.* The rape didn't happen. I was *never* raped by any black guys. Not ever."

The truth was, Larry told Julie, he had had sex with a black kid when he was at Kearney, but the guy was just a little bit older than him, and it was a mutual thing. Larry wanted a picture the guy had, and he had sex with him in order to get the picture. Everything he'd said about being hurt and raped and being torn up and bleeding and going to the infirmary was a lie. The only time he'd been in the infirmary at Kearney was to get glasses. Since that time, he'd also had sex with some other men and he was ashamed of it. When Larry finished this confession, he sobbed and sobbed.

Julie put her arm around him and held him as he rocked back and forth. "Larry, it's okay," she said. "It's okay. I understand. You probably lied because you wanted a reason to hate people. But it's a good thing you're talking about it now. It's good you're letting it out."

"You don't hate me?"

"No, Larry, I love you."

"Could you call everybody in the morning and tell them that was a lie? Please will you do this for me? I can't let it stand the way it was."

"Of course."

"I don't want people to think that happened. It's against black people and black people never hurt me at all. It was so bad of me to say that. Will you please call for me to set the record straight?"

"Larry, you know I'll do that for you. You know I will. I'll make the calls first thing in the morning."

"Promise?"

"I promise."

Julie and Larry sat quietly for a long time after this. His exhaustion and the intensity of his emotional confession made his blood sugar fluctuate wildly, and he began to shake.

"You need to eat something," Julie said.

"Do you think Michael would make me a cheese sandwich?" Larry asked. Michael, who had been downstairs, made Larry a sandwich and sat down with him. After Larry ate half of his sandwich, he began to cry again.

"I've had no reason to hate black people," he said to Michael. "Nobody black has ever done anything bad to me. Not even one black person has ever done anything bad to me. I had no reason to hate black people or to hate anybody in this whole world. I was a hatemonger. I had no excuse for it and I had no reason for it—for my actions. I just did it."

Larry went to sleep sobbing like a little child.

For Julie's fortieth birthday on August 20, Rebecca, Dina and Dave were up at seven-thirty in the morning putting big black and white computer-paper banners all over the front of the house announcing "Lordy, Lordy, Look Who's 40!" "Julie is now 14,600 days old!" "Be Nice, Julie's 40!" Earlier, Larry had gotten Julie a bird named Keppe and a birdcage for her birthday. After he got her Keppe, he got her another bird, Rosie Bourke, to keep Keppe company. On her birthday morning, Julie was cleaning the birdcage, and Larry told her: "Talk to Keppe and give him the equal amount of time you give to Rosie Bourke. They know when you have favorites or when you don't give them equal attention."

Michael got Julie flowers and surprised her with a birthday party. Twenty-five people came over to celebrate. Larry was excited. On his own birthday, May 30, Michael, Julie and the kids had given him a surprise party—the first he'd ever had in his life, and he loved it. He wanted to join this party and have fun, too, but he was too sick to do so.

Throughout the evening, Julie visited with friends in the living room, but she had the sound monitor on, and every few minutes she put it up to her ear. She could hear Larry throwing up, and so she would run into his room to empty the pan as soon as he was done. In between, she'd come back out and visit with everyone. "I feel so sorry for Larry," Julie said. "He's crying and throwing up at the same time all these people are yelling happy birthday and laughing and eating cake and ice cream."

Everything in Larry's body began slowing down. He had a lot of uncomfortable swelling and he was puffy all over. He'd get cold and clammy, and then he'd get the chills. All of these symptoms had to do with the toxins building up in his system because his kidneys and liver weren't functioning to get rid of them. His skin got a yellowish cast, which gave him a jaundiced look.

More and more often, Larry also was having hallucinations. One night Julie came into the room and Larry looked like he was playing the piano at his desk. Julie said, "What are you doing?"

"I'm trying to pick up all these little pieces of paper," he said.

"There are no pieces of paper, Larry."

"How did they get here then?"

Sometimes Larry was conscious of his mind not functioning properly. "I'm having a hallucination," he said another day. "I'm hallucinating. I'm really tired. It's winter outside; there's snow on the ground."

"Larry, flowers are blooming outside. It's August."

Julie watched the deterioration with sadness. "There are times I think his elevator isn't going all the way to the top floor," she said to Michael. "Today he was saying, 'Choo-Choo is like a pig.' I said, 'Larry, you're not quite all there today! Choo-Choo is your cat.' "

"Who's that girl over there?" he said.

"That's not a girl. That's your hamster Isaiah in her cage. You know, Larry, we really should start calling her Alexandria since she had all those babies."

Julie shaved Larry, cut his fingernails, gave him shampoos and cut his hair. "If Larry had feet," Michael said, "she'd cut his toenails." Julie also read to Larry, listened to him, confided in him and, on the really good days, sometimes laughed with him until they both couldn't breathe.

Through sheer will, it seemed, Larry had lived longer than Dr. Fischer or anyone in the medical community believed possible. Finally, however, he began to accept his imminent death. He signed papers releasing the Weissers from having to call 911 when he died. Larry also talked to Michael and Julie about some of the physical things which concerned him. He didn't want to leave the house in a body bag because of the kids—and they promised he wouldn't. He wanted to give certain things of his to friends and he wanted a chance to say goodbye to everyone.

On August 29, Michael and Rebecca drove to Topeka, Kansas, where Michael spoke at a gay rights rally in Gage Park inspired by the fanaticism of a fundamentalist preacher named Fred Phelps, Sr., who had been picketing the park and the funerals of AIDS victims with such signs as "Faggots Are Maggots" and "God's Hate Is Great!"

"Tell them there's no sense fighting hatred with hatred," Larry told Michael before he left. "It's counterproductive. What that man needs is love. Hating him back won't change him. Hate is what he wants—and it only hurts the person who hates him back."

The next day Julie took Larry to the Garden Café for lunch, but while they were eating, Larry started looking for objects in his medicine bag and talking about things that didn't make any sense. When Julie rolled him in his wheelchair out to the car, he asked her why there were soda bottles everywhere.

"There aren't any soda bottles, Larry," she said.

"What's going on with me?" he asked. "This is really scaring me. I'm seeing things that aren't really there. What's happening to me?"

Julie knelt down beside his chair. "Larry, listen to me," she said. "You remember how Dr. Fischer told you this might happen? Your kidneys aren't working right, and the toxins are backing up in your system and affecting your mind. The toxins are making you see things that aren't there. But remember, I'm here. And Michael is. And the kids are."

"Julie, are things getting closer?" he asked. "Am I getting ready to die? I want you to tell me the truth."

"Yes, Larry," Julie said. "You are. But you're going to be okay. We're here for you and we're not going to leave your side for a minute."

Ever since he had made peace with his father and gotten rid of so many of his lies, Larry had also become more accepting of his death. "The shadow has gone," Julie said. "This whole new Larry has arrived. He's like an eight-year-old, but he's gained all this wisdom and insight. If he had time, he could learn so much and contribute so much more, but he doesn't have time."

Larry dreamt he was walking through a neighborhood where everything was white—the houses, lawns, bushes, cars, street—everything was white. At the end of the street, he saw a gate in the distance. On the other side of that gate, everything was in wonderful, bright, dazzling colors, just as it is in real life. Larry wanted to get there, but he couldn't get through the gate because he was carrying a huge bag with all his medicines in it, a bag crucial to his survival. The bag got caught in the gate and he was pulling and struggling to get free so he could get into the land of beautiful colors. Finally, he had to decide whether to let go of the bag and go to the other side or to hold on to the bag and remain struggling where he was.

Another night, Larry woke up and began weeping hysterically again.

He had been hallucinating again, hearing sounds and seeing people who weren't there and experiencing a great deal of disorientation. "I shouldn't have eaten those peanuts," he said, as if that was what had made him so sick. But when Julie logically tried to explain his diabetes, and that smoking and drinking had a lot more to do with his illness than peanuts, Larry waved his hand in the air as if waving away confusion.

"I'm so sick, Julie," he said in a quiet, almost whispering voice. "I love people and I worry about people, but I can't worry anymore. But I have natural worries."

"What are your natural worries? Is there anything I can help you with?"

"I'm not really worried about anything except what's going on with some of these people."

"Like who?"

"Like people in that organization I was in . . . I would never go back to that organization. They're deviant."

"You've already told the police and the FBI everything, so there's no reason for you to even think about that stuff from the past."

"I didn't tell them everything."

"You didn't? I thought you told them everything."

"You don't tell the police or the federal government everything. There are some things I know yet that I will never tell anyone."

"Have you told me?"

"No. But there's nothing I didn't tell you that would harm you in any way."

"There's stuff you haven't told me?"

"I don't know if you should ask me about it. I did terrible things in the past. If there was something that would hurt you or Michael or the kids, I'd tell you in a minute, you know that, don't you?"

"This seems so strange."

"I didn't tell the ADL either. I didn't tell because I didn't trust federal agencies too much. I did wrong."

"The ADL is not part of the government. The ADL is a Jewish-sponsored organization that fights hate crimes and the Ku Klux Klan and the Nazi Party."

"Nobody has the answers to the questions I have. Not even God has the answers to the questions I have."

"Yes, He does. Why do you think He doesn't? Have you asked God?"

"I don't need trains."

"What do you need?"

"There's a lot more important things. I want you and Michael and all the people I love to be okay. I want the world of people to be okay. I like my hamster. I want a kid to have my little hamster."

"Hey, Lar, I want you to be alright. I don't want you to be worried."

"I'm going through the same thing Mom did, and she made it through."

"Do you want me to stay in here with you?"

"No. Go do what you have to do. But soon, let's go to Holmes Park Lake and catch a big fish. I just want to fish. I want things to be the way they used to be. I want to catch five, six, seven, eight, nine fish. All the fish I can catch. Or maybe we'll go to Salt Creek. There are some big fish down there. Catfish. Bass. . . . There'll be a high breeze. I still have some hip waders somewhere. I used to wear them. You can wear them and it'll be fun. When can we go fishin'?"

"Maybe as soon as it gets a little cooler. It's supposed to be hot the next couple of days."

"It doesn't matter how big the fish are," Larry said. "Just going and having fun matters. Fishin's not for everybody, but now it's time to go to bed."

Larry's voice was quiet, almost inaudible. He seemed to know the past somehow didn't matter anymore and soon he would rest—soon the Weissers would rest.

On Sunday morning, September 6, 1992, Julie and Michael were awakened before dawn by the sound of Larry moaning. It was the Nebraska State Fair weekend and the night before, about ten o'clock, Julie had called Jan Branting and told her Larry had slept all day and hadn't been responsive. When he coughed, she said, it smelled like cigarettes and smoke came out of his mouth. He had stopped smoking four years before, but smoke still was coming out of his lungs. A few times during the day, he spoke incoherently, but once he'd opened his eyes, looked at Julie and said, "I miss you already."

Since Friday, Larry hadn't been able to swallow. Dr. Fischer and Jan Branting told Julie that trying to regulate Larry's insulin was a lost cause. It wasn't going to make any difference; his body was shutting down.

"Julie, you know he might not make it through the night," Jan said.

"Can you get some sleep?" Later, Jan would remember her suggestion seemed ludicrous given Julie's anxiety over Larry's death. But in fact, Julie did go into her room after talking to Jan. She worked on a scrapbook she was putting together of Larry's pictures, and then she and Michael went to bed. They had a sound monitor in their bedroom, and they could hear the sound of Larry's breathing as they fell asleep.

Shortly after 5 A.M., Julie and Michael sat up in bed, rested and wide awake. Larry was moaning as if he were trying to call them, and they got up and went into his room. Larry seemed to be asleep but trying to wake up. Michael began to talk to him and say some prayers. Julie said, "Larry, I want you to know we all really love you."

Larry shook his head no. Michael didn't see it, but Julie did. Later, Julie remembered that little flicker and wondered what was going through Larry's mind. Maybe he simply thought he was shaking his head yes.

It was quiet. Michael and Julie watched Larry breathe small, shallow breaths. Julie opened Larry's curtains as the dark predawn sky began to get slightly lighter. Michael noticed Larry holding up his hand as if he wanted someone to hold it, which Michael did. A bit later, Michael went out in the driveway to smoke. He lit his cigarette and was standing there peacefully, looking up at the sky when he noticed Orion, a cluster of stars referred to as "the Hunter." As he was looking, he saw a shooting star pass right in front of Orion. He thought about how Larry was a hunter, and he took it as a sign. He went back inside and told Julie about the shooting star. He kissed Larry on the forehead and sat down. About ten minutes later, as he and Julie were sitting beside Larry, holding his hands, Larry stopped breathing.

After Larry died, Michael sat in Larry's wheelchair by his bed and said the Kaddish, the Jewish prayer recited in the memory of the dead which praises the greatness of God: " '*Yitgadal ve-yitkadash, Shmei rabbah*—May His name be magnified and made holy . . .' " When he finished praying, Michael began to sob.

Julie cried, too, but she was calm as she tucked Larry's quilt around his body, kissed him, set his yarmulke straight on his head and put his trainman's cap under her own pillow. Michael went downstairs and woke Rebecca, Dave and Dina, and they pulled on their robes and came upstairs. They each went into Larry's room to stand by him and to say goodbye. Dave was wearing a silver onyx ring Larry had given him, which he said he would always keep.

Two nurses from hospice came, and then the people from the funeral home. Before Larry was taken from the house on a gurney, Julie tucked the patchwork quilt from his bed around him. Michael walked out of the house alongside the gurney to make sure Larry would not leave their house unaccompanied by family.

Dina, who couldn't stop crying, fed Larry's hamsters and took a walk around the block. Keeping most of her tears inside, Rebecca carried Choo-Choo around in her arms and forlornly agreed to be a pallbearer at Larry's funeral, along with Alan Frank, Charles Griffin and Bob Wolfson.

CROWN OF AN HONORABLE MAN

Chapter 26

I only ask for last kind words from you. We were neighbors for so long, but I received more than I could give. Now the day has dawned and the lamp that lit my dark corner is out. The summons has come and I'm ready for my journey.

— RABINDRANATH TAGORE

Julie opened the door for Mrs. Evans, her eighty-five-year-old neighbor who came over in pink rollers and her apron after she saw the funeral parlor's hearse take Larry away. "Don't you be upset," she said, giving Julie a hug. "His body was just all worn out. Now you can get some rest, too. I watched you take that wheelchair in and out of your car and I worried about your back!"

The phone and the doorbell at the Weissers kept ringing. When it wasn't friends or relatives, it was the news media. One television reporter called and said, "Can we just come over and shoot some footage showing his room and all?" Julie said no, and he couldn't believe it. A few minutes later, he called back again.

"He's a member of our family, and he just died," Julie said. "Can't you understand that?"

"It wouldn't take long," he insisted. "We could be in and out of there in fifteen minutes; we wouldn't intrude."

"How would you feel if someone in your family just died?"

"Well, I'd want to let people know how he passed away," the reporter said. "We could share this with other people . . ."

"No," Julie said, "the answer is no."

The fog of activity and confusion which so often blankets the emotions of the living after the trauma of death descended on the house at Randolph Street. Friends came in and out of the house with food and comforting words as Michael and Julie planned Larry's funeral. Ron Drury, who had his fishing rods in the back of his truck for a hoped-for fishing trip with Larry, agreed to conduct the services along with Michael. Julie had wanted the Lincoln Community Gospel Choir to sing "This Train Is Bound for Glory" at Larry's funeral, but the choir couldn't get together during the week because of their jobs. Leslie Young offered to sing instead. Donna Polk also volunteered to speak.

At the Roper and Sons mortuary later that day, Julie set out framed pictures of Larry all around the room. The pictures were of Larry when he was a little boy, Larry with his father and mother, Larry in his police uniform, Larry fishing. More recent pictures showed Larry with the kids, with her and Michael, with John Ways and Norman Leach and with his father and Margaret.

By that afternoon, the funeral home had shaved Larry and dressed him in the suit, shirt and tie he'd worn at the Martin Luther King Service and on the Fremont dinner train. Tucked up to his waist was the patchwork quilt that had been on his bed since he'd moved into Randolph Street. He had on his prayer shawl and his yarmulke—the blue embroidered one that had his name, Keter Hillel—"Crown of an Honorable Man"—and he was wearing the brotherhood ring Michael and Julie had given him, as well as a silver chain and locket Julie had given him.

John Trapp had requested to see his son one last time, and at 2 P.M., he and his wife Margaret went to the funeral home. When Michael and Julie arrived a short while later, they were surprised to see the casket open. In Jewish tradition, there is no "viewing," nor is a casket ever open during a funeral. They knew Mr. Trapp wanted to see Larry, but they had assumed it would be done in private.

Nonetheless, Michael walked with Mr. Trapp up to Larry's casket. As John Trapp stood looking down at his son's body, he began sobbing and his knees began to collapse. Michael put his arm around Mr. Trapp and held him up. Within a few minutes, Mr. Trapp dried his eyes and said he needed to get back to Omaha. He thanked Julie and Michael for all they had done for Larry.

Julie walked up to the casket and looked at Larry to make sure he had on his rings and necklace, but then she backed away from where he was. "He looked like a wax figure—the color of milk," Julie said. "His sweet beautiful face wasn't there. His dimples weren't there. Larry had this neat face that was so changeable; it showed what he felt. And that wasn't there. I was sitting across the room, and I got this overwhelming wave of Larry saying, 'Stop looking at this body. This is not me.' And I realized the essence of who Larry was is not his body. It is not that person with no legs who was blind."

At Larry's funeral on Tuesday, Rev. Ron Drury, Larry's good friend and a Lutheran minister, shared the bimah with Michael. In his white robe, with a large Christian cross around his neck, Ron Drury stood under the Star of David and spoke with emotion of his friendship with Larry. "The newspapers proclaimed, 'Jewish Family Takes in KKK Member,' but what it was, it was God carrying them all along," he said. "The Weisser family could not have done this on their own. It was God working through them, an awesome God, a God who carries us when we are no longer able to carry ourselves. In the past two weeks, Larry was having trouble getting in and out of bed and Julie and Michael put their arms underneath Larry, carrying him from one place to another, and it was God carrying them so they could do that."

The closed cherry wood casket containing Larry's body sat on rollers at the front of the synagogue, its gleaming surface blending into the beautifully aged Nebraska walnut of the sanctuary. The synagogue was filled with family and friends who came to pay their last respects.

"Many of us have had the opportunity of seeing God in our lifetime," Ron Drury said, "for when we see God in one another, we have the beauty of seeing a glimpse of God. My prayer is that you might see the awesome work of God that can change a man who for all sorts of reasons, and we don't know all of them, was so full of hatred at one time in his life, and was able to laugh and hug and embrace, with words and arms, people he despised just a few months earlier. Mother Teresa in Calcutta put it this way: she said, 'Many people are hungry in the world and they suffer much, but there are many people hungering for love who suffer even more.' "

Leslie Young, dressed in a small black hat and a white jacket, walked up the stairs to the bimah and stood behind the podium, her guitar strap over her shoulder. "This song was real special to Larry because it's a song about the love between him and the Weissers and the love that transformed him into the person we came to know and love," Leslie said into the microphone. "Larry always feared not being loved just for who he was. I'm proud to say I was Larry's friend and I, like the Weissers, came to love Larry as he was. It wasn't hard to love him. He was like a little kid. He was very honest and you knew exactly what he was feeling, 'cause he'd let you know whether you wanted to know or not. The son of a gun had a wicked and wonderful sense of humor, and he had a heart of pure gold.

"The real Larry was the good Larry we came to know this past year. The old Larry was not the true Larry, but as he told me, 'Maybe God let me go through all this stuff just so He could use me.' I think God was using Larry in a mighty way. He touched a lot of people, and I think Larry is going to touch a lot of people probably forever. He's touched me and I passed that on to my daughter, and she'll pass it on to her kids and on and on. Larry's taught us what true love can do for us. I hope that, because of Larry, we'll all try a little harder to lay aside such senselessness as intolerance and hatred. . . . This song is for Larry." Then Leslie sang "What Love Has Done," ending with the chorus:

> It used to be, you hated me
> You didn't understand
> That every race and every man
> Were fashioned by His hand
> That we're all the same within
> 'Neath the color of our skin.
> Yes you and I, we're all the same to Him.

When it was Donna Polk's turn to speak, she stood at the front of the sanctuary in a simple blue silk dress, her hands folded in front of her.

"I'm really grateful to be here today," Donna said. "It has been eight and a half months since I met Larry Trapp at this temple. I tried to pick out the man who had terrorized me so severely. In my mind, I pictured him to be a big man with the scars of racism he had lived with for so long. But when I looked over there to see the man who had to be Larry Trapp, I was amazed. Here was a kind man, with skin that looked so soft with just the most serene look on his face.

"I had the great fortune to get to know him better, to get to understand him. Larry and I talked about his past and it was the same story we often hear—that his hate came out of unhappiness and fear.

"But the thing that makes Larry so unique is that he *changed.* He *changed.* He became a one-person crusade. He tried to get other people to change. He said hatred and racism would end when people understood what they were doing.

"I'm going to say with all my conviction that Larry was a good man. He was a good man. And I want to say to all of you that we must work a lot harder. We must do what Larry did—we must become one-person crusades in our commitment to let people know how important it is to love one another. To reach out. To go into each other's homes and have dinner. To go into churches, synagogues, mosques and temples to spread the word that only through love can we survive.

"I'm grateful to be here today because I feel confident that Larry has gone on to a better place. And perhaps today he's speaking with Malcolm, Martin and Harriet. And they're commiserating about their experience and what they did to change the world. Larry is in good company."

Michael, wearing his black robe, white prayer shawl and a white yarmulke, invited everyone in the synagogue to the Weisser home that evening for "a service which we in the Jewish faith call a minyan, or a shivah—which is sort of a memorial to help us all get through this hard time."

Michael spoke of Larry's life, of the little boy who brought home everything from white rats to a six-foot bull snake, and how his own home had been transformed since Larry had arrived—from being a home with one dog and one cat, to now having two additional cats, three birds, a hamster and her ten babies. He spoke of Larry's life during the past ten months—the time he truly *lived.*

"Sometimes it's really good to think carefully before remembering someone at a time like this," Michael said. "We go back to the past to bitter and angry times and we might have a glimpse that was true, but it would be something that was true no more. The past, as they say, is past. And sometimes it's good to think only of those things of a person that are positive and wonderful. But if we do this, then we tend to create a saint instead of a memory that is real and true. So perhaps what we should do is try and be aware that people are very complex. As we are taught in the Jewish faith, we are born with a dual nature—the propensity for both good and evil. And throughout our lives, we are presented with many choices, many paths upon which to set our feet, and sometimes we make wise choices and sometimes not. I know it's that way with me, and I know it's that way with you, and I know it's that way with everyone of us who live on this earth.

"We are born. We find ourselves in a set of circumstances. We make our choices," Michael continued. "We fill the days of our lives with our activities and then someday we begin to fade, and finally we close our eyes for the last time. We draw in that last earthly breath and we die. And that's the same for me and you and everyone who lives on this planet. Those of us who remain behind ask the question, 'O Lord, what is man? That you take knowledge of him and the children of mankind, that you take account of them, for we are like a breath, like a shadow that passes away. . . .' And yet, somehow, we know there is more to our lives than what first meets the eye. . . ."

After the funeral, Bill Brda, who had been attending services at B'nai Jeshurun for more than three years, dreamt Larry came to say goodbye to him. Larry was dressed in blue jeans and he had his legs and his eyes were perfectly clear. He was completely wholesome and healthy, a "fruitful kind of healthiness," according to Bill.

"Larry, what's it like being on the other side?" Bill asked in his dream.

"It's like being in the sanctuary where there are no distractions and you know everything you need to know," Larry said. In Bill Brda's dream, Larry said, "I'm going to leave you a note on the bedside table." Bill looked and on the desk was a card. He got up and read the note, even though it was written in Hebrew and in real life he can't read Hebrew. Nevertheless, in his dream, the name on the card was "Acor."

When Bill woke up from his dream, he remembered the Hebrew name written on the card sounded like "Achor." When he looked up Achor in the Bible, he found that in the Book of Joshua, the family of Achan had broken the rules, and they'd been cursed and executed. But by the book of Hosea, the name Achan meant "Door of Hope."

Julie dreamed she went looking for Larry. "I went from house to house looking for him," she remembers. "Finally, I came to a house and he was there, and he was really, really happy. He got up from his wheelchair—he had his legs—he got up and gave me this big hug. He was really peaceful. There were all these loving people around him who were his friends, and it was wonderful. After that I knew he was all right."

Traditionally, the unveiling of the stone for someone Jewish takes place on the first *yahrzeit,* the anniversary of a person's death—which ends the full mourning period, observed according to the Hebrew calendar. This hadn't happened because Michael and Julie couldn't afford to buy the marker in September.

As it turned out, delaying the unveiling until November turned out to be perfect, because November 16 was the anniversary of the day Larry felt his life *really* had begun.

And so it was that on November 16, 1993, Michael and Julie, along with Dave, a freshman at the University of Nebraska, Dina, a junior at East High, and Rebecca, a senior, drove to the Wyuka Cemetery in Lincoln. At Larry's grave, which sat under a giant maple, they were joined by several friends, including Charles "Griff" Griffin and Leslie Young. It was a bitterly cold day, but the group had gathered for the unveiling of Larry's stone, and they stood shivering close together across from a tombstone that said "Friend."

It was a solemn moment. Michael lifted the cover off the marker and said the opening words of the Kaddish, " '*Yitgadal ve-yitkadash, Shmei rabbah*—May His name be magnified and made holy.' "

Suddenly, at that instant, a small red fox flashed into view behind the gravestone. It stopped, startled, looked up at the group and then ran on across the cemetery.

Everyone burst out laughing—and then kept on laughing. As many times as they'd been at that cemetery, they'd seen squirrels and a stray cat or two, but never a fox. "Larry is with us," Griff said, and they all laughed harder. Somehow it did seem Larry was there.

We can do no great things.
Only small things with great love.
—MOTHER TERESA

Notes and Sources

These notes and the following bibliography are meant as an informal guide and reference to sources I've used in writing this book. Unless otherwise indicated, I have reconstructed scenes and dialogue based on in-depth interviews and on material taken from audiotape recordings, videotapes, radio and television news reports, newspaper articles, letters, calendars, medical records and court transcripts.

Prologue: The Place and the People (pages 13-22)

Willa Cather's quote "I had the feeling that the world was left behind . . ." is in *My Ántonia,* Book I, "The Shimerdas," p. 7.

The old tribes who roamed through Nebraska became known to English-speaking people as the Pawnees, Kaws, Otoes, Missourias, Osages, Quapaws, Omahas, Poncas, and Iowas. Mandans, Arikaras, Hidatsas, Chippewas, Ottawas, Dakotas, Potawatomis, Kickapoos, Sacs, Foxes, Peorias, Piankashaws, Kaskaskias, Miamis, Oglalas, Santees, Nez Percés, Assiniboines, Crows and Winnebagos. The names they called themselves, such as Ne-yu-ta-ca (Camping at the Mouth of the River) and Ka-za (Swift), came from records of the Nebraska State Historical Society in 1885 and 1886.

The tribes remaining in Nebraska include the Santees, a branch of eastern Sioux, the Omahas, Winnebegos and the Teton Sioux. Many of the 5,000 Plains Indians in Nebraska live on the Santee Reservation or on the Winnebego and Omaha reservations in the northeastern part of the state. Others who do not live in cities stay on the small Iowa Sac and Fox Reservation, which juts into a small southeastern corner of the state, or on the large Rosebud and Pine Ridge reservations that spill over from South

Dakota into Nebraska's northwest corner. Information on current Native American tribes and their history in Nebraska came chiefly from "Indians: The Beauty of the Unbroken Hoop" by Galen Buller in *Broken Hoops and Plains People.*

The quote on p. 14 comes from pioneer J. W. Pattison, in *The Omaha Arrow,* Vol. 1, No. 1, July 28, 1846. I found it reprinted in *Transactions and Reports of the Nebraska State Historical Society,* Vol. II, 1887.

Information on Nebraska's history comes from a variety of sources, including James Olson's *History of Nebraska;* early volumes of *Nebraska History,* the Nebraska State Historical Society's journal; Chudacoff's *Mobile Americans,* which focuses on Omaha; and a collection of essays in *Broken Hoops and Plains People.* Jim Potter, historian at the Nebraska State Historical Society, was most helpful, as was Bertha Calloway at the Great Plains Black Museum.

I recommend Ian Frazier's *Great Plains;* I learned a lot about Custer and Crazy Horse from his wonderful discussion of these people, and also learned from Stephen Ambrose's large and interesting book *Crazy Horse and Custer.*

Information on Omaha, the "Gate City to the West," came from *Mobile Americans.*

Information on "York" came from Lerone Bennett's book *The Shaping of Black America.* Bertha Calloway at the Great Plains Black Museum says the first African-Americans to settle in Nebraska were slaves or indentured servants. She says any stories about free blacks living in Nebraska during the 1700s are pure conjecture.

Information on the sympathies of early Nebraskans and John Brown's route with escaped slaves across Nebraska came from "John Brown in Richardson County," by A. R. Keim, in *Transactions and Reports of the Nebraska State Historical Society,* Vol. II (Lincoln: State Journal Co., 1887).

Nell Painter's *Exodusters: Black Migration to Kansas after Reconstruction* is an extraordinary portrait of the post-Reconstruction South and was essential to my understanding of the forces that produced the migration of blacks from the South to the Midwest. Painter's book *Standing at Armageddon* is also essential reading for anyone interested in Southern history.

The history of the Jews in Nebraska was drawn chiefly from "The Jews of Omaha: The First Sixty Years," by Carol Gendler, M.A. thesis, presented to the Department of History and the faculty of the College of Graduate Studies, the University of Omaha, 1968; and Ella Fleishman Auerbach's "Jewish Settlement in Nebraska," unpublished typescript, 1927. Another good resource on Jewish migration to America is Howard M. Sachar's *A History of Jews in America.*

The story of Julius Meyer is cited in several different places, mainly Gendler. Although Meyer's death was reported as a suicide, it was rumored that in fact he was murdered by a Native American who had been spurned by an Indian woman Meyer planned to marry.

The story of the Klan surrounding the Littles' house, when Malcolm X's mother was pregnant with him, came from *The Autobiography of Malcolm X.* Although there have been some questions about the veracity of this story, it is totally consistent with the Klan history in the state. Newspaper accounts from the spring of 1925 document cross burnings, public Klan gatherings and initiations.

I found a number of different figures on the number of Klan members in Nebraska during the 1920s, but Dr. Michael Schuyler at the University of Nebraska at Kearney says the number was probably 45,000.

The biggest Klan gathering in Lincoln in the 1920s was reported in "Big Klan Picnic and Fireworks," *Lincoln Star,* July 6, 1926.

In researching the history of Klan members who had sought or won important state or national posts, *Mother Jones* ("Klandidates," March–April 1992, p. 15) discovered that President Warren G. Harding was initiated as a Klan member in a White House ceremony in 1921. *Mother Jones* also reported that in 1922, Harry S. Truman paid Klan dues during an election campaign for a judgeship in Missouri, but never became an active member. They also found that Supreme Court Justice Hugo Black was a Klansman in Alabama in 1926, before he was elected to the U.S. Senate, and that today's U.S. Senator Robert Byrd of West Virginia, reelected to his sixth term in 1990, was a KKK Kleagle in 1942–43. According to David Chalmers in *Hooded Americanism,* Klan lecturers made claims that congressmen, senators, high military officers and members of the Cabinet, as well as President Harding and his attorney general, had been initiated into the Klan. The White House denied this, however, and the attorney general wrote to U.S. attorneys stating neither he nor President Harding were Klansmen.

Historian Michael Schuyler relays details of the lynching of William Brown in his paper "The Ku Klux Klan in Nebraska, 1920–1930," *Nebraska History,* Vol. 66, No. 3 (Fall 1985). It is also documented in Frank Shay's *Judge Lynch: His First Hundred Years* (New York: Ives Washburn, 1938), in other records of documented lynchings, and in newspaper accounts of Brown's death. See the *Omaha World-Herald,* September 19, 1919, and October 6, 1919.

Henry Fonda's account of having witnessed the lynching was written by Howard Teichmann in *My Life: Henry Fonda.*

The quote about the riots after the lynching comes from *Mobile Americans.*

Chapter Two (pages 26–37)

The Golden Rule of Judaism—originally "What is hateful to you, do not do to your fellow creature"—came from Rabbi Hillel, 100 B.C.E., *Sab. 31A.*

An essay on sayings from that period can be found in Rabbi Herst's *Authorized Daily Prayer Book* (New York: Bloch, 1974).

Information on the role of cantors came from conversations with members of the American Conference of Cantors and discussions with Jewish scholars. Cantor Linda Shepherd at the Emanuel Congregation in Chicago also was most helpful in this regard. Cantor Shepherd gave me information about the history of cantors in the reform movement and confirmed my impression that rabbis and cantors are becoming more and more mobile. She said cantors traditionally move a lot—either because the congregation gets tired of the cantor's voice or the cantor and rabbi don't see eye to eye on various issues. Rabbi David Straus at Temple Har Sinai in Trenton also helped confirm this information.

The size of Lincoln and various details on Lincoln's commercial life, its universities and colleges, comes from the Lincoln Chamber of Commerce, from records supplied by the Lincoln Public Schools and from observations and discussions in Lincoln.

The history of Congregations B'nai Jeshurun and Tifereth Israel comes from Carol Gendler's very helpful master's thesis, "The Jews of Omaha: The First Sixty Years," as well as from Ella Auerbach's 1927 survey on "Jewish Settlement in Nebraska."

The story of "the Village of Lancaster" becoming Lincoln and the state capital is well documented in *Transactions and Reports of the Nebraska State Historical Society* and in James Olson's *History of Nebraska.*

The origin of the name *nebrathka* is explained in *Flat Water: A History of Nebraska and Its Water* and in James Olson's *History of Nebraska.*

What Michael Weisser told the board of directors during his interview, as well as what he said in his first sermon, is reconstructed from interviews with Michael Weisser about his religious philosophies.

Statistics on the makeup of Lincoln's religious population comes from the 1990 Census and from Interfaith Council reports.

The history of Lincoln's Interfaith Council comes from newspaper reports, the Interfaith Council's newsletters and from interviews with Norman Leach and others.

Gary Rex "Gerhard" Lauck of Lincoln, Nebraska, is still the world's biggest supplier of Nazi propaganda. Information on Lauck and his National Socialist German Workers Party—Overseas Organization (NSDAP-AO) comes primarily from "A Nebraska Nazi's Global Reach," A Special Report by the Anti-Defamation League of B'nai B'rith, and from "The Midwest's Top Neo-Nazi: Gerhard Lauck and the NSDAP-AO," in Klanwatch's *Intelligence Report,* published by the Southern Poverty Law Center. I also learned more about Lauck from news articles in the *Lincoln Journal Star* and the *Omaha World-Herald.*

Chapter Three (pages 38–48)

The quote "Because we all share this small planet earth . . ." comes from the Nobel Peace Prize lecture of the Fourteenth Dalai Lama, Tenzin Gyatso, religious and political leader of the Tibetan people, in *The Nobel Peace Prize and the Dalai Lama* (Ithaca, New York: Snow Lion Publications, 1990) p. 35.

The flyers, pictures and other propaganda mentioned in this chapter are among the actual material the Weissers received from Larry Trapp in 1991.

For more information on the myth regarding Jews as slave-traders and slave-owners, read Rabbi Bertram Korn's essay, "Jews and Negro Slavery in the Old South" in *The Jewish Experience in America,* edited by Abraham J. Karp, 1969, and *Jew-Hatred as History,* a publication of the Anti-Defamation League in 1993. It is interesting to note that Minister Louis Farrakhan and the Nation of Islam use basic Ku Klux Klan propaganda to advance the anti-Semitic thesis that Jews initiated and profited from the slave trade. Of course, Klan members and white supremacists are delighted to see blacks and Jews at each other's throats; it feeds their efforts to stimulate dissention and race war within the United States.

Statistics on the numbers of people who were murdered by the Nazis during the Holocaust can be found in dozens of books on the subject. For more information on the Holocaust, read Martin Gilbert's excellent book *The Holocaust: A History of the Jews of Europe During the Second World War.*

Comments about anti-Semitism in Nebraska are drawn from a variety of interviews with both Christians and Jews in Lincoln and Omaha, as well as from relevant articles and editorials in Nebraska newspapers from 1919 to 1994. Laurence Thomas' essay "The Evolution of Anti-Semitism" in *Transition* provides an excellent discussion of the historical aspects of anti-Semitism and racism.

For more on the Greensboro massacre, read Emily Mann's documentary play *The Greensboro Massacre.* In a civil trial, it was found that although local police and federal agents knew a caravan of armed Klansmen and neo-Nazis were heading to an anti-Klan rally, and although they expected violence, no law-enforcement officers stopped the caravan or confiscated the Klansmen's weapons. Local police officers assigned to keep peace at the anti-Klan march failed to appear at the time of the massacre. Two local police officers who had followed the Klan caravan stayed in their car and watched as Nazis and Klansmen got out of their cars and trucks, pulled out their weapons, shot and killed five unarmed demonstrators, wounded many others and terrorized residents of a black housing project.

Chapter Four (pages 49–62)

Albert Memmi's quote "From the greed of one Jew the anti-Semite concludes . . ." comes from *Dominated Man,* p. 188. Memmi is a Tunisian Jew
who has struggled brilliantly with the psychological and emotional dynamics of racism, anti-Semitism and sexism in this and other books, including *Portrait of a Jew, The Liberation of the Jew* and *The Colonizer and
the Colonized,* translated by Howard Greenfeld and published by Orion
Press.

Although this and other scenes in Larry Trapp's apartment most likely
did not occur in this sequence, everything in the scene has been taken
from factual sources. The T-shirt Larry was wearing, for instance, is one I
found among his possessions. It was so well worn, it was frayed. Also, he
said that as a Klansman and Nazi, he wore his gold swastika medallion
every day.

I've chronicled Trapp's life as a Klansman in this chapter and in following chapters based on interviews with him, with law-enforcement officers,
Klan observers and people who knew him at the time. I built the scenes
and details of his daily life by piecing together evidence and dialogues
from his tape recordings, pamphlets, handwritten enemies lists, the way
he used lights to read and write, and clothes that were among the boxes of
his possessions he made available to me.

In some cases, as indicated in later chapters, I've reconstructed dialogues based on actual recordings made by Larry when he was a Klansman. He authorized my use of these tapes, as well as use of all his
belongings, which included boxes filled with his records, letters, files, calendars, sales slips and notes.

I've quoted passages from Larry's books which were underlined, starred
and annotated in his distinctive, wavery handwriting.

The 350 white separatist groups are listed by Klanwatch. Larry had materials from dozens and dozens of these groups.

Larry told the story of how he used to "sap" Indians to Jack Levine, who
shared the story with me. Larry Trapp's feelings and past experiences with
women came from interviews with him, stories he told Julie Weisser and
direct observations and candid recollections from Larry's sister, Candace
Trapp Bywater.

Donna Polk supplied me with copies of the hate mail sent her by Larry
Trapp.

The history of Klan violence can be read in any number of sources, including Chalmers' *Hooded Americanism: The History of the Ku Klux Klan.*
Klanwatch supplied the statistics of the murders of 300 people attributed
to the Klan since 1964.

Chapter Five (pages 63–82)

Albert Memmi's quote "Everyone looks for an inferior rank . . ." comes from *Dominated Man,* p. 201.

The scene of Larry Trapp handling and cleaning his guns is as I imagine it from watching Larry handle other objects, from seeing his cleaning rags, his receipts from gun purchases and from listening to him describe his guns. His patterns of pawning his guns, lanterns and other items came from an interview with Sheldon Kushner at the Royal Jewelry and Loan Company.

The "Vigilante Voices of Nebraska—Where the truth hurts" and other hotline messages used throughout the book come from actual tape recordings Larry Trapp made or recorded when he was a Klansman.

Larry Trapp told me about the loss of his toe and his amputations and phantom itching.

Larry later admitted to having studied killing techniques, and this is confirmed by the starred and underlined sections in his books on killing skills. These included *Hit Man: A Technical Manual for Independent Contractors* and *Covert Material on How to Kill.* Larry Trapp told me: "I wanted to know how, if I wanted to do away with someone, I could do it. For me, it was like job skills."

Larry Trapp's view of his Klan work as a full-time job was useful. With only the one amputation, he'd been able to use a prosthetic wooden leg and get around pretty well with a cane for balance. But when they took his second leg off, he had to face a real loss of mobility.

Larry told Julie and others about having shot the squirrels and dogs. I found sales slips for his various weapons and the diagram he used for building a silencer on his gun.

Information on Larry's hunting and trapping habits and his environmental concerns came mainly from an interview with Gary Svoboda, "Trapper Refuses to Let Blindness Halt Hunting," *Lincoln Journal Star,* January 19, 1986, p. 4B. Larry discussed the bunker he built, and notes on his bunker were among his records.

Information on Farrands and the Invisible Empire came from Klanwatch. Information on NAPA and Arthur Kirk, and the Posse Comitatus and Michael Ryan's case, came from Bob Wolfson at the ADL, as well as from Rod Colvin's *Evil Harvest,* which recounts the story of Michael Ryan's cult. Other helpful documents were "The American Farmer and the Extremists" and "Extremist Group Outreach to Rural Americans," two special reports of the Anti-Defamation League of B'nai B'rith's Civil Rights Division.

Information on Larry's Klan "naturalization" ceremony came from interviews with Larry, plus a ceremony found among his papers. It seems interesting that a group traditionally against foreigners uses the same term for inducting new members as the U.S. government does when it "naturalizes" new citizens.

These examples of Klan language—words starting with *K*—are abundant in newspaper articles in the early 1920s. The particular examples I use here come from a July 15, 1926, issue of the *Lincoln Star.*

The Klan's entry into Lincoln in 1921 is thoroughly documented in newspaper reports from that time.

Linda Thomson's article about Larry Trapp, titled "Soft-spoken Lincoln Man Peddles Ku Klux Klan," was published in the *Lincoln Star,* February 20, 1990, p. 11.

Dr. Jack Kay's observations regarding the rhetoric of hate groups are further explored in his "Arguing for and Against a White Homeland: The Aryan World Congress versus the Kootenai County Task Force on Human Relations." Dr. Kay is at work on a book about the public/private face and rhetoric of hate groups.

These quotes from the antiracism rally in September 1990 come from articles by Linda Thomson, who covered the rally for the *Lincoln Star,* and Jolene Daib, who covered it for the *Lincoln Journal.*

Chapter Six (pages 83–98)

Albert Memmi's quote "Not enough emphasis has been placed on a particular ingredient of racism . . ." comes from *Dominated Man,* p. 201.

Larry Trapp's recruiting of members and his attitudes toward explosives are based on retrospective interviews and on the actual materials he had read on explosives. Information on Glen Miller and the White Patriot Party comes from newspaper accounts and Klanwatch.

Information on Lincoln's Vietnamese community comes from articles and bulletins, as well as interviews with Phong Huynh, Lincoln Police Department's community liaison Maria Goretti Vu, Norman Leach and others. Copies of hate mail to the Vietnamese center, which had been turned over to the police, were shared with me by the ADL, CARP and the Interfaith Council.

The Dial-A-Racist messages used here came from recordings made by Larry Trapp of the public hotlines of the White Knights of the KKK and from Tom Metzger's WAR hotline.

Information on Tom Metzger and WAR comes from WAR pamphlets, posters, hotline messages and videos, from news articles, the Klanwatch Intelligence Reports and from Morris Dees and Steve Fiffer's *Hate on Trial.*

The quote from the WAR computer bulletin board comes from James Ridgeway's extremely informative book *Blood in the Face.* The message goes on to suggest ways to kill, by loosening a car's cylinders, setting fires or filling a lightbulb with gunpowder so "When the light goes on, he goes out. GFTT."

According to James Ridgeway, Tom Metzger supposedly was one of the recipients of the millions of dollars stolen by the far-right-wing group, the Order. If this is true, it may explain how Metzger was able to afford to set up his computer network and finance the making of videos and "Race and Reason" programs.

For further information on the way white supremacists use computers to communicate, see also Jack Kay's "Communicating Through Electronic Bulletin Boards in the White Supremacy Movement: Creating Culture via Computer" and "Electronic Hate," by the Civil Rights Division of the Anti-Defamation League of B'nai B'rith.

The selection from *The Turner Diaries*, by William Pierce, comes from pages 161–64.

The article "Nebraska Hero—True and Loyal Klansman" was published in *The Klansman*, Issue 147 (September–October 1990), p. 3.

The poem "Rolling Thunder" by Jeffrey Smith is reprinted here with permission of his grandmother Rebecca Fortenbury.

Information on Dennis Mahon and the Kansas City White Knights of the KKK came from Bob Wolfson, regional director of the ADL for Kansas, Iowa and Nebraska, as well as from tapes and materials about the White Knights belonging to Larry Trapp. Information on the activities of the Oklahoma chapter and the activities of the Mahon brothers came from the Tulsa Police Department and newspaper accounts. Currently, Dennis Mahon identifies himself as "Heartland Director of WAR" or WAR's "Ambassador-at-Large."

The Southern Poverty Law Center's Klanwatch has identified at least twenty-eight different Klan groups.

The White Beret, the publication of the White Knights of the KKK, is my source for their views on the environment and their "back to the land" stance.

Chapter Seven (pages 99–107)

Michael Schwerner's quote "You want to kill those people? . . ." comes from William Bradford Huie's *Three Lives for Mississippi*. Schwerner was murdered, along with his friends and coworkers James Chaney and Andrew Goodman, in Mississippi in 1964 by members of the White Knights of the Ku Klux Klan.

The KKK "REAL HERO" posters put up on the university campuses in Lincoln and Omaha were reported on the news and in the university newspapers as well.

Colonel Delmar Gilkensen gave copies of the letter he received from the Klan ("Filthy Race-Mixing Scum . . .") to the police and to reporters. Jeff Gauger wrote about it in the article "Racist Threat Worries Omaha Man," *Omaha World-Herald*, July 27, 1991.

The route of the skinheads from California to Lincoln via Fallbrook, California, and Tulsa, Oklahoma, was traced by police intelligence and by the Midwestern ADL.

For a thorough examination of Tom Metzger's career, the murder of Mulugeta Seraw and the civil case against Tom and John Metzger for Seraw's death, read *Hate on Trial: The Case Against America's Most Dangerous Neo-Nazi* by Morris Dees and Steve Fiffer.

Chapter Eight (pages 108-15)

The description of the destruction of the Vietnamese center came from newspaper accounts and accounts of observers.

The background on the Vietnamese and other immigrant communities in Lincoln came from discussions with a number of people, including children in Ann Kennedy's classes at the Elliott School, who shared stories about their countries and about the effects of war on their lives.

The visual descriptions of the skinheads and their behavior comes from Dave Grooman of public-access Cable Vision and others who observed them. As in Chapters Four and Five, the sequences here are pieced together from many small facts and details, news stories, messages from Trapp and observations from others. While Larry Trapp never admitted his responsibility for the destruction of the Vietnamese Center, enormous circumstantial evidence, including his handwriting in warnings and on envelopes, tape recordings of his and his Klansmen and skinheads' calls and letters, points to his culpability.

Information on the skinheads' role and Larry Trapp's leadership comes in large part from Bob Wolfson, regional director of the Anti-Defamation League. Larry Trapp confirmed a great deal of information on the numbers of skinheads and Klansmen, and in a recording he left on Bob Wolfson's message machine when he was Grand Dragon of the Klan, he acknowledged the skinhead-Klan connection. Other information on skinheads came from articles in the *Omaha World-Herald*.

Dave Grooman recalled in vivid detail his meetings with Larry Trapp and the skinheads. As far as I know, Dave Grooman had more of a business contact with these white supremacists than any other "outsider."

Information on Larry Trapp's sexual habits and interests came from retrospective discussions.

Trapp's vicious attack on Donna Polk was on a tape recording I found among his possessions after his death.

Chapter Nine (pages 116-23)

Larry Trapp's Vigilante Voices hotline messages come again from audiotape recordings he made. Michael's responses come from his memory and

New Haven Free Public Library

www.cityofnewhaven.com/library

Ives – Main Library

133 Elm Street
New Haven, CT 06510

Monday	12-8
Tuesday	10-6
Wednesday	10-6
Thursday	10-8
Friday	Closed
Saturday	10-5
Sunday	Closed

Branch Libraries

Monday	10-6
Tuesday	10-6
Wednesday	12-8
Thursday	10-6
Friday	Closed
Saturday	1-5
Sunday	Closed

Fair Haven Library
182 Grand Avenue
New Haven, CT 06513

Mitchell Library
37 Harrison Street
New Haven, CT 06515

Stetson Library
200 Dixwell Avenue
New Haven, CT 06511

Ives – Main Library	
Children's Room	946-8129
Fair Haven Library	946-8115
Mitchell Library	946-8117
Stetson Library	946-8119

LIVE HOMEWORK HELP FREE ONLINE HELP FROM REAL TUTORS

is **1** click away!

www.cityofnewhaven.com/library

Use it at home
with your valid
New Haven library card
from 3 PM – 9 PM, *everyday*
(in Spanish Sunday – Thursday)

Use it in the library
from 3 PM until closing
(hours on reverse)

Grades 4-12
GED, College Intro.

Math, Science, Social Studies,
Essay Writing or English

Students, Parents, Adult Learners

Chat with a real tutor!

A SERVICE PROVIDED BY

New Haven Free
Public Library

were confirmed by Julie and others who remember what he said at the time.

Larry Trapp later told Dave Grooman and others that using the 1989 Aryan Fest for his first "Race and Reason" show was "a mistake" because it seemed "too violent." The scenes quoted here are from a video of the show, copied by Trapp.

Rebecca Nelms' letter regarding "Race and Reason" was printed in the *Lincoln Star.*

Scott Michaels' interview with Larry Trapp in his Klan robe, hood and mask on Channel 11 news was reproduced here from a videotape recording of that show. Dave Grooman supplied me with videos he had made of various interviews with Larry Trapp, including this one.

Trapp's hotline message, again, came from his own tapes.

Much later Larry Trapp told Julie and Michael Weisser about his wife leaving him, and his wish to die in the cul de sac, as well as his story about killing his cat Max. He told them and Dave Grooman about more than once sitting up all night in his wheelchair with his gun ready.

Chapter Ten (pages 124-37)

"Honoring one another, doing acts of kindness . . ." comes from *Gates of Prayer: The New Union Prayerbook,* p. 441.

Larry Trapp never admitted his responsibility for the Molotov cocktail attacks and arsons that took place in Lincoln and Lancaster County in August, September and October 1991, but cumulative evidence makes it clear he was behind most if not all of these attacks. His recipes for Molotov cocktails are clearly starred and the pages are worn from use—and during later interviews, he told me about making Molotov cocktails and made some of the remarks used here. Lancaster County Sheriff Tom Casady and Police Chief Allen Curtis noted that the timing of the arsons paralleled the showings of "Race and Reason"—a significant detail—but they couldn't prove a direct connection to Trapp.

Larry Trapp later confessed his plot to assassinate Jesse Jackson to Julie and Michael Weisser.

Most of the dialogue between Bill Rush and Larry Trapp included in this chapter is taken with Bill Rush's permission from his unpublished story "Love Thy Neighbor," and from interviews.

Information on Bill Rush's history comes from correspondence with him, as well as from his compelling autobiography, *Journey Out of Silence,* and his manuscript in progress, "A Place of My Own."

Bill's apartment also is set up with a phone-alert system that controls his lights and appliances, asks him if he needs help and calls an emergency center for help at the press of a button. With the help of an automatic door opener, and wheelchair access, Bill is able to come and go independently in his motorized wheelchair.

Donna Polk's friend, Gary Cardori, who was investigating a scandal involving the Franklin Credit Union and possible tie-ins with right-wing Republicans and the white supremacist movement, died when his plane was blown out of the air with Cardori and his eight-year-old son in it. For more about this story, read *The Franklin Cover-up* by John W. DeCamp (Lincoln: AWT, 1992).

Public Defender Susan Tast was most helpful in describing her interactions with her new client.

Accounts of the courtroom interaction come from court transcripts, from Bill Rush's description and from descriptions by Susan Tast.

Bill Rush's feelings about pressing charges, testifying in court and winning his case against Larry Trapp come from his article "My Turn to Speak."

Because Trapp had never signed the certified mail telling him when to appear in court, he was found not guilty of failure to appear. The articles "Klansman Found Guilty for Abusive Message" and "KKK Recruiter Convicted for Menacing Phone Call" appeared in the *Lincoln Star* and *Lincoln Journal,* September 16 and 17, 1991.

Chapter Eleven (pages 138–44)

Long after this time, Larry Trapp talked about his previous fear of dying, his fear of dying in jail and his general anxiety level, which also may have been related unconsciously to an awareness of the severity of his medical condition.

In later interviews, and in tape recordings he made at the time, Larry Trapp expressed his disgust with Tom Metzger and the lack of discipline among his followers.

Trapp's dialogue with Dave Grooman about the inefficiency of the skinheads comes from Grooman's memory of these conversations.

In later interviews, Larry Trapp talked about his previous plan to poison the dogs next door and said he had asked one of his nurses to read him the directions for poisoning "rats."

Larry Trapp taped all of his messages and conversations relating to the murder of Jeffrey Smith. A newspaper article among Trapp's belongings, which lacks an identifying date and name, documents the details of the Klansmen being sentenced for Smith's death.

In his recorded conversation with Jeffrey Smith's grandmother, Trapp said, "That's what we had in common; we both loved the Klan with all our heart and all our soul."

Larry Trapp related the incident with his nurse Cathy Carson. In a telephone interview with Cathy, she said, "The first time I took care of Larry, I was scared to death of him. The director had called us in to prepare us, and she told us, 'He's active Klan and he has an Uzi hanging on his door.' Larry acted tough, but inside that mean exterior, he was a big pussy cat." Cathy said she and her director often went together so one of them could stand outside while the other one went inside, "because with the threats on Larry's part and the threats against him, we didn't know who could be shot." Cathy said Larry became a good friend to her and her director.

Chapter Twelve (pages 145–58)

Martin Luther King Jr.'s quote "Let us not seek to satisfy our thirst . . ." comes from his famous speech "I Have a Dream," delivered from the steps of the Lincoln Memorial during the March on Washington in August 1963.

The article "Local Sponsor Pulls 'Race and Reason' " by L. Kent Wolgamott appeared November 13, 1991, in the *Lincoln Journal*.

I found Monica Kuhn's letter to Larry Trapp among his possessions. Larry told me this letter had a significant effect on him. The letter is reprinted here with Ms. Kuhn's permission.

Trapp's behavior in the Lancaster County Courthouse was well documented by television footage and from newspaper articles and interviews. His statements in court, as well as Judge Mary Doyle's statements, come from transcripts of the court proceedings.

Information on the history of Afro-Americans in Lincoln came from a variety of sources, including my interviews with Lenora Letcher and Leola Bullock, and a series of fine articles by journalist Martha Stoddard in the *Lincoln Journal Star* in June 1992, including "Lincoln Blacks Marking Time: Little yet much has changed in a century of change."

Chapter Thirteen (pages 159–69)

The quote "The seed of hate is within us all. But so, too, is the light of love . . ." comes from my husband, Ron Sitts, who has a rare capacity for going to the heart of any issue and reminding me of what really matters.

I have written the account of Michael and Julie Weisser's remarkable first meeting with Larry Trapp from separate interviews with each of these three participants.

For more on Jewish children who survived World War II, read Howard Greenfeld's excellent book *Hidden Children*.

Chapter Fourteen (pages 170–87)

The quote "Our definition of healing is to touch with softness and kindness . . ." comes from Stephen and Ondrea Levine's *Relationships as a Path of Awakening*, Warm Rock Tapes, 1990.

Larry's exit from the white supremacist, neo-Nazi movement is based on interviews with Larry Trapp as well as copies of his letters and tape recordings.

David Duke is still closely allied with the National Association for the Advancement of White People but now is publicly affiliated with the Office of the Conservative Network. He writes the *David Duke Report* and hosts a talk show in New Orleans.

Greg Withrow had founded the White Student Movement in California before he worked with Tom and John Metzger in setting up the White Aryan Youth Movement. He left this neo-Nazi movement after he fell in love with a young woman who couldn't understand his racism. Withrow has said his father, an adamant racist who raised him to be an Aryan leader, had died earlier that year. After his father's death, Withrow said, he began to think and feel for himself and to question a lot of his previous training. For more on this, see Morris Dees and Steve Fiffer's *Hate on Trial: The Case Against America's Most Dangerous Neo-Nazi* and James Ridgeway's *Blood in the Face.*

Chapter Fifteen (pages 188–96)

Stephen Levine's quote "Love is greater than any emotion . . ." comes from his book *Who Dies?,* p. 210.

John Ways, Norman Leach, Larry Trapp, C. J. Schepers and Julie and Michael Weisser all gave me details about the dinner at the Weisser home.

C. J. Schepers' story, "Grand Dragon Quits, Takes Jew as Friend" appeared November 24, 1991, in the *Lincoln Journal Star.*

Randall Balmer's story on Trapp's metamorphosis was syndicated by the Religious News Service and distributed by the New York Times News Service in 1991.

Chapter Sixteen (pages 197–210)

Rabindranath Tagore's quote "The faith waiting in the heart of a seed . . ." comes from his book *Fireflies,* p. 87.

John Newton was a prolific writer who kept not only a daily journal, but a volume of letters documenting the slave trade. Information on Newton comes from *Amazing Grace: The Story Behind the Song,* by Jim Haskins, and from a televised exploration of the song "Amazing Grace" with Bill Moyers.

Charles Griffin, Leslie Young, Eva Sartori, Cybele Londono and other members of B'nai Jeshurun's congregation generously shared their feelings about Larry Trapp and his presence at the temple.

Leslie Young, Julie, Michael and Larry all told stories about Larry's experiences at his apartment on J Street after he left the Klan.

Larry's tapes on identifying and caring for African violets are mixed in with his hate tapes.

Chapter Seventeen (pages 211-20)

I have pieced together Larry Trapp's medical history in this and in later chapters from his medical records, from Julie's thorough notes on his condition during the period of time she took care of him, his sister Candace Bywater's recollections of her brother's health in previous years and from recollections of Jan Branting, his hospice nurse.

Daniel Levy's article "The Cantor and the Klansman" appeared in *Time* on February 17, 1992. He shared his responses to the cantor, the Klansman and the cantor's family with me during an interview. Daniel Levy became such close friends with the Weissers following his story that when he got married in 1993, Michael and Julie flew back for the wedding so Michael could officiate.

Chapter Eighteen (pages 221-34)

The quote, "And I tell you the good in us will win . . ." comes from *Gates of Prayer: The New Union Prayer Book,* p. 707.

Stories about the previous experiences of Michael Weisser and Larry Trapp come from interviews and letters, stories from siblings, court records, prison records and news articles.

Cantor Glatzer talked fondly about Michael Weisser during an interview about their days at Hebrew Union College.

Rabbi Isaac Moseson, who made such a difference in Michael Weisser's life, currently lives in Cheltenham, Pennsylvania, where he is rabbi to Congregation Melrose B'nai Israel-Emmanuel.

Chapter Nineteen (pages 235-44)

I found Rabbi Gerondi's thirteenth-century quote "The repentant sinner should strive to do good . . ." in Rabbi Joseph Telushkin's *Jewish Literacy.*

Rebecca Nelms, Dina Weisser and Dave Weisser all talked to me during interviews about their own histories and the effect of Larry Trapp's presence on their lives.

The Sh'ma—"Hear O Israel, the Lord is our God, the Lord is one!" is an expression of faith in the ultimate unity of God and the "watchword" of the faith. It comes from the book of Deuteronomy, Chapter 6, Verse 4. Jews recite these words during nearly every synagogue service.

Chapter Twenty (pages 245-54)

Malcolm X's quote "If I can die having brought any light . . ." comes from the essay "1965," by Malcolm X, included in Schwartz and Disch, *White Racism: Its History, Pathology and Practice,* p. 530.

Shortly before his death, Malcolm also said, "I believe in recognizing every human being as a human being—neither white, black, brown or red; and when you are dealing with humanity as a family there's no question of integration or intermarriage. It's just one human being marrying another human being. . . ." (*The Autobiography of Malcolm X,* p. 424)

The Martin Luther King Service was reported in "Dream Comes Alive at Interfaith Service: Ex-Klansman Urges Tolerance for All," by C. J. Schepers, in the *Lincoln Journal,* January 15, 1992. I've transcribed and edited speeches used here from a videotape of the service.

The exchange with Larry Trapp at the NAACP meeting was recounted by members John Ways, Lenora Letcher, Leola Bullock and Donna Polk. They shared information and a tape recording made of the first meeting attended by Larry Trapp. Apparently, Larry went to as many meetings as he could while he was still well enough to go, and was deeply moved and gratified that NAACP members were willing to accept him after all the harm he had done them.

Chapter Twenty-One (pages 255-64)

"In the faces of men and women, I see God," comes from Walt Whitman's *Song of Myself,* St. 48.

I witnessed a great deal of banter between Larry and Rebecca, Dina and Dave during my visits to Lincoln. I also interviewed most of Larry's regular visitors, such as Charles Griffin, Cybele Londono, Leslie Young and Bill Brda.

Julie's personal history and earlier life struggles came from our interviews. She also shared observations about her intense caretaking of Larry and subsequent interactions involving all the family.

Chapter Twenty-Two (pages 265-70)

The quote "In the sayings of the Fathers . . ." comes from Martin Buber's *Ten Rungs: Hasidic Sayings.*

Information on the incident with swastikas being spray-painted on the South Street temple came from interviews and from articles by C. J. Schepers ("Cantor Says Swastikas Not Representative of City") and Bill Kreifel ("Swastika Painters to Learn from Crime Through Study of Judaism, Holocaust") in the *Lincoln Journal,* March 9, 1992, and May 14, 1992.

Since the incident involving State Senator Elroy Hefner's anti-Semitic statement and his meeting with Michael Weisser, Senator Hefner invited Cantor Weisser to give the invocation at a Nebraska business organization's breakfast meeting.

Paul Hammel's story, "Racism Wound Heals; Family Rift Doesn't," was in the Sunday *Omaha World-Herald,* March 1, 1992. Larry showed me previous correspondence from his father severing their relationship and discussed the difficulties he and his father had communicating with one another. John Trapp has maintained that Larry's characterizations of him are unfounded and unfair.

The story in *People* magazine was published June 1, 1992.

Chapter Twenty-Three (pages 271–82)

The quote "It's a basic Jewish Law. . . ." comes from Rabbi Joseph Telushkin, *An Eye for an Eye.*

Most Americans call the small head covering, worn as a sign of respect to God, by its Yiddish name—yarmulke. In Israel, the yarmulke is known by the Hebrew term *kippah*. Michael and Julie refer to the small round hat as a *kippah*.

The definition of the mezuzah comes from Rabbi Joseph Telushkin's *Jewish Literacy.*

Alan Frank, David Gasser, Bob Wolfson and others at Larry's conversion ceremony shared their observations and insights with me about this occasion.

Chapter Twenty-Four (pages 283–94)

The quote "In every man there is something precious . . ." comes from Martin Buber's *Ten Rungs: Hasidic Sayings.*

Again, the details of Larry's medical condition and deterioration come from medical records, from Julie's records and reports, from R.N. Jan Branting and from interviews with other observers and participants, including Larry Trapp.

Larry talked freely and enthusiastically to me and to others about his trains and train collecting. He showed me all of his trains and told me their various histories. And while he mentioned his grandfather and grandmother to me, details from his childhood here come from his conversations with Julie Weisser and Jack Levine, who shared what he told them with me.

Chapter Twenty-Five (pages 295–305)

Larry told Julie his dreams and his nightmares.

The exchange between Larry and Julie concerning his guilt from lying about what had happened to him at Kearney and his not telling about other things he had done has been recalled in detail by Julie. She called me the day after he told her the truth about Kearney because he specifically asked her to tell me. He wanted it known that no black person had ever wronged him.

Chapter Twenty-Six (pages 306-12)

The quote "I only ask for last kind words from you. . . ." comes from Rabindranath Tagore's *Fireflies.*

I attended Larry Trapp's funeral and took excerpts from various speeches verbatim from a videotape of the event.

Bill Brda and Julie Weisser both told me their dreams during interviews after Larry's death. Several people reported the incident at the cemetery.

Bibliography

The following books and articles have been useful in understanding the issues, history and implications of this story:

"The American Farmer and the Extremists." A Special Report by the Anti-Defamation League of B'nai B'rith's Civil Rights Division. New York, January 1986.

Ames, Jessie Daniel. *The Changing Character of Lynching: Review of Lynching, 1931–1941.* Atlanta, Ga.: Commission on Interracial Cooperation, July 1941. Mrs. Ames refutes the "reasons" given for lynchings ("It's murder, not lynching") and includes chapters on media coverage of lynchings and chapters titled "Lynching and the Price of Cotton" and "Mob Violence Masquerading as the Champion of Southern Women."

"Appeals Court Upholds $12.5 Million Judgement Against Metzgers," in Klanwatch's *Intelligence Report.* Montgomery, Ala., May 1993.

Auerbach, Ella Fleishman. "Jewish Settlement in Nebraska, General Survey." 1927. This undocumented but informative compilation of information is housed at the Jewish Federation Library in Omaha.

The Autobiography of Malcolm X, as told to Alex Haley. New York: Ballantine Books, 1973.

Beam, Louis R. *Essays by a Klansman: A Compendium of KKK Ideology, Organizational Methods, History, Tactics, and Options.* Hayden Lake, Idaho: A.K.I.A. Publications, 1983. This book demonstrates the paranoid fanaticism that drives white supremacists. One chapter is headed "Understanding the Struggle or Why We Have to Kill the Bastards!" Beam, a devout Klansman, calls for "Knives, Guns, and Courage" to "take our country back from the illegal Washington government."

Becker, Ernest. *Denial of Death.* New York: Free Press, 1973.

———. *Escape from Evil.* New York: Free Press, 1975.

Black Women in White America: A Documentary History. Edited by Gerda

Lerner. New York: Vintage Books, 1992.

Blacks in America 1492–1970: A Chronology and Fact Book. Compiled and edited by Irving J. Sloan. Dobbs Ferry, N.Y.: Oceana Publications, 1971.

Blacks in Bondage: Letters of American Slaves. Edited by Robert S. Starobin. New York: Markus Wiener Publishing, 1988.

Blee, Kathleen M. *Women of the Klan: Racism and Gender in the 1920's.* Berkeley: University of California Press, 1991.

Block, Gay, and Malka Drucker. *Rescuers: Portraits of Moral Courage in the Holocaust.* New York: Holmes & Meier, 1992.

Broken Hoops and Plains People: A Catalogue of Ethnic Resources in the Humanities: Nebraska and Surrounding Areas. Edited by Paul A. Olson. Nebraska Curriculum Development Center, 1976. This book—found through interlibrary loan services—is an interesting collection of essays examining various ethnic backgrounds of people in Nebraska.

Calbreath, Dean. "Kovering the Klan: How the Press Gets Tricked into Boosting the KKK." *Columbia Journalism Review,* March–April 1981.

Chalmers, David M. *Hooded Americanism: The History of the Ku Klux Klan.* New York: Franklin Watts, 1981.

Chancer, Lynn S. *Sadomasochism in Everyday Life: The Dynamics of Power and Powerlessness.* New Brunswick, N.J.: Rutgers University Press, 1992.

Chudacoff, Howard P. *Mobile Americans: Residential and Social Mobility in Omaha 1880–1920.* New York: Oxford University Press, 1972.

Colvin, Rod. *Evil Harvest: The Shocking True Story of Cult Murder in the American Heartland.* New York: Bantam Books, 1992.

Cone, Molly. *The Mystery of Being Jewish.* New York: Union of American Hebrew Congregations, 1989.

Connell, Evan S. *Son of the Morning Star.* San Francisco: North Point Press, 1984.

Courage to Care: Rescuers of Jews During the Holocaust. Edited by Carol Rittner and Sondra Myers. New York: New York University Press, 1986.

DeCamp, John W. *The Franklin Cover-Up: Child Abuse, Satanism, and Murder in Nebraska.* Lincoln: AWT, Inc., 1992

Dees, Morris, with Steve Fiffer. *A Season for Justice.* New York: Charles Scribner's Sons, 1991.

Dees, Morris, and Steve Fiffer. *Hate on Trial: The Case Against America's Most Dangerous Neo-Nazi.* New York: Villard Books, 1993.

De Lange, Nicholas. *Judaism.* Oxford: Oxford University Press, 1986.

Deloria, Vine, Jr. *Custer Died for Your Sins: An Indian Manifesto.* New York: Macmillan, 1969.

"Electronic Hate." A Special Report by the Anti-Defamation League of B'nai B'rith's Civil Rights Division. New York, 1987.

Epstein, Helen. *Children of the Holocaust: Conversations with Sons and Daughters of Survivors.* New York: Penguin Books, 1979.

Flat Water: A History of Nebraska and Its Water. Edited by Charles A. Flowerday. Lincoln: Conservation and Survey Division, Institute of Agriculture and Natural Resources, University of Nebraska, Resource Report No. 12, March 1993.

Fontenelle, Henry. "History of the Omaha Indians." In *Transactions and Reports of the Nebraska Historical Society,* Vol. I. Lincoln: State Journal Co., 1885.

Frazier, Ian. *Great Plains.* New York: Farrar, Straus & Giroux, 1989.

Fuller, Edgar I., *The Visible of the Invisible Empire: "The Maelstrom."* Denver: Maelstrom Publishing Co., 1925. This exposé of the Klan by a former KKK member is filled with detailed records, analysis of Klan propaganda and copies of speeches and letters condemning the Klan. It includes Fuller's resignation letter to the Imperial Wizard: "I have fully realized my error, and am taking this means of lifting the 'sign of secrecy' calling on all honest men who are members of this organization, or in any way connected with the Knights of the Ku Klux Klan, to do likewise."

Gates of Prayer: The New Union Prayerbook. Weekdays, Sabbaths, and Festivals, Services and Prayers for Synagogue and Home. New York: Central Conference of American Rabbis, 1975.

Gendler, Carol. "The Jews of Omaha: The First Sixty Years." A thesis presented to the Department of History and the Faculty of the College of Graduate Studies, University of Omaha, March 1968.

Gilbert, Martin. *The Holocaust: A History of the Jews of Europe During the Second World War.* New York: Holt, Rinehart & Winston, 1985.

Goldberg, Robert Alan. *Hooded Empire: The Ku Klux Klan in Colorado.* Urbana and Chicago: University of Illinois Press, 1981.

Greenfeld, Howard. *Chanukah.* New York: Holt, Rinehart & Winston, 1976.

———. *Hidden Children.* New York: Ticknor & Fields, 1993.

———. *Passover.* New York: Holt, Rinehart & Winston, 1978.

———. *Rosh Hashanah and Yom Kippur.* New York: Holt, Rinehart & Winston, 1979.

Hallie, Philip. *Lest Innocent Blood Be Shed: The Story of the Village of Le Chambon and How Goodness Happened There.* New York: Harper Colophon Books, 1979.

Hargrove, Jim. *Nebraska.* Chicago: Childrens Press/Regensteiner Publishing, 1989.

Haskins, Jim. *Amazing Grace: The Story Behind the Song.* Brookfield, Conn.: Millbrook Press, 1992.

Hate Crime Statistics, 1990: A Resource Book. Prepared by the Association of State Uniform Crime Reporting Programs and the Center for Applied Social Research, Northeastern University. Washington, D.C.: U.S.

Department of Justice, Federal Bureau of Investigation, 1992.

Hearing on the KKK, 1921, Washington D.C.: U.S. Government Printing Office, 1921.

Heat-Moon, William Least. *PrairyErth (a deep map).* Boston: Houghton Mifflin, 1991.

Heschel, Abraham Joshua. *Man Not Alone: A Philosophy of Religion.* New York: Farrar, Straus & Giroux, 1951.

Horner, John R., and James Gorman. *Digging Dinosaurs.* New York: Workman Publishing Co., 1988.

Huie, William Bradford. *Three Lives for Mississippi.* New York: WCC Books, 1965.

Jews of the United States. Edited by Priscilla Fishman and with an introduction by Arthur Hertzberg. New York: Quadrangle/New York Times Book Company, 1973.

Johnson, Paul. *History of the Jews.* New York: Harper & Row, 1987.

Kaplan, Aryeh. *The Infinite Light: A Book About God.* New York: National Conference of Synagogue Youth, 1981.

Kay, Jack. "Arguing for and Against a White Homeland: The Aryan World Congress versus the Kootenai County Task Force on Human Relations." Paper presented at the Fifth SCA/AFA Conference on Argumentation. Published by Speech Communication Association, 5105 Backlick Road, Suite E, Annandale, VA 22003, August 1987.

———. "Communicating through Electronic Bulletin Boards in the White Supremacy Movement: Creating Culture via Computer." Presented at the International Communication Association Conference, Mass Communications Division, New Orleans, June 1988.

———. "To Legislate or Educate: Thoughts on Fighting Words, Politically Correct Speech, and the Language of Oppression." *Alumni Magazine of Wayne State University,* Vol. 5, No. 2 (Fall 1991).

Keim, A. R. "John Brown in Richardson County," in *Transactions and Reports of the Nebraska State Historical Society,* Vol. II. Lincoln: State Journal Co., 1887.

"Klandidates." *Mother Jones,* March–April, 1992

Korn, Rabbi Bertram. "Jews and Negro Slavery in the Old South" in *The Jewish Experience in America.* Edited by Abraham J. Karp. Waltham, Mass.: American Jewish Historical Society, 1969.

"The Ku Klux Klan: A History of Racism and Violence." A special report compiled by the staff of the Southern Poverty Law Center. 4th ed. Edited by Sara Bullard. Montgomery, Ala.: Klanwatch, 1991.

Langmuir, Gavin I. *Toward a Definition of Antisemitism.* Berkeley: University of California Press, 1992.

Lester, Julius. *Lovesong: Becoming a Jew.* New York: Henry Holt & Co., 1988.

Letters of the Scattered Brotherhood. Edited by Mary Strong. New York: Harper & Row, 1948.

Leubke, Frederick C. "Political Response to Agricultural Depression in Nebraska, 1922." *Nebraska History,* March 1966.

Levine, Stephen. *A Gradual Awakening.* New York: Anchor Books, 1979.

———. *Healing into Life and Death.* New York: Anchor Books, 1987.

———. *Who Dies? An Investigation of Conscious Living and Conscious Dying.* New York: Anchor Books, 1982.

Levine, Stephen, and Ondrea Levine. "Relationships as a Path of Awakening." Chamisal, N.M.: Warm Rock Tapes, 1990.

Levy, Daniel S. "The Cantor and the Klansman." *Time,* February 17, 1992.

Lovato, Rumaldo L. "Ethnic Assimilation and Pluralism in Nebraska: A Replication and Extension." A thesis presented to the Faculty of the Graduate College of the University of Nebraska. Lincoln, May 1980.

Lynching, Racial Violence, and Law. Edited by Paul Finkelman. Vol. 9 of *Race, Law, and American History 1700–1990: The African American Experience.* New York: Garland Publishing Co., 1992. This chilling collection of essays documents lynchings throughout the United States.

Macdonald, Andrew. *The Turner Diaries.* Washington, D.C.: The National Alliance, 1978. This book reflects the extremism of the New Order and militant white separatists.

Mann, Emily. *The Greensboro Massacre* (a play). Unpublished manuscript. The McCarter Theatre, 91 University Place, Princeton, New Jersey 08540, 1995.

Massengill, Reed. *Portrait of a Racist: The Man Who Killed Medgar Evers?* New York: St. Martin's Press, 1994.

Matthews, Anne. *Where the Buffalo Roam: The Storm over the Revolutionary Plan to Restore America's Great Plains.* New York: Grove Weidenfeld, 1992.

Memmi, Albert, *Dominated Man.* New York: Orion Press, 1968.

———. *The Liberation of the Jew.* New York: Orion Press, 1966.

———. *Portrait of a Jew.* New York: Orion Press, 1962.

"The Midwest's Top Neo-Nazi: Gerhard Lauck and the NSDAP-AO," in Klanwatch's *Intelligence Report,* May 1993.

Miller, Jean Baker. *Toward a New Psychology of Women.* Boston: Beacon Press, 1986.

Nathanson, Donald L. *Shame and Pride: Affect, Sex and the Birth of the Self.* New York: W. W. Norton & Co., 1992.

"A Nebraska Nazi's Global Reach." A Special Report by the Anti-Defamation League of B'nai B'rith's Civil Rights Division. New York, February 1993.

Neihardt, John G. *Black Elk Speaks.* Lincoln: University of Nebraska Press, 1972.

Nelson, Jack. *Terror in the Night: The Klan's Campaign Against the Jews.* New York: Simon & Schuster, 1993.

Neusner, Jacob. *The Way of the Torah.* Encino, Calif.: Dickenson Publishing Co., 1974.

Nhat Hanh, Thich. *The Miracle of Mindfulness!* Boston: Beacon Press, 1976.

The Nobel Peace Prize and the Dalai Lama. Edited by Sidney Piburn. Ithaca, N.Y.: Snow Lion Publications, 1990.

Olson, James C. *History of Nebraska.* Lincoln: University of Nebraska Press, 1955.

Painter, Nell Irvin. *Exodusters: Black Migration to Kansas After Reconstruction.* Lawrence: University Press of Kansas, 1986.

————. *Standing at Armageddon: The United States, 1877–1919.* New York: W. W. Norton & Co., 1987.

Peck, M. Scott. *People of the Lie: The Hope for Healing Human Evil.* New York: Simon & Schuster, 1983.

Polk, Donna Mays. *Black Men and Women of Nebraska.* Lincoln: Nebraska Black History Preservation Society, 1981.

Prager, Dennis, and Joseph Telushkin, *Nine Questions People Ask About Judaism.* New York: Simon & Schuster, 1981.

————. *Why the Jews? The Reason for Antisemitism.* New York: Simon & Schuster, 1983.

Race-ing Justice, En-gendering Power: Essays on Anita Hill, Clarence Thomas, and the Construction of Social Reality. Edited by Toni Morrison. New York: Pantheon Books, 1992.

Rank, Otto. *Beyond Psychology.* New York: Dover Books, 1958.

Ridgeway, James. *Blood in the Face.* New York: Thunder's Mouth Press, 1990.

————. "Murder Won't Out." *Village Voice,* October 1, 1991.

Rush, William L. *Journey Out of Silence.* Lincoln: Media Productions & Marketing, 1986.

————. "My Turn to Speak." *Communication Outlook,* Vol. 13, No. 3 (Spring Special Issue), 1992.

————. "Love Thy Neighbor." Unpublished, 1993.

Sachar, Howard M. *A History of the Jews in America.* New York: Alfred A. Knopf, 1992.

The Sayings of GOD. Compiled and translated by Yehoshua Persky. London: Jason Aronson, 1990.

Schepers, C. J. "Grand Dragon Quits, Takes Jew as Friend." *Lincoln Journal Star,* November 24, 1991.

Schuyler, Michael W. "The Ku Klux Klan in Nebraska, 1920–1930." *Nebraska History,* Vol. 66, No. 3 (Fall 1985).

Schwartz, Barry N., and Robert Disch. *White Racism: Its History, Pathology and Practice.* New York: Dell Publishing Co., 1970. This important collection of essays, available only through libraries, should be put back into print.

Shay, Frank. *Judge Lynch: His First Hundred Years.* New York: Ives Washburn, 1938.

Slobin, Mark. *Chosen Voices: The Story of the American Cantorate.* Urbana and Chicago: University of Illinois Press, 1989.

Steinberg, Milton. *Basic Judaism.* New York: Harcourt Brace, 1947.

Stoddard, Martha. "Lincoln Blacks Marking Time: Little Yet Much Has Changed in a Century of Change." *Lincoln Journal Star,* June 21, 1992.

Tarrants, Thomas Albert, III. *Conversion of a Klansman.* New York: Doubleday & Co., 1979.

Teichmann, Howard. *My Life: Henry Fonda.* New York: New American Library, 1981.

Telushkin, Joseph. *An Eye for an Eye.* New York: Bantam Books, 1991.

———. *Jewish Literacy.* New York: William Morrow & Co., 1991.

———. *The Unorthodox Murder of Rabbi Wahl.* New York: Bantam Books, 1987.

Ten Rungs: Hasidic Sayings. Collected and edited by Martin Buber. New York: Schocken Books, 1947.

Terkel, Studs. *Race: How Blacks and Whites Feel About the American Obsession.* New York: New Press, 1992.

Thomas, Laurence. "The Evolution of Anti-Semitism," in *Transition, An International Review,* Issue 57. New York: Oxford University Press, 1992. Thomas examines the historical and conceptual features of anti-Judaism and anti-Semitism since early Christianity.

Thompson, Jerry. *My Life in the Klan.* New York: G. P. Putnam's Sons, 1982.

Thompson, Kathleen. *Nebraska.* Milwaukee: Raintree Publishers, 1988.

Trager, James. *The People's Chronology.* New York: Henry Holt & Co., 1992.

Transactions and Reports of the Nebraska State Historical Society, Vol. II. Lincoln: State Journal Co., 1887.

Tucker, Richard K. *The Dragon and the Cross: The Rise and Fall of the Ku Klux Klan in Middle America.* Hamden, Conn. Archon Books, 1991.

Turner, John, et al. "The Ku Klux Klan: A History of Racism and Violence." Edited by Randall Williams. Montgomery, Ala.: Klanwatch, 1982.

U.S. Commission on Civil Rights. *Intimidation and Violence: Racial and Religious Bigotry in America.* Washington, D.C.: U.S. Commission on Civil Rights, 1983.

Wade, Wyn Craig. *The Fiery Cross: The Ku Klux Klan in America.* New York: Simon & Schuster, 1987.

Welsch, Roger, and Paul Fell. *You Know You're a Nebraskan . . .* Lincoln: Plains Heritage/J & L Lee, 1993.

West, Cornel. *Keeping Faith.* New York: Routledge, 1993.

———. *Race Matters.* Boston: Beacon Press, 1993.

Wiesel, Elie. *Night.* New York: Hill & Wang, 1982.

Williams, Patricia J. *The Alchemy of Race and Rights.* Cambridge: Harvard University Press, 1991.

Wolpe, David J. *The Healer of Shattered Hearts: A Jewish View of God.* New York: Henry Holt & Co., 1990.

Wouk, Herman, *This Is My God: The Jewish Way of Life.* New York: Pocket Books, 1974.

Zona, Guy A. *The Soul Would Have No Rainbow if the Eyes Had No Tears: And Other Native American Proverbs.* New York: Simon & Schuster, 1994.

Acknowledgments

During several trips to Nebraska, I interviewed more than one hundred people, including Donna Polk, Lenora Letcher, Norman Leach, Leslie Young, Alan Frank, John Ways, Sr., Phong Huynh, Nancy Hicks and others whose names don't appear on these pages. I am grateful for the openness with which they all shared their thoughts and experiences. Candace Trapp Bywaters, Larry Trapp's sister, was a remarkable resource, and I appreciated meeting Larry's father and stepmother, Mr. and Mrs. John Trapp. I met and talked extensively with Larry several times before his death, and he and the Weisser family gave me access to all relevant documentation, as well as the vivid recall of incidents in their own lives. Julie, Michael, Dina, Rebecca and Dave also gave me enormous amounts of their time and an equal share of friendship and fun over the past two and a half years. I couldn't have written this book without their extraordinary generosity.

In addition to sources cited in my Notes, I want to thank Nell Painter at Princeton University and Leigh Beinen at Princeton's Woodrow Wilson School. I'm also grateful to Leola Bullock in Lincoln; Jim Potter at the Nebraska State Historical Society; Bertha Calloway at the Great Plains Black Museum; various officers with the Lincoln Police Department—particularly officers William Larsen and Maria Goretti Vu; administrators in the Lincoln Public Schools; Dr. Michael Schuyler at the University of Nebraska at Kearny; Dave Grooman, at Public Access Cablevision in Lincoln; Daniel Levy, of *Time* magazine; Ann Kennedy, English-as-a-Second-Language teacher, and her students at the Elliott School in Lincoln; members of the Lincoln Interfaith Council, the Lincoln Chapter of the NAACP, congregants of B'nai Jeshurun and the staffs of the Jewish Federation Library in Omaha and of Princeton's Firestone Library, which was a treasure trove for my research. I'm also grateful to Laura Woods and Angie Lowry at Klanwatch, the investigative arm of the Southern Poverty Law Center, and to Marc Caplan and Tom Halpern at the Anti-Defamation League of B'nai B'rith, for their information on current Klan and neo-Nazi hate groups.

This book came to me by some magic spun by Jack Levine and Phil Pachoda, who continue to be wonderful allies. Ann Patty first believed in this book, and Bob Bender became its good shepherd. Lee Gruzen dove with me into the slimy muck of Larry's Klan history and rescued me at many points by discussing the complex layers of this story. Marie Stoner, who has always been my first reader, once again responded with insights that led to significant changes in the manuscript in its various stages. Jane Nakashima and Suzi Sato Nakashima's black rock centered me as I wrote about the ugly history of the Klan, and Jaime Manrique, Jan Clausen, Jane Nakashima, Jane Bernstein, Susan Danoff, Michael Kanaly, Howard Greenfeld, Jane Shapiro, Jane Silverman, Mary Bralove and Helen Ahern Mahoney also read and discussed some or all of this manuscript as it progressed. I'm also grateful to Emily Mann for trading insights with me as she worked on her play about the Greensboro massacre, to my Goddard friends for their inspiration and enthusiasm and to the Ocean Gate crowd for their summertime support.

I want to pay special tribute to my exceptional mother, Grace Watterson Landis, who actively sustained my work on this book. Over and again, she searched out books and information in the library for me, photocopied passages and quotes, discovered films and other relevant resource material, read and gave me useful feedback on my writing. My sister, Alice Watterson, also helped me and shared in the excitement of this story, as did my brother, John Watterson, a dabbler in Judaica, by his own description, and my niece Sarah, who sustained me with a barrage of love and encouragement from Micronesia.

Thanks also are due to Elsa Hoffstad, Edie Innes and Terry Grillo, who transcribed my interviews with care and good humor, to Sam Wineburg, who dug up old articles and buried theses I wanted from Nebraska libraries and to Emily Remes, Johanna Li, Gypsy da Silva, Fred Wiemer, Victoria Meyer and Karolina Harris for their fine work during the production of this book at Simon & Schuster.

I thank my husband, Ron, for unearthing the title *Not by the Sword* and for his compassion, hilarity and involvement. I also thank my son, Zachary, for his support and for the joy he brings into my life on a daily basis.

Index

Photo Credits

DATE DUE		
FEB 10 2004